RORSCHACH CONTENT INTERPRETATION

RORSCHACH CONTENT INTERPRETATION

Edward Aronow, Ph.D.
Assistant Professor of Psychology
Montclair State College
Upper Montclair, New Jersey
and Senior Clinical Psychologist
St. Vincent's Hospital
New York, New York

Marvin Reznikoff, Ph.D.
Professor of Psychology
and Director, Doctoral Training Program in Clinical Psychology
Fordham University
Bronx, New York
and Clinical Consultant for the State of Connecticut
Franklin S. Dubois Day Treatment Center
Stamford, Connecticut

GRUNE & STRATTON
A Subsidiary of Harcourt Brace Jovanovich, Publishers
New York   San Francisco   London

Library of Congress Cataloging in Publication Data
Aronow, Edward.
 Rorschach content interpretation.

 Bibliography: p.
 Includes index.
 1. Rorschach test. I. Reznikoff, Marvin, joint
author. II. Title.
 BF698.8.R5A76   155.2'842   76-25544
 ISBN 0-8089-0961-4

Grune & Stratton, Inc.
111 Fifth Avenue
New York, New York 10003

Distributed in the United Kingdom by
Academic Press, Inc. (London) Ltd.
24/28 Oval Road, London NW 1

Library of Congress Catalog Number 76-25544
International Standard Book Number 0-8089-0961-4
Printed in the United States of America

To
Audrey and David Aronow
and
the Reznikoff family and friends

CONTENTS

ACKNOWLEDGMENTS

We gratefully acknowledge permission granted by the authors and publishers to reprint uncopyrighted and copyrighted material.

The following scoring systems are presented in detail: De Vos's system, set forth in Chapter 3, reprinted by permission of the publisher from "A quantitation approach to affective symbolism in Rorschach responses" by George De Vos in *Journal of Projective Techniques,* 1952, **16,** 133–150; Schafer's themes, also set forth in Chapter 3, reprinted by permission of the author and publisher from *Psychoanalytic Interpretation in Rorschach Testing* by Roy Schafer, © 1954 by Grune & Stratton, Inc., New York; Burt's system, presented in Chapter 4, by permission of Grete Archer from an unpublished monograph, *The Rorschach Test;* abbreviated summaries of the Zubin content scales, also presented in Chapter 4, by permission of the authors and publisher from *An Experimental Approach to Projective Techniques* by Joseph Zubin, Leonard D. Eron, and Florence Schumer, © 1965 by John Wiley & Sons, New York; Elizur's hostility and anxiety scales, set forth in Chapter 5, by permission of the author and publisher from "Content analysis of the Rorschach with regard to anxiety and hostility" by Abraham Elizur in *Rorschach Research Exchange and Journal of Projective Techniques,* 1949, **13,** 97–126; the Barrier and Penetration scales, set forth in Chapter 6, by permission of the authors and publisher from *Body Image and Personality* (2nd ed.) by Seymour Fisher and Sidney E. Cleveland, © 1968 by Dover Publications, New York; the Wheeler signs, presented in Chapter 8, by permission of the author and publisher from "An analysis of Rorschach indices of male homosexuality" by William M. Wheeler in *Rorschach Research Exchange and Journal of Projective Techniques,* 1949, **13,** 97–126; the Endicott scales of depression and suspiciousness, also presented in Chapter 8, abstracted from unpublished scoring materials by permission of Noble Endicott; summaries of the communications defects and deviances system, also presented in Chapter 8, by permission of the authors and publisher from "Principles for scoring communication defects and deviances in parents of schizophrenics: Rorschach and TAT scoring manuals" by Margaret T. Singer and Lyman C. Wynne in *Psychiatry,* 1966, **29,** 260–288; the Δ-scale, presented in Chapter 9, by permission of the authors and publisher from "An index of pathological thinking in the Rorschach" by John G. Watkins and James C. Stauffacher in *Journal of Projective Techniques,* 1952, **16,** 276–286.

FOREWORD

For many years, reviewers of projective techniques have been deploring the schism between psychometric research findings and clinical practice; as the negative results accumulated, clinical use of instruments like the Rorschach continued with apparently undiminished vigor. The schism was intensified by the cultism and esoteric, near-magical approach of some exponents of particular projective techniques. Against such a background, the authors have taken a cool, dispassionate, and nonpartisan look at the current status of the Rorschach. Their examination of the vast literature on this instrument led them to two major conclusions: (1) interpretation of responses in terms of their content has more to offer than do formal scoring systems based on the perceptual determinants of responses; (2) at least in its present form, the Rorschach can serve best as a standardized clinical interview.

The book begins with a survey and critical evaluation of content scoring systems and specially developed content scales, drawing upon published and unpublished research on both the Rorschach and the Holtzman Inkblot Technique. In terms of their psychometric properties, these content scores are judged to be more promising than the majority of perceptual scores. Nevertheless, none of the available content scales or scoring systems is considered to be ready for routine clinical use. All need more research and development before they can be confidently applied in individual diagnosis.

The major contribution of the book, in my opinion, is found in Chapters 10, 11, and 12, which focus on the clinical use of the Rorschach as a means of enhancing the idiographic understanding of the individual case. The authors observe that this is, in fact, the way most clinicians use the Rorschach, and that in this approach they rely chiefly on the content of the responses and on accessory verbal and nonverbal behavior. On the basis of available research and clinical experience, the authors provide a set of guidelines for more effective and dependable idiographic interpretations. For example, responses that depart from the commonplace and those less closely bound to the stimulus characteristics of particular blots are more likely to be significant in the individual case. Similarly, the authors caution against rigid adherence to universal systems of symbol interpretation and offer instead procedures for investigating the significance of responses within the individual's own experiential history. The proposed procedures should also serve to curb the wildly imaginative and highly subjective interpretations which have all-too-often rendered projective techniques more highly projective for the examiner than for the subject.

Combining psychometric sophistication with clinical expertise, the authors are especially qualified to evaluate such a technique as the Rorschach and to offer constructive recommendations regarding its potential values. The refreshing, well-balanced approach represented by this book argues well for the scientist-professional model in the training of clinical psychologists.

Anne Anastasi
Fordham University

PREFACE

Given the large number of previously published textbooks that deal with the Rorschach test, one might well ask if another such treatment is needed. The justification and raison d'être for the present book are found in the lack of attention devoted to content approaches in almost all of the previous Rorschach texts.* This inattention has existed despite the presence of the most consistently positive inkblot validity evidence with respect to content interpretation and despite the quite heavy reliance of psychologists on the analysis of content and accompanying verbalizations in the clinical setting. *Rorschach Content Interpretation* attempts to fill this gap by systematically mapping content and contextual approaches that have been proposed by various workers in the field. We hope that this text will contribute to a kindling of interest in the complex and significant clinical procedure that constitutes the Rorschach test.

The history of inkblot techniques is presented in the first chapter in order to set the Rorschach Test and its content approaches in their proper historical perspective.

The various scales that have been constructed to measure content and contextual aspects of test behavior (the most notable among the latter being the subject's verbalizations) are presented in Chapters 2 through 9; this coverage includes an evaluation of reliability, validity, and Rorschach normative data for the scales. The simple content scales proposed by Hermann Rorschach are discussed first, in Chapter 2. Chapters 3 and 4 present the attempts to construct numerous content scales designed to measure multiple aspects of test performance or personality; we have dubbed these scales the "Content Category Systems." Chapters 5 through 8 discuss the various attempts to construct content and contextual scales that are designed to measure intensively a more limited aspect of test performance or personality. Chapter 9 presents the evidence bearing on two approaches to scaling pathological verbalizations, the Rorschach Δ-scale and the Holtzman Inkblot Technique (HIT) V-scale.

Approaches to the clinical use of the Rorschach as a type of standard interview that will provide the skilled clinician with idiographic informa-

*With the exception of: Schafer, R. *Psychoanalytic interpretation in Rorschach testing.* New York: Grune & Stratton, 1954.

tion about the subject's unique personality also are discussed extensively in this volume. As noted by Anastasi, projective tests can be used to both provide measuring scales, as objective tests do, and furnish the clinician with a tool with which to probe for information of psychodynamic relevance.* Chapter 10 presents this latter use of the test and discusses the types of information that can be provided by applying the test as a standard interview; in addition, ground rules and procedures that have been suggested by experts in the field are also reviewed. Chapter 11 presents what is currently known about the stimulus properties of the 10 Rorschach blots based on the research studies carried out to date: such information is likely to be of particular value to the clinician who seeks to tease out the projective aspects of the Rorschach response from its nonprojective aspects. Chapter 12 discusses modifications in the Rorschach administration procedure that are likely to enhance the quality of information elicited in applications of the test as a standard interview. Finally Chapter 13 reviews the literature on the Consensus Rorschach with particular emphasis on idiographic applications. Chapters 10 through 13 in addition include clinical examples and test protocols that demonstrate use of the Rorschach as a potent clinical tool.

The clinician and clinical student are likely to profit most from those chapters that deal with the idiographic clinical use of the test. We believe that a consistent application of the principles discussed in Chapter 10 that takes into account the blot stimulus properties presented in Chapter 11 and modifies the administration procedure as discussed in Chapter 12 is likely to lead to more accurate clinical assessment and to a diminution of "wild analysis" in Rorschach interpretation. While many of the content and contextual scales reviewed in Chapters 2 through 9 look promising in terms of reliability and validity, the absence of sufficient psychometric and normative information as discussed herein renders them of little immediate use in the clinical context.

This volume offers the researcher a compendium of the existing reliability and validity data on inkblot content and contextual scales as well as suggestions concerning the directions in which relevant inkblot research might be moving most productively. Also of special interest to the researcher is the survey presented in Chapter 11 of empirical work on the stimulus properties of the Rorschach blots. Finally we suggest that research efforts can be applied more effectively in the area of idiographic Rorschach interpretation.

*Anastasi, A. *Psychological testing.* (3rd ed.) New York: Macmillan, 1976.

RORSCHACH CONTENT INTERPRETATION

Introduction

In his introduction to the 1970 *Personality Tests and Reviews*, Oscar Buros pointed out the seemingly incredible fact that, after thousands of research studies spanning several decades, there is still little agreement among psychologists as to the basic validity or lack of validity of the Rorschach test.

> The Rorschach [is the] kingpin of all personality tests judging by the vast amount of material written on it. . . . This vast amount of writing and research has produced astonishingly little, if any, agreement among psychologists regarding the specific validities of the Rorschach. It is amazing to think that this voluminous research and experimental writing over a period of nearly half a century has not produced a body of knowledge generally accepted by competent psychologists. . . . It is difficult to understand why the research has been so unproductive. (Buros, 1970, p xxvi)

It is the contention of the present authors that there *is* a body of Rorschach knowledge on which clinicians and researchers can and do agree. As demonstrated by Potkay (1971) and others, Rorschach clinicians rely primarily on content in interpreting the Rorschach test. Studies that have dealt with content interpretation of the Rorschach have found favorable evidence of the test's validity. It is this content approach to Rorschach interpretation which is the subject of this book.

Historically there have been two major approaches to Rorschach interpretation, one based on *perceptual* factors, the other based on *content*. Hermann Rorschach favored the perceptual factors, and the major

1

emphasis of the Rorschach schools and Rorschach textbooks has likewise been on perceptual factors. Consequently most of the research studies on the Rorschach test have dealt with perceptual aspects of the test, particularly determinants. As a result of the negative findings of the great majority of the empirical Rorschach studies, many psychologists have become increasingly critical of the Rorschach test. This development can be seen in many of the reviews of the Rorschach test in Buros's *Mental Measurements Yearbooks,* culminating in Jensen's suggestion that ". . . the rate of scientific progress in clinical psychology might well be measured by the speed and thoroughness with which it gets over the Rorschach" (Jensen, 1965, p 509). Such negative judgments of the test's validity and value filter down to students, who are then left with the impression that the Rorschach is an invalid test. As noted by Harris,

> One need only turn to a text in introductory or developmental psychology to find uncomplimentary summary statements about the coveted Rorschach test, statements which are being presented regularly to successive classes of . . . students. (Harris, 1960, p 417)

There is no question but that the research literature on the Rorschach test is, on the whole, highly discouraging. However this judgment only applies to that body of research that has investigated the validity of the *formal scoring categories* of the Rorschach test (notably determinants). In contrast, research on the validity of *content interpretation* has produced encouraging results. And because it has been repeatedly demonstrated (Potkay, 1971; Powers & Hamlin, 1957; Symonds, 1955) that clinicians in the field rely most heavily on content for their Rorschach interpretations, it would seem that pessimism about the Rorschach test is not warranted.

The present authors believe that there are two essential approaches to inkblot content interpretation. One approach is normatively based, utilizing scales on which inkblot responses can be scored, thereby enabling the psychologist to compare an individual's score with those of other subjects in order to gauge the degree of a particular characteristic. The second approach uses the inkblots for the intensive study of the individual case, rendering information about the unique pattern of psychodynamics of the individual subject — information that cannot be culled from objective tests. This distinction between the two major Rorschach content approaches is similar to Allport's (1937; 1961) distinction between the *nomothetic* and the *idiographic* approaches to personality description. Chapter 12 presents methods of test administration that serve to enrich the content of material gleaned from a Rorschach administration, particularly with respect to the *idiographic* information which the Rorschach can provide.

It should be noted that content interpretation, as presented herein, may be used in conjunction with traditional Rorschach scores and ratios in interpreting personality structure and dynamics; it need not be seen as an exclusive procedure. The present authors recognize that a few formal aspects of the system have some validity. A good example is $F+\%$, for which the validity evidence is impressive (Berkowitz & Levine, 1953; Friedman, 1952; Knopf, 1956; Rickers-Ovsiankina, 1938). Other aspects of formal scoring appear to have some validity, but the validity evidence (notably for Rorschach's M) is inconsistent. The current presentation assumes that the reader is acquainted with traditional Rorschach administration and scoring procedures.

Although the title of this book is *Rorschach Content Interpretation*, it does not deal solely with what the testee reports seeing in the inkblots. This volume also discusses various approaches to understanding the verbal and nonverbal context of test responses. Verbalizations accompanying the response are considered primarily, but nonverbal behavior occurring during testing is also dealt with. Zubin in particular (Chapter 4) has attempted to analyze such verbal and nonverbal Rorschach behavior in assessing the subject's test-taking attitudes and certain psychological characteristics of the subject's response process (e.g., affect of the subject and mood of the response). In addition to the Zubin approach, three other attempts to develop contextual scales are described herein: the Rorschach Index of Repressive Style (Chapter 8), the Communication Defects and Deviances system (Chapter 8), and the analysis of pathological verbalizations (Chapter 9). The importance of the subject's verbalizations is also accorded recognition in Burt's content category system, which is presented in Chapter 4. An analysis of the subject's verbalizations must also be acknowledged as a major part of the idiographic approaches to both individual and consensus Rorschach interpretation (Chapters 10 and 13 respectively). Based on the importance of contextual analysis in the interpretation of the Rorschach test, some have suggested (Reznikoff, 1972; Zubin et al. 1965) that the Rorschach test can be conceptualized as a special type of standard interview.

As *Rorschach Content Interpretation* does not deal solely with the interpretation of content, neither does it deal entirely with the Rorschach test. Included in the discussion of the reliability and validity of content approaches are studies that have utilized the Holtzman Inkblot Technique (HIT). The authors chose to include HIT studies because HIT content scales are largely based on corresponding Rorschach scales and because of the impressive correlations found between HIT and Rorschach content scales in the few studies that have been conducted thus far in this area (Holtzman et al., 1961; Whitaker, 1965). In addition it should be recognized, particularly in regard to reliability data, that evidence concerning HIT scales is available, whereas similar evidence for the corresponding Rorschach scales generally is not. Although it would not have been justifiable to ignore this body of literature in considering research on the Rorschach test, we recognize that one can never be completely sure that conclusions about HIT content scales are applicable to the corresponding Rorschach scales.

Not all content approaches have proved as promising as those presented in this volume. For example, research has not demonstrated the success of content inquiries such as the investigation of suicide potential (Neuringer, 1974) or the diagnosis of alcoholism (Ackerman, 1971). Such generally unsuccessful content approaches are not covered in this volume. In the interest of brevity, we have also been selective in the content approaches that are presented. We have typically chosen to exclude or give minimal coverage to content scales for which little or no reliability and validity data are available. Finally, it should be noted that some value judgments are inherent in our choice of material covered, particularly in the section on the interpretation of individual psychodynamics by means of content. We find Schafer's approach to be the most incisive. His presentation is therefore covered in the greatest detail, while the contributions of other investigators in this area are covered more briefly.

1

A Brief History of Inkblot Techniques

EARLY HISTORY OF INKBLOT TECHNIQUES

The pre-Rorschach use of inkblots and similar ambiguous stimuli has a long history (Tulchin, 1940; Zubin et al., 1965). Zubin and Eron (cited in Holtzman et al., 1961) divide the history of inkblot usage into three distinct periods. In the pre-experimental period, inkblot usage was characterized by "occasional observations that inkblots and other vague, formless stimuli were useful to the artist, the poet, and the spiritualist to stimulate the imagination, foretell the future, or communicate with spirits" (Holtzman et al., 1961, p 3). In the fifteenth century, Leonardo da Vinci quoted Botticelli as stating that when a sponge full of various colors is thrown against a wall, a blot is produced in which figures of people, various animals, etc., may be perceived. Da Vinci suggested the use of such perceptions as these for artistic inspiration (cited in Zubin et al., 1965). The nineteenth century poet Kerner produced inkblots by folding paper over drops of ink. The figures so produced stimulated him to poetry. Many of these poems and the accompanying blots were subsequently printed. The use of these inkblots in parlor-games became popular, with each person trying to use the blots to foretell the future (Zubin et al., 1965).

The second stage denoted by Zubin and Eron, the experimental period, began when Binet and Henri took a psychometric approach to inkblots, utilizing them as a test of imagination in their search for a valid test of intelligence (Binet & Henri, 1896). In America, Dearborn (1897;

1898) used inkblots to study the "content of consciousness" — i.e., memory, imagination, after-images, and associative processes. He also used inkblots to test for differences of reaction time in his subjects. Kirkpatrick (1900) found that young children and older children were more certain in their responses to an inkblot task than were children in grades four to six. Pyle (1913; 1915) noted that dull children responded in the same manner as younger children — they were uncritical and gave many responses. Whipple (1910) and Sharp (1899) used inkblots as measures of imagination. Bartlett (1916) and Parsons (1917) analyzed inkblot responses primarily on the basis of content. Bartlett distinguished between specific responses (i.e., personal reminiscences) and general responses. Parsons classified her subjects' responses into such categories as animal associations, human beings, and architecture.

HERMANN RORSCHACH

The third period in inkblot usage discussed by Zubin and Eron began with the work of Hermann Rorschach. Rorschach was born in 1884, in Zurich, Switzerland, the son of an art teacher. In school Rorschach was nicknamed "Klex," meaning "inkblot" or "painter," an appellation possibly indicating his classmates' expectation that he would follow his father's profession (Zubin et al., 1965). Rorschach decided in favor of medicine and attended universities between 1904 and 1909. From 1909 to 1913 he worked as a resident in psychiatry at an asylum. He received his M.D. in 1912, having written a dissertation under Bleuler entitled "On Reflex-Hallucinations and Kindred Manifestations." During this time Rorschach carried out several inkblot studies, but he was primarily interested in psychoanalysis.

In 1913 Rorschach worked in Russia, his wife's native country. But one year later he returned to Switzerland, where he began to experiment with his patients' inkblot perceptions. Rorschach worked with many inkblots, which he administered to a variety of patients with varying diagnoses. On the basis of his observations, Rorschach incorporated response categories into his scoring system which seemed to differentiate between diagnostic groups. He further refined his scoring categories by administering the test to individuals of supposedly known characteristics, such as mental defectives and artists. "Rorschach's methodology thus represented an early, informal, and relatively subjective application of criterion keying" (Anastasi, 1976, p 560). Rorschach was so encouraged by his results that he decided to write a monograph describing his findings. However, before Rorschach completed his work, a report by Hens was published in 1917 dealing with the use of inkblots with children, normal adults, and the mentally ill. Rorschach was critical of this approach because of its emphasis on content and the relation of responses to such factors as vocational interest and current events.

Rorschach's monograph, *Psychodiagnostik*, was published in 1921. His initial experimentation had been done with 15 blots, but he was only able to have his work printed by agreeing to limit the test to 10. The printer also reduced the blot cards in size and altered their colors. In addition an imperfect printing process resulted in varieties of shading that were not originally intended by Rorschach (Ellenberger, 1954). These altered and imperfect reproductions of Rorschach's plates constitute what is now known as the Rorschach test. Rorschach presented his test before the Swiss Psychiatric Society and the Swiss Psychoanalytic Society, but not many of his colleagues were interested in his work. Few copies of the book were sold. The test was described to the German Society of Experimental Psychology, but it was attacked by William Stern. Hermann Rorschach died in 1922.

RORSCHACH'S TEST

Hermann Rorschach wrote that "in scoring the answers given by subject, the content is considered last. It is more important to study the *function* of perception and apperception" (Rorschach, 1921/1942, p 19). Rorschach thus held that the test was essentially perceptual in nature. Four types of questions were to be asked with respect to Rorschach protocols.

1. How many responses are there? What is the reaction time? How frequently is refusal to answer encountered for the several plates?
2. Is the answer determined only by the form of the blot, or is there also appreciation of movement or color?
3. Is the figure conceived and interpreted as a whole or in parts? Which are the parts interpreted?
4. What does the subject see? (Rorschach, 1921/1942, p 19)

Rorschach's preliminary answers to these questions and sample protocols comprise the bulk of the *Psychodiagnostik*. Rorschach concluded that the answers to the questions would reveal which of the so-called types the subject belonged to (e.g., introversive versus extratensive experience type). Rorschach further held that the formal characteristics of the responses reveal aspects of the individual under study. For example, "the more color responses predominate over kinaesthetic responses, the more unstable the affectivity of the subject" (Rorschach, 1942, p 182). Finally

Rorschach asserted that the test was considerably useful in diagnosis and as a test of intelligence.

THE RORSCHACH TEST IN AMERICA

Emil Oberholzer, a coworker of Rorschach, introduced the test to David Levy, an American psychiatrist studying in Switzerland. In 1921 Levy brought a set of Rorschach blots home with him to America. While working as Chief of Staff at the Institute for Child Guidance in New York, Levy taught the test to Samuel Beck, a psychology trainee. At about the same time, Manfred Bleuler, a psychiatrist, introduced the test at the Boston Psychopathic Hospital.

In 1930 Beck published a Rorschach study involving the diagnosis of the feebleminded; it was the first published Rorschach research in the United States. Beck received a fellowship in 1934 which enabled him to study the test with Oberholzer in Zurich. In his intensive efforts at developing and encouraging the use of the Rorschach test in America, Beck was soon joined by Marguerite Hertz and Bruno Klopfer. Major Rorschach scoring systems in the United States were put forward over the years by Beck, Klopfer, and Piotrowski. Other systems include those of Hertz and of Rapaport and Schafer. A recent work of Exner (1969) has admirably summarized the differences between the various Rorschach systems.

CHANGING ATTITUDES TOWARD
THE RORSCHACH TEST

After the death of Rorschach, his test gradually came to assume a prominent place among instruments used by clinicians in the United States and in other parts of the world. However the test was subject to a number of criticisms even during the early period of its use. The present authors surveyed book reviews dealing with the Rorschach test (Aronow & Reznikoff, 1973) and a number of trends were found. In early reviews, dated from before to soon after World War II, considerable optimism characterized the field of Rorschach psychology. In some instances the Rorschach test was compared favorably with the Stanford–Binet in importance and usefulness. The major criticism of the test in the early reviews accused its users of being a "cult of the initiated" who employed complex terminology undecipherable to outsiders. A need for comprehensive norms was also voiced in the early reviews, as was a somewhat defensive posture toward criticism from the academic community. As stated by Holtzman et al. (1961, p 4), "the main stream of academic psychology looked askance at the Rorschach movement, criticizing its cultist character and lack of scientific discipline."

World War II brought with it a great need for psychodiagnostic testing in the armed services. The Rorschach became the major psychodiagnostic tool during the war; training manuals were rushed into print and many people were trained in Rorschach procedure. Following the war, graduate training in psychology increased tremendously, and the Rorschach test became one of the major clinical tools.

In the postwar period, however, failure to validate many of Rorschach's hypotheses became increasingly known in the field, and that knowledge was reinforced by the many doctoral dissertations that resulted in negative findings. Thus in the later book reviews surveyed by Aronow and Reznikoff, one finds a shift from optimism to pessimism about the test's value. The Rorschach test was described by many reviewers as invalid. Rorschachers were criticized for their resistance to modifying their interpretive systems in light of new research findings, for the rivalry that existed between the major Rorschach schools, for the overemphasis on scoring, and for the lack of links with theoretical psychology as a whole.

Consequently, use of the Rorschach test in research began a period of decline, as did other projective tests. This decline in popularity has been documented by a survey of test references in the psychological literature carried out by Buros (1970). Rorschach references as a percentage of all test references went from 18.4 percent in 1939 to a high of 36.4 percent in 1954. After this peak, the percentage gradually dropped back to 11.3 percent in 1968. Thelen, Varble, and Johnson (1968) observed that projective techniques declined substantially in use and importance among academic clinical psychologists. In a later survey of a similar sample reported by Thelen and Ewing (1970), the respondents favored an emphasis on instruction in research and therapy in lieu of diagnosis. Biederman and Cerbus (1971) have noted a corresponding decrease in the number of Rorschach courses offered in clinical training programs. The decline of the Rorschach has also been apparent, although less pronounced, in the strictly clinical sector of psychology. Sundberg (1961) surveyed 185 clinical settings and reported that the Rorschach was used in 92 percent of them; 59 percent reported that the Rorschach test was used "in a majority of cases." Lubin, Wallis, and Paine (1971) repeated the Sundberg survey on 251 clinical settings. This later survey found that, although 91 percent still used the Rorschach, only 35 percent now reported that they used the test with a majority of cases. As stated by Holt

(1968), there are a number of reasons for this decline of the Rorschach and of projective tests in general, including the expansion and acceptance of the clinical psychologist's role to include functions other than diagnosis. However it is also likely that the discouraging validity evidence has played a prominent role in the declining fortunes of the Rorschach test.

THE HOLTZMAN INKBLOT TECHNIQUE

Although a number of inkblot scales have been proposed since the advent of the Rorschach Test — e.g., the Bero test (Zulliger, 1941/1969) and the Howard Inkblot test (Howard, 1953) — the Holtzman Inkblot Technique has been by far the most successful of these additional inkblot scales. Wayne Holtzman and his coworkers published *Inkblot Perception and Personality* in 1961. This book presented the Holtzman Inkblot Technique (HIT), an inkblot test specifically designed to avoid the psychometric deficiencies of the Rorschach test. The HIT has two parallel forms, A and B. Each form contains a series of 45 cards. The parallel forms make it possible to assess the temporal stability of the HIT and also facilitates the test's use as a before-and-after measure in experimentation. The HIT permits only one response per card, and thus test productivity (R) is held constant for all subjects.

Other problems of the Rorschach test that are specifically dealt with in the HIT are the lack of objectivity in the inquiry period and the lack of agreement on scoring criteria, particularly with respect to the determinants. The HIT provides for an inquiry immediately after each response. This inquiry invariably consists of three standard questions, and the scoring procedures are standardized in terms of rating scales. The HIT manual allows for the scoring of 22 variables. Extensive data on reliability are presented and validity data are also available (Gamble, 1972; Holtzman, 1968). Anastasi (1976) describes both the reliability and the validity data for the HIT as "promising."

The major criticism of the HIT pertains to the loss of information that may be entailed in limiting the subject to one response per blot. "The clinician accustomed to subjective analysis may feel that something vital has been lost if he cannot observe a sequence of responses to a single stimulus" (Coan, 1965, p 440). Martin (1968) has also pointed to the loss of potential for sequence analysis inherent in the HIT. Hayslip and Darbes (1974) administered the HIT under an altered procedure requiring five responses per blot. These researchers found that there was a tendency for responses from the first through the fifth to become more dissimilar, a finding implying that quantitative and qualitative information may be lost through the established HIT procedure.

THE CONTENT APPROACH

Hermann Rorschach's neglect of content led to little interest in the content approach for many years, although it appears that Rorschach's own attitude toward content interpretation was undergoing a change prior to his untimely death (Brown, 1953/1960). The shift to increased interest in content began in the late 1940s with several important events in the history of content interpretation. Lindner (1946) wrote of the possible symbolic meaning of specific Rorschach responses; Hertzman and Pearce (1947) published a quasi-experimental study demonstrating types of personality interpretations that can be made from the content of certain test responses. Rapaport, Gill, and Schafer (1946) emphasized the importance of the subject's verbalizations during testing.

The year 1949 witnessed the publication of two major content approaches: the anxiety and hostility scales of Elizur, and the Wheeler signs of homosexuality. In 1950 Sen published an article reporting a study in which content scales developed by Burt (Note 1) demonstrated considerable validity in contrast to Rorschach perceptual scales. De Vos (1952) produced a series of scales of affective symbolism, and Schafer (1954) published his well-known exposition of Rorschach interpretation from a psychoanalytic perspective. In 1958 Fisher and Cleveland published their Barrier and Penetration scales, which were conceptualized as measures of the permeability of body boundaries. Other major content and contextual scales developed over the years include the elaborations of the Zubin scales (Zubin et al., 1965), Holt's Primary and Secondary Process scoring (Holt & Havel, 1960), the Rorschach Index of Repressive Style (Levine & Spivack, 1964), the Endicott scales of depression and suspiciousness (Endicott, 1972), and the Singer and Wynne (1966b) Communication Defects and Deviances system.

With the availability of a wide variety of content scales, research interest, in the Rorschach test has increasingly shifted toward content and analysis of verbalizations. As noted by Ogdon (1975), most Rorschach research studies in recent years have dealt at least in part with the interpretation of content. Anastasi (1976), Eron (1965), Klopfer (1968), and Zubin et al. (1965) have pointed out that the validity evidence thus developed on content scales is quite impressive. This circumstance has led several investigators to suggest that the analysis of content and verbalization may indeed offer the most productive approach to the Rorschach test (Aronow & Reznikoff, 1973; Eron, 1965; Zubin et al., 1965).

2

Hermann Rorschach's Content Categories

Hermann Rorschach's treatment of content (1921/1942) was extremely limited in scope, consisting largely of an assignment of content to one of six categories: Animal content, human content, animal detail, human detail, inanimate object, and landscape. Such workers as Beck, et al. (1961) and Klopfer et al. (1954) have added to the number of scored content categories. Holtzman et al. (1961) included five simple content categories as variables in the HIT: Human, Animal, Anatomy, Sex, and Abstract responses.

In addition to these simple content categories, Rorschach's category of the Popular response can also be considered largely based on content. Rorschach (1942) defined a popular or "vulgar" response as one that occurred in at least one test record out of every three. Some workers have adhered to this criterion of one-in-three, while different criteria have been suggested by others in the field. The two most commonly used lists of populars are those put forward by Klopfer et al. (1954) and by Beck et al. (1961). Klopfer presented a list of 10 popular responses, with no evident arithmetic basis for selection. Beck, in contrast, proposed 21 popular responses based on a complex arithmetic procedure. Beck's populars were derived from the protocols of 157 normal adults. His criteria include the requirements that the area must have been chosen by at least 6 percent of the subjects and that the response itself must have been given by at least 14 percent of the subjects. Despite the apparently differing criteria for selection between the Klopfer and Beck populars, it should be noted that all but essentially two of Klopfer's populars are contained in the Beck list.

Despite the very rough and simple nature of Rorschach's content categorization, the research literature appears to support at least some of the interpretations that have been suggested for content categories. The categories of human content *(H)*, animal content *(A)*, and anatomy content *(At)* are common enough in test protocols and have been empirically investigated to the point where it is possible to draw some conclusions about their validity. The literature on the popular response *(P)* is also extensive enough to allow some tentative conclusions.

THE CONTENT SCALES

Human Content *(H)*

Rorschachers have consistently interpreted human content as an indication of the ability to empathize with and relate to other people (Klopfer et al., 1954; Phillips & Smith, 1953; Piotrowski, 1957). Phillips and Smith have stated that "H implies interest in and sensitivity to others" (1953, p 138). The capacity for mature interpersonal relations is thus held to be indicated by $H\%$. However it is pointed out that having the capacity does not necessarily mean that these tendencies will be manifested in overt behavior. "The interests . . . may be expressed in fantasy rather than social contact" (Weiner, 1966, p 162).

Animal Content *(A)*

Rorschach held that animal content generally indicates stereotypy in normal as well as patient populations. Individuals scoring an $A\%$ rating of more than 50 were said to be characterized by stereotypy of thought, the tendency not to go beyond the obvious. Subjects with $A\%$ below 30 were seen as imaginative individuals "who turn away from reality to a greater or lesser degree" (Rorschach, 1921/1942, p 62). Later Rorschachers have agreed with this contention. Thus Klopfer states that $A\%$ over 50 ". . . tends to be associated either with low intellectual capacity or disturbed adjustment . . . This high an $A\%$ indicates a stereotyped view of the world" (Klopfer et al., 1954, p 314). Piotrowski remarks that "the $a\%$ increases when there is an unwillingness to exert oneself intellectually and a tendency to intellectual comfort either because of a neurosis or because of a lack of training in intellectual discipline" (Piotrowski, 1957, p 341).

Anatomy Content *(At)*

Rorschach workers have generally tended to interpret the anatomic response as an indication of concern with bodily integrity (Allen, 1954; Rapaport et al., 1968). It has also been suggested that feelings of intellectual inadequacy may be reflected by a profusion of anatomic percepts (Piotrowski, 1957; Rapaport et al., 1968).

Popular Response *(P)*

Rorschach (1942) described the popular response as indicating "the share in the collective or common way of sensing or perceiving things" (p. 198). This emphasis on *P* as an indication of whether the subject perceives in a manner similar to other people is seen in the interpretations of most Rorschach experts. Thus, Piotrowski refers to "the degree to which the subject shares the common ideas of his social group" (1957, p 108). Klopfer and Davidson describe *P* as a measure of "the subject's ability to view the world in the same way as most other people do" (1962, p 139). Molish views *P* as the "ability to adapt one's thinking to that of one's fellow man" (1951, p 253). The popular response is one of the more commonsense approaches to the Rorschach test; it directly measures the communality of the subject's percepts.

Holtzman et al. (1961) included Popular (*P*) as one of the scoring variables on the HIT. The criterion used for inclusion was that the response had to occur in at least one of seven protocols in each of two samples of subjects. Holtzman provided a list of 26 popular reponses for Form A and 29 popular responses for Form B.

RELIABILITY

Interscorer Reliability

The scoring of the various simple content categories is relatively easy, unlike the scoring of determinants which is notoriously ambiguous. Ramzy and Pickard (1949) studied the scoring reliability of various Rorschach categories using 50 Rorschach protocols. With respect to content, only 8 disagreements out of 673 scored responses were found for the categories of *H*, *Hd*, *A*, and *Ad*. Thus, agreement was approximately 99 percent. The few disagreements mainly involved the decision of whether "leg" should be scored as *Hd* or *Ad*. Rieman (1953) reported 92 percent agreement in the scoring of Rorschach content, and 82 percent in the scoring of populars (according to the Hertz criteria).

Holtzman et al. (1961) reported on interscorer reliability for the HIT content categories. These investigators found that with two highly trained scorers both working with the HIT protocols of 40 schizophrenic subjects, the resultant correlations were .995 for Human responses, .994 for Animal responses, and .98 for Anatomy responses.

Test–Retest Reliability

Results on the test–retest reliability of the simple content scales have been inconsistent and in general disappointing. Kagan (1960) administered the Rorschach test to the same set of 37 male and 38 female subjects at median ages of 10.5, 13.5, and 16.5. Fifty-two of these subjects were also administered 32 modified Rorschach stimuli at a median age of 25 years. While most of the Rorschach categories investigated involved determinants or thematic categories of content, Kagan also included *H* and *At* responses. Between the first and second administrations, an interval of 3 years, the reliability coefficients for *H* were .25 for males and .00 for females; for anatomy they were .30 for males and .21 for females. Between the first and third administrations, an interval of 6 years, the coefficients for *H* were .12 for males and .04 for females; for Anatomy responses the coefficient was .22 for both males and females. Between the third Rorschach administration and the modified blots, an interval of 8.5 years, the coefficients for *H* were .20 for males and .23 for females; for anatomy they were .18 for males and .02 for females. None of these coefficients were statistically significant.

Eichler (1951) has also provided test–retest data on various Rorschach categories. The subjects were 35 male college students who were administered the Rorschach test with a median interval of 21 days between administrations. The reliability coefficients were .76 for *H*, .74 for *A*, and .76 for *At* responses. Holzberg and Wexler (1950) presented data on test–retest reliability with 20 chronic schizophrenic subjects. There was a 3-week separation between test and retest. Correlations of .60, .94, .71, .72, and .98 were found for *H, Hd, A, Ad,* and *At* respectively.

Swift (1944) has reported the test–retest reliability of *A%* among a group of 41 children between the ages of three years, 1 month and 6 years, 4 months. With approximately a 30-day gap between administrations, the resultant reliability coefficient was .83. With a 10-month gap, using 20 subjects, the coefficient was .53. A 14-day retest was also run and the coefficient was .71. Swift also presented equivalent data for *P*.

With a 2-week interval, a coefficient of .70 was obtained; the coefficients were .70 with a 30-day gap and .51 with a 10-month retest.

Because many of the lower coefficients were obtained when the test–retest interval was longer and when the population was composed of samples of children and adolescents, it could be argued that differences in the Rorschach categories over time might reflect developmental changes in the subjects. However the very low magnitude of many of these coefficients is disturbing and raises serious questions as to how much precision can be expected of these measuring scales. It could also be argued that the applicability of test–retest reliability with the Rorschach is as questionable as it is with many other psychological tests (Anastasi, 1976), because subjects might merely be recalling previous responses. However this possibility should logically result in spuriously high estimates of test–retest reliability, rather than the type of coefficients that have been obtained for these scales.

Split-Half Reliability

Results of trials of split-half reliability have been more promising. On the negative side, Vernon (1933) split the test into two sets of five blots each. For his 90 adult subjects, Vernon found an average corrected reliability coefficient of .48 for $A\%$, and .64 for $P\%$. In contrast, Hertz (1934) reported the split-half reliability of various Rorschach scores for 100 high school subjects. The split was made between even and odd-numbered cards. The corrected split-half reliability coefficients found by Hertz for the content categories were .86 for $H\%$, .83 for $A\%$, .97 for $At\%$, and .67 for $P\%$.

Using a method that assigned consecutive responses in an odd-even split, Zubin, Eron, and Sultan (1956) found that, for the protocols of 44 "superior" subjects, corrected split-half reliability coefficients of .74, .59, and .62 were obtained for human, animal, and anatomy content respectively. For the communality scale (a scale for scoring popular responses), a coefficient of .71 was found. These results compared favorably with the split-half reliabilities of perceptual Rorschach scales included in Zubin's study, but they were not as high as the coefficients of other content-oriented scales.

Holtzman et al. (1961) have reported on the split-half reliability of the HIT content scales. Split-half reliability for the human content category ranged from .66 among elementary school children to .93 among schizophrenic subjects; most of the coefficients clustered in the .70s and .80s. For animal content, the split-half coefficients ranged from .53 among school children to .95 among retarded subjects with a median of .70. With respect to anatomy, the coefficients ranged from .54 among school children to .94 among schizophrenics with a median of .71. For populars, the coefficients ranged from .00 among college students to .77 among depressed patients with a median of .51.

It has been argued (Goldfried, Stricker, & Weiner, 1971; Rosenzweig, Ludwig, & Adelman, 1975) that split-half reliability measures are inapplicable to broadly conceived thematic scales of content in the Rorschach and other projective tests. It is doubtful that this reservation would also apply to such narrowly defined categories as *H, A, At,* and *P.*

Alternate Form Reliability

Because the HIT has two forms, it is possible to estimate the amount of error variance attributable to the combined effects of temporal fluctuations and content sampling. Holtzman et al. (1961) have reported that among 120 college students with an interval of 1 week, the obtained coefficient for *H* was .69; among 72 11th graders with a 3-month interval it was .60; among 42 elementary school students with a 1-year interval it was .64; and among 48 college students with a 1-year interval the coefficient was .64. With respect to *A,* the coefficient among the college students, with a 1-week interval was .41; among the 11th graders it was .62; among the elementary students it was .60; and among the college students with a 1-year interval, the coefficient was .42. The corresponding coefficients for *At* responses for the same four groups were .24, .25, .11, and .15 respectively. (These latter correlations are phi coefficients.) As for *P,* Holtzman et al. found a coefficient of .36 among the college students with a 1-week interval, .19 among the 11th graders, .28 among the elementary students, and .24 among the college students with a 1-year interval.

There are also some data available on the correlations between the Rorschach test and the Behn–Rorschach for various content categories. In the Swift reliability study (1944), the Behn–Rorschach was used as an alternate form. A 1-week interval between Rorschach and Behn administrations (*N* = 49) resulted in a correlation of .54 between Rorschach *A%* and Behn *A%*. When a further Rorschach administration was carried out 1 week later, the correlation between the Behn test and the second Rorschach was .74.

Eichler (1951) has also presented data on the correlations between the Rorschach and Behn–Rorschach for various categories. Median time intervals of approximately 3 weeks separated the two tests. The subjects consisted of two groups of 35 male undergraduate students. Reliability coefficients of .54 and .56 were found for *H*; .74 and .55 for *A*; and .43 and .46 for anatomy responses.

It is useful to compare the data of Holtzman et al. on alternate form reliability with the split-half coefficients reported above. The differences between these two classes of coefficients should indicate the extent to which temporal fluctuations add to error variance. The alternate form coefficients are indeed considerably lower than the corresponding split-half coefficients, a fact indicating that the scales do seem to have serious difficulties in terms of temporal stability (although the phi-coefficient data on At are difficult to interpret).

VALIDITY

H

The validational literature generally supports the relationship between $H\%$ and a desire to relate to other people (social interest), although many studies have yielded rather tangential evidence in this regard. The results of research studies in this area do not indicate that individuals with a high $H\%$ tend to be more empathic than individuals with low $H\%$. In fact, in one investigation, ratings of empathy were found to be negatively related to $H\%$ (Rosenstiel, 1969).

With respect to the relationship between empathy and H, three studies are of direct relevance: Haan (1964), Fernald and Linden (1966), and Rosenstiel (1969). Haan (1964) investigated the relationship between various Rorschach scores and 10 coping mechanisms, including empathy. The coping mechanisms were rated on the basis of interview data from 88 adult participants in the Oakland Growth Study. Haan found no significant relationship between the ratings of empathy and the number of H-responses.

Fernald and Linden (1966) hypothesized that H would vary directly with capacity for empathy, social interest, social isolation, and pathology. Although the HIT was the inkblot test employed, H-responses were scored according to the usual Rorschach rules, with H, Hd, and (H) responses receiving equal weight. The subjects of this investigation were college students, hospitalized patients, and firemen. Empathy was measured by means of paired comparison ratings; social isolation was measured through the use of sociometric preferences; social interest was assessed by scores on the Strong Vocational Interest Blank; pathology was defined in terms of a contrast between hospitalized schizophrenics and firemen. The variables of social interest and pathology were found to be significantly related to H in the expected direction. The authors raised questions as to the adequacy of their criteria for measuring empathy and social isolation.

Rosenstiel (1969) also related H-responses to empathy. The subjects were 113 students at the University of Munich (60 males, 53 females). The HIT and the 16PF were administered to all subjects, who were also interviewed for 1 hour by two psychologists. Capacity for empathy was rated. An anxiety score was secured from the 16PF. Rosenstiel found that ratings of empathy were indeed related to H, but in a negative direction for subjects high in 16PF anxiety ($r = -.50, p < .01$) and subjects low in 16PF anxiety ($r = -.55, p < .01$). The correlation was not significant for subjects intermediate in 16PF anxiety. Rosenstiel asserted that subjects with very low anxiety scores were probably responding defensively and were therefore actually high in anxiety. He also emphasized the nature of the sample, students in psychology who "hope that a study of psychology will help them to overcome their problems" (Rosenstiel, 1969, p 341). High need for contact with others was thus seen as a factor leading to unsuccessful contact behavior, which in turn led to even greater need for contact.

As noted above, Fernald and Linden (1966) found H to be significantly related to social interest as measured by the Strong Vocational Interest Blank. Further evidence on the social interest correlates of H have been revealed in studies in four major areas: interpersonal distance; occupational differences; the H-characteristics of antisocial individuals; and the H-responses of schizophrenic subjects. There are also several studies relevant to the validity of H which are not classifiable under the above rubrics.

Greenberg and Aronow (Note 2) investigated the relationship between several HIT variables and two measures of interpersonal distance, one live and the other projective. The subjects of this study were 65 college students (41 female, 24 male), although only 30 of the women and 22 of the men participated in the live distance measure. Greenberg and Aronow found a significant negative correlation between the projective distance measure and H ($r = -.25, p < 05$). Thus subjects with higher H used less interpersonal distance. However the correlation was not significant for the live measure of distance ($r = -.06$). It is interesting to note that projective indices of interpersonal distance are sometimes thought to measure the degree of closeness that individuals wish to have with others, while live distance measures indicate the distance an individual actually keeps between himself and others (Aronow, Reznikoff, & Tryon, 1975). Greenberg and Aronow's finding of a significant correlation between H and projective distance, but not between H and live distance, may thus parallel the observation of Rorschach clinicians that a subject displaying social interest as measured by H does not necessarily manifest this interest in overt behavior (Weiner, 1966).

There is also some evidence to suggest that workers in technical fields provide relatively few *H* responses. Rieger (1949) studied Rorschach differences between applicants for jobs in six major fields. She reported finding that engineers had rather low *H* in comparison with the other groups. Draguns, Haley, and Phillips (1967) reported a foreign language study which also found engineers to have few *H* responses. Roe (1952) compared the Rorschach protocols of workers in psychology, anthropology, biology, and physical science. With respect to *H%*, psychologists and anthropologists were found to be higher than physical and biological scientists. Roe also found that clinical psychologists had significantly more *H* responses than other psychologists, although Roe correctly pointed out familiarity with the Rorschach test could have biased these last results. In a similar vein, Dörken (1954) found that interns who intended to specialize in psychiatry had more *H*-responses than did the general group of young physicians.

With respect to the *H*-responses of antisocial individuals, Geil (1945), Lindner (1943), and Walters (1953) have all reported on *H%* in various groups of prison inmates. The inmates were said by these investigators to be low in *H%* (6.98 percent for Walters, 8.42 percent for Lindner, and 5.57 percent for Geil), but no statistical comparisons were made with control groups and these percentages do not include *Hd* responses. Endara (cited in Draguns et al., 1967) found that *H%* was related among prisoners to severity of offense and recidivism. Horn, Bona, and Tarkovass (cited in Draguns et al., 1967) found that institution-reared subjects differed from foster-reared subjects in having fewer human content responses.

As might be expected, several studies have dealt with the *H*-characteristics of schizophrenic individuals. Sullivan (1962) has written on the importance of interpersonal factors in treating and understanding the schizophrenic patient; Cameron (1947) speaks of desocialization as the major causative factor in schizophrenia. Disturbed object relations is commonly recognized as among the hallmarks of schizophrenia (Weiner, 1966). Surprisingly, *H* does not have a good track record in this regard.

Rieman (1953) included human content in studying the Rorschach test's effectiveness in discriminating between neurotic and ambulatory schizophrenic subjects. One hundred male neurotic and 100 male schizophrenic subjects were employed. This investigator found that human content discriminated between the groups in only one of two comparisons. The significance of the difference is stated as being only "at the 10 percent level or better." Furthermore Rieman has stated that the Rorschach protocols may have influenced the diagnoses.

Wittenborn and Holzberg (1951) compared the Rorschach protocols of patients in five diagnostic groups: paranoid schizophrenic, manic-depressive psychosis in the manic phase, involutional psychosis, simple schizophrenia, and manic-depressive psychosis in the depressed phase. Neither *H* nor *Hd* proved to be related to diagnosis, nor did they correlate with various symptom clusters.

Knopf (1956) investigated the diagnostic differentiating power of various Rorschach indices, including *H*. The subjects of this study were 131 neurotics, 106 psychopaths, and 100 schizophrenics. Knopf reported that the groups differed in terms of sex ratio, but there was no apparent attempt to control for sex. *H%* was not found to differentiate between the diagnostic groups. Armitage and Pearl (1957) also found that *H* was not useful in discriminating between paranoid schizophrenics, unclassified schizophrenics, neurotics, and character disorder subjects. However Draguns et al. (1967) have reported two foreign language studies in which schizophrenics were found to have lower *H* than normals, both among adults and children.

Friedman (1952) contrasted schizophrenic subjects with two groups of normals. *H* responses differentiated between schizophrenics and normals only when demographic variables were not controlled. When the schizophrenics were compared with normal subjects similar in terms of IQ, age, and sex, diagnosis was not related to *H*.

Although evidence of the value of *H* in diagnosing schizophrenia is not encouraging, *H* does appear to be more successful as an indicator of prognosis in schizophrenia. Halpern (1940) related various Rorschach scores to improvement following insulin therapy for schizophrenia. Fourteen male patients were the subjects. Seven were rated as unimproved, seven as improved. Halpern found that those subjects who later improved in response to insulin therapy had three times more *H%* than those who did not later improve (14.9% versus 4.9%).

Goldman (1960) compared improved and unimproved schizophrenic patients at the time of hospital discharge. Using a combined index of *M* + *H* as a composite measure of "attitude toward people," Goldman found the improved subjects to be higher in this index than unimproved subjects ($p < .04$, one-tailed test). It will be recalled that a response must contain *H* in order for it to be scored *M*.

Stotsky (1952) studied the test performance of remitting and nonremitting male schizophrenic patients. Two samples of both remitting and nonremitting subjects were used. With respect to human content, the remitting subjects in both samples had more human responses. But the differences for only one sample reached significance at .05, and this value was found with the one-tailed test of significance.

Piotrowski and Bricklin (1958; 1961) have reported on the discriminating capacity of a prognostic index for schizophrenic patients. One of the signs used was the "absence of human content" in Rorschach protocols. The authors found this sign to discriminate between improved and unimproved schizophrenics ($p < .01$).

Rickers-Ovsiankina (1954) studied schizophrenics who had improved and schizophrenics who had not. All subjects were male. Most of the improved patients had left the hospital, whereas most of the unimproved patients remained hospitalized. The interval between the first and second Rorschach tests varied from 1 to 10 years. Rickers-Ovsiankina found that the total schizophrenic group showed a significant decrease in $H\%$ over time ($p < .05$). Although the unimproved schizophrenics displayed a greater loss in $H\%$ than the improved subjects, this difference was not significant at the .05 level.

Among the miscellaneous studies relevant to the meaning of H-responses, is a report by Fisher (1962), who studied the relation of H to four self-concept indices. The subjects of this investigation were 63 college students (33 female, 30 male). The self-concept measures were obtained from the subjects' descriptions of themselves wearing masks. The four self-concept measures scored were positive attitude (number of masks referred to in a positive way), sex confusion (sex of a mask misidentified), vulnerability (injury or disfigurement described), and immaturity (masks perceived as children). This investigation controlled for the effect of R by asking each subject to give three responses per blot. Three of Fisher's four predictions were confirmed: there were significantly more instances of positive attitude ($p < .01$) and significantly fewer cases of sex misidentification ($p < .05$) and vulnerability ($p < .05$) for subjects high in H. The prediction for immaturity was not confirmed.

Richter and Winter (1966) studied differences in HIT profiles between women with high creative potential and those with low creative potential. Creative potential was assessed by means of the Myers–Briggs Type Indicator. There were 15 subjects in each group. The groups were matched for age and verbal ability. With respect to H, Richter and Winter (1966) found that the creatives had significantly more such responses than the noncreatives, as predicted ($p < .005$).

Rawls and Slack (1968) compared the group Rorschach protocols of 12 artists and 12 nonartists. There were no differences between the two groups in sex, age, verbal intelligence, and education. One of the variables expected to differentiate between the groups was human content. H did indeed differentiate significantly: the artists had a higher mean H ($p < .01$).

Morris (1952) studied the ability of Rorschach factors to predict the personality attributes of psychology trainees. The subjects were 120 male trainees. The criteria in this study were personality ratings. For $H\%$, the criterion was the rating of "motivation for scientific understanding of people." The correlation did not prove to be significant. Morris acknowledged, however, that the criterion for $H\%$ was only an approximation of what H purports to measure. $H\%$ also proved to be unrelated to another important personality rating in the Morris study, viz., social adjustment.

Ames (1959) contrasted the Rorschach records of 50 emotionally disturbed boys between the ages of 6 and 12 with those of 50 control subjects matched for age, sex, intelligence, and socioeconomic status. The pairs of records were compared for presence of 16 so-called danger signals of disturbance, one of which was the absence of H responses, or an Hd:H ratio of 2:1 or more. This particular sign did significantly discriminate the disturbed children from those who were not disturbed $(p < .01)$. Ames did not indicate the extent to which each of the two elements of this sign contributed to the discrimination.

Shatin (1955) correlated Rorschach categories with a number of TAT scoring variables. The subjects were 90 hospitalized male patients. With respect to H — excluding (H) responses — 8 of the 40 TAT variables were found to be related at or beyond the .05 level: mean deviation of initial response time, mean level of interpretation, emphasis on action and movement, picture criticisms, unpleasant feeling tone, intensity of feeling tone, strength of attack on conflict issues, and unreal or fantasied achievement. All eight correlations were positive. Shatin viewed these significant correlations as confirmation of standard Rorschach views of H, e.g., reflecting "the capacity to give goal-directive release to inner tensions . . . [and] potentiality for rich fantasy creations" (Shatin, 1955, p. 327). However Shatin's post hoc explanations are not convincing; it is questionable whether many of these correlations would have been predicted a priori. H was not found to be related to TAT "strength of interpersonal relationships," although (H) responses in this study were indeed significantly related $(p < .05)$ to this TAT variable. There was apparently no attempt to control for Rorschach R.

Burnham (1949) related Rorschach $H\%$ to subjects' scores on the Picture Arrangement subtest of the Wechsler–Bellevue. This subtest was described by Wechsler as a measure of social intelligence. Among 90 male veteran outpatient subjects, the correlation was .09. For 54 subjects in a delimited IQ range, the correlation proved to be .08.

Gibby et al. (1953) worked with three groups of male patients. One group had been in therapy continuously for at least 6 months $(N = 33)$; the second group terminated therapy before the sixth session, against the therapist's advice $(N = 33)$; the third group refused psychotherapy altogether $(N = 33)$. These investigators determined that the first group had significantly more H-responses than either of the other two groups.

However the differences evaporated when R was controlled by computing H as a percentage. Rogers, Knauss, and Hammond (1951) also found H to be unrelated to tendency to terminate psychotherapy.

A

A number of studies have investigated the link between $A\%$ and the prevailing interpretation of stereotypy of thought and poor intellectual functioning. Many of these studies must also be considered tangential to the Rorschach propositions regarding $A\%$, although the general trend of the results tends to support the hypothesized relationship.

Several investigations have explored the relation between $A\%$ and intelligence. In one such study Wysocki (1957) correlated $A\%$ on a group Rorschach with the scores on a verbal intelligence test — the S.P. 15 — and scores on a nonverbal intelligence test — Raven's Matrices. The subjects were 132 men and 85 women. Correlations of -.29 $(p <$ .01) for males and -.21 for females were found in the verbal intelligence test; in the nonverbal intelligence test, the correlations were -.12 for males and -.18 for females. Wishner (1948) correlated $A\%$ on the Rorschach with Wechsler–Bellevue scores, using a sample of 42 neurotic outpatients. The resultant correlations were not significant for the verbal subtests, but they were significant for the Object Assembly subtest ($r = -.48, p < .01$). Sommer (1957) has reported finding a clearly nonsignificant correlation of .02 between $A\%$ and intelligence in a sample of 123 psychiatric patients. The Wechsler–Bellevue verbal scale was the measure of intelligence. Draguns et al. (1967) have suggested that restrictions of range of intelligence in these samples may explain the dearth of positive findings in this area. Consalvi and Canter (1957) worked with 45 adult subjects with a large range in educational level. The Rorschach test, Raven's Progressive Matrices, and the vocabulary test of the Wechsler–Bellevue were administered to all subjects. Consalvi and Canter found correlations of -.38 $(p < .05)$ and -.33 $(p < .05)$ between $A\%$ and the matrices and the vocabulary test respectively. In short the findings on the relationship between intelligence and $A\%$ are inconsistent; results have been most encouraging with a large range in educational level. These findings may indicate a weak negative relationship between $A\%$ and intelligence.

Other studies have dealt with $A\%$ as a prediction of successful or unsuccessful schoolwork and general intellectual achievement. Margulies (1942) found that eighth- and ninth-grade boys who were rated successful in their work had a lower $A\%$ than students rated unsuccessful. This study was controlled for the intelligence of the subjects.

In the Morris (1952) study discussed above, $A\%$ was related to ratings of the subjects' "quality of intellectual accomplishments." Although $A\%$ was related to the ratings in the predicted direction, the correlation was not significant at .05 ($r = -.18$). Because the subjects of this study were graduate students, the range was reduced, and that factor may have resulted in the low correlation.

Steinzor (1944) similarly compared the Rorschach protocols of 15 achieving and 15 nonachieving college students, all of high ability. The nonachievers were determined to have a higher $A\%$, but the difference fell slightly short of significance at the .05 level. The high ability of these subjects was determined by scores on the Ohio State University Psychological Examination.

Rust and Ryan (1953) used the Davidson adjustment signs, which include $A\%$ to contrast underachieving college students ($N = 29$), normal achievers ($N = 36$), and overachievers ($N = 35$). Rust and Ryan found that $A\%$ significantly discriminated between the three groups ($p < .01$); the normal achievers had an $A\%$ less than 50 more often than the underachievers or overachievers. Surprisingly, the overachievers had the higher $A\%$.

In the Richter and Winter study (1966) of college students with high or low creative potential, it was predicted that the two groups would differ in A responses on the HIT. The groups did not differ significantly in A, although the low creative subjects had more A responses.

In the Haan study (1964) A-responses were also related to the measures of coping mechanisms. Haan found that there was indeed a significant relationship, but in an unexpected direction. Males who gave a large number of A-responses were characterized by "cognitive mechanisms, objectivity, intellectuality, logical analysis, and by tolerance of ambiguity, empathy, free expressive coping, and suppression of impulse" (Haan, 1964, p. 435). These surprising findings were ascribed to the growth study context of the investigation and to the high A subjects' lack of defensive concern in producing a childlike response.

Several studies of psychiatric samples have also been carried out with $A\%$. In the Rickers-Ovsiankina study (1954), $A\%$ was studied in relation to course of schizophrenic illness. Those schizophrenic subjects who improved between first and second testing demonstrated a significant increase in $A\%$, a fact suggesting that these subjects were increasingly able to fall back on the obvious.

Kobler and Stiel (1953) found that depressed, involutional melancholic patients had a higher $A\%$ than paranoid involutional subjects, but the difference fell short of significance at the .05 level. In the Knopf investigation mentioned above (1956), $A\%$ was included as one of the Rorschach indices used to differentiate between the neurotic, psychopathic, and schizophrenic subjects. $A\%$ discriminated significantly between the psychopaths and schizophrenics $(p < .01)$, but it did not succeed in the other two contrasts. Armitage and Pearl (1957) did not find $A\%$ useful in discriminating between four diagnostic groups. In the Friedman study mentioned above (1952), $A\%$ did not discriminate between schizophrenic and normal subjects when demographic variables were controlled.

Booth (1946) contrasted the Rorschach protocols of 60 arterial hypertension patients (tension in the vascular system-V group) with 60 patients suffering from Parkinsonism or chronic arthritis (tension in the locomotor system-L group). Unfortunately, Booth did not indicate whether the groups were equated in terms of relevant demographic and other variables. With respect to animal content, this author found an average $A\%$ of 30 in the L group and 51 in the V group $(p < .001)$. $A\%$ was interpreted to represent stereotypy of thought, and thus the L group was considered more individualistic and autonomous. Booth found further support for this view in the fact that the L group had a tendency to project images of two animals commonly associated with force and independence — eagles and pigs. By contrast the V group tended to see more sheep and cows.

Other research has considered the question of the relationship between $A\%$ and therapy prognosis. The findings generally indicate a negative relationship. As part of a study on the validity of Rorschach signs of adjustment, Davids and Talmadge (1963) investigated the $A\%$ of 28 women who showed evidence of casework movement with a social worker, and 22 women who did not display such movement. The two groups of subjects did not differ in intelligence. These authors found that the former group displayed significantly less $A\%$ on the Rorschach $(p < .001)$. In an investigation by Gibby et al. (1953), the patients who continued therapy had significantly lower $A\%$ than those who either terminated or refused to begin. Intelligence was not directly controlled, but the three groups did not differ in level of education.

Bloom (1956) compared the Rorschach protocols of normally productive and unproductive male outpatients who had good and poor therapy histories. Forty-six males served as subjects. Bloom found that among the normally productive patients, those with poor treatment histories scored higher in $A\%$ $(p < .05)$ than those with good treatment histories. However there were no differences in $A\%$ between good and poor history patients who had underproductive Rorschach protocols. Patients with a poor treatment history had significantly lower IQs, and thus the meaning of these results is unclear.

Two interesting studies have explored the relation between $A\%$ and personality measures. Gardner (1951) correlated $A\%$ with ratings of impulsivity in 10 college and graduate students. Rated impulsivity was found to correlate at .52 with $A\%$ and at .64 ($p < .05$) with impulsivity, as measured by the Rosenzweig P-F test.

In the Shatin investigation discussed above (1955), $A\%$ was also one of the Rorschach scores correlated with the TAT variables. $A\%$ was found to be significantly and positively related to the number of TAT pictures rejected and negatively related to unpleasant feeling tone, degree of inner conflict, unreal or fantasied achievement, and verbal and emotional aggression. Shatin's post hoc explanations here seem more consistent with the data; he viewed his research as a confirmation of the impression that $A\%$ is related to restrictive and inhibitory trends.

At

A number of validity studies on the At response have dealt with the so-called body concern hypothesis. The most direct test of this hypothesis has been carried out by Endicott and Endicott (1963). In this investigation 84 psychiatric patients were clinically rated on severity of somatic preoccupation and were administered the Rorschach, TAT, and MMPI, each of which was scored for somatic concern. After a treatment or waiting period, the patients were again rated and administered the psychological tests. These authors found that Rorschach $At\%$ correlated significantly with the hypochondriasis scale of the MMPI on both the first and second test occasions ($r = .24, p < .025$; and $r = .38, p < .0005$), and with the ratings of somatic preoccupation on both occasions ($r = -.19, p < .05$; and $r = -.40, p < .0005$). The negative correlations with the rating scale resulted from the scale's reversal of the usual polarity. Although $At\%$ did not significantly predict changes over time in the ratings of somatic preoccupation, the observed At changes were in the predicted direction. Endicott and Endicott also presented two clinical examples in which $At\%$ was able to predict severe somatic concerns, while the objective procedures were not able to do so. These authors concluded that Rorschach $At\%$ may be particularly useful in measuring the unconscious somatic preoccupation that objective test methods do not reach.

In a later study Endicott and Jortner (1967) investigated the relationship of At responses and other inkblot content to rated degree of somatic preoccupation. In this experiment, 90 inpatients and 40 outpatients were first rated as to somatic preoccupation on a 6-point rating scale. The HIT served as the inkblot test. The raw number of At responses was found to correlate at .26 ($p < .05$) and the HIT At score correlated at .27 ($p < .05$) with rated somatic preoccupation among the inpatients.

The correlations among the outpatients, however, were not significant.

In a study with a similar focus, Cleveland and Johnson (1962) contrasted the Rorschach records of 25 male subjects hospitalized after acute myocardial infarction with the records of 25 male presurgical patients and 25 patients hospitalized for various skin diseases. Both subject groups in distressing and possibly life-threatening medical circumstances — the myocardial and presurgery subjects — had significantly more Anatomy responses than did the patients with skin disorders.

Shatin (1952) contrasted the Rorschach records of 33 neurotic and 24 psychosomatic male subjects. The groups were equivalent in age, education, and intelligence; neither were there significant differences in total number of responses. The psychosomatics were found to have significantly more Anatomy responses $(p < .02$; with a coefficient of association of .45).

Anatomy responses have also been found to be negatively related to likelihood of rehabilitation success. Levi (1950; 1951) found high $At\%$ to be strongly linked to medical rehabilitation failure. Carnes and Bates (1971) studied the case histories of 112 patients with an $At\%$ over 30. All of these subjects were found to have been judged rehabilitation failures. Carnes and Bates interpreted their striking findings in terms of hypochondriacal personality organization which produced resistance to rehabilitation efforts.

Draguns et al. (1967) have reported several foreign language studies that found heightened At in women suffering from psychiatric complications due to pregnancy, in Parkinsonian patients, in women during their menstrual periods, and in patients awaiting surgery who suffered from chronic disabilities. On the other hand, Weiss and Winnik (1964) did not find any relationship between At and the diagnosis of hypochondriasis. Allardice and Dole (1966) likewise found that 26 hospitalized male patients suffering from leprosy did not significantly differ from 26 control subjects in At score on the HIT.

In a 1963 multitrait – multimethod matrix study, Wallace and Sechrest included the Rorschach test and the trait of somatic concern. Among the 72 freshman nursing students, At was not found to correlate significantly with somatic concern on either self-description, peer reputation, an incomplete sentences blank, or TAT measures. Anatomy responses in the Rorschach test also failed to correlate significantly with either the number of visits to health services or a medical symptom checklist. The findings of this study are by no means encouraging in regard to the somatic concern correlates of the At response. However the fact that the subjects of this study were nursing students may help account for the dearth of significant findings, because the At response may have had a specifically occupational meaning for this subject group.

Draguns et al. (1967) have suggested that a high occurrence of anatomic content may be more generally indicative of self-absorption, whether physiological or autistic in character. Such individuals might thus be expected to be characterized by a loss of interest in the external world. Few empirical studies are relevant to this enlargement of the hypothesis. The general findings of *At* as high in schizophrenics (Draguns et al., 1967; Shereshevski-Shere et al., 1953; Weiner, 1966) would appear to support this view. Also relevant is a study by Rav (1951) which related *At*% to other Rorschach variables and found significant correlations with *H*% ($r = -.25$, $p < .01$), $F+\%$ ($r = -.21$, $p < .01$), and *M* ($r = -.25$, $p < .01$). Because these other Rorschach variables are often interpreted in terms of object relations and the testing of reality, some support for the extended hypothesis of Draguns et al. is seen. But the hypothesis must await further confirmation.

Phillips and Smith have proposed that "anatomy content reflects a sensitivity to, and concern with, the expression of destructive impulses" (Phillips & Smith, 1953, p 123). Such individuals were characterized by an emphasis on bony or visceral anatomic responses. Phillips and Smith interpreted bony responses as an indication of the individual's fear of losing control of hostility. Such an individual would thus be expected to be extremely rigid in avoiding the expression of hostility. Visceral *At* responses were seen to represent a failure to repress aggressive urges. Such individuals would thus be expected to express hostility openly. Phillips and Smith tied in their aggression-*At* hypothesis with the *At*-bodily concern hypothesis by noting that "destructive impulses lead to concern about the integrity of the body and its parts" (Phillips & Smith, 1953, p 124). In a factoral study Sandler and Ackner (1951) did find a relationship between rated aggressive tendencies and a factor defined primarily by internal anatomy. This *At* hypothesis must also await further validation.

Rorschach (1942) suggested that, in rare instances, individuals of low intelligence may try to impress the examiner by reporting many anatomic percepts. Rorschach termed this the intelligence complex. Other authors (e.g., Beck, 1967) have cautioned that *At* responses may sometimes reflect a vocational interest, particularly among physicians and nurses. It is interesting to note that there is some disagreement about the extent to which medical training predisposes subjects to perceive *At* responses on the Rorschach. Molish et al. (1950) reported a relatively high frequency of *At* responses among fourth-year medical students (mean = 4.83, *At*% = 8.2). They noted that this high figure was still considerably lower than that reported by Harrower-Erickson and Steiner (1945). However Rossi and Neuman (1961) reported a mean *At* of only 2.5 among fourth-year medical students, a finding that does not differ much from that found among other highly educated groups (Roe, 1951; 1952). Because profession-related responses may be an attempt to avoid revealing oneself, it is possible that motivational differences in the subjects may explain the different results. Phillips and Smith assert that bony anatomy responses in such individuals still signify hostility; these individuals "enter medicine or nursing because these fields provide a solution to adjustment problems, problems implied in the bony anatomy content" (Phillips & Smith, 1953, p 126).

P

Surprisingly little study has been directed toward explaining the meaning of the popular response. Perhaps because of the common sense nature and face validity of this category, psychologists have seen little need for specific validation. In a novel study which is quite relevant to common assumptions about the meaning of P, Tutko (1964) found the number of P responses to be elevated among subjects who scored high on the Marlowe–Crowne social desirability scale. However Schwartz and Giacoman (1972) found nonsignificant correlations of .04 and .08 respectively between Rorschach P (as scored by Beck), and the Marlowe–Crowne and a TAT index of social desirability. The two latter indices of social desirability correlated significantly with one another.

The most common type of study involving P has dealt with the question of whether low P can be used as a sign of schizophrenic illness. Beck (1938) found that P significantly discriminated between schizophrenics and normal control subjects. Beck (1954) has similarly reported that P discriminated between schizophrenics and normals, and between schizophrenics and neurotics.

In like manner, in the Friedman investigation (1952), P (as scored by Beck) was one of the few Rorschach variables that discriminated significantly $(p < .02)$ between schizophrenic and normal subjects. As expected, the schizophrenics had fewer P responses. In the Knopf diagnostic study (1956), P as scored by Hertz was also included. Median P discriminated significantly between the schizophrenics and the other two diagnostic groups, with schizophrenic subjects scoring the lowest P. Knopf did indicate that the groups did not differ significantly in Rorschach R. Bradway and Heisler (1953) also studied the relation of various Rorschach content categories to psychiatric diagnosis. With respect to P (scored according to Klopfer), these authors found that none of the psychotic subjects $(N = 22)$ had seven or more populars, whereas 6 of the neurotics $(N = 27)$ did so.

As part of a study by Bloom (1962), populars were related to severity of psychopathology among 101 schizophrenic subjects. Among female patients, there was relatively little relation of P to severity of psychopathology. Among the males, however, a nonlinear relationship was found. The severely disturbed schizophrenics evidenced the fewest P responses. Bloom also suggested that a weighted P score should be developed, in order to give greater weight to the appearance of highly popular responses (e.g., Card V-bat).

Berkowitz and Levine (1953) compared the Rorschach protocols of 25 neurotics and 25 schizophrenics. All subjects were hospitalized patients, but these authors did not report the length of time that the subjects were hospitalized. The groups were apparently not equated for relevant control variables. P (as scored by Klopfer) was found to discriminate between the groups $(p = .03)$, with the schizophrenics giving significantly fewer popular responses.

In a Japanese investigation, Kataguchi (1959) examined the usefulness of various Rorschach scoring categories in discriminating hospitalized schizophrenics $(N = 30)$ from neurotic $(N = 30)$ and normal $(N = 30)$ subjects. The schizophrenic subjects were found to have significantly lower P and $P\%$ than the neurotics and the normal subjects $(p < .01)$. Populars were scored according to the Klopfer system.

Warner (1951) investigated P (as scored by Klopfer) to see if it would discriminate between 60 neurotic and 60 ambulatory schizophrenic outpatients. The groups were equated for age and intelligence. Warner did not find P to be effective in this discrimination. $P\%$ was likewise ineffective in differentiating the groups. He concluded that length of withdrawal through hospitalization may have been the causative factor in the previously observed low P of hospitalized schizophrenics. This result is consistent with Phillips and Smith's caution that "the obtained P is remarkably impervious to the impact of psychopathology" (Phillips & Smith, 1953, p 320). In a more equivocal vein, the Rieman study discussed above reported that popular responses (scored according to Hertz) were able to discriminate between neurotic and ambulatory schizophrenics in one sample "at the 10 percent level or better," but not in a second sample (Rieman, 1953).

Results have also been equivocal in the study of the relationship between P and prognosis for recovery in schizophrenic illness. In the Stotsky investigation mentioned above (1952), the remitting and nonremitting schizophrenics were found to differ in frequency of popular responses, with the remitting subjects perceiving significantly more Beck popular responses in both samples. However Goldman (1960) has reported no significant differences in popular responses between improved and unimproved schizophrenic patients leaving a psychiatric hospital. In the Rickers-Ovsiankina study noted above (1954), the improved schizophrenics showed a greater increase in $P\%$ than the unimproved schizophrenics. However the difference was not significant at .05.

In a study unrelated to schizophrenia, the Gardner investigation mentioned above (1951) found $P\%$ (using the Rapaport criteria) to be correlated at .67 $(p < .05)$ with rated impulsivity, and at .86 $(p < .01)$ with impulsivity as measured by the Rosenzweig P-F Test. In the Steinzor investigation (1944), the nonachievers had higher $P\%$ than the achieving college students, but the difference was not significant at .05. P was scored according to the Klopfer criteria.

In the research of Gibby et al. (1953), P was also included as a Rorschach variable (Beck criteria). With P scored as a percentage of R, Gibby et al. found that the patients who continued in psychotherapy had significantly lower $P\%$ $(p < .01)$ than patients who refused psychotherapy.

NORMATIVE DATA

Over the years various Rorschach workers have attempted to provide workable norms for the Rorschach scoring categories, including the simple content categories and the popular response. It is the impression of the present authors that many of the norms provided are flawed by inadequate consideration of such demographic variables as intelligence, social class, and race. It is also true that many available norms must now be considered somewhat dated, because they were first collected many years ago. Nonetheless the available norms do provide at least some help to the practicing clinician, provided that their limited applicability is kept in mind.

The most comprehensive set of norms for children has been presented by Ames, Métraux, Rodell, and Walker (1974). These authors have worked with the Rorschach records of 650 children aged 2 to 10 years, of "mostly highly educated parents" (Ames et al., 1974, p xiii). These records were supplemented by the addition of 900 protocols at various levels of socioeconomic status. Levitt and Truumaa (1972) surveyed 162 sources that provided normative data on the Rorschach records of children and adolescents. Using strict criteria for the inclusion of data, these authors reduced the studies to only 15 investigations, with the normative studies of the Ames group included. Although Levitt and Truumaa distinguished between the records of subjects of average and above average intelligence, they did not take into account the variables of race and socioeconomic status.

Comprehensive norms for adolescents have also been provided by Ames, Métraux, and Walker (1971) in a study of 700 children aged 10 to 16. The Levitt and Truumaa volume (1972) likewise deals with normative data on adolescents. Comprehensive norms for elderly individuals have been prepared by Ames, Métraux, Rodell, and Walker (1973) using 200 subjects over age 70.

H

Ames et al. (1974) have reported a slow but steady increase in $H\%$ from age 2 (average $H\% = 3$) to age 10 (average $H\% = 16$). However this age trend appears to be very much a function of the high socioeconomic status of these children. The age trends in H were more obscure in children from working class backgrounds, and they were actually reversed among inner city children, dropping from 22 percent at age 5 to 5 percent at age 8 and increasing again to 12 percent by age 10. One could question whether a white examiner testing a black child may have been a determining factor in the inner city age trend. In the summarized Levitt and Truumaa data, no age trends in $H\%$ were found in children of average intelligence. ($H\%$ of 11.2 would be expected at all the ages.) In children of above average intelligence, $H\%$ was noted to increase with age, from 10.3 percent at age 5 to 18 percent at age 10.

Ames et al. (1971) reported a relative stabilization of $H\%$ for adolescent boys and girls combined. When the sexes are considered separately, however, they found that the boys dropped from a high of 19.5 percent at age 10 to 13.9 percent at age 15 (16.1 percent at age 16). On the other hand, girls passed from 18.2 percent at age 10 to 21.9 percent at age 15 (20.1 percent at age 16). "Girls in general tend to give an increasing, boys in general a decreasing number of H responses" (Ames et al., 1971, p 73).

Levitt and Truumaa (1972) found no relation between age and $H\%$ among adolescents of average intelligence; 11.2 percent was expected. They did find that the increase of $H\%$ leveled off with age among adolescents of above average intelligence; it leveled off at about 20 percent in the teenage years.

In summarizing normative data on adults, Ames et al. (1974) stated that the general expectancy is of 10–15 percent for $H\%$. Levitt and Truumaa (1972) also reported an expectancy of 10–20 percent in adults, the more intelligent subjects being in the upper part of the range.

Among elderly subjects Ames et al. (1973) measured $H\%$ at 24 percent, 17 percent, and 5 percent for normal, presenile, and senile subjects respectively. $H\%$ also increased with age among the elderly, from 16 percent at age 70, to 18 percent at age 80, and 24 percent at age 90. This increase with age was also found in the longitudinal data.

Norms for human responses on the HIT are consistent with the population trends noted above. Holtzman et al. (1961) found that 5-year-olds had the lowest number of human responses among eight groups studied, and that college students the highest.

A

Ames et al. (1974) found that $A\%$ described a fairly steady pattern from age 2 through 10; it varied irregularly from a low of 41 percent to a high of 56 percent. $A\%$ was also found to vary with socioeconomic status, being higher in the lower social classes. (Among inner city children, the average $A\%$ was as high as 71 percent at age 8.) Levitt and Truumaa reported little relationship between age and $A\%$ among children of either average or above average intelligence. ($A\%$ was nearly 50 percent in these children.) Interestingly, these authors did not find that $A\%$ varied with intelligence.

Ames et al. (1971) reported that $A\%$ remained relatively stable in the adolescent years, again at approximately half the test responses. The data of Levitt and Truumaa (1972) are consistent with the Ames data. Ames et al. (1974) suggested an expectancy of 35–50 percent for $A\%$ in the adult years. Among elderly subjects, Ames et al. (1973) measured $A\%$ at 46 percent, 55 percent, and 40 percent for normal, presenile, and senile subjects respectively. There was a slight increase with age, from 52 percent at age 70, to 53 percent at age 80, and 56 percent at age 90. This tendency of $A\%$ to increase slightly with age among the elderly was confirmed by longitudinal findings.

At

Ames et al. (1974) found an average of less than one anatomic response per record for all the childhood age groups except age 9, where the mean was 1.2. "Anatomy responses . . . come in conspicuously at 8, 9, and 10 years, approximating about one response per child at each of these ages. A few girls at 10 years give *only* anatomic responses" (Ames et al., 1974, p 82). Unfortunately the variable of socioeconomic status was not considered with respect to the *At* response. Levitt and Truumaa (1972) reported a similar finding of less than one *At* response at all ages.

In the adolescent period (Ames et al., 1971), anatomic responses remained fairly static, averaging below one response per record except at age 14, where the mean was 1.21. Levitt and Truumaa reported means below 1.00 for all the adolescent ages.

Among elderly subjects (Ames et al., 1973), a decided increase in anatomy percepts was found with progressive senility; the average responses per record were 0.5, 1.4, and 8.4 for normal, presenile, and senile subjects respectively. In fact, anatomic responses were the most common responses in the records of senile subjects. In contrast, $At\%$ decreased with age, from 12 percent at age 70, to 10 percent at age 80, and 0% at age 90. This decrease is confirmed by the longitudinal data. These authors also reported that $At\%$ increased with decreased socioeconomic status, from 8.16 percent to 15.79 percent. The institutionalized elderly also were found to have higher $At\%$ than the noninstitutionalized subjects — 17.63 percent versus 6.38 percent.

The HIT norms on At are consistent with the Rorschach norms in that few At responses are noted for any of the eight subject groups. (The 50th percentile At score is no more than 2 for any group.)

P

The responses scored popular in the Ames collection of normative studies were specifically chosen using statistical criteria from the test responses of the normative samples. The actual frequencies and percentages thus obtained are therefore likely to be of little value to the psychologist who uses other lists of populars. However the general trends found are worth noting. Ames et al. (1974) found that $P\%$ doubled from age 2 to age 10. Levitt and Truumaa (1972) also found a substantial increase with age during childhood. Lower socioeconomic subjects in the Ames investigation were generally higher in $P\%$ than subjects from the higher social classes. P stayed relatively constant through the adolescent years according to the Ames data (Ames et al., 1971), though Levitt and Truumaa found a slight increase with age. Among the elderly (Ames et al., 1973), popular score was found to drop from the normal, to the presenile, to the senile subjects. $P\%$ did not seem related to socioeconomic status among the elderly. Noninstitutionalized subjects gave significantly more popular responses than did the institutionalized.

For those choosing to work with Beck's populars, there is a rule of thumb table (Beck et al., 1961) which takes into account total R.

GENERAL EVALUATION

Although the data are at times inconsistent, it seems appropriate to draw some tentative conclusions about the reliability of the content scales proposed by Hermann Rorschach. The interscorer reliability of the scales appears to be quite high and poses no problems, except perhaps for *P,* for which only HIT-based evidence is available. In a more negative vein, however, both content sampling and temporal instability appear to be significant sources of errors in measurement. To judge from available data, these sources of error may at times account for up to 40 percent or more of the variance in human, animal, and anatomy scores. The reliability of *P* appears to be particularly poor, at least with respect to the HIT. The fact that HIT populars were carefully chosen by procedures similar to those recommended by most Rorschach workers may indicate major reliability difficulties for the populars category. Although the reliability data are at times inconsistent and post hoc reasons can perhaps be found for some of the poor reliability findings — e.g., the specialized nature of the sample used by Kagan (1960) — it should be noted that reliability coefficients for these Rorschach scales have rarely been reported above .80, which is often considered the minimum necessary for reliable individual prediction. Cronbach and Gleser (1965) have characterized projective tests as instruments that provide high breadth of coverage at the expense of lowered fidelity or dependability of information. The available data on the reliability of these content scales are certainly consistent with this "lowered fidelity" view of projective techniques.

There are several problems in reaching conclusions about the validity of these scales. First, many of the validational studies discussed above were carried out many years ago, when controlling for relevant variables in a Rorschach investigation was not regarded as standard operating procedure. Second, many of the studies reported above must be considered tangential to the general hypotheses concerning content categories. In line with the holistic emphasis of traditional Rorschach interpretation, many of the early validational studies correlated numerous Rorschach scores with a particular criterion. Although the results are certainly valuable in drawing conclusions about the meaning of scores, they do not provide the focused testing of a hypothesis that is most useful, such as that exemplified in the Endicott and Endicott study on *At* (1963). In addition, of course, the so-called shotgun approach to Rorschach validation raises the probability of a Type I error in evaluating those few statistical tests that do turn out to be significant.

The validational literature generally supports the hypothesized relationship between *H* and social interest, but it does not support the concept that *H* is an index of empathy. The association of *H* with social interest is seen most clearly in the data on occupational groups, the Fernald and Linden (1966) findings on social interest and pathology, the relationship of *H* to desired interpersonal distance (Greenberg & Aronow, Note 2), the data on antisocial individuals, and the relationship of *H* to prognosis for schizophrenic subjects. Draguns et al. have concluded that "the research investigators and textbook authors are substantially in agreement; the principal meaning of *H* appears as an index of social maturation" (Draguns et al., 1967, p 23). The present authors are largely in accord with this statement, but we must add the caution that the studies supporting this particular Rorschach hypothesis consist in great measure of indirect tests of the hypothesis relevant to the construct validity of *H%*.

The most discouraging findings on *H* have come in the area of the diagnosis of schizophrenia. As noted above, the weight of the evidence does not favor *H* as a useful index for this purpose. Weiner (1966) has suggested that *H* may vary between different types of schizophrenic patients − e.g., acute versus chronic. In light of the importance of social functioning in discriminating between reactive and process schizophrenics (Higgins, 1968; 1969; Kantor & Herron, 1966), it is quite possible that *H%* may prove valuable in the diagnosis of schizophrenia if this particular distinction is taken into account. The findings on the value of *H%* in predicting improvement in schizophrenia are consistent with this approach.

The literature on *A%* is generally even more tangential to the relevant hypothesis than is the literature on *H%*. It is noteworthy that most of these studies generally support the theory that *A%* is an indication of stereotypy of thought − e.g., the investigations on school achievement, improvement in schizophrenia, therapy prognosis, and the Booth (1946) and Shatin (1955) studies. However *A%* does not appear to be strongly related to intelligence. The only conclusion that would be justified by the evidence is the statement that, although the research literature is somewhat supportive of the link between stereotypy and *A%*, this link remains to be more firmly established by clearly relevant studies. It is somewhat incredible that among the more than 4000 Rorschach publications, so few are directly relevant to this important hypothesized relationship.

More definite conclusions can be reached about *At%*, largely because of the Endicott and Endicott (1963) and Endicott and Jortner (1967) studies, which were directly related to the validation of *At%*: each was a test of the concurrent validity of *At%*. *At%* was shown to be significantly related to ratings of somatic concern and to the *Hs* scale of the MMPI. The impression conveyed by Endicott and Endicott (1963) that the Rorschach *At%* was clinically useful because it supplemented the information provided by the MMPI is a fascinating proposition. In the clinical setting, of course, psychological tests serve to supplement one another. Some statistical evidence of the extent to which inkblot *At%* predicts unique aspects of the clinical ratings not predicted by the MMPI was provided by Endicott and Jortner (1967), who found that the multiple correlation was significantly raised when inkblot content variables were added to the MMPI in predicting the clinical ratings.

The results of the Cleveland and Johnson (1962), Shatin (1954), and the various foreign language studies are also consistent with the At hypothesis, as are the studies of rehabilitation success. Three studies do not support the hypothesis (Allardice & Dole, 1966; Wallace & Sechrest, 1963; Weiss & Winnik, 1963).

There is very little literature that is highly relevant to the validity of P, perhaps because few have felt it necessary to validate this common sense scoring category. Several studies dealing with P have viewed the absence of such responses a possible characteristic of schizophrenic illness. As summarized above, these results by no means fully support the value of P in diagnosing schizophrenia. The Warner (1951) findings and those of Rieman (1953) are particularly disturbing, in that they suggest that length of hospitalization may have been the decisive factor in previous research rather than schizophrenia per se.

In view of the inconclusive findings in this one area, the lack of more extensive relevant research, and the indications that P may have major problems in terms of reliability, the present authors do not think it advisable to draw conclusions about the usefulness of P at this time. Considerable research remains to be done in this area. In such research we view the Beck populars as preferable to those presented by Klopfer, both because of the more specific statistical criteria used in setting up the Beck populars, and because of the greater possible range of scores for Beck's P.

Because normative data are available for Hermann Rorschach's content categories, they have a major advantage over the other content scales presented in this volume. However clinicians must be particularly careful in applying these norms to test subjects without regard to relevant demographic variables. Those psychologists wishing to provide more up-to-date norms would do well to consider such variables as race, intelligence, and socioeconomic status in their research design.

3

Rorschach Content Category Systems.
I: De Vos and Schafer

This chapter and the following chapter discuss four category systems for the scoring of Rorschach content. These systems are characterized by an attempt to assess many aspects of personality or test behavior based on Rorschach content. The category systems presented in these two chapters are those of De Vos (1952), Schafer (1954), Burt (Note 1), and Zubin et al. (1965). Arnaud (1959) has likewise published a Rorschach category system which, although not entirely based on content, relies heavily on content. Because Arnaud's content-oriented categories are largely duplicated by other scales presented in this volume and because reliability and validity data on the Arnaud scales are so sparse, these scales are not discussed.

DE VOS'S CONTENT SCALES

De Vos (1952) presented a system for scoring Rorschach content in seven categories: hostility, anxiety, bodily preoccupation, dependency, positive feelings, miscellaneous, and neutral.[1] Each of these categories includes subcategories that "record more precise inferences as to how affect is expressed, blocked or toned in the content symbolism" (De Vos, 1952, p 135). Capital letters are used to symbolize the major categories, followed by two or three letter abbreviations for the subcategories. A summary of De Vos's seven category content system follows.

[1]A more comprehensive exposition of these content categories was subsequently written by De Vos (Note 3).

HOSTILITY

De Vos noted that there is some difficulty discriminating between hostile and anxious responses. Responses are scored for hostility when a hostile element is prominent in the response. When one figure is seen attacking another, one must question with which figure the subject identifies.

Hor.   Hor are oral aggressive responses. In these the teeth are used in an act of biting, for example, a "couple of caterpillars eating something."

Hdpr.   Hdpr responses show depreciation or dehumanization of figures and imply indirect hostility. An example is "birds dressed in men's clothes."

HH.   HH are responses in which direct hostility is expressed, as in fighting, conflicts, or arguments. An example is "a couple of fighting cocks."

Hh.   Hh responses show indirect hostility, as in weapons, fires, knives, or indefinite hostile implications. An example is a "spear used by Indians."

Hha.   Hha are indirect hostility-anxiety responses. They include certain mythical figures and cutting weapons that might imply an underlying castration threat. They also include blood that is unrelated to other content. An example of this type of response is "an alligator's head."

Hhad.   Hhad responses are distorted figures or figures with parts missing, for example, "a distorted dog."

Hhat.   Hhat are responses indicative of inner tension, for example, an "eruption of a mountain."

Hsm.   Hsm are sado-masochistic responses and are scored where there is violation of living tissue and responses such as ripping cloth. An example is a "bat with a wing shot off or torn off."

ANXIETY

Test behavior that is symptomatic of anxiety, such as card turning, are noted marginally in the record but are not scored.

Adis.   Adis are responses that include disgusting or phobic material with either oral or tactual connotations, as it "looks like a slimy reptile."

AA.   AA are direct anxiety – fearful scenes or figures that are directly threatening and fearful, as a "huge bird clutching in toward this figure of a man here."

Aa.   Aa show indirect anxiety with figures suggestive of anxiety or usually deemed phobic in nature. An example is "pointing fingers."

Afc.   Afc are faces or profiles in unusual details (Dd) indicative of underlying anxiety regarding human relations. An example is "a bearded man."

Aev.   Aev are evasive responses. Subject avoids the blot by becoming vague, as by saying "a map."

Arej.   Arej is rejection of the card.

Agl.   Agl are responses emphasizing gloom or sadness and include cold and ice responses. An example is "eroded soil, barren and sterile."

Abal.   Abal are responses that show lack of balance or instability, as in "a mouse treading precariously."

Acon.   Acon is confusion or indecision verbalized as part of a response. An example is a "group of insects milling about not knowing what to do."

Asex.   Asex responses show confusion over the sex of a figure.

Adeh.   Adeh are percepts that are usually seen as human dehumanized: statues. An example is the inability to see popular figures on Card III.

Ahyb.   Ahyb are autistic or mythological combinations of animals, humans, or plants that create some kind of hybrid. An example is "half cobra, but from the legs down a woman in an evening dress."

BODILY PREOCCUPATION

Bb.   Bb is bone anatomy, as a "backbone."

Bf. Bf is flesh anatomy and includes all internal organs except the sexual organs. An example is it "looks like a liver."

Bs. Bs is internal sexual anatomy, as a "uterus."

Bso. Bso are sexual organs and intercourse responses, as "a cow's udder."

Ban. Ban are anal or fecal responses.

Bdi. Bdi is disease and, by analogy, rotting, putrification, or decomposition. An example is "a wasting of flesh."

Bch. Bch is childbirth or pregnancy and autistic preoccupation with birth processes.

DEPENDENCY

Df. Df are fetal, embryonic, or early infant responses. They suggest strong regressive tendencies or primitive fixations. An example is "pig embryos."

Dor. Dor are various oral responses that reflect a concern with such activities as drooling, licking, or sucking. An example is "a bee sucking nectar out of a flower, through a long proboscis."

Dcl. Dcl are clinging, hanging, or leaning responses. An example is "a man holding onto a tree."

Dch. Dch are childishly toned responses not pleasurable in content, as "a gremlin peering out from behind a rock."

Dlo. Dlo are responses that suggest longing, as "the enchanted hills, a mist setting in."

Dsec. Dsec are responses suggesting wish-fulfillment activities. An example is "this looks like a fireplace."

Drel. Drel are religious responses.

Daut. Daut are authority responses, as a "crown."

PLEASURABLE OR POSITIVE FEELINGS

Por.   Oral pleasure responses, such as "beer in ice."

Ps.   Ps responses are pleasure in sensual sensations, such as "velvety material."

Pch.   Pch responses are pleasure in childish games or content, as in "like a game where you clap hands. Two kids, I guess."

Prec.   Prec are recreational activities, cultural objects or activities, and musical instruments, as "a violin."

Pnat.   Pnat is pleasure in the beauties of nature and living things, as "a beautiful sea shell."

Porn.   Porn is pleasure in ornaments, designs, vases, bowls, etc., as "a necklace."

MISCELLANEOUS

Mst.   Mst are striving responses, as in "two animals climbing a hill — a sack race."

Mor.   Mor are responses emphasizing oral content but not specifically oral dependent or oral aggressive.

Mnar.   Mnar are narcissistic responses, usually of a bodily nature. An example is "a well-developed male physique."

Mip.   Mip are responses that show intellectual pretentiousness, as "an armadillo — it's a form of anteater, you know."

Msex.   Msex are responses of indirect sexual interest, as "panties."

Mi.   Mi are indeterminate responses having some symbolic affective significance that can't be determined, as in "Siamese twins."

NEUTRAL RESPONSES

Neutral responses include the majority of responses in a record (approximately 50 percent). Animal and human responses form the majority of neutral responses. De Vos computed total indices for each category by counting the number of responses falling into each category, and then dividing each by the total number of responses in the record.

Reliability of the De Vos Scales

To check the interscorer reliability of the scales, De Vos gave a series of 20 records to four judges, all experienced Rorschachers, for independent scoring. The mean correlation between ratings for hostility was found to be .77; for anxiety, .88; for bodily preoccupation, .99; for dependency, .68; for positive feelings, .91; and for neutral responses, .85. De Vos also computed an index composed of the combination of the categories of hostility, anxiety, and bodily preoccupation. This summary score was designated the "unpleasant affect" category. The mean correlation between the judges' ratings for this category was .88. De Vos further indicated that "disagreements as to what subcategory a response belonged to were fairly common" (De Vos, 1952, p 144), but he presented no statistics on this point. Nor did he provide data on the test–retest or split-half reliability of the scales.

Levitt, Lubin, and Zuckerman (1962) simplified the De Vos scoring system for dependency into 3 primary categories and 12 subcategories. A group Rorschach was administered to two classes of student nurses ($N = 72$, $N = 74$). These authors determined the interscorer reliability of their scale by computing the correlations between two raters, which were found to be .83 for the first class and .76 for the second.

Validity of the De Vos Scales

To determine the validity of his scales, De Vos used the Rorschach records of 60 normals, 30 neurotics, and 30 schizophrenics. Unfortunately De Vos does not make clear the extent to which demographic and other variables were controlled.

De Vos first tested for significance the difference between the mean percentages of each content category. The bodily preoccupation scale, the total unpleasant affect scale, and the positive affect scale discriminated significantly between all three groups of subjects. The anxiety scale and the neutral affect scale were successful in two of the three possible discriminations, whereas the hostility scale and the dependency scale were not successful in any of the three discriminations.

De Vos next directly investigated the discriminating capacity of the various indices by tabulating the number of subjects in each of the three groups who scored 1 *SD* and 2 *SD* above or below the mean of the normal group. Chi square statistics comparing frequencies in the three groups lying beyond these *SD* units were then computed. Of particular interest in these reported results is the relative absence of positive content among the schizophrenic subjects. A positive affect score above 20 percent excluded all of the schizophrenic subjects, whereas 17.1 percent was the mean of the normal subjects on this index. The bodily preoccupation scale also differentiated very well between the schizophrenic and the other two groups: 50 percent of the schizophrenics scored more than 2 *SD* above the mean, whereas only 5 percent of the normals and 17 percent of the neurotic subjects did likewise. The total unpleasant content scale also did a reasonably good job of differentiating: 53 percent of the schizophrenics, 30 percent of the neurotics, and only 5 percent of the normals scored more than 2 *SD* above the mean.

De Vos also compared the differentiating power of the content scales with that of $F+\%$. Taking only those subjects with two or more affective indices more than 2 *SD* from the means of the normal group, De Vos found that this included 5 percent of the normals, 40 percent of the neurotics, and 60 percent of the schizophrenics. Subjects scoring below 60 or above 96 in $F+\%$ included 5 percent of the normals, 23 percent of the neurotics, and 47 percent of the schizophrenics. In this respect the content indices clearly compared favorably with $F+\%$.

Finally this investigator correlated the total unpleasant affect category with Fisher's configural maladjustment score (Fisher, 1950). The correlation was found to be .63 when interdependent items were removed. De Vos does not report whether this correlation is based on all the subjects in his three groups.

In another study of validity, Speisman and Singer (1961) used the De Vos categories of hostility, anxiety, bodily preoccupation, positive affect, and dependency to discriminate between the following subject groups: 46 duodenal ulcer patients, and 14 patients with comparable digestive diseases; 28 patients with hypertension, and 13 patients with various heart disorders; and 20 subjects facing surgery for pulmonary and cardiac lesions. Ages for these male subjects were reported, but no effort was made to equate groups in this respect. Speisman and Singer stated that they used modifications of the 1952 content scales at the suggestion of De Vos. A chi square analysis was performed on the means from the five groups of patients on each of the five Rorschach content scores. The overall chi square proved to be statistically significant. Mann-Whitney U-tests were performed comparing all these illness categories; among the 40 possible group comparisons for the hostility, bodily preoccupation, positive affect, and anxiety content scales, only four were statistically significant $(p < .05)$. For the dependency scale, however, 6 of the 10 group comparisons resulted in significant discriminations. The ulcer patients had the greatest frequency of dependency responses, a finding consistent with expectations.

Taniguchi, De Vos, and Murakami (1958) required 100 subjects (50 delinquents and 50 nondelinquents) to choose which of the Rorschach blots reminded them of their father and which of their mother, and to state the reason why. The results of this aspect of the investigation are presented in Chapter 11. In addition, Taniguchi et al. found that, with respect to the De Vos content categories, significantly more anxious responses were given by the nondelinquent group to the cards chosen as "father card" than to the remainder of the cards $(p < .001)$. The delinquents, on the other hand, showed more anxiety in response to the "mother card" than to other blots. The nondelinquents were also found to give significantly more dependent responses, while the delinquents had more unpleasant responses to the "mother card" than to the other blots. In a direct contrast between the delinquents and nondelinquents, Taniguchi et al. noted a significantly greater percentage of anxious and unpleasant responses to the "father card" and significantly greater dependent and pleasant content to the "mother card" on the part of the nondelinquent subjects. The delinquents manifested a significantly greater percentage of neutral content in response to the chosen "mother card."

Zuckerman, Levitt, and Lubin (1961) administered measures of dependency, which included the Rorschach test, to 72 student nurses. The measures used were self-ratings and peer ratings on scales derived from Leary's Interpersonal Adjective Check List, the Gough Dominance and Navran Dependency questionnaires, the Edwards Personal Preference Schedule, the Rohde Sentence Completion test, and a group-administered Rorschach and TAT. An adaptation of the De Vos 1952 scale was used to measure dependency on the Rorschach test; unfortunately these authors do not specify the precise nature of the modifications. This study found that the more direct measures correlated significantly with the peer ratings, whereas the Rorschach, TAT, and sentence completion tests did not. The Rorschach protocols of 20 subjects at extremes in terms of peer ratings were then sorted by two experienced clinical psychologists. The judges were not able to sort subjects better than chance, and there was little agreement between the judges. These authors also cite an unpublished study in which they determined that only the De Vos dependency scale was able to discriminate between volunteers and nonvolunteers in this same group of subjects.

Pruitt and Van de Castle (1962) administered the Navran Dependency scale, the WAIS verbal scale, and the Rorschach test to 30 male welfare clients. These 30 subjects consisted of a group of 15 chronic welfare cases and 15 nonchronic cases. The groups were matched to control for ethnic classification, age, and verbal IQ. The chronic welfare subjects scored significantly higher on the Navran scale $(p < .05)$, but the De Vos content scale of dependency and a scoring of Rorschach shading responses did not discriminate between the groups. However Pruitt and Van de Castle did report suggestive findings in the predicted direction for the Rorschach scores. These authors also noted that their subjects were low in verbal IQ and gave relatively short Rorschach protocols, and thus the potential effectiveness of the Rorschach measures may have been limited.

In the Levitt et al. (1962) study discussed above, the authors hypothesized that individuals who volunteered as subjects for a hypnotism experiment would manifest more dependency on the Rorschach dependency scale than subjects who would not volunteer. The volunteers in two studies did in fact have higher dependency scores on the De Vos scale $(p < .01$ and $p < .05)$ than did the nonvolunteers.

Rothstein and Cohen (1958) compared peptic ulcer patients, schizophrenics, nongastrointestinal psychosomatics, and normal control subjects for hostility and dependency as measured by the De Vos scales. There were 20 male subjects in each group. Analyses of variance indicated that there were significant differences between the groups on both the De Vos hostility $(p < .01)$ and dependency $(p < .01)$ scales. Of the 10 possible intergroup contrasts, 6 were significant with respect to the hostility scale, and 5 were significant for the dependency scale.

As part of a general study of measures of aggression and hostility in psychiatric patients, Buss, Fischer, and Simmons (1962) administered the Rorschach test individually to 96 patients (33 men and 63 women) and scored the protocols according to both the De Vos (1962) and the Elizur (1949) scoring scales. The resulting correlation between the two hostility scales was .74. Because the correlation was so high, Buss et. al. proceeded to use only the Elizur scale in later parts of this study.

Bolgar (1954) collected 10 dreams from each of 30 adult psychiatric patients to whom the Rorschach test had been administered. The Rorschach protocols and the dreams were scored for affective content according to De Vos's scoring system. Bolgar did not report her findings separately for the various affective categories, but she did report a high overall degree of consistency between the affective content of the dreams and that of the Rorschach protocols. This investigator also found that judges were able to match the dreams and the Rorschach protocols significantly more often than would be expected on the basis of chance $(p < .01)$.

General Evaluation of the De Vos Scales

Because of the relatively small amount of data available on the De Vos scales, it is difficult to evaluate their effectiveness and potential usefulness. Reliability data are quite minimal, although information is available on the interscorer reliability of the scales. From data presented on this by De Vos (1952) and by Levitt et al. (1962) the interscorer reliability of most of the scales seems adequate, with the dependency and hostility scales evidencing the most difficulty in this regard.

Validity data are also quite sparse. The De Vos findings on the ability of the scales to discriminate between diagnostic groups is quite encouraging, although as noted there is some question as to the comparability of groups. The anxiety and hostility scales of De Vos, although more inclusive than the corresponding scales of Elizur to be discussed in Chapter 5, are nonetheless quite similar in form and apparently correlate well with the Elizur scales. There is no evidence that the De Vos scales are any more valid than the corresponding Elizur scales. Because far more empirical information is available on the Elizur scales, it is not likely that the De Vos scales will supplant them.

Several other of the De Vos scales are quite original, however, and may prove to be useful. De Vos's distinction between content categories suggesting pleasant and unpleasant affect is interesting and original. His findings on the particular diagnostic usefulness of the pleasant content scale certainly call for further research with this scale.

De Vos's dependency scale is also potentially useful for clinical purposes. Dependency is a major personality construct utilized by clinicians, and De Vos's scale is one of the few attempts to quantify the measurement of this construct by means of inkblot content. It is thus not surprising that most validity studies on the De Vos scales have dealt with the dependency scale. The results of these investigations have been mixed: the studies of Levitt et al. (1962) and Speisman and Singer (1961) yielded positive findings with the scale in various situations; however Pruitt and Van de Castle (1962) and Zuckerman et al. (1961) did not report encouraging results, although the limitations of the sample used by Pruitt and Van de Castle should be kept in mind.

The failure of the dependency content scale to relate to other measures of dependency is not encouraging, although Zuckerman et al. (1961) note one instance in which only the De Vos scale was able to predict a relevant criterion. In terms of interscorer reliability, the content scale of dependency does apparently have some difficulties. These difficulties may also help to explain the inconsistent validity findings on the dependency scale.

SCHAFER'S CONTENT THEMES

In his 1954 book *Psychoanalytic Interpretation in Rorschach Testing,* Roy Schafer presented a listing of Rorschach content that suggested 14 major personality themes. It should be noted that Schafer's themes were not presented as a psychometric scale but rather "as an illustration of a way of thinking about Rorschach responses" (Schafer, 1954, p 138). Schafer recommends that content interpretation be carried out flexibly and that the context of the responses be taken into account. His approach emphasizes the interpretation of idiosyncratic dynamics. This approach to Rorschach interpretation is discussed further in Chapter 10.

Schafer's content categories are presented in this chapter for two principal reasons. First, the few attempts to quantify and empirically investigate Schafer's themes have met with no small measure of success. Second, Schafer's listing covers areas which hold considerable interest for psychoanalytically oriented psychologists and which might fruitfully be explored in future research.

Schafer's 14 themes and some scoring examples follow.

DEPENDENT ORIENTATION, ORALITY, AND PREOCCUPATION WITH SUPPLY AND DEMAND

Supply; oral-receptive orientation.
Food: These include meat, vegetables, candy, ice cream, and boiled lobster.
Food sources: These include breasts, udders, nipples, and corn fields.
Food objects: These include syrup jars, frying pans, decanters, cornucopias, and table settings.
Food providers: These include waiters, bakers, cooks, and mother birds with worms.
Passive food receivers: These include chicks with open beaks, nursing lambs, fetuses, fat persons, big bellies, pigs, and persons eating.
Food organs: These include mouths, lips, tongues, throats, stomachs, umbilical cords, and navels.
Supplicants: If thematic context is conspicuously oral, these include beggars, persons praying, and hands raised in supplication.
Nurturers, protectors: These include nurses, cows, mother hens, birds in nests, good fairies, and protective angels.
Gifts, givers: These include Santa Claus, Christmas trees, and Christmas stockings.

Good luck: These include wishbones (other than near-popular middle orange on card X) and horseshoes.

Oral erotism: These include figures kissing or nuzzling, lips, and lipstick.

Demand; oral-aggressive orientation.

Devourers: These include birds, beasts, and persons of prey and their oral and clawing parts, such as lions, tigers, sharks, crocodiles, vampires, Dracula, wolves, coyotes, vultures, octopuses, wild boars, tapeworms, crabs (other than the popular side blue crab and the common side gray and upper gray crab on Card X), spiders, spider webs, claws, teeth, eagles' beaks, fangs, tusks, jaws, and cannibals. Tomoto worm, mosquito, and the like may be regarded as defensively minimized devourers.

Devouring: This category includes carcasses and animals clawing, biting, chasing, or eating other animals or persons.

Engulfing, overwhelming figures and objects: These figures include women with enveloping cloaks, witches, octopuses, pits, vises, traps, and spiders.

Depriving figures and objects: Included here are breastplates or brassieres (in heavily oral contexts, brassieres seem to stand for barriers to the desired object — the breast), flat-chested (breastless) women and witches.

Deprivation: Typical objects of deprivation are beggars, scarecrows, emaciated faces, wasteland, and steer skulls in the desert (if the prevailing emphasis is on oral rather than decay themes.) See also masochism, and concern with aging and death below.

Impaired or denied oral capacity: This category includes mouthless or toothless faces, false teeth, and dentists' tools.

Oral, verbal assault: Included here are persons or animals arguing, spitting, yelling, sneering, or sticking out their tongues.

Burdens: These include oxen, yokes, camels, mules, men weighted down by packs, and Atlas. (If oral themes are emphasized, these images may relate to feelings of being drained or sucked dry.)

ANAL ORIENTATION AND PREOCCUPATION

Direct anal reference. These images include the anus, rectum, colon, buttocks, feces, toilet seats, persons or animals defecating, bustles, and rear ends of creatures.

Anal contact and perspective. Included in this theme are figures seen from behind or with their backs turned, buttocks touching or bumping, and persons back-to-back.

Dirt.   Images of mud, dirt, smears, stains, and splatters compose this category.

Assault; explosion.   Included here are bleeding rectums, creatures with talons around an anus, erupting lava, flaming tails of rockets or jets, and gas masks.

SADOMASOCHISTIC ORIENTATION

Sadism with an emphasis on hostility, attack, violence, or destructiveness.

> *Oral attack:* Images suggest devouring, stinging, biting, or tearing objects or creatures, as in the oral-aggressive examples cited in the section on the oral-aggressive orientation of demand, above.
>
> *Anal attack:* Bombs, explosions, torpedoes, volcanos, poison gas, and gas masks are included here. (Also see the above section on assault and explosion.)
>
> *Phallic attack:* Images include piercing, cutting, bludgeoning, and shooting objects and creatures, such as arrows, spears, cannons, rifles, knives, hatchets, saws, pliers, shears, clubs, stingers, horns, rhinoceroses, centaurs, and charging bulls.
>
> *Aggressive primitive men:* The category includes Mr. Hyde, cavemen, Ku Klux Klan figures, Prussians, savages, demons, devils, King Kong and Joseph Stalin.
>
> *Aggressive primitive women:* These include shrews, witches, Amazons, Medusa, Charles Addams's cartoon woman, and other menacing female figures.
>
> *Miscellaneous:* Included here are images of blood, tanks, steam rollers, animals colliding head-on, legs smacking together, and persons fighting or wrestling.

Protection and defense.   Examples are shields, armor, shells, camouflages, visors, helmets, hip guards, shoulder pads, breastplates, moats, fortresses, turrets, porcupines, and sheltering features of the terrain such as valleys or thickets.

Masochism: Emphasis on victimization, damage, punishment and defeat.

Deprived, devoured, burdened: See the examples listed under demand and oral-aggressive orientation in the section on dependent orientation and orality.

Mutilated: Included here are mangled wings, bleeding legs, squashed tomcats, bleeding vaginas, peg-leg sailors, headless women, split-open skulls, and persons being torn in half.

Worn, diseased, ruined, dead: This theme includes images of tattered clothes, falling birds shot in flight, mummies, inflamed tissue, gangrenous tissue, pus, ruined walls, bombed buildings, war-torn and devastated terrain, eroded pelvises, rubble, withered leaves, autumn leaves and stagnant water.

Oppressed: Images of oppression include slaves, climbing animals being pushed down or held down, oxen, and yokes.

Punished: Hell, fire and brimstone, persons on racks exemplify this theme.

AUTHORITARIAN ORIENTATION

Authority.

Power: Included here are God, Jehovah, kings, queens, crowns, thrones, scepters, generals, admirals, Napoleon, Prussians, policemen, Ku Klux Klan figures, seals of state, fierce or huge or otherwise threatening figures, and persons giving orders or addressing a multitude.

High social status: This category includes crests or coats of arms, derbies, top hats, mink coats, castles, palaces, and butlers. References are made to the pride, elegance, richness and formality of figures and objects.

Subjugation.

Submission: Images here include slaves, servants, kneeling or servile positions, squashed or crushed figures, chains, prison bars, yokes, robots, parrots, chess pawns, trained seals or monkeys, marionettes, clipped French poodles (regarded as an utterly and humiliatingly domesticated beast).

Low social status: Included here are torn or ragged clothing and objects, huts, beggars, slaves, servants, and peasants. References are made to the coarseness, dirtiness, and clumsiness of figures and objects.

Rebellion.   Typical images for this theme are the liberty bell, and other references to the American Revolution; the Confederate flag or hats and other references to the rebellion of the South; American Indians and other references to defiance of white man's authority; the hammer and sickle and other references to the Communist revolution or to overthrow of established social and economic authority; the devil, Loki, and other references to religious and mythological figures of rebellion; and gangsters, a person sticking out his tongue, cracked yokes, and broken chains.

SUPEREGO CONFLICTS

Guilt. Hell, purgatory, Satan, cloven hooves, fire and brimstone, black sheep, and stains exemplify this theme.

Morality. Jehovah, prophets, Puritans, policemen, the Decalogue, and inquisitors fall into this category.

Projected superego. Pointing fingers, eyes, and ears are characteristic of this theme.

Innocence; denied guilt. Images include Jesus, the Madonna, saints, angels, cherubs, nuns, monks, cathedrals, halos, good fairies, Alice in Wonderland, lambs, bunnies, "snow-white buttocks," and Snow White.

Masochism. See the masochistic categories in the above section on sadomasochistic orientation.

GENERAL WEAKNESS AND STRENGTH

Weakness.
   Inadequacy, impotence: Typical images of this theme are straw man, scarecrows, jellyfish, bodies without backbones, "ghosts without muscles," drooping arms, wings too large or heavy for their body, birds without wings, dunce caps, dangling legs, "mice barely hanging on"; emphasis placed on bad construction or preparation, as in a badly tied bow tie, a badly smeared slide, a crudely skinned animal, or badly baked cookie.
   Fearfulness: Images of fear are ugly, weird, loathsome, huge, menacing, sinister, frightening, or frightened figures such as gorillas, ghosts, Dracula, dragons, monsters, dark caves, fleeing deer, dogs scampering away, or a bat coming toward one.
   Need for support and guidance: This need is visualized in beacons, handles, lighthouses, canes, and crutches.

Strength.
   Physical power; potency: Included here are powerful wings, mus-

cular figures, lumberjacks, truck drivers, Atlas, Hercules, stags, and charging bulls.

Wisdom: Socrates, Buddha, Christ, Shakespeare, Lincoln, Einstein, and similar persons are seen in this category.

Leadership; forcefulness; heroism: Napoleon, George Washington, Teddy or Franklin Roosevelt, kings, crowns, Norsemen, and warriors are typical images of leadership.

Counterphobic attitude: This theme includes toy gorillas, comic book monsters, "ridiculous ghosts," "an ancient tribal mask that once was frightening," and similarly belittled phobic images. (Also see the theme of fearfulness in the above section on general weakness and strength.)

FEAR OF AND REJECTING ATTITUDE TOWARD MASCULINE IDENTITY, AND FEMININE IDENTIFICATION IN MEN

Reversal, combining, blurring and arbitrary assignment of sex characteristics. The middle figure on Card I is seen as a man; the popular figure on Card III is seen as a woman or bisexual; the lower middle of Cards II and VII and the upper middle of Card IV are viewed as a penis; the lower middle of Card I and the upper middle of Card II appear to be a vagina; the upper middle of Card IV is seen as an ambiguous sex organ. Other images include men in gowns, such as mandarins and monks; figures that change from the sex originally specified; symmetrical figures seen as one man and one woman; mixed-species figures such as mermaids or centaurs. (Mixed-species figures may refer to feelings of being part man and part woman. They may deny sexual identity by eliminating human sex organs. Such images may state a more general theme regarding impulses, however, such as half-human and half-inhuman or half-good and half-bad.)

Feminine emphasis. Images in this category include brassieres, bed jackets, corsets, stockings, gowns, materials and textures (silk, taffeta, and tulle), jewelry, perfume bottles, cosmetics, images of pregnancy, and decorative objects and plants, such as vases, chandeliers, candelabra, and pretty flowers. Careful attention is paid to the details of the dress of female figures.

Reference to perversions. Such references are typically visualized as lesbians embracing, men embracing, women masturbating men, bestiality, men with cosmetics, frank transvestism, and androgyny.

Hostile, fearful conception of masculine role; phallic-aggressive emphasis.   Included here are images of a gigantic penis, bleeding hymens, clubs, arrows, drills, cavemen, apemen, fighting cocks, and double-barreled shotguns. (Also see the above subsections on phallic attack and aggressive primitive men in the first section under sadomasochistic orientation.)

Hostile, fearful, rejecting characterizations of women.   These include Amazons, witches, Medusa, shrews, gossips, "old hens," webs, traps, and a vagina with hooks in it.

Equating passivity and/or exhibitionism with femininity; preoccupation with feminine bodies and pleasures.   This theme includes images of woman reclining, sunbathing, sleeping, eating, or having a gay time. Chorus girls, ballerinas, nudes.

Anal perspective and preoccupation.   See the above section on anal orientation and preoccupation.

"Castration" emphasis.   Images include amputated, crippled, stunted, withered, deformed, or missing limbs or heads; nutcrackers, pliers, tweezers, and trusses; stumps of trees, and dead branches; cuts, wounds, scars and missing or blind eyes; and unfinished figures. (Also see the above subsection on inadequacy under the theme of general weakness and strength.)

General increase in sexual, anal, and oral imagery.   Included here are images of penises, testicles, vaginas, wombs, sexual intercourse, anuses, colons, mouths, food, breasts, and devouring.

FEAR OF AND REJECTING ATTITUDE TOWARD
FEMININE IDENTITY, AND MASCULINE
IDENTIFICATION IN WOMEN

Reversal, combining, blurring or arbitrary assignment of sex characteristics.   See the corresponding category in the preceding section on masculine identity.

Masculine emphasis.   This theme is visualized in images of mechanical objects, especially if specifically named, such as in "the wings of a DC-3" or "a mechanical governor." Also included are athletic objects and figures, such as baseball bats, umpires, bowling pins, ice skaters, and mountain climbers.

Reference to perversion.   See the corresponding category in the preceding section.

Hostile, fearful conception of masculine role; phallic-aggressive emphasis.   See the corresponding category in the preceding section.

Warding off intrusion.   Included here are images of shields, dragons at the entrance to a building, and gargoyles over a doorway.

Disparagement (symbolic castration) of men.   This theme is characterized by gnomes, dwarves, gremlins, dunces, boys, Little Lord Fauntleroy, Andy Gump, a man with no chin or a receding chin, dandies, little men, artificial antlers, and deer without antlers.

Disparagement of maternal figures.   Flat-chested women, bony chests.

Rejecting attitude toward conventional feminine role and status.   Included here are images of women engaged in trivial gossip and vacuous-looking women. There is revulsion in the response to images of menstruation or of a vagina.

Castration emphasis.   See the corresponding category in the preceding section.

Sensuous attention to physical, feminine detail.   Responses here include fine descriptions of the dress, grooming, shapes, and attractiveness of female figures.

General increase in sexual, anal and oral imagery.   See the corresponding category in the preceeding section.

REJECTING ATTITUDE TOWARD ADULT,
NURTURING PARENTAL ROLE

Regressive preoccupation with childhood imagery.   Such images are typified by witches, dragons, wizards, elves, ogres, Alice in Wonderland, Snow White, children bundled up, cradles, bunnies, leggings, circuses, fireworks, candy, and ice cream.

Devouring characteristics of children.   Baby crocodiles, little demons, fat-bellied devils, tiny lions, fat-cheeked pussy cats, and lizards are examples of images in this category.

Feelings of being devoured.   Included here are visualizations of bones or chicken necks, with the meat removed; "the skin eaten away by bugs," mice tearing down a house; emaciated cow head.

General oral emphasis.   See the first section, dependent orientation.

NEGATIVE IDENTITY: DEFIANT, OSTENTATIOUS,
CHRONIC FAILURE AND INADEQUACY AS A
LIFE ROLE

Weakness.   See the corresponding category under the above section on general weakness and strength.

Castration emphasis.   See the corresponding category under the above section on masculine identity.

Subjugation.   See the corresponding category under the above section on authoritarian orientation.

Masochism.   Emphasis on victimization, damage, defeat, punishment, and ruin characterize this response. (Also see the corresponding category under the above section on sadomasochistic orientation.)

Deprivation.   See the corresponding subsection under the above theme of dependent orientation, orality, and preoccupation with supply and demand.

Decline.   See the section below on *concern with aging and death.*

BODY NARCISSISM AND SENSUALITY

Images of this theme include jewelry, dress forms, hairdressers' head rests, and perfume bottles; clothing and other decorative objects, especially with emphasis on their sheen, iridescence, fragility, delicacy, and texture; peacocks, exotic scenes, and persons or objects from *The Arabian Nights*; chorus girls, sunbathers.

CONCERN WITH REPRODUCTION OR
GENERATION

This concern is visualized in ovaries, uteri, wombs, swollen or pregnant abdomens, eggs, storks, fetuses, semen, stamen, pistils, pollen, seeds, a woman in a delivery position, and umbilical cords. Emphasis is placed on big, hollow, empty, or cleaned out internal spaces, or on worn, broken or distorted pelvic anatomy.

CONCERN WITH AGING AND DEATH

Concern with death is expressed in worn, torn, and decayed persons, anatomy, animals, plants, and objects, as in a withered leaf, old posts, worn-out skin, mangy fur, eroded pelvises, ragged boots, and frayed garments. (Also see the examples in the section on masochistic imagery, under the theme of sadomasochistic orientation.)

EMOTIONAL TONE AND INTERPERSONAL ATMOSPHERE

Sad.   Tears, crying, mourning, desolation, ruins, decay exemplify this response.

Gay, warm.   Included here are images of carnivals, circuses, clowns, frolicking, dancing, embraces, snuggling, kissing, toys, and childhood references as in the above section on regressive preoccupation, under the theme of a rejecting attitude toward the adult role.

Cold.   Eskimos, ice, icebergs, snow, and polar bears characterize this category.

Barren, lonely.   Deserts, little islands, wasteland are typical images.

Controlled.   Images here include governor or steam engines, anemometers, walls, shells, and other geometrically precise objects.

Cautious, timid, slow.   Turtles, snails, rabbits, mice, and masks are common in this category.

Turmoil.   Images of turmoil include thunderstorms, high winds, storm clouds, lightning, fire, explosions, volcanos, and chaos.

Active.   Leaping, springing, dancing, playing, pushing, and charging images exemplify this response.

Inert.   This theme is visualized as lying or sitting down, resting, or sleeping or as images of a snail or sloth.

Validation of the Schafer Themes

Only a few studies have empirically investigated the Schafer themes. These investigations have dealt with two major issues: the measurement of dependent orientation and the use of Schafer's themes in differentiating homosexuality.

MEASUREMENT OF DEPENDENCY

Masling, Rabie, and Blondheim (1967) related Schafer's Rorschach thematic categories of oral dependence and oral sadism to obesity and TAT measures. Twenty obese Israeli subjects (18 female and 2 male) and 18 control subjects (16 female and 2 male) were contrasted in this study. Because the experiment concerned obesity, Schafer's subcategory of food images was not included in the scoring. Masling et al. reported 93 percent agreement for two scorers with respect to scoring reliability. Obese subjects were found to have given significantly more oral-dependent responses ($p < .01$), but the two groups did not differ in oral-sadistic Rorschach responses. Correlations of .58 for oral dependence ($p < .01$) and .51 for oral sadism ($p < .01$) were found between the Rorschach content scores and corresponding TAT indices.

Masling, Weiss, and Rothschild (1968) used Schafer's dependency categories (oral dependence and oral sadism) with a group of 23 male yielders and 21 male nonyielders in an Asch conformity experiment. All subjects were college students to whom the Rorschach test had been administered. These authors found the yielders to have significantly higher oral dependence percentages on the Rorschach ($p < .05$), as was predicted. No differences in oral sadism between the two groups were noted. Later-born subjects were found to have significantly higher oral dependence Rorschach percentages than firstborn or only children ($p < .05$). Masling et al. (1968) also report 89 percent agreement in the scoring of oral percepts. The correlation coefficients for the agreement of the scores of two raters were determined to be .89 for oral dependence and .87 for oral sadism.

Bertrand and Masling (1969) reported on the oral-dependent and oral-sadistic Rorschach responses of alcoholics. Twenty alcoholics were compared with a matched control group of 20 subjects; all subjects were male. A separate Rorschach category, consisting of alcohol, drinking, and liquid percepts was also scored. Bertrand and Masling report 96 percent agreement in scoring for orality. A correlation of .62 was noted ($p < .005$) between oral responses and total Rorschach R, and an insignificant correlation of .32 was found between oral-dependent and oral-sadistic responses. With R controlled, the alcoholic subjects gave significantly more oral-dependent responses than the control subjects ($p < .02$). There were no differences in oral-sadistic responses.

Weiss and Masling (1970) investigated oral imagery in the Rorschach records of 23 heavy drinkers (including 9 diagnosed as alcoholic), 6 asthmatics, 13 obese patients, 6 who stuttered, 10 with ulcers, and 16 thumb-sucking patients. To each of these experimental subjects, a control subject was matched for sex, age, education, marital status, and diagnosis — except in the case of diagnosis for the 9 alcoholics. All subjects were receiving outpatient psychotherapy. The Rorschach records were scored for oral-dependent and oral-sadistic imagery according to the Schafer criteria. However obese subjects and controls were not scored for food and eating responses and alcoholics and controls were not scored for liquor and drinking responses. Productivity was controlled by computing the content categories as percentages. These authors found no significant differences between the experimental and the control groups in Schafer's oral sadistic category, although the asthmatics were found to give significantly more hostile and destructive responses than the corresponding control subjects ($p < .04$). However four of the experimental groups — obese patients, stutterers, ulcer patients and alcoholics — had significantly more oral-dependent responses than the controls.

Wiener (1956) studied the oral Rorschach percepts of neurotic depressives and alcoholics. In this study the Rorschach protocols of 42 subjects were scored in a manner that differed somewhat from that of Schafer; Weiner scored food objects, parts of the anatomy used for ingestion, acts of eating or preparing food, use of the mouth for eating or noneating purposes, and eating and cooking implements. Once a response was scored as oral, it was designated as either positive, neutral, or hostile. Wiener found that the depressives had a significantly greater percentage of hostile oral responses ($p < .01$), significantly more neutral oral responses ($p < .01$), and significantly less positive oral responses ($p < .01$) than the alcoholics.

DIFFERENTIATION OF HOMOSEXUALITY

Andersen and Seitz (1969) investigated the usefulness of Schafer's content category *fear of and rejecting attitude toward masculine identity* in differentiating homosexual, sex-role disturbed, and heterosexual subjects. Forty-five male psychiatric patients served as subjects. There were no significant differences between the three groups in age, education, intelligence, or number of hospitalizations. The Schafer signs were found to discriminate significantly between all groups in the expected directions. Unfortunately these authors do not indicate whether Rorschach productivity was controlled.

Raychaudhuri and Mukerji (1971) studied the diagnostic usefulness of both the Wheeler signs of homosexuality and Schafer's *fear of and rejecting attitude toward masculine identity.* Fifteen active homosexuals, 15 passive homosexuals, 15 sex-role disturbed persons, and 15 heterosexuals were the male subjects of this study. All subjects were convicts in West Bengal, India. The Schafer signs of homosexuality for the Rorschach test were able to discriminate significantly between active homosexuals and sex-role disturbed subjects ($p < .025$), between active homosexuals and heterosexuals ($p < .01$), between passive homosexuals and sex-role disturbed subjects ($p < .025$), and between passive homosexuals and heterosexuals ($p < .025$). The Schafer signs were not able to discriminate between active and passive homosexuals or between sex-role disturbed subjects and heterosexuals. The Schafer category proved to be superior to the Wheeler signs in that the former made four significant discriminations, whereas the latter made only two. However, like Anderson and Seitz, these authors do not indicate whether Rorschach productivity was controlled.

Hooker (1958) used six major Schafer themes in her well-known study of male homosexuality. The subjects of this investigation were 30 homosexual males matched for age, intelligence, and education with 30 heterosexual males. The six themes used were *dependent orientation, anal orientation, sadomasochistic orientation, fear of and rejecting attitude toward masculine identity, negative identity,* and *body narcissism.* Three of the six *(dependent orientation, anal orientation,* and *fear of and rejecting attitude toward masculine identity)* differentiated between the homosexuals and heterosexuals at or beyond the .05 level. Hooker notes that the significant differences are consistent with psychoanalytic views of homosexuality. However she also questions the usefulness of the Schafer themes in identifying homosexuality in individual cases.

Armon (1960) used several of Schafer's themes in an investigation of overt female homosexuality. In this work 30 female homosexuals were compared with 30 mothers whose children were participating in a preschool program. There were no significant differences between the groups in age, education, socioeconomic level, or cultural status (foreign born versus first-generation American). Based on psychoanalytic views of female homosexuality, Armon predicted that on the Rorschach test the homosexual group would display significantly more *dependency orientation (supply and demand), hostile-fearful conception of the feminine role, disparagement (symbolic castration) of men, hostile-fearful conception of the masculine role, rejection of feminine identification,* and *limitations in personal-social adjustment.* Armon's themes were largely based on those presented by Schafer (1954). Although psychologists serving as judges were not able to sort the records better than chance, Armon found significant differences in the predicted direction between the two groups in the major categories of *hostile-fearful conception of female role* ($p < .01$) and *disparagement of men* ($p < .05$). There were no significant differences in *dependency orientation, hostile-fearful conception of female role,* or *rejection of feminine identification.* In two of the subcategories of *limitations in personal-social adjustment,* significant differences were again found. Because of the highly exploratory nature of this research, it is not possible to determine if those scales that did not discriminate significantly failed to do so because of shortcomings in the scales or because of errors in the theoretical conceptualization of female homosexuality.

Evaluation of the Schafer Themes

For a content system so firmly based in Freudian theory, Schafer's themes have proved to be surprisingly robust in the few empirical studies carried out to date. No evidence is available on the reliability of Schafer's themes, except with respect to the interscorer reliability of oral dependency. The interscorer reliability for the Schafer themes of oral dependency appears to be quite acceptable, in contrast to that found with the De Vos dependency scale.

The validity of the oral-dependent (receptive) theme has been shown in four investigations (Masling et al., 1967; Masling et al., 1968; Bertrand & Masling, 1969; Weiss & Masling, 1970) to be high in obese subjects, in yielders in an Asch-type experiment, in alcoholics, in stutterers, and in ulcer patients. Schafer's theme of *fear of and rejecting attitude toward masculine identity* has been found to be useful in differentiating homosexual from heterosexual subjects in three studies (Andersen & Seitz, 1969; Hooker, 1958; Raychaudhuri & Mukerji, 1971). Raychaudhuri and Mukerji (1971) have cited two other foreign language studies that have also found the Schafer themes useful in differentiating homosexuals. Armon's (1960) study of female homosexuals and Hooker's study also found several other of Schafer's categories to discriminate significantly between groups. Although these studies constitute only a handful of empirical investigations, two of which did not control for productivity (Andersen & Seitz, 1969; Raychaudhuri & Mukerji, 1971), and although the meaningfulness of differentiating homosexuality is questionable (see Chapter 8), the present authors believe it is notable that not one study has yet been reported which has found evidence militating against the validity of the Schafer themes. This track record compares quite favorably, of course, with studies of the validity of traditional Rorschach scores, and even with validity studies of other content scales. Given the interesting psychoanalytic approach of the Schafer themes, their diagnostic impact, and the positive validity evidence for at least some of them, it seems clear that they merit considerable attention in future Rorschach research.

4

Rorschach Content Category Systems.
II: Burt and Zubin

One English Rorschach investigator whose work with the test has received little attention in the United States is Professor Cyril Burt of factor-analytic fame. In an unpublished monograph (Note 1), Burt presented a system for the interpretation of Rorschach content and test behavior. He held that the Rorschach determinants do not correlate significantly with independent assessments of the individual, and that it is therefore

> ... not on scores, but on impressionistic judgements ... and still more on a study of the content (much as one would study a letter of literary composition) that ... most stress should be made. The value of the blots is that it [sic] gives the interviewer a plausible, interesting, and harmless point of departure to set the testee talking freely — more freely than he would if questioned about real problems or asked to discuss his dreams or day-dreams. (pp 1–2)

Burt utilized three sources of information in his system of content interpretation. First he looked at what he called the subject's "mode of attack." By this is meant the subject's general manner of handling the problem presented by the inkblots. Burt urged the psychologist to ask himself questions of the following nature.

Does the testee jump to stock conclusions rapidly and unreflectingly, relying chiefly on the inner workings of his mind to suggest what he says? ... Is he hesitant, reserved, suspicious, reluctant to give himself away (inhibited type)? Does he cooperatively enter into the fun of the thing freely and without restraint (unrepressed type)? Is he concerned more with his emotional reactions (assertions of pleasure, unpleasantness, critical and personal judgements ...)? Is he influenced more by the flow of the words in his mind (verbal type)? Or by the actual spatial patterns in front of him (spatial type)? Does he ... try to impress others (or himself) with his own mental skill (exhibitionistic type)? And if so, what impression does he predominantly wish to convey? (e.g., "See what cultured or casual words I use? How wide my knowledge is of foreign languages, geography, literature, art? See what interesting places abroad I have visited? See how cautious and scientific I am? ...") Does he treat the whole thing humourously and facetiously, and if so, why? (because he is a merry, humourous creature, or because by refusing to take the matter too seriously, he can preserve his dignity or avoid giving himself away, because he is intellectually too high and mighty to allow his whole personality to take part in a trivial test). (p 5)

The second source of information utilized by Burt is the actual *blot content*. For example, does the subject refer to cognitive aspects of common life — concrete things seen or imagined — or does he refer largely to affective aspects — "rather a pleasant shape," "a most unpleasant blot," "a very exciting pattern"?

Lastly, Burt looks to the subject's *life content* as revealed in his responses to the blots. The subject's phraseology may reflect his education, his occupation, his leisure pursuits, his interests, and the events that have impressed themselves upon his memory. "Do [the responses] ... suggest an interest in other persons and their activities? Do they reflect a morbid interest in his own person, in his emotions, diseases, etc.? Do they exhibit a defiance of taboos?" (p 5).

One means by which Burt pursued the *life content* meaning of Rorschach percepts was by eliminating the standard Rorschach inquiry following the association phase. Instead of inquiring about the source of the percept *in the blot,* Burt chose to look for it *in the subject's experience.* In searching for the origin of the percept, he deemed it especially important to distinguish between those percepts that appear because of recent memory from those percepts based on remote memory. The latter were thought to be more important because they represent experiences that made lasting impressions. Burt also distinguished between content derived from artificial sources (e.g., a book, movie, or play) and content derived from the subject's inner imagination. Burt further asserted that the two distinctions often coincide, with the themes borrowed from books and movies usually introduced because they were recently experienced. To find the source of the percept, Burt suggested free association starting from notable percepts. He presented as an example three subjects who interpreted Card II as (A) a lamp, (B) a top, and (C) a large house with a pointed roof.

> [Subject]
> A explains that the lamp was like the white oil-lamp in his study which he had to fill and light himself when he first went into lodgings 25 years ago. Why this lamp? He hated the responsibility of having to fill it, for fear it should catch fire; in fact, he hated all responsibility. (B) "Just like a top my elder brother had for Christmas when I was about seven" (a long-forgotten jealousy of the supposed favorite of the family). (C) "Mrs. X used to live in a house like that — a lovely house." (The testee is a spinster — and used to cherish a yearning to be happily married like Mrs. X.) (p 2)

Burt further suggested that such questioning about the source of the percept in the subject's past could be adapted to group testing.

The major part of Burt's monograph is concerned with the exposition of a "Psychographic Schedule" for use with the Rorschach test. The following is a brief summary of Burt's presentation.

BURT'S PSYCHOGRAPHIC SCHEDULE

Intellectual (Cognitive)

INNATE ABILITIES

General intelligence.   The intelligent testees exhibit attention to relations, such as with time, cause, and evidence, and often demonstrate this concern by using the word "because." They also exhibit originality of responses; attention to the realities of the blots; specificity of content (e.g., "Herman and Helena just waking up in the wood" rather than just "two people"); a particular situation or activity cited to account for symmetry and shape distortions (e.g., "two clowns dancing and bowing to each other"); good vocabulary and general verbal expression, with elaborate sentences linked with conjunctions; use of abstract terms; adjectives and adverbs used to qualify even unoriginal percepts; and a variety of content categories from which responses are drawn. Burt rejected the number of whole responses as an index of intelligence, stating that "it is rather the compact and plausible organization of accurately perceived details that is significant" (p 6).

In contrast, Burt viewed the following characteristics as indications of poor general intelligence: slowly given, difficultly expressed interpretations; percepts not fitted to the blot contours; absence of activity (Burt asserted that activities inappropriate to the blot contours are usually due to emotional interference); origination of the entire percept in a trifling detail of the blot; suggestion of two or more ideas that are not combined in a sensible way (e.g., "a hat and two stockings and two dolls lying on a heap of stones with a house at the top"); original responses due to the lack of an adequate fund of appropriate ideas; brief and general interpretations; the absence of many verbs expressing movement or relationship; few fantasies; perseveration of the same field of experience or even the same item within the field (e.g., "a doggie," "a dog kennel," "another doggie"); lack of emotional interest or liveliness of expression; color naming (e.g., "That's a red one"); monotonous, stereotyped phrases (e.g., starting each response with "that one looks like a . . ."); childish interests — i.e., a preponderance of animals, humans, and clothing in the content categories; childish vocabulary and grammar.

Special capacities.

Observation: The observant individual follows a systematic apperceptive procedure. Content described is complete, realistic, and almost literally accurate. Responses based on the larger details suggest a practical type of observation, whereas those based on rarer or more minute details suggest more patient habits of observation.

Verbal capacity: This aptitude is demonstrated by wide vocabulary and free flow of words.

Imagination and inventiveness: These qualities are suggested when the patient offers numerous or ingenious responses, percepts referring to persons and active movement, or elaborate, embellished replies. Imaginative patients make free use of lively or graphic adjectives, and draw content from the world of imagination rather than from objects of everyday life; for example, visualization of a Chinese woman would not suggest imagination if the testee lived in a Chinese community. Lack of imagination is indicated when the subject immediately takes refuge in standard replies, such as diagrams, maps, clouds, or mist. But if such replies are made after an embarrassed delay, a repression of imagined ideas is suggested. Also suggestive of poor imagination is a stereotyped adherence to one field of thought, most notably animals.

Quickness: Quickness is shown by prompt, quickly elaborated replies, with no hesitation between responses or between blots.

Imagery type: The distinction here is between the visualizer and the verbalizer. Burt asserts that it is difficult to make this distinction with inkblot responses.

Memory: As with the previous category, Burt believes the blots are of little use in assessing memory.

Relations: More intelligent individuals attend explicitly to relations — space, time, cause, and evidence.

Artistic aptitudes: The artistic individual does not jump to simple and immediate interpretations, but is more influenced by inner details of light, shade, and coloring. Artistic subjects tend to comment on the aesthetic characteristics of the blots — their colors or excellence of the composition. The content will also indicate familarity with art and its techniques.

ACQUIRED KNOWLEDGE AND INTERESTS

Educational. This characteristic can be seen in the content of replies, for example, in references to geography and science, the less familiar animals, and famous names in history, literature, and art. Education is also evidenced by the form of the replies, by the accuracy and variety of grammatical constructions.

Vocational. The testee's occupation is almost always reflected in the replies.

Cultural. The subject's vocabulary and content reveal his or her cultural level, or, if the subject is young, that of the home.

Emotional

MAINLY INNATE

General emotionality. This quality is seen in animated descriptions, glowing rapturous terms ("a lovely little . . ."), a tendency to dramatize the scene, constant changing of seating position, and constant and rapid turning of the card. Lack of drive — passivity, or lethargy — is seen in a relaxed and bored attitude to the test, a tendency to hold the cards limply, an inclination to gaze listlessly at the blots, a recurring formula of resignation ("that's all — I can't see any more"), initial inability to see anything but smudges followed by a slow emergence of ideas, comments that the blots seem the same, and the absence of energetic postures or actions in the percepts.

Temperamental type.

Extraversion versus introversion: Burt states that introversion is seen in: slowness in reaching and in stating a percept and reluctance to interpret the blots; vague or noncommittal percepts (e.g., "two people doing something"); responses full of negatives (e.g., "it might be a bat, but can't say it really looks like one"); perseveration of ideas and phrasing in order to avoid any commitment.

Repression is seen in such phrases as "I can't think of the names," or "I never saw anything like that," in an inability to locate a percept seen earlier, and in the denial of a response: "It doesn't look like . . ." Repression is also displayed in delayed *RT* and such behavior as blushing and giggling; in white space responses; in the ostentatious presentation of far-fetched percepts, as if the subject were avoiding the obvious reply; in a tendency to look away from the blot or to hold it at arm's length; in failure to mention activity or motion, which suggest exaggerated aloofness to people: "More people; heaven knows what they're doing."

Cheerfulness versus depression: Cheerfulness is seen in frequent, frank reference to direct experience of enjoyable activities, in humorous concepts humorously worded, in frequent smiling and laughter during the test session, in comments of pleased approval, and in the enjoyment of colors in the blots.

Special emotions.

Anger: Good or bad temper is usually seen in the approach the subject takes to testing, for example, annoyance. Burt believes it is rash to assume that reference to quarreling in the percept indicates that the subject is quarrelsome.

Aggressiveness: The characteristic can be judged in reference to aggressive action: if aggressive motions and instruments are described with gusto, aggression is suggested; if they are described with distance, anxiety is suggested.

Curiosity: Curiosity is shown by inquiring attitude toward the blots and toward everyday life; it is also suggested if the testee tends to turn the cards to see if anything else can be discovered.

Sociability: This quality is indicated by social and personal references, and by talkativeness and verbose or gossipy phraseology. The absence of human percepts suggests a nonsociable person.

Sex: Descriptions that suggest interest in the opposite sex, and interpretations of the blots as sexual objects fall into this category, as do such possibly Freudian responses as horns or noses.

Tenderness: Tenderness is implied by reference to animals, especially those that could be pets, and also by the delicate phrasing of these references.

Fear: In children, fear is seen chiefly in unpleased references to dangerous animals and implements of aggression. In adults, it is seen in responses such as dark caves, drowning, and morbid interpretations. Timidity is suggested by cautious preambles or reservations in offering responses.

Disgust: Frank reference to certain blots or colors as unpleasant, and a tendency to see sexual or excretory organs or processes both indicate disgust.

MAINLY ACQUIRED

Sentiments and interests.   Such traits as exhibitionistic mannerisms, and the self-ideal that the subject tries to exhibit are likely to appear in the subject's blot associations. Inadequate self-criticism appears in a similar manner. The individual's ambitions are also likely to be indicated in test responses that are characterized by inaccurate eagerness with reference to an occupation.

Complexes.   Repetitive fantasy themes may be indicative of emotional complexes, but they may also be a hangover from a recent book or film; careful inquiry is needed to establish which is the case. In addition, the testee may not be projecting himself, but someone else into the blot; in describing a sister whom the testee has dominated, he may see her bowing before a queen or humbly agreeing to do what she's told. Burt also states that if a repetitive fantasy theme does reflect a complex, it must be interpreted by quasi-psychoanalytic interpretation of content. An uncompensated inferiority complex is apt to be shown by constant apologetic phrases and excessive self-criticism. An overcompensated inferiority complex is betrayed in a supercilious attitude toward the test, or in a would-be superior turn of phrasing: "I suppose they could be some sort of clown-like creatures, not very well drawn; but the whole thing doesn't convey much to me."

Moral code.   The subject may carry out the test instructions so faithfully and meticulously that he seems to regard it a moral duty. There may also be an open defiance of social, sexual, and religious taboos. The examiner may also observe the testee's tendency to introduce valuation into percepts.

Suggestibility. By suggesting possible percepts, particularly far-fetched ones, the examiner can get an idea of the subject's suggestibility. Negativism may be seen in obstinate efforts to avoid the obvious and to impose the subject's own unconventional notions. Antiauthority complexes are frequently betrayed by children in slight turns of phrasing rather than in actual content: "A rather grim looking lady — she seems to be writing on the blackboard." Caricatural responses also often reflect this complex: "It's a bit like Granny, with a funny long nose."

Neurotic Tendencies

GENERAL

Neurosis is strongly suggested by several factors: failure to interpret some cards, but intelligent interpretations to others; evasive answers (e.g., clouds or maps); mere enumeration of colors; avoidance of the obvious and popular responses, especially if the subject is highly intelligent; morbid or eccentric interpretations such as occult responses presented without humor and references to morbid ideas or attitudes in the individual's life; egocentricity, seen in many explicit self-references; a marked tendency to express personal judgements, for example, frequent reference to the unpleasantness of the cards.

SPECIAL

The anxious neurotic feels insecure during this novel task and may reveal his anxiety in tentative phrasing — fearsome beasts, caves, woods, and the like are typically seen. He also comments on the depressing effect of the blacker cards: "Rather a gloomy thing." His replies are also characterized by insecurity and diffidence. The neurasthenic individual has few lively suggestions; his responses are expressed in curt phrases as if he were too weary to talk or think much. The hysterical subject is in an ever-jovial test behavior and uses superlative expressions ("the sweetest little . . ."). Paranoids are suspicious of the whole situation: "What's this supposed to tell you?" Obsessives may be preoccupied with recurrent themes and give an excessive number of animal responses. The hypochondriac exhibits a morbid interest in human body details: "It looks like a body cut across the middle — you can't see the face."

Validation of Burt's System

The only validation of Burt's system of content interpretation reported in the research literature is a 1950 investigation by Sen. In this study 100 Indian students in England were administered the Rorschach test, two intelligence tests, and Cattell's test of fluency. The subjects were also rated independently by individuals who had lived with them for at least 2 years. The categories of rating were intelligence, verbal ability, imagination, perception of relations, general emotionality, extraversion-introversion, assertion–submission, cheerfulness–depression, sociability, anxiety, neurotic tendencies, and extent of vocational and cultural interests. The Rorschach protocols were scored according to Burt's system and according to Beck's Rorschach scoring system (location, determinants, etc.). Burt's system was found to be by far the better predictor of the judges' ratings and intelligence, yielding respectable correlation coefficients in almost every instance. The correlation between the intelligence tests and Burt's Rorschach ratings for intelligence was .77; the correlations between Burt's system and the ratings varied between .43 and .66. All were statistically significant. Beck's system yielded few significant correlations. The judges were also asked to match personality descriptions, based either on the Beck scoring or on the Burt scoring, with the name of each subject. Again the Burt system proved superior, with every one of the subjects matched correctly with the description.

Unfortunately the evidence for the validity of Burt's system can only be considered suggestive at the present time. Sen's study appears to be the only relevant investigation thus far. Furthermore Sen states that the Burt scoring was accomplished by counting up the number of relevant items in a Rorschach record for each Burt category. Because the Burt system is highly subjective, it is unfortunate that interscorer reliability in Burt's system was not measured in the study. It should also be noted that the categories for validation were specifically chosen with Burt's system in mind; thus the study was somewhat biased in favor of the Burt system.

Evaluation of Burt's System

Burt's presentation of Rorschach content interpretation represents a considerable departure from traditional Rorschach test procedure. In Burt's discussion of the value of the Rorschach procedure, one gets the impression less of a psychometric test than of a task to set the subject talking freely. In this Burt foreshadows the work of later investigators, who have tended to view the test as a type of standard interview (Aronow & Reznikoff, 1973; Reznikoff, 1972; Zubin et al., 1965). Tied in with this standard interview emphasis is Burt's use of the test to focus in on *life content* as revealed by the subject during the test session. By encouraging the subject to talk freely of life events and emotions, Burt uses the test, per se, as a stepping stone to get closer to the subject's experience. Also notable in Burt's presentation is the heavy emphasis placed on stylistic aspects of subjects' responses (e.g., mode of attack) which are largely ignored in the traditional scoring systems.

A particularly fascinating aspect of the Burt system is its author's suggestion of a different method of test adminstration. Instead of the traditional inquiry, Burt used a free association technique to help clarify the content perceived in the blots and to link the percepts to the subject's life experience. This suggestion follows from Burt's rejection of the perceptual foundations of the Rorschach procedure and from his stress on content. Because the traditional inquiry period is perceptually based, Burt held that it should be turned in a more useful direction. This logical extension of the content approach to the Rorschach test will be further discussed in Chapter 12.

A major weakness is also apparent in Burt's presentation. The principal difficulty of his system is its lack of amenability to statistical treatment. There is an absence of precision in the definitions of categories of response. Because slight nuances of speech and behavior are crucial to the meaning of the test response, scoring of a test protocol according to Burt's categories is likely to be a highly subjective affair. At times Burt's presentation becomes so vague and impressionistic that to call it a "system" seems something of a misnomer. This criticism was shared by Burt, who noted that "there seems no simple method of reducing assessments, based on this mode of inference, to a precise quantitative form" (p. 5). Burt suggested establishing a 5-point scale for each category; typical replies suggestive of each point on the scale would be used in assigning ratings. Unfortunately neither Burt nor Sen has presented such scales or scaled examples. Consequently, despite Sen's encouraging findings, the Burt system cannot at this point be assumed to be of practical clinical or research use. Furthermore the strict division specified by Burt between innate versus acquired aspects of functioning represents a somewhat antiquated manner of viewing individual characteristics. The lack of adequate data on the reliability and validity of the system and the absence of norms also clearly militate against clinical use of the scales at this time.

ZUBIN'S CONTENT SCORING SYSTEM

Zubin et al. (1965) have also presented a series of scoring categories for the Rorschach test. They noted that in making interpretations, the

Rorschach worker often takes into account aspects of the response other than those traditionally scored. To supplement traditional scoring, these authors have therefore constructed a number of additional scales. Zubin and coworkers divided these scales into those that deal with the *formal* aspects of the response and those that deal with *content*. In most cases content is scored in each category on a 5-point scale; sometimes note is made of those responses to which the scale does not apply. Among the content scales, there are four major subdivisions: content per se, the psychological characteristics of the response, ratings of the subject's attitude toward responses, and general data.

CONTENT PER SE

In this subdivision Zubin et al. distinguished between *dynamic content* on the one hand, and *objective content* on the other. Dynamic content is defined as being more dependent on internal factors within the subject, and therefore it is quite likely to reveal the personality of the testee. In contrast objective content is more subject to the accidental influence of experience, and therefore it is likely to reveal less of the subject's personality.

The following are the dynamic aspects of content discussed by Zubin et al.

Evaluative.   This aspect is defined as the extent to which the subject evaluates his percept; examples of an extreme evaluative attitude include statements such as "a terrifying gorilla" and "a gorgeous underwater tropical scene."

Humanlike.   This content category measures the extent to which humanlike percepts are described in either a positive or a negative direction. At one end of the scale, "angel" and "clerics" are found, while at the other end, "vampiremen" and "decaying corpses" are described.

Human debasement.   This category evaluates the extent to which humans are described as debased. Examples of extreme debasement are images such as a "man pushing a woman off a cliff"; "Human having sexual relations with an animal."

Ascendance–submission.   An example of extreme submission is the visualization of a "decrepit old man."

Personal distance.   This dynamic aspect is defined as the extent to which the subject expresses distance between himself and his percepts.

Interpretations of the blots as "drawings" and "statues" are examples of extremely distant responses.

Degree of self-reference. The extent to which personal reference is expressed characterizes this category. Examples of extreme self-reference are images of the subject such as "myself as a little child" and "gorilla coming at me."

With respect to objective content, Zubin et al. distinguished between what they call importance scales and type scales. Importance scales require the examiner to rate the objective content categories of *human animal, plant, inanimate, abstract,* and *anatomy* on the extent to which the percept emphasizes the category. Thus the percept " a man's coat" would receive a low rating for *human* and a high rating for *inanimate.* The authors list four *type scales.*

Whole–part. The whole-part scale measures the extent to which whole objects or only parts of objects are perceived. An example of an extreme part-response: the visualization of "a nose," because noses are not ordinarily thought to exist in isolation.

Sex reference. This category evaluates the extent to which the response contains an explicit or implicit sexual reference. Two responses of extreme sex reference are "sexual intercourse," and "the sex organs."

Definiteness of content. This scale rates the extent to which the content is specific on the one hand or vague and amorphous on the other. The subject gives highly specific response if he interprets the blot as the "Arc de Triomphe"; a vague response: "splotches."

Gender of observed figure. Extent to which the gender of a percept is identified characterizes this category.

PSYCHOLOGICAL CHARACTERISTICS
OF THE RESPONSE

Zubin et al. list seven categories under this classification, categories which they believe to be more closely related to content than to perceptual scoring.

Perseverative tendency. This content category measures the extent to which the response is a repetition of previous responses.

Elaborative tendency. This category evaluates the extent to which the response to the blot is elaborated. In its extreme form, the response resembles free association and apperception.

Tendency toward blot description. This response, often seen in schizophrenic patients, measures the extent to which the blot is merely described rather than a scorable response given.

Mood of the response. In this category, the extent to which the percept has a pleasant or unpleasant quality is measured. This response may be a projection of the subject's own emotional state.

Affect of the subject. This content category measures the subject's emotional reaction to the percept. Zubin et al. noted that at times there may be marked incongruity between the mood of the response, per se, and the subject's affective reaction to the response.

Congruousness of response. The extent to which elements in the response hang together is assumed to be a measure of the subject's clarity of association. An extremely incongruous response is "grass bear," an image resulting from the fusion of two percepts.

Communality scale. This scale rates the extent to which the subject's response is one that is frequently given by others. Such responses are scored by reference to commonly used listings of so-called popular responses.

RATING OF SUBJECT'S
ATTITUDE TOWARD RESPONSES

This general classification of Rorschach responses refers to the subject's attitudes, both toward particular percepts and toward the general task of inkblot interpretation.

Self-estimate of the adequacy of the response. This response evaluates the extent to which the subject views his response as adequate or inadequate. Zubin et al. hold that it is useful to compare ratings of this scale with ratings on the quality and congruence scales, in order to judge how well the subject's estimate of response adequacy jibes with those of others.

Interpretive attitude. Under this category the interpretive attitude with which the subject approaches the task is measured. Is the task viewed as an effort to find specific objects in the blots, or to interpret the blots despite a lack of perfect congruity between the blot contours and his mental image? Zubin et al. provide two separate parts for this scale. One deals with the *type of interpretive attitude* — from acceptance of figures as real, to emphasis on the fact of representation. The second deals with the subject's *awareness of interpretive attitude* — the extent to which he reveals awareness of the fact that interpretation is taking place. (Awareness is seen in such remarks as "if you use your imagination . . .")

Reaction time. This category measures the time the subject takes to produce the first response to a card. Reactions are scored in the first, second, third, or fourth quartiles of reaction time.

GENERAL DATA

Ratings in this general classification are made either for the entire test protocol or for the responses to entire blots.

Turning of the card. This scale evaluates the extent to which the subject either turns the card freely at one extreme, or refrains from touching it at the other. This behavior may be an index of his general attitude towards the test. Zubin et al. suggest that card turning be scored for each blot rather than for each response.

Observational data on handling of cards. These data include the numbers of times the subject squints at cards, looks at back of cards, turns cards very rapidly, looks across surface of the flat blots, and moves card to indicate percept's movement.

Subject's readiness to respond. The extent to which the responses flow smoothly and prolifically is evaluated in this category.

Type of responses. The number of responses made during the free association phase, the number of responses made during the inquiry, and number of cards rejected are counted under this category.

Temporal data. The examiner determines total time for each card, reaction time before first response for each card, and average reaction time to chromatic and achromatic cards.

Zubin et al. suggest that means — representing the strength of the tendency measured by the scale — may be computed for the majority of scale scores. If a binomial distribution fits the data, they suggest computing the value of p for the binomial as the measure of strength of tendency. If the scale is bipolar — as is the case with the humanlike scale, the human debasement scale, and the type of interpretive attitude scale

— either the binomial statistic, a percent distribution of the categories, or modes may be utilized as summary statistics.

Reliability and Validity of the Zubin Scales

Nearly all of these scales were first presented in a 1956 article by Zubin et al. Data on the reliability of the scales were reported at that time. The interscorer reliability of the scales was assessed by having two raters who had been trained in the use of the scales rate responses independently. Zubin et al. found that the median perfect agreement on all of the content scales was 95 percent, a finding indicating a very high degree of interscorer reliability.

These authors also evaluated the split-half reliability of the scales. Test protocols of 44 subjects were split in terms of consecutive responses, i.e., subject 1, response 1, card 1, assigned to series A; response 2, card 1, to series B, etc. The content scales fared well with respect to this type of reliability: 20 of 26 scales had significant reliability coefficients (above .30). The reliability coefficients of 10 of the 26 scales were above .80, which is the coefficient necessary for reliable individual prediction with the scales. These 10 coefficients were as follows: degree of self-reference measure .89; sex definiteness, .94; elaborative tendency, .83; tendency toward blot description, .91; mood of response, .97; affect of the subject, .99; congruousness of response, .99; self-estimate of adequacy of the response, .99; interpretive attitude, .98; and awareness of interpretive attitude, .98.

The perceptual scales constructed by Zubin et al. did not appear to have high split-half reliability. Interestingly, the very high reliabilities (above .80) were almost exclusively confined to the general categories of psychological characteristics of the response (5 of 7 coefficients above .80) and subject's attitude toward responses (3 of 3 above .80). The general categories of dynamic and formal content did not fare as well. In the two general areas where high reliability was found, Zubin et al. noted that the coefficients "can be considered high even for intelligence and aptitude tests" (Zubin et al., 1956, p. 779).

Only one validational study by McCall (cited by Zubin et al., 1965), has apparently been carried out with the Zubin scales. In this study ascendance–submission, plant, importance, dehumanization, reaction time, and popularity were found to be significantly related to outcome in psychosurgery; ascendance–submission was the best predictor. Those showing improvement saw more submissive human figures in the blots.

Evaluation of Zubin's System

The scales put forward by Zubin, Eron, and Schumer represent a remarkable effort to quantify Rorschach test procedure. These scales attempt to cover both content per se, and the stylistic and affective aspects of Rorschach test behavior. Psychologists have long bemoaned the absence of quantitative scales to measure these latter aspects of test behavior (e.g., Davis, 1970). The Zubin scales must therefore be regarded as a significant step toward objectification of the test's interpretative procedure. The reliability evidence provided for the Zubin scales in the earlier Zubin et al. article (1956) further attests to the potential usefulness of the scales, particularly for those dealing with the psychological characteristics of the response and the subject's attitude toward responses.

The major shortcoming of the Zubin scales, at this time, is the lack of data on their validity. Norms are of course not available for these scales, and thus they are presently of little practical use to the clinician. In addition, although Zubin et al. (1956) have demonstrated that the scales have high interscorer reliability, it is essential to gather more extensive examples of scorable responses at each point on a particular scale.

GENERAL EVALUATION OF RORSCHACH CONTENT CATEGORY SYSTEMS

The four content category systems discussed in Chapters 3 and 4 are a heterogeneous group. The De Vos, Schafer, and Burt systems are similar in that each is *subject-centered:* every category deals with an aspect of the subject that can be revealed by test behavior. In contrast the Zubin system is *test-centered:* the types of percepts perceived by the subject and the subject's test behavior constitute the units of the system. Although Zubin et al. occasionally discuss the possible meaning of certain classes of responses (e.g., the prevalence of tendency toward blot description among schizophrenic subjects), by and large they do not attempt to translate the test responses and behavior they present into assumed psychological meaning for the subject. Of the three subject-centered systems, the Burt approach is the most inclusive, encompassing everything from intelligence and imagination to morality and neurosis; the price paid for this inclusiveness seems to be a lack of precision within each category. The De Vos and Schafer systems are the most similar of the four, with the Schafer system borrowing more heavily from psychoanalytic theory (e.g., oral and anal preoccupation). The De Vos system uses categories of personality that are less specifically psychoanalytic (e.g., dependency, hostility, and positive feelings).

A further point of contrast between the four systems is their differing amenability to quantification. The Zubin scales are presented as point scales and are therefore easily quantifiable. The Schafer and De Vos systems involve frequency counts within categories and can thus be quantified. At least some evidence on the interscorer reliability of the Zubin, De Vos, and Schafer scales is presently available. Insofar as the Burt system is concerned, however, the picture in relation to quantification is decidedly less optimistic. There are no data on interscorer reliability, and quantification of such diffuse and subjective categories does not appear to be an easy matter. The great difficulty inherent in quantifying the Burt system is rather ironic when one considers the statistical contributions and expertise of the author of the system. The greater quantifiability of the Zubin, De Vos, and Schafer scales also means that, as of this writing, these three systems lend themselves more readily to validation research and the collection of norms than does the Burt system.

These four Rorschach content category systems are neither widely used nor even widely known, although Schafer's approach has been quite influential in the idiographic approach to Rorschach assessment. There has been only one validational study each for the Burt and Zubin systems. Only a few studies have been carried out in relation to the De Vos and Schafer systems in the 20 years since these methods were published. Clearly the content systems that intensively investigate the measurement of more delimited aspects of personality (Chapters 5 through 8) have received far more acceptance.

Reasons for the failure of these systems to catch on are not hard to find. The Burt system, developed in England, was never published, although the Sen article attracted some attention and made known the existence of the system. Burt's view that the Rorschach test is primarily content-based was quite heretical at the time, and it is doubtful that his system would have received favorable response had it been published. Furthermore the great difficulties inherent in quantifying the Burt system would likely have been another factor discouraging its adoption.

The situation appears to be somewhat different with respect to the De Vos, Schafer, and Zubin systems, which have been generally available in this country and can be quantified. The De Vos scales included duplications of Elizur's two scoring methods. Because data on the Elizur themes had already begun to accumulate, the corresponding De Vos scales were neglected. The remaining De Vos scales, except for dependency, were in areas of less intrinsic clinical interest (e.g., positive, neutral content). The Schafer themes were in fact not presented as a scoring system, but rather as a flexible guide to be used by the psychoanalytically-oriented clinician. Several researchers have nonetheless used the themes as scales largely because they deal with core psychoanalytic concepts that are of interest to investigators. The Schafer approach has also influenced the content approach developed by Holt (Chapter 7).

The *test-centered* rather than *subject-centered* quality of the Zubin scales tends to leave the immediate clinical meaning of the measured behavior obscured. Because little validity information is available many clinicians would be at a loss if they wanted to interpret scores on the scales. In addition, as pointed out by Knutson (1972), the numerous Zubin scales require a complicated and lengthy scoring procedure, and thus their use in clinical practice is discouraged further. It should also be noted that the Zubin scales were presented to psychology at a time of decreased interest in and discouragement with the Rorschach test, particularly with respect to the psychometric properties of determinant scores. Although the Zubin system focuses on content, its statistical tone may have resulted in its being grouped with other perceptual psychometric Rorschach approaches that have traditionally appealed more to researchers than to clinicians. It would be most unfortunate for psychology if the trend of research disillusion with the Rorschach test, which is largely based on perceptually-oriented research, should result in a neglect of the content category systems of Zubin and others.

A great deal of work remains to be done if these four sets of content scales are to be used productively. If the Burt system is to be of use, a quantifiable scoring system for it must be developed. Such a scoring system will likely resemble Zubin's, perhaps with a 5-point scale and examples provided for each point on the scale. Far more data on the reliability and validity of all four systems must be collected. Norms are also required if the systems are to be useful to the practicing clinician. Finally, the scales should be refined once enough information on subscale validity and consistency becomes available.

5

Content Measurement of Anxiety and Hostility: The Elizur Scales

In 1949, Abraham Elizur published an article entitled *Content Analysis of the Rorschach with Regard to Anxiety and Hostility.* This article was a watershed in the development of content interpretation. It was a clear empirical demonstration of the fact that core aspects of personality could be reliably and validly scored from the thematic content of Rorschach responses. As such it led to many research studies that utilized the Elizur scales, efforts to develop similar scales of anxiety and hostility, as well as attempts to develop such useful scales in other areas of personality.

ELIZUR'S ANXIETY SCALE

In addition to the Elizur anxiety scale, other measures of anxiety have been put forward by Arnaud (1959) and by De Vos (1952). (See Chapter 3 for a discussion of the De Vos scale.) Holtzman et al. (1961) have included in the HIT a content scale of anxiety that was patterned after the Elizur scale. As noted by Goldfried (1966), these other systems can be considered modifications of the Elizur scale; most of the validity studies have been carried out using the Elizur scale. For these reasons only the Elizur scale is discussed here.

SCORING

Elizur scored responses as anxiety-evincing if they were characterized by the following features.

Anxiety expressed or implied.   A capital *A* would be scored if fear, unpleasantness, sorrow, pity, or similar emotions were expressed in responses. Examples: "A frightening giant"; "A weeping child"; "A dangerous crevice"; "Darkness and gloom."

A lower case *a* would be scored for responses indicating a lesser degree of anxiety, for example, "an unpleasant animal."

Anxious expressive behavior.   If the behavior of the percept figure suggested anxiety, *A* would be scored. Examples of such responses include "a girl escaping"; "a retreating animal"; "a rabbit running away."

Response symbolizing anxiety.   A lower case *a* would be scored for symbolic responses suggesting anxiety, for example, "an unbalanced figure"; "dead leaves"; "scarecrow"; "an impression of coldness."

Cultural stereotypes of fear.   The presence of percepts having a general connotation of fear in our culture would be scored *A* or *a*. Examples of *A* include "bats,"; "snakes"; "monsters"; "atomic bomb." Examples of *a* are "spiders"; "mosquitoes"; "church"; "totem pole."

Double connotation of anxiety and hostility.   Responses containing clear evidence of both anxiety and hostility were scored *a*. Examples of such responses include "headless person"; "injured bear"; "child with cut-off arms"; "a torn butterfly"; "a policeman"; "an animal going to attack you, I feel somewhat scared."

In Elizur's system borderline responses in which there is doubt as to whether anxiety is involved should not be scored. Examples presented by Elizur that suggest neither anxiety nor hostility are the following.

Animals.   Typical examples are frogs, mice, bugs, crabs, and bears.

Anatomic.   Spinal cords, x-ray, bones, and lungs are included here.

Miscellaneous.   Common responses include coats of arms, rocks, and skins of animals.

A subject's total anxiety score is computed by counting each *A* response as two units and each *a* response as one unit. The two resulting sums are added to yield the total anxiety score. Although Elizur did not recommend correcting for the total number of responses in a Rorschach protocol, subsequent studies utilizing the Elizur anxiety scale have found a relationship between anxiety score and Rorschach *R*. Computing anxiety score as a percentage or otherwise correcting for *R* in Rorschach research studies on anxious content would thus appear to be required. This problem is of course largely avoided when the HIT is the inkblot vehicle.

RELIABILITY

Interscorer reliability. To determine the interscorer reliability of his system, Elizur had 8 graduate students independently score 15 Rorschach records. The average intercorrelation coefficient between the eight scorings for anxiety was found to be .77. The correlation between the average of the eight scorings and Elizur's own scoring of the protocols was determined to be .89. Forsyth (1959) has also found high interscorer reliability for Elizur's anxiety content system (r = .90 and .95).

Using the HIT anxiety scale, Holtzman et al. (1961) reported that with two highly trained examiners scoring 40 schizophrenic protocols, a correlation of .99 resulted. With four less highly trained examiners rating 96 protocols from college subjects, an average correlation of .86 was found.

Test–retest reliability. One investigation is of at least some relevance with respect to test–retest reliability. Epstein, Nelson, and Tanofsky (1957) administered an inkblot test to a group of 16 college subjects on 10 different occasions over a 5-week period. The blots were created specifically for the purposes of the experiment. On each occasion 10 different blots were used. These authors estimated the test–retest correlation across all administrations to be .26. Because of the shifting and unusual nature of the test stimuli, however, this finding must be considered of limited value.

Split–half reliability. Elizur also attempted to determine the internal consistency reliability of his anxiety scoring system. Using the split-half (odd–even) method and the Spearman-Brown formula with 30 subjects, he found a correlation coefficient of .48. Holtzman et al. (1961) found the odd–even reliability coefficients for HIT anxiety among various subject groups to vary from .31 to .97, with a median of .66.

Alternate form reliability. Using Forms A and B of the HIT, Holtzman et al. (1961) also reported on the delayed alternate form reliability of the HIT anxiety scale. Among 120 college subjects with a 1-week interval, the reliability coefficient was .55; among 72 11th graders with a 3-month interval, it was .53; among 42 elementary school students with a 1-year interval, it was .49; and among 48 college students with a 1-year interval, it was .52.

VALIDITY

Numerous studies have investigated the validity of inkblot anxiety scoring. These studies are grouped below into six categories, according to the criterion against which the anxiety scoring system was validated. The six classes of criteria are (1) rating of self and others, (2) prognosis, (3) relationships with other tests, (4) diagnosis and symptomatology, (5) experimentally manipulated anxiety, and (6) miscellaneous criteria.

Rating by self and others. Elizur's initial investigation (1949) and a subsequent study by Stewart (cited in Goldfried et al., 1971) have correlated the Rorschach anxiety scoring system with ratings by self and others. An additional study by Zuckerman, Persky, Eckman, and Hopkins (1967) correlated the HIT anxiety scoring system with judges' ratings of anxiety. The two Rorschach studies did find that the anxiety scoring correlated significantly with both self-rating and others' ratings of anxiety. The HIT investigation did not find such a significant relationship.

As part of his original study, Elizur included five self-rating items dealing with fears and insecurities. With 30 volunteers he found the correlation between the five self-rating items and Rorschach anxiety to be .52 ($p < .01$). He also found the correlation between self-ratings of control of dependency and control of depressive moods on the one hand, and Rorschach anxiety on the other, to be .73 ($p < .01$) and .50 ($p < .01$), respectively. Twenty subjects were also interviewed by the investigator and then rated as to their submissiveness, dependency, anxiety, and hostility. Elizur found that the correlation between Rorschach anxiety and rated interview anxiety was .71 ($p < .01$). Interestingly, the correlation between the self-ratings of anxiety and the interview ratings of anxiety was found to be .36 ($p < .05$), a finding suggesting that the Rorschach content scale may give a better measure of anxiety than the self-ratings.

Stewart (cited in Goldfried et al., 1971) obtained therapists' ratings of anxiety for 112 psychiatric outpatients after the patients had been seen for a minimum of eight sessions. The correlation between Rorschach anxiety and a median split of therapists' ratings of anxiety was estimated to be .39.

One study using the anxiety scale of the HIT failed to find a significant correlation with judges' ratings of anxiety. Zuckerman et al. (1967) tested the convergent and discriminant validity of psychological techniques used for the measurement of anxiety, depression, and hostility. The subjects were 29 male psychiatric patients and 25 normal male controls. The measures used with the anxiety variable were a rating scale of anxiety (filled out by two judges following an interview), the Taylor Manifest Anxiety scale (MAS), the anxiety scale of the Multiple Affect Adjective Check List, the HIT Anxiety scale, and ratings of TAT performance for anxiety. The HIT Anxiety scale was not found to correlate significantly with the judges' ratings of anxiety or with the other anxiety measures in either of the two subject groups or in the combined group.

Prognosis. Four investigations have taken up the question of the relationship between anxiety scoring and prognosis. Two studies (Grauer, 1953; Stotsky, 1952) were concerned with using the system to predict length of hospitalization for schizophrenic inpatients. One study (Gallagher, 1954) related anxiety scoring to successful outcome in psychotherapy. One further investigation (Cohen, 1954) related the scoring system to course of illness in tubercular patients. In general the findings do not seem to indicate that anxiety scoring is useful as an indicator of prognosis in these situations.

Grauer (1953) compared groups of improved and unimproved male paranoid schizophrenic patients. The two groups were matched in terms of age, and IQ and years of schooling were also controlled. However the unimproved group had been hospitalized almost twice as long as the improved subjects. There were 18 subjects in each group. Improvement was defined primarily in terms of whether the patient remained hospitalized following shock therapy. Grauer found that, consistent with expectations, the improved patients did indeed have significantly higher anxiety scores ($p < .01$). This result was predicted on the basis that the presence of anxiety in Rorschach protocols could be interpreted as meaning that the patient was still engaged in an active struggle with the psychotic process.

Stotsky (1952), on the other hand, did not find such differences in anxious content between remitting and nonremitting schizophrenic patients. In this study the subjects were white male veterans who had been admitted to a neuropsychiatric hospital. All had been diagnosed as schizophrenics. Two groups of subjects were selected from this pool: those who were subsequently discharged and remained in remission, and those who did not leave the hospital. Forty-six subjects were included in each group. The difference between groups with respect to Rorschach anxious content did not reach significance at the .05 level.

Gallagher (1954) attempted to evaluate the efficacy of the anxiety system for predicting success in psychotherapy. Fifteen highly successful therapy patients were compared with 15 unsuccessful patients and 34 dropouts. Therapy was conducted by a graduate student in a counseling center setting. Success in therapy was determined by ratings of the therapist, judges, the client, and the ratio of positive to negative feelings in the first and the last interviews. Gallagher found no significant differences in Elizur Rorschach anxiety level between the three groups of subjects.

Cohen (1954) used anxious content as one of a number of Rorschach indices used to predict the course of illness in patients with pulmonary tuberculosis. Forty-five male white veterans who were hospitalized and being treated for active pulmonary tuberculosis served as the subjects. Two years after the psychological tests had been administered, three physicians rated the progress of the tubercular process as compared with what might have been expected as the course of the illness. Elizur anxious content was not found to be significantly related to course of illness in this study.

Relationships with other tests. A number of investigations have considered the question of the extent to which anxiety content scoring on inkblot tests relates to other tests of anxiety. The general pattern of results has been confusing because such relationships are found in some studies but not in other similar studies.

Seven investigators have included the inkblot anxiety scale and the Taylor Manifest Anxiety scale (MAS) as measures (Forsyth, 1959; Goodstein, 1954; Goodstein & Goldberger, 1955; Kates & Schwartz, 1958; Mogar, 1962; Westrope, 1953; Zuckerman et al., 1967). Five of these investigations found no significant relationship between the inkblot anxiety scale and the MAS; two do report such a relationship.

In one of the studies with positive results, Goodstein (1954) correlated the MAS, Elizur Rorschach anxiety scoring, and four scales of the Iowa Multiple-Choice Picture Interpretation test (IPIT) among 57 college students. A correlation of .38 ($p < .01$) was found between the Rorschach anxiety measure and the MAS. Goodstein partialed out the effect of Rorschach R, and still found a significant correlation between MAS scores and anxious content ($r = .36$). The anxiety scale of the IPIT did not correlate significantly with either Rorschach anxiety or the MAS.

In another study with positive results, Goodstein and Goldberger (1955) compared the Rorschach anxiety scores of 16 psychiatric patients (7 females and 9 males) who scored high on the MAS with those of 16 patients who scored low. These authors found significantly higher Rorschach anxiety score percentages for those patients who scored high on the MAS ($p < .04$, one-tailed test).

In one of the studies with negative findings, Forsyth (1959) investigated the effects of color, shading, and anxiety level on the production of anxious and hostile Rorschach content. Thirty subjects constituted a high anxiety group, 30 a middle, and 30 a low anxiety group. These groups were selected on the basis of Welsh anxiety scores. All subjects were male. Forsyth found no significant relationship between Rorschach anxiety and anxiety as measured either by the MAS or the Welsh A scale of the MMPI. There was a high and significant correlation between the MAS and the Welsh MMPI scores ($r = .86, p < .01$).

In another such study Mogar (1962) investigated the relationships between Elizur's anxiety scoring, the MAS, and 12 presumed anxiety indicators on the Draw-A-Person test (DAP). This study used 123 male psychiatric subjects. Mogar found that Rorschach anxiety was significantly related to four of the DAP indices and was not significantly related to the MAS. The MAS correlated significantly with only one of the DAP indices. Unfortunately Mogar does not indicate whether Rorschach R was in any way controlled. Mogar concluded that the Rorschach test and the DAP appear to measure anxiety "along the same continuum," whereas the MAS does not.

Kates and Schwartz (1958) studied the question of the relationship between the Elizur anxiety scale and the MAS using female undergraduate subjects as part of a larger investigation. These authors found no significant relationship between these two test measures. Westrope (1953) compared 24 subjects (12 males and 12 females) who scored high on the MAS with 24 subjects who scored low. The Rorschach anxiety scores of the former group were found to be significantly higher than those of the latter. However, the difference between the groups did not remain significant once total Rorschach R had been adjusted for by means of a covariance analysis. As part of the Zuckerman et al. (1967) investigation discussed above, HIT anxiety was likewise found to be unrelated to the MAS.

Two studies have related Rorschach anxiety content to MMPI scales other than the MAS (Forsyth, 1959; Zimet & Brackbill, 1956). As noted above, Forsyth found no significant relationship between Rorschach anxiety and the Welsh scale on the MMPI. Zimet and Brackbill (1956) correlated anxiety content with Welsh's anxiety index and the Pt scale of the MMPI. The subjects of this study were 97 psychiatric patients. These investigators found a significant correlation between Rorschach anxiety and the Welsh index ($r = .25, p < .05$), but the correlation with the Pt scale did not reach significance at the .05 level ($r = .21$).

Nichols and Tursky (1967) studied the relation of anxiety to pain sensitivity as measured by both the HIT Anxiety scale and the MAS. Four measures of pain sensitivity were available; two of the four were significantly related to HIT anxiety, with high anxiety subjects being more sensitive to pain. None of the four correlations for the MAS were significant. HIT anxiety was also found to be related to a paper-and-pencil measure of body anxiety when a one-tailed test of significance was employed; the MAS did not correlate significantly with the body anxiety measure. Nichols and Tursky concluded that symbolic tests of anxiety such as the HIT Anxiety scale may measure unconscious anxiety, whereas tests such as the MAS may measure conscious anxiety.

Three studies have dealt with the relationship between inkblot anxiety and other projective test measures of anxiety. One investigation explored the relationship between Rorschach anxiety content and the IPIT (Goodstein, 1954). As noted above, Goodstein did not find a significant relationship between the two anxiety measures. Also as discussed above, Mogar (1962) found that 4 of 12 relationships between DAP anxiety indices and the Elizur anxiety scale were significant. In the Zuckerman et al. (1967) study, the HIT Anxiety scale was not found to correlate significantly with a TAT anxiety scale. The HIT Anxiety scale was also found to be unrelated to the IPAT Anxiety scale and an anxiety scale of the Multiple Affect Adjective Checklist.

Elizur (1949) found correlations between his anxiety content scale and a 10-item questionnaire measure of anxiety designed specifically for his study. Five of the 10 items dealt with fears and phobias, whereas the remaining 5 items dealt with lack of self-confidence. Elizur found that correlations with the Rorschach anxiety content scale were .58 for items of fears and phobias ($p < .01$), .39 for items of lack of self-confidence ($p < .05$), and .61 for the combined scale ($p < .01$).

Cook, Iacino, Murray, and Auerbach (1973) administered the HIT and the State-Trait Anxiety Inventory (STAI) to 52 college students. Shading and anxiety content were scored on the HIT. The state and trait scales of the STAI were administered to subjects at the outset of the experiment, followed by the HIT; then the state scale of the STAI was readministered and subjects were asked to respond in terms of how they felt during the administration of the inkblots. Only one significant correlation was found between shading and the STAI, and this correlation was in the direction opposite from that predicted. Anxious content correlated significantly with both pre-test state anxiety ($r = .25, p < .05$) and post-test state anxiety ($r = .27, p < .05$). Interestingly, state anxiety scores for subjects increased significantly when subjects were asked to indicate their feelings during administration of the HIT.

In a 1974 study, Iacino and Cook again related HIT measures of anxiety to the STAI, using four HIT variables as potential measures of anxiety: Anxiety, Shading, Movement, and Barrier scores. The subjects were 76 undergraduate students, equally divided between control and experimental conditions. The control and experimental groups were matched on trait anxiety as measured by the STAI. The HIT was administered to the experimental group under neutral conditions and under threat of shock. Iacino and Cook found that, with respect to the relationships between the inkblot scales and STAI scores, the Anxiety scale of the HIT correlated significantly with trait anxiety on both test administrations ($p < .05$). None of the other HIT variables were found to be significantly related to the STAI scores.

Diagnosis and symptomatology. Several investigators have dealt with the ability of anxiety content scoring to predict diagnosis and symptoms. The findings with respect to diagnosis are contradictory and difficult to interpret. Results concerning symptomatology are more encouraging. Elizur (1949) compared the anxiety content of 22 neurotic subjects with that of 22 normal control subjects. The subjects were matched for age, sex, and intelligence. Elizur found that the neurotics had significantly higher anxiety content scores than the control subjects ($p < .01$), as was predicted.

Zimet and Brackbill (1956) compared the Rorschach anxiety scores of 32 psychotics, 32 neurotics, and 33 patients with character disorders. These authors predicted that there would be no significant differences between the three groups; this prediction was confirmed. Ullmann and Hunrichs (1958) similarly compared psychotics, neurotics, and patients with character disorders, but these investigators found that the Elizur scale did significantly differentiate the groups. It should be noted that this latter study was carried out in a neuropsychiatric setting, whereas the former study was conducted in a general medical hospital.

Gorlow, Zimet, and Fine (1952) compared the anxiety content scores of 13 delinquents with those of 13 matched control subjects. The delinquent subjects had significantly higher anxiety scores than the controls. Although the groups did differ in R, the nondelinquents had the greater productivity. Cleveland and Johnson (1962) compared coronary patients with noncoronary patients; it was determined in this study that the coronary patients had significantly higher anxiety content scores.

In the area of symptomatology, three investigations have been carried out: those of Cummings (cited in Goldfried et al., 1971), Page (1957), and Vernallis (1955). Cummings investigated the relationship between anxious Rorschach content and the severity of nail biting among 70 nail biting children between 10 and 14 years of age. This author found a significant correlation between these two variables ($r = .28, p < .05$).

Page (1957) administered a scale of frequency of daydreaming to college females. Twenty subjects with a high frequency of daydreaming were then compared with an equal number of subjects who indicated a low frequency of daydreaming. No significant difference was found between the anxious content scores of these two groups.

Vernallis (1955) compared 40 teeth-grinding college subjects to a normal control group of 40 matched college subjects. With respect to anxiety content, Vernallis found a significant biserial r of .29 ($p < .05$). Vernallis does not indicate whether Rorschach productivity was controlled in this study.

Experimentally manipulated anxiety.   Four studies have attempted experimental manipulation of anxiety level in order to affect inkblot anxiety content. Three of these investigations report negative results, and one was positive. In one of the studies with negative results, Kates and Schwartz (1958) administered an inkblot test to two groups of 12 female college students. The experimental group was then given written accounts, purportedly based on an analysis of the test, which described them as poorly adjusted. An inkblot test was then readministered to the two groups. The Rorschach test and the Behn-Rorschach test were counter-balanced among subjects as the before-and-after measures. The test interval was 2 weeks. Kates and Schwartz found no difference in Elizur anxiety content between the two occasions for either the experimental or the control groups.

Lebo, Toal, and Brick (1960) worked with 24 male prisoners with prominent symptoms of anxiety. In this investigation the experimental group, consisting of 12 prisoners, was given carbon dioxide treatment. The control group was given no treatment. The groups were matched on age and length of imprisonment. The Rorschach test was administered before the onset of the carbon dioxide treatment and afterwards. These authors found that there was a significant decrease in the percentage of Rorschach anxiety content in the experimental group ($p < .05$, one-tailed test). No significant difference in anxiety content for the control group was evident, although the difference would have been significant had a one-tailed test of significance been applied.

In the Iacino and Cook (1974) study discussed above, anxiety was experimentally manipulated by the use of shock threat. This study was unusually well designed in that the investigators were able to demonstrate a significantly greater increase in state anxiety during the experimental condition than in the control condition. Iacino and Cook found that anxiety scores on the HIT for the experimental group did not significantly differ from the anxiety scores of the control group.

Lucas (1961) investigated whether induced frustration would affect the Rorschach scores of 8- and 9-year-old children. The Rorschach test was first individually administered to both the 28 experimental and the

28 matched control subjects. Eight weeks later the experimental subjects were frustrated in a game. The Rorschach was then readministered to all subjects. Lucas found that neither group displayed a significant change in anxiety content between the two administrations.

Miscellaneous studies.   A few studies that have investigated correlates of inkblot anxiety content are not easily classified. In one of these investigations, Forsyth (1959) compared three groups of 30 subjects each, who were administered three different sets of inkblots. One group was presented with the standard Rorschach blots, one with achromatic blots, and one with blots on which shading differentiations had been eliminated. The two nonstandard series of blots were identical to the Rorschach blots except for color and shading. Forsyth found no significant differences between the anxiety content levels of the three groups.

Lit (cited in Goldfried et al., 1971) compared the Rorschach anxiety content of college students on probation with a matched group of dean's list students. Lit hypothesized that because academic failure is often a result of emotional problems, the probationary students would manifest greater anxiety. The hypothesis was not confirmed; there was no significant difference in Rorschach anxiety between the two groups.

In the Greenberg and Aronow study (Note 2) discussed in an earlier chapter, the HIT Anxiety scale was one of the inkblot measures correlated with interpersonal distance. The anxiety scale was found to correlate significantly with both live interpersonal distance ($r = .30, p < .05$) and with projective interpersonal distance ($r = .27, p < .05$). However, Dosey and Meisels (1969) found no significant relationship between the Elizur Rorschach anxiety scale and interpersonal distance as measured by three separate methods. It should be noted that the interpersonal distance measures of Dosey and Meisels did not intercorrelate significantly; however the two measures of Greenberg and Aronow were significantly related ($r = .52, p < .01$).

Sanders and Cleveland (1953) investigated whether examiners' anxiety levels would affect the Rorschach anxiety content of test subjects. Nine male graduate students were first administered the Rorschach test and each in turn administered the test to 30 male undergraduate subjects. The Rorschach anxiety of the nine graduate students was designated their covert anxiety levels. Test subjects' ratings of the examiners' anxiety were designated the overt anxiety levels. Sanders and Cleveland found that the test subjects' Rorschach anxiety was not significantly related to either the examiners' overt or covert anxiety levels.

General Evaluation of Anxiety Scoring

The interscorer reliability of the Elizur scale appears to be within satisfactory limits. Although split-half coefficients obtained by both Elizur (1949) and by Holtzman et al. (1961) are quite low, as noted in Chapter 2, it could be argued that high split-half coefficients should not be expected of an instrument as heterogeneous as the Elizur scale.

A more relevant question is the extent to which temporal fluctuations can be considered a source of error. As discussed above, the investigation of Epstein et al. (1957) estimated a test-retest coefficient of .26, but this finding must be considered of limited value because of the nature of their test stimuli. More to the point is the contrast between the delayed alternate form and the split-half coefficients reported for the HIT Anxiety scale by Holtzman. The gap between these two types of coefficients is typically small, a fact suggesting that lack of temporal stability is not a major problem for this scale.

The evidence is likewise generally favorable with respect to the validity of the anxiety scale. The anxiety scale has been shown to be significantly related to ratings of anxiety by self and others, and to specific symptomatology associated with anxiety. The Elizur anxiety scale does not appear to be a valid indicator of prognosis or diagnosis. However, as noted by Goldfried et al. (1971), there is no reason to expect that a test measuring trait anxiety would in fact be an effective predictor of prognosis or diagnosis. Many of the studies done in this vein appear to have included the anxiety scale as one of many measures, with no strong theoretical justification for expecting a relationship between inkblot anxiety and the variables in question. A survey of the research reveals that the more appropriate the rationale for inclusion of inkblot anxiety in the study, the more likely that the study concluded with significant results.

A more complex question is the matter of whether the Elizur scale can be best understood as a measure of *trait* or *state* anxiety. Elizur stated that his inkblot anxiety scale measures "an internal state of tension within the individual that tends to 'break through' whenever an opportunity is offered" (Elizur, 1949, p 248). It is thus *trait anxiety* that the scale is designed to measure. Auerbach and Spielberger (1972) have discussed the evidence relating to whether the Elizur scale measures *trait* as opposed to *state* anxiety. They concluded that the evidence is most consistent with an understanding of the scale as a measure of *trait anxiety*, though it is possible that the scale may be a confounded measure of both *trait* and *state* anxiety.

As noted above, temporal fluctuations as a source of error appear to be less of a problem for anxiety scoring than for many other content systems discussed in this volume; furthermore the scale does not seem sensitive to experimental attempts to invoke *state anxiety*, particularly as seen in the well-designed study of Iacino and Cook (1974). The present authors thus agree with Auerbach and Spielberger (1972) in seeing the anxiety scale primarily as a measure of enduring *trait anxiety*. The Cook et al. (1973) investigation, however, is also consistent with the Auerbach and Spielberger view that *state anxiety* may also be measured by the Elizur scale. The extent to which state anxiety influences Elizur scale scores remains to be determined by future research in this area. Auerbach and Spielberger suggested that two of the major Elizur scoring categories (cultural stereotypes of fear and symbolic responses) should be expected on a logical basis to be measures of *trait anxiety*. This view suggests that it may be possible to develop relatively more purified measures of *trait anxiety* by refining the scoring categories in future research.

A puzzling phenomenon is the lack of consistency in the relationship between the anxiety content scale and other tests of anxiety, notably the MAS. One possible explanation for the discrepancy may be found in Elizur's initial study. As noted above, Elizur found that his inkblot anxiety scale correlated more strongly with third-party ratings of anxiety than did a self-report measure. Because the MAS is essentially a type of self-report measure, it is possible that the Rorschach scale is actually a more valid index of trait anxiety than the MAS; thus there is a lack of congruence between the two measures. It is also possible that the two tests measure different aspects of anxiety, although there is no indication of what these different aspects might be. The findings of Mogar (1962) are interesting in this regard, in that the DAP and the Rorschach anxiety scale seemed to be measuring the same variable, while the MAS was not related to these two measures. The findings of Nichols and Tursky (1967) are also consistent with this approach. A more complete explanation for the inconsistent relationship of the inkblot anxiety scale with the MAS and other measures of anxiety must await further research in this area.

The Zuckerman et al. study (1967) stands out in its negative implications for the anxiety scoring of content. An explanation for these findings is not immediately evident. The HIT Anxiety scale was not found to relate to judges' ratings of anxiety; this finding contradicts the results of two similar studies using the Rorschach test. It is possible that the HIT anxiety scale measures something different from what the Elizur scale measures, but the great similarities between them do not support such a conclusion.

Finally, a note of caution must be included for the practicing clinician. Validity studies that have been carried out in this area do seem to indicate that Rorschach content can be used as a valid measure of anxiety. However it must also be stated that the usefulness of the Elizur scale as a normative instrument in clinical practice still needs to be proved. There is as yet no way of knowing how sensitive the Elizur anxiety scale is to differing degrees of trait anxiety. Although the scale may be able to discriminate significantly between extreme groups, if there is a considerable amount of group overlap the scale may be of rather limited use in enabling the clinician to estimate the severity of anxiety.

A related problem is the total inadequacy of available norms for the Elizur anxiety scale. In fact such norms do not now exist. Goldfried et al. (1971) have provided the next best thing, viz, a listing of average anxiety scores for the various groups of subjects that are reported in the research literature. Unfortunately the effect of R on total anxiety score is not taken into account in many of these averages. Furthermore a perusal of the Goldfried table of Rorschach anxiety averages indicates considerable disparity between anxiety scores as determined by different studies, even within diagnostic groups. For example, Elizur's initial study reported 12.5 anxiety responses in the average Rorschach protocols of neurotic adults. On the other hand, Zimet and Brackbill (1956) reported 6.7 anxiety responses in the average protocols of their neurotic adults. The reason for such gross disparities is not clear, but they may be due to major demographic differences between samples of subjects or perhaps to differences in subjects' motivations. Adequate norms are a prerequisite for use of the Elizur scale as a measuring instrument valuable to the clinician.

ELIZUR'S HOSTILITY SCALE

Scales of hostility other than that of Elizur have been developed by such investigators as De Vos (1952), Murstein (1956), Storment and Finney (1953), and Towbin (1959). Holtzman et al. (1961) included a Hostility scale in the HIT, patterned after both the Elizur (1949) and the Murstein (1956) scales. The Elizur scale of hostility has met with less universal acceptance by researchers than has his anxiety scale. Scales other than Elizur's have frequently been used in research studies on hostility. These other scales often incorporate elaborations such as Murstein's suggestion of scoring responses for the degree of hostility, and the idea of scoring the directionality of hostility presented in the *Palo Alto scale* (Finney, 1955). The Elizur scale is described below.

SCORING

Elizur scored responses as hostility-evincing if they contained the following characteristics.

Hostility expressed or implied. A capital *H* would be scored if hatred, dislike, criticism, or derogation were expressed in the response. Examples of these responses include "A type of man I hate"; "an ugly figure"; "a stupid animal"; "an angry face"; "a quarrelsome person." A lowercase *h* would be scored for responses indicating such hostility to a lesser degree. Examples of such responses include: "Gossiping women"; "two butlers making each other compliments."

Hostile expressive behavior. If the *behavior* of the percept figure suggests hostility, *H* would be scored. Examples include "two animals fighting with each other"; "they squashed the butterfly"; "a wolf devouring its prey"; "a killed aminal."

Response symbolizing hostility. A lowercase *h* would be scored for symbolic responses suggesting hostility. Examples: "The red represents struggle,"; "a primitive war mask."

Objects of aggression. The presence of objects used for aggressive purposes would be scored *H* or *h*. Examples of *H* include "Arrows"; "gun"; "pistol." Examples of *h* are: "Pliers"; "knife"; "teeth."

Double connotation of anxiety and hostility. Responses that contain clear evidence of both anxiety and hostility would be scored *h*. Examples of such responses include: "Headless person"; "injured bear"; "child with cut-off arms"; "a torn butterfly"; "a policeman"; "an animal going to attack you, I feel somewhat scared."

Elizur believed that borderline responses in which there was doubt as to whether hostility was involved should not be scored. Examples presented by Elizur that suggest neither anxiety nor hostility are the following.

Animals. Frogs, mice, bugs, crabs, and bears are typical examples.

Anatomic. Spinal cords, x-rays, bones, and lungs fall into this category.

Miscellaneous. Coat of arms, rocks, and skins of an animal exemplify miscellaneous responses.

An individual's total hostility score is determined by counting each *H* response as two units, and each *h* response as one unit. The two resulting sums are added to yield the total hostility score.

Research to date on the relationship between Rorschach hostility scoring and R has been contradictory. Sanders and Cleveland (1953) have reported a significant positive correlation, whereas Gorlow et al. (1952) have reported a significant *negative* correlation between these two variables. Goldfried et al. (1971) have suggested that there may be a curvilinear relationship between Rorschach hostile content and R. Use of the HIT as the inkblot vehicle for hostile content is particularly recommended in research studies in this area so that R may be eliminated as a potential confounding variable.

RELIABILITY

Interscorer reliability. To determine the interscorer reliability of his system, Elizur had 8 graduate students independently score 15 Rorschach records. The average intercorrelation coefficient between the eight scorings for hostility was .82. The correlation between the average of the eight scorings and Elizur's own scoring of the protocols was .93. Forsyth (1959) also found high interscorer reliability coefficients for Elizur's hostility system: .94 and .91. Holtzman et al. (1961) reported that when two highly trained examiners scored 40 schizophrenic protocols, a correlation of .96 was found with the HIT Hostility scale. When four less highly trained examiners rated 96 protocols from college students, the average correlation was .88.

Test–retest reliability. One study is tangentially relevant to test–retest reliability. Epstein et al. (1957) administered an inkblot test to a group of 16 subjects on 10 different occasions over a 5-week period. The blots were not the standard Rorschach blots, but blots created for purposes of the experiment. On each occasion 10 different blots were used. These authors estimated the test–retest correlation across all administrations to be .30 ($p < .001$). However it is difficult to evaluate the system's temporal stability on the basis of this study because of the obscure and shifting nature of the inkblot stimuli.

Split-half reliability. Elizur conducted a study to determine the internal consistency of the hostility scale. Using the split-half (odd-even) method and the Spearman-Brown formula with 30 subjects, he found a correlation coefficient of .75. With respect to the hostility scale of the HIT, Holtzman et al. found that the odd-even reliability coefficients for hostility among various subject groups varied from .54 to .89 with a median of .71.

Alternate form reliability.   Holtzman et al. (1961) reported the following data for the HIT Hostility scale: among 120 college students with an interval of 1-week, the reliability coefficient was .59; among 72 11th graders with a 3-month interval, it was .43; among 42 elementary school students with a 1-year interval, it was .47; and among 48 college students with a 1-year interval, it was .47.

VALIDITY

Numerous studies have investigated the validity of hostility content scoring. These studies are summerized below and grouped into six categories according to the criterion against which the hostile scoring system was validated. The six major classes of criteria are (1) a behavior history of aggression, (2) ratings of hostility and aggression by self and others, (3) relationship with other tests, (4) situationally induced aggression, (5) diagnosis and symptomatology, and (6) miscellaneous criteria.

Behavior history of aggression.   Several studies have investigated whether groups characterized by a history of antisocial acts would differ from control subjects in hostile Rorschach content. In general the data seem to indicate that Rorschach content scales of hostility can significantly discriminate between such groups. In one such study, Storment and Finney (1953) investigated whether the Rorschach records of 23 male neuropsychiatric patients with a history of violent, assaultive acts could be differentiated from those of 23 matched patients without such a history. Three methods were used to analyze the Rorschach records: Klopfer's traditional categories, clinical judgment, and a hostile content system developed by the authors. Storment and Finney found that few of Klopfer's scoring categories were able to discriminate between the two groups, and clinical judgments demonstrated only chance correspondence with the criterion. The hostility content analysis, however, discriminated between the two groups at a level of significance greater than .001. The biserial correlation coefficient between the criterion and the aggressive content scores was .71.

Finney (1955) revised the Storment and Finney scale into the *Palo Alto Destructive Content scale.* He investigated whether traditional Rorschach scores, clinical judgment, and his content scale would discriminate between 39 nonassaultive and 78 assaultive hospitalized psychiatric patients. Two of the traditional scores did significantly discriminate the groups, but these scores were not the same traditional scores found to be successful in the previously mentioned study by Storment and Finney (1953). Two of three clinical judges were able to discriminate significantly between the groups, but they were not able to agree among themselves as to the assaultive patients. The modified content scale was not able to discriminate between the criterion groups at the .05 level, but it did discriminate significantly between groups ($p < .01$, one-tailed test) when the subjects of this study were combined with the subjects of the Storment and Finney (1953) investigation.

Gorlow et al. (1952) studied the Rorschach and Symonds Picture Story test protocols of 13 adolescent delinquents and 13 nondelinquent adolescents. Using the Elizur hostility scoring system, these authors found significant differences in the predicted direction between the mean hostility scores of the groups. Content scoring for hostility of the Symonds test was not similarly successful.

Wolf (1957) studied 37 male neuropsychiatric patients divided into two groups on the basis of acting-out history. A scoring method similar to Elizur's hostility system was then related to the criterion. Wolf found that the hostile content system did significantly discriminate between the acting-out and nonacting-out groups ($p < .005$).

Sommer and Sommer (1958) studied the Rorschach protocols of 31 male psychiatric patients who made only nonaggressive color responses in their protocols (e.g., ice cream, orchid) and 26 such patients who made aggressive color responses (e.g., fire, volcano). Ratings of physical and verbal explosiveness were then made on the basis of their social histories. These authors found that the aggressive color subjects had a greater incidence of past physical explosiveness than did the nonaggressive color subjects ($p < .05$). The two groups did not differ significantly on rated verbal explosiveness. However it does not appear that the two groups were equated for a host of potentially relevant control variables.

Towbin (1959) investigated 48 male hospitalized schizophrenic subjects with a history of assaultive behavior on the ward to see if they would differ from 48 similar patients without such a history. He constructed his own Rorschach content scoring system for hostility. Both aggressive percepts and aggressive remarks during the test administration were found to be significantly related to a behavior history of aggression (phi coefficients equal .50 and .26 respectively ($p < .01$). Two other categories of hostile Rorschach responses — aggressive instruments, and responses connoting hostile activity — were also examined in order to determine their relationship to the criterion. The former was found to be significantly related to aggressive ward behavior ($p < .01$), whereas the latter was not.

One investigation reporting a more complex relationship between Rorschach content and a behavioral history of aggression is that of Haskell (1961). Haskell investigated whether the Rorschach test, the TAT, and the Object Relations Technique would be related to ratings of aggression based on patient history, nurses' ratings of ward behavior, and therapists' ratings of interview behavior. Thirty-eight hospitalized schizophrenic patients were studied. The Rorschach variables that were related to these criteria were Towbin's card criticism and aggressive content responses, Sommer's aggressive color content, and various formal Rorschach categories. Haskell found that Towbin's card criticism was significantly related to the social history of aggression and to nurses' ratings of aggressive behavior (contingency coefficients were .30 and .35 respectively, $p < .05$); aggressive color content was significantly related to the nurses' and the therapists' ratings (coefficients were .38 and .35 respectively, $p < .05$); aggressive content per se was only significantly related to the therapists' ratings, and not to the social history or nurses' ratings. Haskell interpreted these findings as suggesting that the Rorschach content indices were sensitive to hostility on deeper levels of the personality. A few of the formal Rorschach categories were found to be related to the criteria of aggression, but most of these were in the opposite direction from what was predicted. Unfortunately Haskell did not indicate whether total R was controlled in this study.

Ratings by self and others. A second major focus of investigations on the validity of inkblot content in scoring hostility has been on the use of ratings as criteria. Although some results in this area have not been positive, most studies have found significant relationships between hostile content and rated aggressiveness and hostility.

As part of his validation of the scales, Elizur (1949) included three self-rating items relevant to hostility for his 30 subjects. The self-rating items asked about the control subjects felt that they had over aggressive feelings toward friends, members of the family, and strangers or members of minority groups. A correlation of .45 ($p < .05$) was found between the self-ratings and Elizur's hostility scoring. A correlation of .41 ($p < .05$) was also found between hostile content and self-ratings of depression.

Elizur (1949) also had 20 subjects interviewed and their hostility rated by three psychologists. When the average rating provided by the three judges was correlated with Elizur's Rorschach hostility scoring, it yielded a correlation of .60 ($p < .01$). As noted above, Haskell (1961) had therapists rate subjects for degree of hostility. Haskell found these ratings to be significantly related to the patients' aggressive content (contingency coefficient was .39, $p < .01$) and to aggressive color content (contingency coefficient was .30, $p < .05$).

Smith and Coleman (1956) studied the Rorschach and MAPS protocols of 30 white male school children, aged 9 to 15. The Rorschach protocols were scored for hostile content using a combination of the methods of Elizur (1949) and Walker (1951). The subjects were also rated for physical hostility, verbal hostility, and quarrelsomeness by five teachers and one graduate student assistant. These authors predicted and tested for a curvilinear relationship between Rorschach hostility and the ratings of hostility. The Rorschach content scale was found to be significantly related to all three of the hostility ratings. Multiple correlations between the Rorschach scale and MAPS hostility scores as predictors, and ratings of hostility as the criterion, indicated that the combined use of Rorschach hostile content and the MAPS yielded the best validity. There is no indication that Rorschach R was considered as a potential confounding variable.

Wallace and Sechrest (1963) constructed a multitrait-multimethod matrix for four traits and five methods. The four traits evaluated were somatic concern, hostility, achievement concern, and religiousness. The five methods used were self-description, peer reputation, content Rorschach, Incomplete Sentences Blank, and TAT. The subjects were 72 freshman nursing students. Wallace and Sechrest utilized Klopfer's delineation of hostile content and Holtzman's category of implements of violence for their Rorschach scale. The Rorschach hostile content scale was found to be significantly and positively related to self-description somatic concern ($p < .05$) and to self-description hostility ($p < .05$).

Rader (1957) correlated the Rorschach hostility scores of 38 state prison inmates with their rated aggressiveness in group psychotherapy. He constructed a hostility and mutilation Rorschach content scale based on the hostility systems of Elizur (1949), Schafer (1954), and De Vos (1952). Rader then scored the Rorschach records for passivity, guilt, depressive, and inadequacy content (PGDI), which he felt might predict low behavioral aggression. Rader found that hostile Rorschach content was significantly related to rated aggression ($p < .01$). He also found that by combining hostility and the PGDI content ratings in a single regression equation, he was able to increase significantly the multiple correlation coefficient.

Abrams (1962) explored whether frequency of hostile Rorschach content would be related to tendencies toward repression-sensitization as determined by peer ratings. Abrams asked 250 female student nurses and oral hygienists to rate themselves and 5 other subjects for hostility. Three groups of 20 subjects each were then selected. Group 1 included those who were rated as very hostile and also perceived themselves as hostile. Group 2 consisted of those who were rated as very hostile, but who did not perceive themselves as hostile. Group 3 was composed of those who were rated average in hostility and also perceived themselves as average. All subjects were group administered the Rorschach test, and two tests specifically constructed for the study — recall and preference tests. Subjects were asked to give three responses to each Rorschach card. The responses were scored for hostility according to responses considered hostile by Phillips and Smith (1953) or Schafer (1954). Both hostile groups (Groups 1 and 2) exhibited a significantly greater frequency of hostile Rorschach responses than did the average hostile subjects (Group 3). There was no significant difference between the hostility scores of Groups 1 and 2.

Walker (1951) investigated the question of whether Rorschach and MAPS content scalings of hostility would be related to psychotherapists' ratings of hostility in their patients. Patients had been seen by the therapists for a median of 19.5 hours. Thirty-six therapists and 40 patients were involved in this investigation. Walker scored the Rorschach protocols for hostility by submitting selected Rorschach responses to a panel of judges who rated the amount of hostility indicated by the responses. The resulting hostility scores were correlated with the criterion. Walker found an estimated Pearson correlation of .78 ($p < .01$) between Rorschach hostile content and the therapists' ratings of their patients' hostility.

Kagan and Moss (1961) administered a 32-card inkblot test to 34 females and 35 males who were members of the Fels Research Institute longitudinal population. The 32 cards were actually the standard 10 Rorschach cards divided into D and d areas. The inkblot protocols were scored for aggressive activity, for example people or animals fighting or arguing. Responses evidencing symbolic or disguised aggression — monsters, guns, blood — were not so scored. It is not clear from the Kagan and Moss presentation whether R was controlled. Subjects were interviewed and then rated on the following relevant characteristics: overt rebellion to male authority, aggressive retaliation, ease of anger arousal, competitive behavior, criticism of father, criticism of mother, and introspectiveness. The other measures included were a weighted TAT affect scale (ascribing emotions to TAT figures), self-ratings on overt aggression and ease of anger arousal, and tachistoscopic recognition of aggressive pictures. For female subjects the only significant correlations between aggressive inkblot percepts and the other measures were correlations of -.37 ($p < .05$, one-tailed) with interview-rebellion to authority, .44 ($p < .02$, one-tailed) with interview-competitiveness, .43 ($p < .02$, one-tailed) with interview-introspectiveness, and .35 ($p < .02$, one-tailed) with TAT weighted affect. None of the correlations for male subjects were statistically significant. However it should be noted that the unusual inkblot stimuli used in this study (divisions of the standard Rorschach cards) and its scoring method (involving exclusion of symbolic aggressive responses) make it difficult to compare this investigation with others in this area.

Gluck (1955) related Rorschach hostile content to hostile behavior among 30 neuropsychiatric patients in an army hospital. Patients were first individually administered the Rorschach test as part of a standard test battery. The Rorschach protocols were scored for covert, overt, and combined hostile content. Subjects were then placed in a stress situation designed to provoke hostile behavior. Gluck found little relationship between hostile content and rated hostile behavior in the stress situation.

In the study of Zuckerman et al. (1967) that was discussed above, a rating scale of hostility and the HIT Hostility scale were among the measures employed with the 29 male psychiatric and 25 normal male subjects. The HIT Hostility scale was not found to correlate significantly with the judges' ratings of hostility in either of the two subject groups or in the combined group.

Relationships with other tests.   A third focus of validational efforts with Rorschach hostile content has been the attempt to relate it to other tests and measures of hostility and aggression. In general the hostility content system does not seem to correlate well with other measures of hostility, and there is even disagreement as to the expected direction of such a hypothetical relationship (Murstein & Wheeler, 1959).

In Elizur's initial validation study (1949), a questionnaire was administered to the 30 volunteers; five of the questions sought to measure indirect evidence of hostility (indirect, because hostility is so condemned in our culture). These questions concerned intrapunitiveness, especially goodnatured behavior to others, and the apparent use of projection. Elizur found a correlation of .74 ($p < .01$) between his 5-item scale and his content scoring for hostility. Elizur further hypothesized that because submissiveness, aloofness, ideas of reference, and depression are often concomitants of hostility, measures of these characteristics would also correlate significantly with his Rorschach hostility scale. Elizur found the following correlations, which by and large supported his reasoning: the correlation with questionnaire submissiveness was .64 ($p < .01$); the correlation with questionnaire aloofness was .43 ($p < .05$); the correlation with questionnaire ideas of reference was .48 ($p < .01$); and the correlation with questionnaire depression was .44 ($p < .01$).

Other studies in this area have tended to use more established measuring instruments than were used by Elizur. Walker (1951) determined the correlations between the various tests used in his investigation. The estimated Pearson r between a modified Elizur Rorschach hostility scoring and MAPS hostility was determined to be .73 ($p < .01$) for the 40 subjects in this study. The estimated Pearson correlation between Rorschach hostility and a hostility questionnaire was determined to be nonsignificant at -.39.

Murstein and Wheeler (1959) administered the Rorschach test and a Thematic Series test (including TAT cards) to a sample of 36 women with breast cancer. Reasoning that a person *free* from hostility would be more able to recognize the hostile stimulus properties of thematic cards, these investigators hypothesized that there would be a significant *negative* correlation between Rorschach and thematic hostility. Thus thematic responses were viewed by these authors as more subject to defensive distortion than were Rorschach responses. Murstein and Wheeler found a correlation of -.41 ($p < .01$, one-tailed test) between Murstein's hostility scoring (Murstein, 1956) and hostility scoring of the thematic responses, and thus their hypothesis was confirmed.

Hafner and Kaplan (1960) related Rorschach scoring of hostile content to hostility scoring of the TAT. These authors first established their own Rorschach and TAT scales of hostility on the basis of eight clinical psychologists' ratings of 200 Rorschach percepts and 100 TAT themes. These eight judges thus established the level of hostility indicated by the percepts and themes and the degree to which the hostility should be considered overt or covert. The TAT and the Rorschach test were then administered to 30 psychiatric patients. Hafner and Kaplan found a nonsignificant Pearson correlation of .32 between the Rorschach and TAT hostile content scales.

In the Wallace and Sechrest (1963) study discussed above, correlations were computed between the various psychological tests administered to the nursing students. A correlation of .00 was found between Rorschach hostility and TAT hostility, and a correlation of .18 was found between Rorschach hostility and incomplete sentences blank hostility.

Goodstein (1954) administered the Taylor Manifest Anxiety scale, the Rorschach test, and the Iowa Picture Interpretation test (IPIT) to 57 undergraduate student subjects. The Harrower group administration of the Rorschach was used, and the protocols were scored according to Elizur's system. Goodstein found a correlation of -.02 between Rorschach hostility and IPIT hostility. Interestingly, a low but significant negative correlation was found between Rorschach response productivity and Rorschach hostility, a result indicating that subjects giving few responses tended to give responses scored in the hostility category.

In an investigation by Buss et al. (1962), Rorschach hostile content was correlated with the Buss-Durkee hostility inventory and with the IPIT on a sample of psychiatric patients. These authors found correlations of .10 and .40 ($p < .01$) between Rorschach content hostility and the Buss-Durkee inventory for male and female subjects respectively; correlations of .18 for male subjects and -.40 ($p < .01$) for female subjects were found between Rorschach hostility and the IPIT.

Siegel (1956) developed a Manifest Hostility scale (MHS) consisting of MMPI items considered to reflect hostility by five judges. This test and the Rorschach test were administered to 60 white male college students and 60 white male veterans applying for treatment at a Veterans Administration mental hygiene clinic. Siegel found no significant correlations between the MHS and Elizur scoring of Rorschach hostility. The rank-order correlation for the students was .17, and for the veterans .01. However, as noted by Siegel, the MHS cannot be considered a validated test of hostility.

Rosenstiel (1973) reported no significant relationship between HIT hostility and the Buss-Durkee factor 1 scale scores (resentment, suspicion) and factor 2 scale scores (assault, indirect, irritability, verbal) among German subjects. However Rosenstiel found that there was a significant correlation between the subjects' increase in HIT hostility following experimental frustration and their Buss-Durkee factor 1 scores, as was predicted. Rosenstiel interpreted this finding by considering the HIT scale as a measure of hostility rather than aggressiveness.

In the Zuckerman et al. (1967) multitrait-multimethod study (1967), correlations were found between the HIT Hostility scale and the hostility scales of the Buss-Durkee, the Multiple Affect Adjective Check List, and the TAT. None of these correlations was significant.

Situationally induced aggression. A few studies have investigated the effect of attempts to evoke aggression on Rorschach protocols. Frustration and post-hypnotically induced hostility have been utilized. The studies in this area have yielded inconsistent results.

In one of these investigations, Lucas (1961) studied whether induced frustration would affect the Rorschach scores of 8- and 9-year-old children. The children were first individually administered the Rorschach test; 8 weeks later the children in the experimental group were subjected to frustration in a special game. The Rorschach test was then readministered to all subjects. Lucas found that the experimental subjects did not evidence more hostility on the second administration. The control subjects, however, produced more hostile responses in the second administration; thus there resulted a significant difference between the groups in the opposite direction from that predicted. Lucas explained his findings by suggesting that his control subjects felt more comfortable in expressing hostility during a second administration.

Pattie (1954) administered the Rorschach test to 14 subjects who were hypnotized and instructed to take the test first in a normal frame of mind, then in a state of post-hypnotically induced hostility toward the examiner. The subjects were also instructed to forget their first set of responses before taking the test a second time. Most of the subjects were also asked to predict how a hostile subject would behave in testing. Scoring according to Beck's categories, Pattie found that 8 subjects showed more than twice the percentage of hostile content under the hostile conditions than they did under normal conditions. Two of the subjects were very uncooperative in the hostile condition, and 4 subjects showed neither of these patterns. These subjects' manner of displaying hostility on the Rorschach conformed in large measure to the individual subjects' predictions of how hostility would be manifested in Rorschach test behavior.

Rosenstiel (1973) investigated the effect of frustration on HIT hostility scores. In this study subjects in the experimental condition were told that they had not performed well on an intelligence test. In a preliminary study the subjects were 46 male German students, mostly medical students; 23 served as controls. In the primary study the subjects were 50 male German students. Rosenstiel found that the number of HIT hostility responses significantly increased among the experimental subjects following frustration ($p < .01$).

Diagnosis and symptomatology.   Diagnosis and symptomatology have also been used as validating criteria for hostility scoring. Whereas two studies found differences between normals, neurotics, and schizophrenics, two studies did not. One investigation also reported more hostile responses in the records of passive–aggressive subjects than in those of paranoid subjects. Results of studies concerning symptomatology have been more consistent — teeth grinding and nail biting have been shown to be related to the presence of hostile inkblot responses.

Elizur (1949) compared the Rorschach hostility scores of matched neurotic and control subjects. As expected, the neurotics proved to have significantly higher hostility scores than the normals. Wirt (1956) compared the Rorschach records of 38 normal, 32 neurotic, and 50 schizophrenic male subjects. Thirty-eight normal female subjects were also included. The records were scored according to Finney's Palo Alto Aggressive Content scale. Wirt found that the aggression means of all three groups were significantly different from each other after adjustment for the total number of responses in the record. The normals' adjusted mean was 6.36, the neurotics' was 9.38, and the schizophrenics' mean was 9.07. In addition the groups showed a significant difference in the direction of punitiveness: the normal group tended to direct hostility outwardly, the schizophrenics directed it inwardly, and the neurotic group revealed no characteristic direction. Wirt's results also indicated that the age, sex, and educational and social status of his subjects were not significantly related to the appearance of aggressive responses in their protocols.

Fisher and Hinds (1951) compared the test records of 26 normal, 25 paranoid schizophrenic, and 20 suicidal schizophrenic subjects with respect to hostility and hostility controls. The Rorschach test was one of the measures used; responses were considered hostile if they contained openly hostile content or symbolic or concealed hostility. The Terman-Miles inkblots were also shown to subjects, who were asked to choose which of four alternatives the blots resembled. One of the four alternatives was a hostile choice. Fisher and Hinds determined that neither their overt–covert scoring of hostility nor the multiple-choice inkblot procedure was able to differentiate significantly between the groups.

Moylan, Shaw, and Appleman (1960) compared the Rorschach protocols of 10 dependent, 13 passive–aggressive, and 12 paranoid male patients in a neuropsychiatric hospital. One of the categories on which the groups were compared was that of aggressive responses, defined by the authors as a percept containing words of an aggressive, destructive, or explosive nature, or animals associated with aggression. Moylan et al. found that the passive–aggressive patients evidenced significantly more aggressive percepts than the paranoid patients ($p < .02$). The passive–aggressive subjects also had more aggressive responses than the dependent patients (20.5 percent versus 12.3 percent), but the difference fell short of significance at the .05 level. It should be noted that the small number of subjects used in this study considerably reduced the power of the statistical test; thus it was very difficult to demonstrate differences between subject groups.

Vernallis (1955) noted that psychoanalysts view teeth grinding as a result of fixation at the oral-sadistic stage of psychosexual development. He therefore hypothesized that teeth grinding would be related to hostility as measured by Elizur's content system. Vernallis compared 40 teeth grinding college students to 40 matched control subjects, using biserial correlation. He found a correlation of .57 ($p < .01$) between Rorschach hostility and teeth grinding/nonteeth-grinding status. However R does not appear to have been controlled in this study.

Cummings (cited in Goldfried et al., 1971) similarly assumed a relationship between hostility and a behavioral characteristic — nail biting. The severity of nail biting was rated in 70 subjects between the ages of 10 and 14, and their Elizur Rorschach hostility scores were calculated. Cummings found a correlation of .34 ($p < .01$) between Rorschach hostility and nail biting.

Miscellaneous.   Four miscellaneous additional sets of findings are relevant to the validity of hostility content scoring. In the study of Kagan and Moss (1961), 26 male and 30 female college subjects were administered inkblots derived from various sources, they were also given a concept formation task. Five concepts were used: anger, sexual excitement, number, texture, and happiness. The authors found that aggressive inkblot percepts were positively associated with early acquisition of the concept of sexual excitement among both males and females; they were also associated with early acquisition of the concept of anger among female subjects. Kagan and Moss concluded that the production of blatantly aggressive inkblot responses may reflect minimal repression of sexual as well as aggressive thoughts.

Kagan, Sontag, Baker, and Nelson (1958) compared the projective test protocols of subjects whose IQ increased with those of subjects whose IQ decreased. The study involved subjects at Fels Research Institute. Rorschach responses were considered to be aggressive if they involved either overt physical or verbal aggression, explosive objects or explosions, or objects or animal parts associated with aggression. Kagan found that the frequency of aggressive Rorschach responses was significantly associated with an increase in IQ in boys ($p < .07$ for the initial sample, $p < .01$ in a later follow-up of 20 of these subjects). The higher incidence of aggressive imagery in boys whose IQ increased was interpreted by the authors as a reflection of stronger competitive motivation.

The above-mentioned study by Towbin (1957) also investigated what effect the subject's perception of the examiner's power and status had on the Rorschach responses. The subjects were exposed to a conversation between the examiner and a confederate immediately before the test administration. Five experimental treatments were thus utilized: (1) high power, high status, (2) high power, low status, (3) high status, low power, (4) low status, low power, and (5) control condition, no confederate. Towbin found that neither the perceived status of the examiner nor the perceived power affected the frequency of hostile Rorschach responses.

The HIT Hostility scale was included in the Greenberg and Aronow (Note 2) investigation. HIT hostility was found to correlate significantly with both live interpersonal distance ($r = .29, p < .05$) and projective interpersonal distance ($r = .27, p < .05$).

General Evaluation of Hostility Scoring

As is the case with the content scales of anxiety, most of the reliability evidence for the hostility scales pertains to the HIT. In general the inter-scorer reliability coefficients that have been reported are within acceptable limits. With respect to temporal stability, however, the HIT Hostility scale appears to have more difficulty than does the HIT Anxiety scale. The split-half coefficients reported for the hostility scale are consistently and considerably greater in magnitude than the corresponding delayed alternate form coefficients. However it should also be recalled that the HIT Hostility scale is by no means identical to the Elizur scale of hostility, and one must be more careful than usual in generalizing from the apparent reliability of the HIT scale to that of a corresponding Rorschach scale.

The validational evidence on hostility scoring must be considered highly encouraging, particularly in light of the diverse scales used to measure hostile content. That significant results emerge so often despite the diversity of content scales is testimony to the strength of the effect being measured. The evidence of validity is most convincing in studies of the scales' ability to differentiate subjects with a behavioral history of aggression. Of the seven investigations in this area, five reported strongly positive findings, and the remaining two were at least partially supportive. Those studies that used ratings as the criterion also supported the validity of hostile content. Of nine reported investigations in this area, six resulted in positive findings, and one other was partially supportive. The results have been far less positive when hostility scoring has been related to a group of self-rating scales, objective tests, and projective tests designed to measure hostility. It is unclear why the hostility scales fare so much better when validated against criteria other than strictly test measures.

The results of studies of situationally induced aggression have been inconsistent. Aside from the question of whether the methods used were adequate to provoke aggression, one could argue that hostile content actually should not be very much affected by these experimental techniques because the Elizur scale in particular is designed as a measure of long-term hostility in subjects. Studies of the diagnostic usefulness of hostility scoring are likewise inconsistent. It is possible that the use of diverse techniques in measuring hostile content may have played a role in the divergence of these findings. The two studies of symptomatology have strongly supported the validity of hostile content: symptoms thought to be characteristic of hostile individuals were shown to be associated with the appearance of hostile Rorschach content. The miscellaneous studies likewise generally support the construct validity of Rorschach hostile content.

Evaluation of the literature on hostility content scales poses more problems than does evaluation of the literature on anxiety content, largely because of the profusion of scales in the area. The Elizur anxiety scale established an early position of dominance in the inkblot measurement of anxiety; this is less the case in the measurement of hostility. Many experimenters have apparently felt the need to construct additional scales of hostility. This fact may reflect the feeling that aspects of hostility are left unmeasured by the Elizur hostility scale. The inclusion of the dimension of internally versus externally directed anger, as in the Palo Alto scale, is certainly an interesting elaboration of hostility scoring. The finding of Wirt (1956) that the direction of hostility served to differentiate diagnostic groups suggests that this sort of elaboration may be clinically useful. Considerable further work remains to be done in this area.

Although the most consistently positive validational evidence with respect to hostile content was found in differentiating subjects with a history of acting out aggression, one must be cautious in expecting behavioral aggression because of high hostile content scores. Such an approach would not be consistent with a dynamic understanding of aggressive behavior. Hostile drive as measured by inkblot scales is clearly involved in aggression: witness the relationship found between aggression and hostile Rorschach content. However, there is another aspect of the personality that is intimately involved in the question of whether aggression takes place, namely, the control aspect of the personality. As can be seen from the studies done in this area, the relationship between aggression and hostile content has been largely investigated in samples of hospitalized psychiatric patients and among prison inmates — precisely those groups in which ego controls are likely to be most deficient. This approach to the understanding of aggression was partially confirmed by Rader's (1957) finding that including a consideration of control added to the predictability of aggression. The careful clinician must thus consider the nature and quality of the subject's ego controls before predicting potential for aggression based on the presence of hostility. The prediction of aggressive behavior based on a composite measure of hostility and impulse control as demonstrated by Rader (1957) is another fertile area for future research.

As was noted in the discussion of anxiety content, the absence of norms and information on the differentiating precision of hostility scoring makes these scales of little use at this time to the clinician in search of psychometric instruments.

6

Barrier and Penetration

Fisher and Cleveland's Barrier and Penetration Rorschach scores evolved from an intensive study of patients with rheumatoid arthritis. Fisher and Cleveland observed that a great deal of these patients' emotional energies seemed to be tied up with bodily concerns. Their Rorschach records were characterized by an unusual number of responses having to do with the periphery of objects. These investigators saw a possible link between the patients' arthritic symptomatology and their pattern of Rorschach responses. On the basis of this research, Fisher and Cleveland attempted to construct a rating scale of definiteness of body boundaries. By intensive study of the arthritics' Rorschach records, Fisher and Cleveland developed two scales which seemed to be measuring the definiteness of body boundaries: the Barrier scale and the Penetration scale. In general terms, Barrier responses are those in which the peripheries of percepts are stressed. Penetration responses are those emphasizing the penetrability of boundaries.

SCORING

Barrier Scale[1]

All separate articles of clothing are scored on Barrier scale, as are all articles of clothing worn by animals and birds. If the clothing is being worn by a person, however, it is scored only if it is unusual in its covering

[1]The Barrier and Penetration scales presented are those in Fisher and Cleveland's latest revision (1968), which includes several changes from the 1958 scales.

111

or decorative function. (Popular boots on Card IV and bow tie on Card III are not scored for Barrier.) Examples of responses scored for Barrier are a woman in a high-necked dress, a man in a robe, an imp with a cap that has a tassel on it, and people with mittens or gloves. Examples of responses not scored for Barrier are a woman in a dress, a man with a coat on, and a man with a hat.

Animals or creatures whose skins are distinctive or unusual are scored only if the response includes more than the head of the animal. Examples of such animals are alligators, beaver, chameleons, rhinoceroses, scorpions, weasels, and zebras. Any animal skin (except the bearskin on Card IV) is scored for Barrier if unusual emphasis is placed on the textured, fuzzy, mottled, or striped character of the surface. Examples include fuzzy skins, skins with spots, and skins with stripes. All shell creatures except crabs and lobsters are scored for Barrier. Crabs and lobsters are scored for Barrier only if the shell alone is seen. Snails, mussels, shrimps, clams, and turtles are all examples of shelled animals that are scored for Barrier.

References to enclosed openings in the earth are scored for Barrier, for example, valleys, ravines, mine shafts, wells, and canals.

References to unusual animal containers are scored in the Barrier scale. Examples include bloated cats, pregnant women, kangaroos, and udders.

All references to overhanging or protective surfaces are scored for Barrier. Examples of such references are umbrellas, awnings, domes, and shields.

Another group of Barrier responses are references to things that are armored or very dependent on their own containing walls for protection. Tanks, battleships, rocket ships in space, armored cars, and men in armor are typical.

References to things being covered, surrounded, or concealed are scored in the Barrier scale. Some examples are bowls overgrown by plants, houses surrounded by smoke, a person behind a tree, someone peeking from behind a stone, or a donkey with a load covering his back.

References to things with unusual containerlike shapes or properties are also Barrier responses. Bagpipes, thrones, ferris wheels, and chairs are examples of this type of response.

Score Barrier for all references to buildings and to vehicles with containing attributes, for example, automobiles, airplanes, and rockets.

Do not score Barrier for masks.

Do not score Barrier for instruments that grasp or hold, such as pliers, tweezers, or tongs.

Additional general examples of Barrier responses include baskets, bays, bells, bottles, bubbles, cages, candleholders, caves, cocoons, fuzzy poodles, globes, helmets, inlets, land surrounded by water, mountains covered with snow, nets, urns, wallpaper, and wigs.

Penetration Scale

All references to the mouth being opened or being used for intake or expulsion are scored on the Penetration scale. Examples are a dog eating, a dog yawning, a man sticking out his tongue, a man vomiting, a boy spitting, a person with his mouth open, and an animal drinking. Penetration is not scored for references to the use of the mouth for singing or talking.

All references to evading, bypassing, or penetrating through the exterior of an object and getting to the interior should be scored for Penetration. Examples include x-rays, a body seen through a fluoroscope, a cross-section of an organ, a body cut open, and an autopsy.

Score for Penetration any references to the body wall being broken, fractured, injured, and damaged. All references to loss of a body member are also scored for Penetration. Typical references in this group are a mashed bug, a wounded man, a person bleeding, a wound, a stabbed man, a man's skin stripped off. Also score for Penetration when some kind of degeneration of surfaces is involved, for example, diseased skin, withering skin, a withered leaf, and deteriorating flesh.

Another group of Penetration responses is characterized by openings in the earth that have no set boundaries or from which things are being expelled. Examples include a bottomless abyss, a fountain shooting up, and an oil gusher coming in.

All openings should be scored for Penetration. Typical examples are an anus, a birth canal, a doorway, an entrance, and the act of looking into a throat, nostril, rectum, vagina, or window.

References to things that are insubstantial and without palpable boundaries are scored for Penetration. Examples of this group include cotton candy, ghosts, shadows, and soft mud.

All references to transparency should be scored for Penetration. Examples are transparent windows and the ability to see through a dress.

Further general examples of Penetration responses are an animal chewing on a tree, a jigsaw puzzle that is not put together, a doorway, a fish with meat taken off, a bat with holes, a torn fur coat, frayed wings, a harbor entrance, and a man defecating.

Responses that can be scored for both Barrier and Penetration are scored on both scales.

As might be expected, both Barrier and Penetration have been found to be positively correlated with Rorschach R, a fact necessitating the control of productivity in Rorschach research studies in this area. Fisher and Cleveland (1958/1968) have noted three major techniques for controlling R: requiring a fixed number of responses for each blot; eliminating from the study all test records with fewer than 15 responses and reducing all records with more than 25 responses to 25; and using neither of the above techniques but demonstrating that the groups to be contrasted do not significantly differ in R. Use of the HIT as the inkblot vehicle would, of course, eliminate this difficulty.

RELIABILITY

Interscorer Reliability

Studies of the interscorer reliability of these two scales have in general indicated scoring consistency within acceptable limits. Both Fisher and Cleveland (1958/1968) scored a series of 20 test records. The rho correlation between the two sets of Barrier scores was found to be .82; the rho correlation for Penetration was .94. On a second series of 20 records also scored by both of these researchers, the rho correlations between their ratings were determined to be .97 for Barrier and .99 for Penetration. Fisher and Cleveland concluded that "carefully trained and well motivated judges can generally agree somewhere in the .90s" (Fisher & Cleveland, 1958/1968, p 64).

Several other investigations have reported on the interscorer reliability of the Rorschach Barrier and Penetration scales. Ramer (1963) had three judges score the Rorschach records of 96 female undergraduates for Barrier. The correlations between the three sets of scoring were .96, .81, and .90 (mean: .89). Daston and McConnell (1962) also investigated the interscorer reliability of the Barrier and Penetration scales. The Rorschach protocols of a previous study were used. The subjects were 20 males with physical disorders. Each subject had been tested twice, 2 months apart. The Pearson r's between raters were .84 for Barrier and .61 for Penetration. The raters thereafter clarified differences in interpretation, and the correlation for Penetration rose to .79 on a further set of 48 records.

Eigenbrode and Shipman (1960) found that their Barrier scorings correlated at .80 for 83 protocols. Goldfried et al. (1971) reported on two additional Rorschach investigations in which interscorer reliability coefficients for Barrier and Penetration were found to be .97 and .92 respectively in one investigation (Landau) and .89, .94, and .95 for Barrier in another study (Sieracki).

Holtzman et al. (1961) included Barrier and Penetration scales in the HIT, closely modeling them after the Fisher and Cleveland scales. As part of their data gathering for the HIT, Holtzman et al. had two highly trained scorers independently score 40 protocols drawn randomly from the protocols of 99 schizophrenic males. The correlations for Barrier and Penetration were found to be .95 and .92 respectively. Megargee (1965) found that the correlation between his scoring of 75 HIT protocols for Barrier and that of another scorer was .86.

Split-Half Reliability

As is the case with the Elizur anxiety and hostility scales, it is questionable whether the Barrier and Penetration scales should be expected to have high split-half reliability. The Rorschach research literature does not, in fact, report split-half reliability for the Barrier and Penetration scales. Holtzman et al. (1961), however, do include these data for the scales on the HIT. The odd–even reliability coefficients for 15 different subject groups on the Barrier scale ranged from .47 to .85, with a median correlation of .70. For Penetration the coefficients ranged from .41 to .92, with a median of .62.

Test–Retest and Alternate Form Reliability

Two studies of the test–retest reliability of the Rorschach scales have been published, and Holtzman et al. (1961) have reported on the delayed alternate form reliability of the corresponding Holtzman scales. In addition Fisher and Renik (1966) and Renik and Fisher (1968) have likewise provided data on the temporal stability of the HIT Barrier scale.

In the Daston and McConnell (1962) study discussed above, test–retest correlations on the Rorschach for Barrier and Penetration were computed. For rater A, the test–retest correlations were .90 and .82 for Barrier and Penetration; for rater B, the correlations were .88 and .79. Fisher and Cleveland also scored these protocols, and test–retest correlations were determined to be .93 for Barrier and .90 for Penetration. The Penetration score showed evidence of decrease on retest, possibly reflecting an improvement in health. This decrease suggested to these authors that the Penetration score is a more sensitive indicator of change than the Barrier score.

Cleveland (1960) analyzed data from a previous investigation in which the Rorschach test was administered to 50 schizophrenic female inpatients on two occasions 5 days apart. Cleveland reports that test–retest reliability for the Penetration score was .89, and for the Barrier score, .65. The low test–retest reliability of Barrier is blamed by Cleveland on the very limited range of Barrier responses.

Holtzman et al. (1961) have presented data on the delayed alternate form reliability of the HIT Barrier and Penetration scales. Their data reveal that among 120 college students retested within a 1 week interval, the correlations were .38 for Barrier and .43 for Penetration. In a group of 72 eleventh graders reexamined within a 3-month interval, the correlations were .51 and .34 for the two scales. Among 42 elementary school students with a 1-year interval between tests, correlations were .42 for Barrier and .43 for Penetration. Lastly, for a group of 48 college students, again retested after a year, the correlations were .40 for Barrier and .37 for Penetration.

As part of an experiment Fisher and Renik (1966) found alternate form correlations for Barrier on the HIT. Only the data for the control group are relevant because the experiment was designed to alter the Barrier score for the other groups. A short experimental task intervened between the two HIT administrations. Only the first 25 blots of Forms A and B were used. A correlation of .85 was found for the 20 female subjects. In a similar experiment with males, Renik and Fisher (1968) found that the alternate form HIT correlation for the control group was .87.

The test–retest findings of Daston and McConnell (1962) can certainly be considered to within acceptable limits. However, as is the case with many psychological tests (Anastasi, 1976), the applicability of test–retest reliability to the Rorschach is questionable. The subjects in the Daston and McConnell investigation may merely have been recalling specific percepts from the first administration. In fact Holtzman's data on the delayed alternate form reliability of the scales suggest that there is a major problem with these HIT scales. It will be recalled that time and content sampling are the sources of error in delayed alternate form reliability. The alternate form coefficients reported by Holtzman et al. (1961) for Barrier and Penetration are substantially lower than most of the corresponding split-half coefficients. Further evidence that the scales present difficulties in terms of time sampling was uncovered by Fisher and Renik (1964), whose findings on alternate form coefficients with immediate administration were far higher than the delayed alternate form coefficients found by Holtzman et al. However this conclusion must be considered tentative because of the small number of studies in this area. At this time it suffices to note that there are some doubts as to the adequate stability of these scores over time.

VALIDITY

The research literature on the validity of the Barrier and Penetration scores is quite extensive and covered very comprehensively by Fisher (1970), Fisher and Cleveland (1958/1968), and Goldfried et al. (1971).

Therefore only selected validity studies will be presented here. In general the present authors discern eight broad classes of criteria against which Fisher and Cleveland's scores have been validated: diseases, direct and indirect bodily measures, reaction to stress, personality characteristics, measures of social interaction, psychopathology, sex, and various miscellaneous criteria.

Diseases

Fisher and Cleveland and other investigators have produced strong evidence that the Barrier and Penetration scores are related to location of psychosomatic disorder. There is also some tentative evidence that these scores are related to site of disorder in a disease not usually thought of as strictly psychosomatic, i.e., cancer. The results of several studies also appear to indicate that the Barrier score is not much affected by situational body concern.

As might be expected with a scoring system that was developed on a group of patients with a presumably psychosomatic disorder, several investigations of the scales' validity have examined their psychosomatic correlates. Fisher and Cleveland (1958/1968) hypothesized that patients with exterior symptoms would have higher Barrier and lower Penetration scores than subjects with interior symptoms. Five groups of patients were compared: 25 subjects with stomach disturbance, 20 subjects with ulcerative colitis, 25 subjects with rheumatoid arthritis, 25 subjects with neurodermatitis, and 20 subjects with conversion hysteria. The first two groups were regarded as having interior symptoms, the latter three groups, external symptoms. By chi square analyses the patients with exterior symptoms were found to have significantly higher Rorschach Barrier scores ($p < .001$) and significantly lower Pentration scores ($p < .02$) than the patients with interior symptoms. In addition the Barrier scale significantly discriminated between each interior and each exterior group at or beyond the .02 level. For Penetration, three of the six possible group discriminations were significant at or beyond the .02 level. Furthermore three clinical psychologists were successful in sorting the protocols of five exterior and five interior patients based on the scoring system; two of the psychologists sorted the records perfectly.

In a cross-validation of their initial research, Cleveland and Fisher (1960) compared the Barrier and Penetration scores of 26 male arthritic patients with those of 31 ulcer patients on the HIT. The arthritic group again was found to have significantly more Barrier responses ($p < .01$), but the difference in Penetration scores between the groups was not significant, although it was in the predicted direction ($p < .10$).

One study that did not find a relationship between Rorschach Barrier score and psychosomatic disorder has been reported in the literature. Eigenbrode and Shipman (1960) compared 54 patients with external psychosomatic disorders with 29 patients who displayed internal psychosomatic disorders. The Rorschach test was used as the Barrier measure. The Barrier scores of the two groups were not found to differ significantly. These authors discussed several possible reasons for these findings, including instability of scores because of low Barrier frequencies, ambiguities in the scoring system, and a possibly heterogeneous scoring system. Fisher and Cleveland (1968) have also noted that Eigenbrode and Shipman included in the internal category a variety of symptoms (e.g., genitourinary) that had not been included in prior studies.

In an experiment inspired by the failure of Eigenbrode and Shipman (1960) to differentiate patients with internal and external symptoms by means of Barrier and Penetration, Cleveland, Snyder, and Williams (1965) compared similar psychosomatic groups. First, 18 male rheumatoid arthritics were compared to 20 male patients with peptic ulcers or ulcerative colitis. As predicted, the arthritics significantly exceeded the internal symptom patients in Rorschach Barrier score ($p < .001$). There was no significant difference in Penetration score. In addition 20 rheumatoid arthritics were then contrasted with 20 patients with peptic ulcers. This time the subjects with external symptoms had both significantly more Barrier responses ($p < .001$) and significantly fewer Penetration responses ($p < .02$).

Malev (1966) also studied the relation of Rorschach Barrier and Penetration to symptoms in 6- and 8-year-old boys. He found that in the 30 6-year-olds both Barrier and Penetration were significantly related to the frequency of the exterior type of symptom ($p < .05$), both in the predicted direction. However these relationships were not found to be significant among the 30 8-year-old boys.

Fisher and Cleveland (1958/1968) have taken the position that the Barrier score reflects long-term body attitudes and is not affected by situational body concern; thus internal or external physical disorders should not affect the Barrier scores of patients. Several studies have investigated this view of Barrier, beginning with Fisher and Cleveland (1958/1968) who studied the question of whether their observed Barrier differences in symptom groups might be attributable to a reaction to having lived with the symptoms.

Fisher and Cleveland compared the Rorschach test records of their rheumatoid arthritic patients with a group of 20 patients who experienced back pain due to mechanical trauma; the patients with neurodermatitis were compared with 22 patients with skin difficulties due to external causes (burns and chemicals). Total R was not found to differ in the two groups of subjects, but the two functional groups were determined to have significantly higher Barrier scores than the two comparison groups. Clinical psychologists were again asked to sort test records and were essentially successful in differentiating between the different types of patients on the basis of the Barrier concept. These authors did note that the functional patients had symptoms for longer periods than did the control patients. However duration of symptom was not found to be related to Barrier score. Finally the authors compared the protocols of back pain and skin damage patients with those of the patients with stomach disturbances and colitis. The groups were not found to differ in Barrier.

Allardice and Dole (1966) compared 26 hospitalized male patients suffering from leprosy with a matched group of 26 control subjects. The groups were matched for age, race, education, and socioeconomic level. Using the HIT, these researchers found no significant differences between the groups in either Barrier or Penetration scores, nor did the length of hospitalization relate to these scores. Allardice and Dole concluded that their study constitutes further evidence that the scales measure fundamental body attitudes rather than situational body concern.

Orbach and Tallent (1965) have reported on the Rorschach Barrier and Penetration scores of 31 patients (18 male, 13 female) who had had colostomies 5 to 10 years before the test. The median age of the group was approximately 60, and the subjects were primarily Jewish and had been born in Europe. In comparing these subjects to a normal group of Fisher and Cleveland (200 subjects), Orbach and Tallent found that their colostomy patients had significantly fewer ($p < .0005$) Barrier responses than the normals; no significant differences in Penetration were found. This finding is not consistent with the view that Barrier is insensitive to situational bodily concerns. However this clinical paper does not indicate whether there were differences in total R between the groups, or whether the groups were comparable with respect to demographic and other variables.

In a further extension of the research on the bodily correlates of Barrier and Penetration scores, Fisher and Cleveland (1958/1968) related these scores to site of cancer, with the assumption that site of cancer can be influenced by psychological factors. First these authors sorted 17 test records of cancer patients with exterior and interior sites. All but two of the cases were sorted correctly. Next the Rorschach records of 59 patients with exterior cancer and 30 patients with interior cancer were compared. The exterior group was found to have significantly greater Barrier scores ($p < .001$) and significantly lower Penetration responses ($p < .01$) than the interior group. To investigate the influence of symptoms on the Penetration score, the authors also compared the Rorschach records of 28 colostomy patients (approximately 10 years after the operation) with the scores of the patients with interior cancer. No differences in Penetration scores were noted, and thus Fisher and Cleveland were lead to conclude that the symptomatology did not seem to be the causal factor in the observed differences between groups.

Physiological Measures

Several studies have related a variety of physiological measures to the Barrier and Penetration scales. Although there are inconsistencies, on the whole the results suggest that high Barrier subjects are more reactive to external than internal bodily events. The opposite seems to be the case for low Barrier subjects.

In one study that used physiological measures, Davis (1960) investigated nine measures and their relation to the Rorschach Barrier score. The nine physiological measures were observed in 50 normal male subjects. Physiological indices related to exterior and interior physiological responsivity were. abstracted from the nine measures. Davis determined that subjects high in Barrier had greater physiological reactivity in the exterior indices under stress, whereas subjects low in Barrier correspondingly displayed greater reactivity in the internal indices. However these differences did not appear under a nonstress condition.

In another such study, Fisher (1959) examined the GSR reactivity and heart rate of 30 Girl Scouts during an anxiety phase and a rest phase. As predicted, the Rorschach Barrier score was found to be positively and significantly correlated with GSR (rho = .46, $p < .01$) and negatively and significantly correlated with heart rate (rho = .51, $p < .01$) during the anxiety phase. Thus high Barrier was once again found to be associated with a tendency to external rather than internal reactivity. Again the relationship only held up at a statistically significant level under stressful conditions.

Zimny (1965) researched the physiological reactivity of interior and exterior body sites in their relation to Rorschach Barrier and Penetration. Heart rate and skin resistance were the physiological measures observed in 24 female college students. The subjects were observed preceding and during the performance of a stressful task. Zimny determined that during the period preceding the stressful task, Barrier was positively correlated with skin resistance ($p < .05$). None of the other three correlations for Barrier was found to be significant. Using the method of extreme groups, Zimny also found that results for exterior and interior measures were significant in the predicted direction of relationship to Barrier. Penetration was not related to any of the physiological measures observed.

Fisher and Fisher (1964) carried out a series of four studies which explored the relation of Rorschach Barrier to patterns of body perception. In the first study, subjects were asked to make a mark whenever a prominent sensation was felt in the skin, stomach, muscle, or heart. A significant relationship between Barrier and exterior versus interior sensation was found ($p < .01$) in that the high Barrier subjects had a greater tendency to report exterior sensations. In the second study, subjects had to remember where they had felt sensations at various times in the past. Barrier was again found to be significantly related in the predicted direction. In the third study, subjects were given a (placebo) drug and asked to describe their body symptoms in response to it. Among male subjects, more exterior than interior bodily symptoms were noted for the high Barrier subjects ($p < .01$); this result was not found with the female subjects. In the last study, subjects were required to try to remember a list of body-related phrases, for example, "stomach pain" and "muscle stiff." High Barrier subjects recalled a significantly greater proportion of exterior and fewer interior sensations than did low Barrier subjects.

Shipman, Oken, Goldstein, Grinker, and Heath (1964) studied 15 depressed patients (eight females and seven males) who were measured for heart rate, blood pressure, movement, and surface action potential from seven muscles. Both the Rorschach Barrier and the Holtzman Barrier scales were among the psychological measures employed. These researchers found correlations of overall muscle tension with the Rorschach Barrier to be as follows in four situations: .14 in an affect arousal situation; .71 ($p < .05$) in a session aimed at inducing self-control; .83 ($p < .05$) in a neutral conversation; and .65 ($p < .05$) in neutral rest. When overall muscle tension was broken down into the three separate muscles in four experimental situations, 7 of the 12 resulting correlations were significant at the .05 level. (All of these 7 were positive correlations.)

Fisher and Cleveland (1958/1968) reported asking 75 college subjects to indicate by a check mark whenever they experienced sensations in the heart, muscle, stomach, or skin. This marking was done for a period of 3 minutes. No significant differences between high and low Rorschach Barrier subjects were observed, but the authors noted tendencies in the expected directions.

Cassell (1966) investigated the tachistoscopic recognition times for pictures depicting exterior and interior body parts. There were 104 (61 male and 43 female) subjects, and the Rorschach test was administered to each. Cassell found that high Barrier subjects were able to recognize exterior body photographs at significantly lower exposure times than were the low Barrier subjects. The male subjects recognized the internal organ pictures significantly faster than did the female subjects.

In the context of a more general study of body reactivity and attitudes, Fisher (1960) related the Rorschach Barrier and Penetration scores to right–left differentiation in body image and to differential GSR responsiveness on the right versus the left side. The subjects were 36 male and 42 female college students. Neither Barrier nor Penetration proved to be significantly correlated with the former measure, but the Penetration score was significantly related to right–left GSR reactivity: high Penetration subjects were significantly less left-GSR-reactive than were low Penetration subjects ($p < .01$).

Fisher and Fisher (1959) used a variety of body image and body reactivity measures on a sample of 53 boys and 66 girls ranging in age from 5 to 17. Rorschach Barrier, a puppet measure of masculinity-femininity, a measure of perceived distortion in body sides, and a GSR measure of right–left reactivity were the body measures used. Barrier was related to the GSR measure for the 13–17 age group ($p < .05$). Neither of the other two body measures was significantly related to Barrier.

Using data obtained by a previous investigator, Fisher and Cleveland (1958/1968) were able to study the relationship between the Rorschach Barrier score and Sheldon's somatotypes. No significant relationship was found; the authors' presentation implies that this was the expected result.

Relationship to Measures of Similar Constructs

Although no instruments can be said to deal with precisely what Barrier and Penetration purport to measure, several studies have related these scales to various body indices. The results to date have been encouraging, though by no means uniformly so.

Positive results were found by Fisher and Cleveland (1958/1968), who studied a sample of 30 heterogeneous hospitalized patients. These subjects were individually administered the Rorschach test and the Projective Movement Sequence (PMS). The PMS consists of projected scenes for which the subject must compose a story. The number of body-dissolution stories composed on the PMS was scored. The authors found a significant rho correlation of .45 ($p < .02$) between Barrier scores and PMS body-dissolution. Fisher and Cleveland also determined that the Barrier scale did not correlate significantly with the frequency of stories of inanimate dissolution.

Using incomplete sentences relating to the skin (e.g., "The skin can start to . . ."), Fisher and Cleveland (1958/1968) hypothesized that low Barrier subjects would have a greater tendency to complete the sentences with themes involving body vulnerability. After eliminating some items and clarifying the scoring procedures with an initial sample of 25 subjects, these investigators administered the sentence test and a group Rorschach to 39 college students. Low Barrier subjects were found to construct significantly more sentences involving body vulnerability ($p < .05$) than subjects with high Barrier.

As part of a larger investigation, Fisher and Cleveland (1956) studied the relationship between their measures of body boundaries and the body complaints of normal subjects. The Rorschach test was administered on a group basis to 87 undergraduate subjects. A checklist of body complaints was also administered, including seven exterior and interior areas of the body. The high Barrier subjects reported significantly more exterior body complaints than did the low Barrier subjects ($p < .02$), but there were no significant differences in terms of interior body complaints. No significant differences in body complaints were found with the Penetration scale.

In another investigation with positive findings, Fisher and Cleveland (1958/1968) also related their Rorschach Barrier scale to the Secord Body Cathexis test, a list of homonyms that can be interpreted as either bodily related or nonbodily related (e.g., colon). Using a group Rorschach with 62 college students (33 females and 29 males), the authors found that high Barrier subjects gave more body associations to the words than did low Barrier subjects ($p < .001$). This result suggested that the low Barrier students had weaker security feelings about the body.

Fisher and Cleveland (1958/1968) also looked into the relationship of the Rorschach Barrier score to performance in drawing tasks. Although drawings of human figures did not relate to the Barrier score, the authors did have success with drawings of a house done by 38 female schoolteachers. Elaboration of boundaries and surroundings of the house was significantly related to Barrier score ($p < .001$); high Barrier subjects displayed the greater elaboration.

Using a subject pool consisting of 6 female and 14 male college students, Fisher and Cleveland (1958/1968) related Rorschach Barrier scores to the subjects' reported dreams. Four psychologists were asked to categorize the dreams according to the degree in which physical boundaries and behavior sequences were intact. The results were in the predicted direction, but only one of the raters' classifications bore a statistically significant relationship to Barrier ($p < .02$). However two others approached significance.

Hartley (1967) attempted to develop a homonym test as an objective measure of the Barrier variable. The homonym task was found to correlate at .80 and .56 with HIT Barrier for male and female subjects respectively, and at .67 ($p < .01$) when the two sexes were combined into one group.

The most discouraging evidence in this area has been presented by Jaskar and Reed (1963), who compared 30 female psychiatric patients to 30 control subjects with the Barrier and Penetration scales of the Rorschach, the Drawing Completion test, the Homonym Word Association test, and the Body Cathexis scale. There were no significant correlations between the Barrier and Penetration scales and any of the other body measures.

In another study with negative findings, Fisher (1966) investigated the relationship between the HIT Barrier and Penetration scales and the Body Experience Questionnaire as part of a larger study of psychiatric patients. No significant relationships were noted.

Stress

Several investigations have dealt with the relation of stress to the Barrier and Penetration scales. Although the studies in this area are few, it would appear that high Barrier subjects respond more favorably to various forms of stress − experimental frustration, illness, amputation − than do low Barrier subjects. One study (McConnell & Daston, 1961) found evidence that the Penetration score varied in response to the stress of pregnancy and birth. Reitman and Cleveland (1968) noted that the differential effect of sensory deprivation on Barrier and Penetration was mediated by psychiatric diagnosis.

In one such investigation of stress, Fisher and Cleveland (1958/1968) analyzed previously collected data on the Rorschach test and the SAM Pseudoscope, a mirror-drawing task. The subjects were 90 ROTC cadets. Although the time scores of high and low Barrier subjects did not differ, the error score did significantly differentiate the groups in the expected direction. In a different type of stress study, Fisher and Cleveland (1958/1968) reanalyzed data from a previous investigation in which 20 normal women succeeded at a motor task and then failed very badly. They determined that the high Rorschach Barrier subjects adjusted more realistically to the failure than did the low Barrier subjects ($p < .05$).

Ware, Fisher, and Cleveland (1957) also reported a study wherein response to the stress of being hospitalized with poliomyelitis was studied in its relation to the Barrier score. The Barrier scores of 59 such patients were calculated from individual Rorschach administrations, and these scores were compared with ratings for adjustment to the situation carried out by physicians, a psychologist, and a social worker. The Barrier score significantly differentiated the well-adjusted patients ($p < .01$): the high Barrier subjects displayed better adjustment. The length of time between development of acute symptoms and Rorschach administration did not relate significantly to the Barrier scores, nor did seriousness of disability.

In a somewhat different vein, using data previously collected on 24 unilateral above-elbow amputees, Fisher and Cleveland (1958/1968) studied the perception of phantom limb in its relation to the Rorschach Barrier score. Twelve subjects drew their phantom limb outside the stump, and the remaining 12 drew it inside the stump. Fisher and Cleveland theorized that the former patients were having more difficulty in reorganizing their body boundaries and were therefore likely to have lower Barrier scores than the patients who drew the phantom limb in the stump. Scoring the records of these patients for Barrier, the authors confirmed their theory ($p < .01$).

Fisher and Cleveland (1968) also reported on studies by Fisher and Bialos, Landau, Shipman, and Sieracki which found that high Barrier subjects responded more favorably to the stress of gynecologic examination, paraplegia, distraction, and physical disability, respectively.

McConnell and Daston (1961) studied changed perception of body image as a result of pregnancy. Twenty-eight multiparous pregnant women were administered the Rorschach test and other measures during the eighth or ninth month of pregnancy. The Roschach and other measures were readministered three days after delivery. These authors found a statistically significant ($p < .05$) decrease in Rorschach Penetration scores after delivery. Barrier scores were not found to change in any systematic manner. McConnell and Daston explained these findings by assuming that the Barrier score refers to slowly changing aspects of the body image, whereas the Penetration score can be affected by situational factors threatening the ego.

Reitman and Cleveland (1964) have reported the effects of sensory deprivation on the HIT Barrier and Penetration scores. In this study 40 schizophrenic and 20 nonpsychotic psychiatric patients served as subjects. Schizophrenic subjects were found to give significantly more Barrier responses and significantly fewer Penetration responses following sensory deprivation. Among the nonpsychotic subjects, however, the opposite was true: subjects gave significantly more Penetration and fewer (though not significantly fewer) Barrier responses following the sensory deprivation. Reitman and Cleveland explained these findings by suggesting that sensory deprivation "[provides] the schizophrenic patient with a uniform, nonthreatening pattern of stimuli which, so to speak, offers him a chance to pull himself together (Reitman & Cleveland, 1964, p 175). Among the nonpsychotics the sensory deprivation serves to disorganize the body image, because "normal incoming stimuli useful in orienting and determining one's body boundaries are diminished" (Reitman & Cleveland, 1964, p 175).

Cleveland and Johnson (1962) contrasted the Rorschach records of 25 male subjects hospitalized following acute myocardial infarction with the records of 25 male presurgical patients and 25 male patients hospitalized for various skin diseases. The Barrier scores of the two groups were not significantly different. The Penetration scores of the coronary patients were, however, significantly higher among the presurgery subjects ($p < .01$).

Nichols and Tursky (1967) related Barrier score on the HIT to four measures of sensitivity to pain. The four measures of sensitivity to pain included the levels at which discomfort and pain were reported while subjects were being given electric shocks. The subjects of this experiment were 30 male college students. Three of the four correlations were significant; high Barrier was associated with greater tolerance to pain.

Personality Characteristics

A great variety of studies have dealt with the personality characteristics of individuals differing in Barrier. Many of these investigations have focused on what Fisher and Cleveland have called the self-steering behavior that is held to be characteristic of high Barrier subjects. These authors define self-steering behavior as that which involves "the individual's desire and ability to steer his own special course through the variety of alternatives he encounters in life" (Fisher & Cleveland, 1958/1968, p 118). Such individuals have a greater tendency to lead their lives forcefully and successfully and to satisfy their needs. The research studies summarized below suggest that high Barrier subjects more often than low Barrier subjects are characterized by high levels of aspiration, independence, a need for task completion, low suggestibility, insight, ability to communicate, clarity of identity, ability to express and satisfy sexual and other needs, and the capacity to express anger. Barrier has not been proved to be related to field-dependence–field-independence.

In one such study using the TAT Aspiration Index, Fisher and Cleveland (1958/1968) reported that among 42 members of families of individuals who had sought psychiatric treatment, high Rorschach Barrier subjects had significantly more aspiration themes than did low Barrier subjects ($p < .05$). In a study by Appleby cited by Fisher and Cleveland (1958/1968), the high Barrier subjects among the 60 college students also tended to produce more high aspiration themes, but the difference fell short of being statistically significant.

Findings have been less encouraging with respect to the McClelland n Achievement measure. Fisher and Cleveland (1958/1968) found that the Rorschach Barrier scores of 30 subjects were significantly related to the n Achievement measure ($p < .05$); they also cited the Appleby investigation, in which the relationship was significant only for the male subjects.

Reanalyzing other previously collected data, Fisher and Cleveland (1958/1968) compared the Rorschach Barrier scores of college over-achievers and underachievers; these categories were defined by comparing actual college grades with predicted grades. The resulting chi square approached but did not reach the .05 level of significance. Fisher and Cleveland (1958/1968) also reported on the relationship between Barrier and an instructor's ranking of 11 female college students on achievement goals and independence. A nonsignificant correlation between Barrier and achievement ranking was found, but the correlation between Barrier and independence ranking was significant ($p < .01$).

In the 1956 Fisher and Cleveland study, six TAT variables were included: high aspiration level, inactivity of story characters, deception, hostility toward father, hostility toward mother, and definiteness of attitude toward parents. Level of aspiration, deception, and definiteness of attitude were found to be significantly related to Barrier scores. High Rorschach Barrier subjects had high levels of aspiration, more instances of deception in their stories, and more definite attitudes toward their parents than did low Barrier subjects. All these differences between high and low Barrier subjects were significant. Only level of aspiration was significant on the Penetration scale: high Penetration subjects had the higher levels of aspiration ($p < .05$). In a cross-validational study with 38 undergraduate female subjects, the relationships between TAT level of aspiration and TAT definiteness of attitude toward parents on the one hand, and Barrier score on the other, were again significant ($p < .05$).

Again reanalyzing data collected by another investigator, Fisher and Cleveland (1958/1968) studied the relationship between Rorschach Barrier and three measures of suggestibility. The subjects were 50 undergraduates (30 males and 20 females). High Barrier subjects were significantly less suggestible on the Inkblot Suggestibility test and the Postural-Sway test ($p < .05$). No significant differences were found in the perception of autokinetic movement. Cleveland and Morton (1962) similarly found a significant negative relationship between Barrier and suggestibility. However Hartley (1967) found that suggestibility of postural sway was not related to HIT Barrier among college students.

In another investigation Fisher (1964a) studied the judged behavioral patterns of subjects differing in Rorschach Barrier. One hundred and twenty-three college men and 72 college women were interviewed and then rated on three variables. High Barrier subjects were rated significantly higher than low Barrier subjects in ability to communicate ($p < .02$), insight ($p < .05$), and clarity of identity ($p < .05$).

Reanalyzing data collected by other researchers, Fisher and Cleveland (1958/1968) investigated the relationship between the Rorschach

Barrier score and manner of handling anger. Sixty-nine undergraduates were exposed to a situation designed to elicit strong feelings of anger. Fisher and Cleveland found that the Barrier score was significantly related ($p < .02$) to the manner in which the anger was expressed: high Barrier subjects tended to express the anger outwardly and low Barrier subjects tending to express it inwardly.

Fisher and Cleveland (1958/1968) have also described an investigation in which they studied the extent to which high Rorschach Barrier subjects had a strong orientation to self-gratification. Thirty-eight graduate students, mostly schoolteachers and female were asked to describe how they would spend their time if they had only one month to live, and what they would do if they had an unlimited amount of money. The subjects' replies were then differentiated into two groups: self-gratifying and self-denying. A significantly larger proportion of high Barrier subjects gave self-gratifying answers on the two questions combined ($p < .02$).

In one experiment with negative results, Fisher and Cleveland (1958/1968) tested for the relationship between the Rorschach Barrier score and measures of field-dependence–field-independence. Analyzing previously collected data on the rod-and-frame and the tilting-room-tilting-chair tests, Fisher and Cleveland found only a chance relationship between Barrier and these measures of field independence.

In addition to the above studies that focused on self-steering personality characteristics, several investigations have dealt with the relationship of other personality variables to Barrier and Penetration. Two studies have investigated the relations of the Rorschach Barrier scale to the F scale. In the investigations of Fisher and Cleveland (1956) and Appleby (cited in Fisher and Cleveland, 1958/1968), the F scale was included as one of the test measures. In both investigations the F scale was found to be unrelated to Barrier. The Fisher and Cleveland study also found that the F scale was unrelated to Penetration.

Several reseachers have explored the values and interests of subjects differing in Barrier. In the study by Appleby cited by Fisher and Cleveland (1958/1968), the Allport-Vernon Study of Values and the Thurstone Interest Schedule were investigated in their relationship to Rorschach Barrier score among a group of 30 male and 30 female undergraduates. Appleby found a phi coefficient of -.27 between Barrier and the Theoretical score on the Allport-Vernon Study of Values. With the Thurstone Interest Schedule, Barrier had significant positive correlations with the *humanitarian* and *linguistic* categories, and a significant negative correlation with the *physical sciences* category. Fisher and Cleveland interpreted these results as signifying that high Barrier subjects are interested in activities that involve communicating with people about emotionally significant matters, and are less interested in value orientations that stress the importance of "things and abstractions."

In another reanalysis of previously collected data, Fisher and Cleveland (1958/1968) compared the Rorschach Barrier scores of 123 psychology trainees with the subjects' scores on the Allport-Vernon Study of Values and the Strong Vocational Interest Blank. None of the Allport-Vernon scores were significantly related to Barrier, although two (social and political) came quite close. On the Strong test, Group I (professional), Group II (quantitative science), Group IX (sales), and the sales manager scale were significantly related to Barrier. Low Barrier subjects scored higher in the first two Strong scales, whereas high Barrier subjects scored higher in the latter two. The results with the Strong scale dovetail nicely with the conclusions drawn by Fisher and Cleveland from the Appleby study, namely, that high Barrier subjects prefer occupations in which interaction with people is maximized and avoid the objective-theoretical occupations.

In the 1956 Fisher and Cleveland experiment, it was hypothesized that high Rorschach Barrier subjects would have greater interest in athletics, law, and cooking. The hypothesis was confirmed for athletics ($p < .05$) but not for cooking and law.

Using data previously collected by other investigators, Fisher and Cleveland (1958/1968) have also compared the Rorschach Barrier scores of persons in various fields. These authors determined that a combined group of eminent psychologists, anthropologists, and artists scored significantly higher on Barrier than did a combined group of eminent mathematicians, biologists, chemists, and physicists ($p < .05$). Among non-eminent persons, psychologists had significantly higher Barrier scores than did physicists and biologists ($p < .05$). When eminent and non-eminent groups were combined, psychologists greatly exceeded physicists and biologists in Barrier ($p < .001$). The combined psychologist–anthropologist group exceeded the physicist–biologist group in Barrier score ($p < .001$). All of these results further support the contention of Fisher and Cleveland that high Barrier subjects are oriented toward people and away from things and abstractions.

Compton (1964) related the Barrier and Penetration Rorschach scales to color, fabric, and design preferences among a group of 30 female psychiatric patients. Subjects were asked to choose the fabric or design that they would prefer in clothing for themselves. Compton found that preferences for saturated colors and strong contrasts between figure and ground were negatively related to Barrier scores. Preferences for warm colors and large patterns were positively related to Penetration scores. This investigator also found evidence of a positive relationship between the patients' weight to height ratios and their Barrier scores. Compton interpreted her findings as evidence that clothing fabrics may function to strengthen weak body boundaries for female psychiatric patients.

There is some confusion about the relationship between Barrier and anxiety measures. Goldfried et al. (1971) have cited a study by Sieracki in which a nonsignificant correlation was found between Rorschach Barrier and anxiety scores on the IPAT. Shipman et al. (1964) found a significant negative correlation between Rorschach Barrier and the Taylor Manifest Anxiety scale.

Measures of Social Interaction

A few studies have dealt with the qualities of social interaction characteristic of high and low Barrier subjects. Several investigations have dealt specifically with the behavior of subjects in small groups. Fisher and Cleveland (1958/1968) report on a study in which the subjects were 11 men and 12 women being seen in group psychotherapy. The therapist had been asked to choose from each of five groups the two patients who ranked highest and lowest in encouraging the group to deal with problems and in interest and concern for other group members. The Rorschach Barrier score was found to be significantly related to the former variable ($p < .02$), but the differences on the latter variable did not reach statistical significance.

In a further study related to group behavior reported by Fisher and Cleveland (1958/1968), the Rorschach test was administered in a group setting to 24 participants (12 male and 12 female) in a human relations training situation. The subjects were divided into three groups, which met 1.75 hours per day for 10 days. Other measures used included a sociometric questionnaire, a language facility test, and a measure of ascendancy-submission. Fisher and Cleveland predicted that high Barrier subjects would differ from low Barrier subjects in 17 items of the 22-item sociometric questionnaire. High Barrier subjects were found to differ significantly from low Barrier participants on eight of these items on the 10th conference day, all in the predicted directions. High Barrier subjects were more often described as wanting a warm group, being active in resolving differences, putting group goals above personal goals, operating independently of the group leader, and being accepted in the group. Low Barrier subjects were more frequently characterized as clashing with the group and putting personal goals above group goals. There were no significant differences between high and low Barrier subjects on the language facility test and the measure of ascendancy-submission.

Cleveland and Morton (1962) similarly evaluated 69 psychiatric patients participating in group therapy. The HIT was the inkblot measure of Barrier. In the fourth week of interaction, subjects filled out a sociometric questionnaire. Cleveland and Morton found that 9 of their 13 hypotheses were confirmed. High Barrier subjects received significantly more nominations than low Barrier subjects for ability to influence the opinion of others, degree of acceptance by the group, ability to operate effectively without direction from the group leader, setting group goals above individual goals, desire to accomplish something, helping in the resolution of group differences, keeping the group "on the ball," and preference as a recipient of discussion.

Fisher and Cleveland (1958/1968) carried out three other investigations on the performance of subjects differing in Rorshcach Barrier in small groups. In each of these investigations two small groups were set up, one consisting of high Barrier individuals, the other of low Barrier subjects. There were five to eight persons in a group. University students served as subjects in the first two studies, while student dieticians from a VA hospital were used in the third study. The subjects in each group were asked to work together to construct two spontaneous stories and to discuss and cite traits that lead to success in our culture. The student dieticians were also asked to discuss ways of improving relationships on the job. Four psychologists then rated the spontaneous stories and discussion material on scales of concern with achievement and with the philosophy of humanitarianism. Groups of raters were also asked to make the same judgments. As they had expected, Fischer and Cleveland found that the raters judged the material of the high Barrier groups to be significantly more concerned with achievement and humanitarianism than that of the low Barrier groups ($p < .001$).

Frede, Gautney, and Baxter (1968) studied the relationship between 30 male students' Barrier scores on the HIT and their performance on the MAPS test. It was found that high Barrier subjects tended to place MAPS characters closer to each other ($p < .025$) and expressed more approach and overall incidents of interaction than did low Barrier individuals ($p < .05$).

In a study discussed in an earlier chapter, Greenberg and Aronow (Note 2) correlated several HIT measures including the Barrier scale with interpersonal distance as measured by both paper-and-pencil and live measures. These authors found that among the college student subjects, Barrier was significantly correlated with the paper-and-pencil measure of interpersonal distance ($r = -.47$, $p < .01$), but the correlation with the live measure was not significant at the .05 level ($r = -.15$). The direction of the findings in both instances was that high Barrier subjects used less interpersonal distance.

Dosey and Meisels (1969), however, reported only chance correlations between the Rorschach Barrier scores of 186 undergraduates and their interpersonal distance as measured by three separate methods. No ready explanation is available for the discrepant findings of these authors. It is perhaps notable that they used the Rorschach test, whereas the two studies with positive findings used the HIT. Cleveland and Fisher (1960) have suggested that because of the broader range of Barrier scores found with the HIT, it should be considered the superior measure. As stated in Chapter 5, it should also be noted that the Dosey and Meisels measures of interpersonal distance demonstrated poor convergent validity.

Finally, in a study of the communications of subjects differing in Barrier, Ramer (1963) related the Rorschach Barrier score to quantity and quality of communication in an experimental situation. Ninety-six college females served as subjects. The students were asked to write stories based on photographs presented to them and then to engage in a story discussion with another subject via slips of paper. The subjects supposedly received no replies, positive replies, or negative replies from the other subject. Ramer found that the high Barrier students sent significantly more messages and more units of information, and that they sent significantly more messages in which they gave their opinions than did low Barrier subjects.

Psychopathology

A number of investigations have studied the relationship of Barrier and Penetration to psychopathology. Whereas an initial study of Fisher and Cleveland (1958/1968) in this area suggested rather clear-cut differences between schizophrenic and nonschizophrenic subjects in both Barrier and Penetration, later studies have produced conflicting results.

In their encouraging initial study, Fisher and Cleveland reported an investigation that compared the Rorschach Barrier and Penetration scores of normals, neurotics, and schizophrenics. The normal subjects were 30 women and 20 men whose Rorschach records had been already collected by another investigator. Forty male veteran patients constituted the neurotic group, 30 male and 10 female patients composed an undifferentiated schizophrenic group, and 28 male and 12 female subjects made up a paranoid schizophrenic group. The Barrier score was found to differentiate significantly both schizophrenic groups from the neurotics, and the combined schizophrenics from the combined normals and neurotics. Penetration significantly separated the normals from both groups of schizophrenics, the neurotics from both groups of schizophrenics, and the combined normal and neurotic group from the combined schizophrenics.

As part of the same study with these patient groups, the authors compared the extent to which they displayed Penetration responses that directly reflected destruction of the body. Some 93 such responses were found in the 80 schizophrenic test records, 9 such responses were discovered among the neurotics, and only one was found among the 50 normals; the differences were all statistically significant.

Later studies have been less encouraging. In a study by Jaskar and Reed (1963), no significant differences in Barrier and Penetration scores were noted in a comparison of 30 female psychiatric patients with a control group of 30 applicants for employment. In an investigation by Reitman cited by Fisher and Cleveland (1968), schizophrenic subjects had significantly higher Penetration scores than neurotics, but the difference between groups in Barrier was neither statistically significant nor in the expected direction.

Fisher (1966) studied the Barrier and Penetration scores of 40 neurotics (20 males and 20 females) and 91 schizophrenics (45 males and 46 females). The HIT was used as the Barrier and Penetration measuring instrument. Fisher found that Penetration did not discriminate between the neurotics and the schizophrenics. Barrier discriminated between neurotics and schizophrenics only for the female subjects ($p < .05$), and in the opposite direction from that predicted. However Barrier did significantly discriminate between paranoid and nonparanoid subjects ($p < .05$); the paranoids scored higher on Barrier. Barrier correlated significantly with Grandiose Expansivness on the Lorr Inpatient Multidimensional Psychiatric scale, but not with other Lorr scales. Neither Barrier nor Penetration was determined to be significantly related to ratings of ward behavior.

This finding of differences between paranoid and nonparanoid schizophrenic subjects may help to explain the above inconsistent results. Other studies have confirmed the importance of type of schizophrenic illness in reference to Barrier and Penetration. Fisher and Cleveland (1968) cited a study by Conquest in which paranoid schizophrenic subjects scored significantly lower on the Penetration scale and significantly higher on the Barrier scale than did nonparanoid schizophrenic subjects. Fisher (1964) also found that paranoid schizophrenics had higher scores than nonparanoids in a combined Barrier minus Penetration scale.

One study has dealt with the relationship between personality reorganization in schizophrenics and the Barrier and Penetration scores. Cleveland (1960) studied the Rorschach records of 24 newly hospitalized schizophrenics. The HIT was administered to the subjects before they began drug therapy, and on several other occasions in the course of their drug treatment. Two criteria of personality reorganization were used: the

Lorr Rating scale and a psychiatrist's global evaluation of the patient at the close of the study. Patients improving during hospitalization demonstrated significant decrements in Penetration score. No relationship was found between patient improvement and an increase in Barrier score.

Megargee (1965) administered the HIT and other measures to 75 male juvenile delinquents. Additional measures used included ratings of aggressiveness filled out by the delinquents' counselors and behavior checklists of aggressiveness. Megargee reported that the delinquents' Barrier scores were significantly lower than those of normal subjects ($p < .001$). An extremely delinquent subgroup ($N = 28$) was also determined to have significantly lower Barrier scores ($p < .001$) than less seriously delinquent subjects ($N = 44$). Barrier was also observed to correlate significantly ($r = .23$, $p < .05$) with the overall ratings of aggressiveness, but not with the behavior checklists of aggression. Fisher and Cleveland (1968) have also cited a study by Leeds in which delinquents and narcotic addicts were observed to have significantly lower Barrier scores than normals.

Cleveland and Sikes (1966) compared 70 hospitalized male chronic alcoholics with nonalcoholic patients. All subjects were administered the HIT, from which four scores were derived: Barrier, Penetration, responses involving deterioration and decay, and water responses. The alcoholics had significantly more Penetration responses ($p < .02$), deterioration and decay responses ($p < .001$), and water responses ($p < .001$). There were no significant differences between the groups in Barrier score.

Two recent studies have dealt with the effect of body awareness training and a physical development program on the Barrier and Penetration scores of pathological groups. Each study found one of the inkblot variables to be affected in the predicted direction by the experimental program.

In a 1970 study Darby investigated whether schizophrenics' Barrier and Penetration scores would be affected by body awareness training. Fifteen schizophrenic subjects were randomly assigned to each of five different groups. The HIT was administered as both the pre- and post-training measure. Barrier scores increased significantly in groups that experienced actual physical stimulation. The Penetration score for these groups, however, was only slightly affected by the experimental manipulations.

Chasey, Swartz, and Chasey (1974) studied the effects of a physical development program on the Barrier and Penetration scores of trainable mentally retarded subjects. Three groups of subjects were used: 16 subjects — the experimental group — who participated in a daily 5-week physical development program; 15 subjects — the Hawthorne control group — who participated in a daily 5-week sedentary recreation program; and 13 subjects — the control group — who took part in no specialized program. While the three groups were homogeneous with respect to most possible confounding variables, sex does not appear to have been adequately controlled in this investigation. The findings indicated that the number of subjects giving HIT Penetration responses decreased significantly only in the experimental group. This result suggested to the authors that the physical development program had resulted in a more positive body image.

Sex Differences

Fisher and Cleveland (1958/1968) initially stated that there were evidently no differences between male and female adult subjects in Barrier and Penetration scores. Other studies, however, have found that female subjects are higher in Barrier and lower in Penetration than males.

Fisher and Cleveland (1958/1968) reported there were no differences attributable to sex in their many surveys of college samples, and in a group of working adults. Holtzman et al. (1961) also failed to find significant differences between males and females in Barrier and Penetration. Greenberg and Aronow (Note 2) likewise reported no significant sex differences in Barrier on the HIT.

However several other studies have indeed found sex differences. As part of a larger investigation, Fisher (1964b) studied sex differences in the Rorschach Barrier and Penetration scores. The subjects were 564 college students (274 men and 290 women). Males had both significantly lower Barrier scores ($p < .001$) and significantly higher Penetration scores ($p < .001$) than females. Fisher argued that possible causes for this difference include the cultural encouragement of women to be strongly interested in their bodies and generally more involved in bodily events. Hartley (1967) similarly found that female college subjects scored significantly higher than male college students on HIT Barrier.

In analyzing data collected by a previous investigator, Fisher and Cleveland (1958/1968) were able to compare the Rorschach Barrier responses of 16 men and 21 women from a Japanese village, 26 male and 24 female Japanese immigrants to the United States, and 25 male and 25 female American-born Japanese. No sex differences were found among the village and immigrant samples, but the female American-born subjects were significantly higher in Barrier than the males ($p < .05$). The authors explain this difference by noting the greater difficulty American-born Japanese males have in coping with American customs.

There is no ready explanation for the contradictory evidence on sex differences in Barrier scores. Goldfried et al. (1971) have suggested that the size of the sample may be a factor, with sex differences tending to be found when the sample is very large. However this hypothesis would not explain why the study of Holtzman et al. (1961) did not find sex differences (N = 120), nor why the Hartley investigation (1967) did find such differences (N = 57 and N = 83 in two samples). The finding of Fisher and Cleveland (1958/1968) that sex differences in Barrier vary considerably in Japanese subjects differing in acculturation suggests that Barrier and Penetration may likewise be sensitive in our general American culture to differences in the sex role characteristics of various subcultures.

The results obtained with respect to sex differences in Barrier and Penetration among children seem to vary with the age of the children. Fisher and Cleveland (1958/1968) analyzed normative Rorschach data collected by other investigators in order to relate the variable of sex to Barrier and Penetration scores. Between the ages of 5 and 7, boys gave significantly more Penetration ($p < .01$) and significantly fewer Barrier responses ($p < .02$) than did girls. Between the ages of 10 and 13, however, the findings with respect to Barrier reversed: boys now gave significantly more Barrier responses than did girls ($p < .05$). Between ages 8 and 10 and between ages 13 and 17, no differences in Barrier and Penetration scores were found between the sexes. Fisher and Cleveland suggested that these findings may indicate disruption in body boundaries resulting from castration anxiety in boys between 5 and 7 and the onset of puberty in girls between 10 and 13.

Two studies have taken up the question of the relation of the Rorschach Barrier score to masculinity–femininity. Fisher and Cleveland (1958/1968) reported the analysis of a set of data collected from 96 ROTC cadets. No significant relationship was found between Barrier and the M-F scale of the MMPI. These same authors, utilizing a second set of data, found no relationship between Barrier and masculinity–femininity as measured by the Terman-Miles scale in a group of 72 male college students.

Miscellaneous

Correlates of Barrier and Penetration have also been investigated in other areas. The research literature includes three investigations that have related the Barrier and Penetration scores to measures of intelligence. Ware et al. (1957) and Fisher and Cleveland (1958/1968) found no significant relationships between measures of intelligence and the Rorschach Barrier and Penetration scales. The Appleby study cited by Fisher and Cleveland (1958/1968) also found no relationship between the Barrier scale on the Rorschach test and the Wonderlic Personnel test, which is largely a measure of verbal intelligence.

As reported by Fisher and Cleveland (1958/1968), Appleby did find a significant relationship (phi coefficient = .46) between Barrier score and number of words in Rorschach protocols. Appleby's subjects were 60 college students. However Fisher and Cleveland (1958/1968) note that there was no significant relationship between the Rorschach Barrier and Penetration scores and total word count in two separate samples of 40 subjects each. As further evidence of the Barrier and Penetration scores' independence of verbal productivity, Fisher and Cleveland related that in one sample, only 1 percent of the responses scored for Barrier involved phrases of over four words, whereas none of the Penetration responses involved more than four words. These same authors also reported that in a sample of 24 mental health professionals, the Barrier and Penetration scores from a group Rorschach were unrelated to scores on a difficult language facility test.

In an investigation of Barrier patterns within families, Fisher and Cleveland (1958/1968) studied the Rorschach Barrier scores in the families of patients seeking psychotherapy. The data analyzed had been collected earlier. None of the correlations between Barrier scores of various family members proved to be statistically significant, although two were of borderline significance (the father–mother correlation and the average of the father-and-mother–adolescent-children correlation).

In further analysis of the same data, these investigators compared the mothers of high and low Barrier patients with respect to their Fisher Maladjustment and Fisher Rigidity scores on the Rorschach. The mothers of the low Barrier children were determined to have significantly higher Maladjustment scores ($p < .01$) and significantly higher Rigidity scores ($p < .05$) than the mothers of the high Barrier children. TAT stories of these parents differed in that there was significantly more ($p < .05$) family closeness described on Card 2 by the mothers of high Barrier subjects, as well as more story definiteness ($p < .05$). Predicted differences in TAT level of aspiration fell just short of significance at the .05 level.

Fisher and Cleveland (1958/1968) also report on the extent to which clinical reports based on projective test data differed for 20 high and 20 low Rorschach Barrier subjects. The low Barrier subjects made more explicit references ($p < .01$) both to the mother and the father as threatening, destructive, and disruptive.

Fisher and Renik (1966) conducted an experiment that investigated the effect that directing attention to interior versus exterior body site had on the Barrier scale. Twenty subjects were directed to pay special attention to their skin and muscles; 21 were directed to focus on the body interior; and 20 were not asked to direct attention to any specific body area. All subjects were female; the HIT was used as the inkblot measure. The instructions to direct attention to the exterior of the body resulted in an increased Barrier score on retest: the difference between the exterior group and the control group was significant at the .05 level by use of a one-tailed test. The group that was directed to pay attention to the body interior did not produce significantly fewer Barrier responses on the retest than did the control group.

Renik and Fisher (1968) used this same methodology with male subjects. Sixteen subjects were asked to direct their attention to their skin and muscles, 15 were told to focus upon the body interior, and 15 were not asked to focus on the body. Again the HIT was the inkblot measure. The authors determined that the group asked to focus on the body interior produced, on retest, significantly fewer Barrier responses than did the control group ($p < .01$, one-tailed test). The retest Barrier difference between the exterior and the control group was not found to be significant.

To test the effect that examiners had on the Rorschach Barrier score, Eigenbrode and Shipman (1960) analyzed the protocols of subjects seen by seven examiners. A Kruskal-Wallis H was not found to be statistically significant, a result suggesting that differences between examiners did not cause differences in the subjects' Barrier responses.

In analyzing data collected by various investigators, Fisher and Cleveland (1958/1968) were able to compare the Rorschach Barrier scores of six cultural groups (Bhil of India, Hindu of India, Navaho of United States, Zuni of United States, Tuscarora of United States, and Haitian) with three general American groups. Of 21 contrasts, 5 were found to be significant at the .05 level. The Bhil group was significantly higher in Barrier than each of the three American samples; the Zuni group was higher in Barrier than one of the American samples; and the combined Bhil, Navaho, and Zuni groups were higher in Barrier than the combined Haitian and three American samples.

Hartung, McKenna, and Baxter (1970) investigated the effects of LSD on Barrier score. Forty-thre subjects (26 males and 17 females) who had consumed LSD twice or more were compared with a control group that had been matched on the basis of age, sex, and college credits. The HIT was individually administered to each subject. They found no significant differences between the groups in either Barrier or Penetration scores.

GENERAL EVALUATION

The Barrier scale does appear to be valid; that is, it appears to measure what it is supposed to measure. Fisher and Cleveland and numerous other investigators have presented strong evidence that Barrier is related to location of psychosomatic disorder, sensitivity to external versus internal bodily events, measures of similar constructs, reaction to stress, self-steering and other personality characteristics, and measures of social interaction.

It is in the area of psychopathology that the results with the Barrier scale have thus far been most discouraging. Fisher and Cleveland (1968) suggested that the scales could be of considerable use for diagnosis, particularly the diagnosis of schizophrenia. Such use might have been expected on a priori theoretical grounds because the maintenance of ego boundaries is considered by psychologists to be a function of the ego (e.g., Federn, 1952) and because ego pathology is a hallmark of the schizophrenic process (e.g., Bellak & Loeb, 1969). Weiner (1966) has also suggested that Barrier and Penetration could be of use in the diagnosis of schizophrenia. However later studies have not tended to support Fisher and Cleveland's highly encouraging findings. It is conceivable that if a distinction is made between paranoid and nonparanoid subjects, Barrier and Penetration may still be of use in discriminating between these two types of schizophrenics. Another possibility is to take into account the Barrier and Penetration scores of schizophrenics classed as either process or reactive. Further research is obviously necessary in this area.

The Penetration scale has been something of a disappointment to workers in this field. It has often been shown not to relate consistently to relevant criteria. There are some indications (e.g., McConnell & Daston, 1961) that it may be more sensitive to situational body concern. Surprisingly, studies of the relationship between the Barrier and Penetration scales have revealed either no significant correlation (e.g., Compton, 1964; Jaskar & Reed, 1963) or a positive correlation (Fisher & Cleveland, 1958/1968). These results make little sense in terms of the theoretical underpinnings of the scale, because Barrier is assumed to measure the firmness of body boundaries and Penetration is supposed to measure the corresponding lack of firmness.

A possible explanation for these unexpected results has been proposed by Cassell (1964), who criticized the Penetration score as a heterogeneous measure that encompasses percepts suggestive of both boundary indefinitness and awareness of body interior. Cassell (1964) modified the Penetration score so that only the latter percepts were scored: in addition, percepts which referred to the interior of the body were scored (e.g., heart, spinal cord). Cassell called this new index the Body Interior scale. It was hypothesized by Cassell that Barrier would be inversely related to this new scale. Among the 185 undergraduate subjects (115 men and 70 women), low Barrier individuals did indeed score higher than high Barrier subjects ($p < .001$) on Cassell's scale. Cassell's work in this area certainly appears promising. Further research is necessary to determine if the Body Interior scale could serve as a theoretically and practically appropriate substitute for the Penetration scale. It is also interesting to note that Cassell found males to be significantly higher than females in bodily interior awareness; this finding is consistent with those studies that have found females to be higher in Barrier.

A further puzzling aspect of the research literature on Barrier and Penetration lies in the inconsistent findings on sex differences. As discussed above, no ready explanation for the inconsistency is apparent. It is possible that sex differences in Barrier vary from subculture to subculture within our country.

As mentioned above, it seems that at least with respect to the HIT both the Barrier and the Penetration scales have a significant problem of temporal consistency. Although some questions have been raised about the appropriateness of expecting a heterogeneous projective scale to have high split-half reliability, there should be no question about temporal stability. If the Barrier and Penetration scales do indeed measure a long-term body attitude, then Barrier and Penetration measures taken at different points in time should show a high degree of correspondence, regardless of the objective or projective nature of the test in question. If deficient temporal stability is determined by further research and in fact proves to be a characteristic of the scales, it would suggest that while the Barrier scale may be sufficiently valid for research purposes, it may not measure with enough consistency to be useful to clinicians.

Possibly the greatest potential clinical use of the scales is as an aid in the diagnosis of schizophrenia and types of schizophrenia. Given psychoanalytic theory in the areas of schizophrenia and ego boundaries, the theoretical rationale is strong. The initial data presented by Fisher and Cleveland (1958/1968) was indeed encouraging. By distinguishing between types of schizophrenia (notably paranoid versus nonparanoid and process versus reactive) in future research, it is possible that the scales may one day attain the usefulness suggested by Weiner (1966) in the psychodiagnosis of schizophrenia.

As is the case with most other content scales, no actual norms are available for either the Barrier or Penetration scales. A table prepared by Goldfried et al. (1971) shows that considerable variability has characterized median Barrier scores found in various studies, although the nature of the sample (e.g., college students versus general adults) and the total number of Rorschach responses must be taken into account. Surprisingly, treating Barrier and Penetration responses as percentages of total responses has not been favored as a technique for controlling for Rorschach *R*.

At this time neither the Barrier scale nor the Penetration scale can be used clinically. The presentation of favorable data on temporal stability, and the availability of adequate Rorschach norms and data on overlap between clinical groups are necessary before either the Barrier or the Penetration scale can be regarded as a useful clinical scale for the Rorschach test.

The present authors recommend that future research in this area direct considerable effort toward establishing norms for the Rorschach Barrier scale in various subject groups. Further data on the temporal stability of the Barrier scale must also be provided in order to evaluate the potential usefulness of the scale in a clinical setting. It is also suggested that research efforts be directed toward exploring the potential for replacing the Penetration scale with the Cassell scale. The characteristics of the "items" on these scales have not been sufficiently investigated. Therefore the final recommendation is that item analysis procedures be applied to the Barrier, Penetration, and Cassell scales in order to determine whether more valid scales can be derived from those already extant.

7

Holt's Assessment of Primary Process Manifestations

HISTORICAL BACKGROUND

From a historical perspective it is noteworthy that in an early publication (Holt & Havel, 1960) Holt referred to his scale as a procedure for evaluating both primary and secondary process. Subsequently, however, the emphasis has been entirely on primary process manifestations. No scoring categories have been specifically developed to measure the impact of secondary process per se; Holt explained that, in essence, he was merely concentrating on a portion of the primary-secondary continuum, "leaving most of the secondary part of it undifferentiated" (Holt & Havel, 1960, p 269).

Holt differentiates between primary and secondary process as Freud did. Primary process is described as being at variance with the principles of logical thinking and reality appreciation, and dominated by a desire to achieve immediate gratification of sexual and aggressive desires and impulses. Furthermore it is characterized by ideational fluidity, unreflectiveness, and magical and arbitrary thinking. The secondary process, in contrast, reflects a rational approach and reality-bound ideation under rigorous ego controls. It implies mature, socially responsive, goal-directed behavior and appropriate delay of impulse gratification.

According to Holt (1966/1975) his method of scoring the Rorschach started as an "index of neutralization," by which is meant the degree to which motives are socialized. It then developed into a mode of assessing

142

content and formal manifestations of the primary process and the ways in which an individual endeavors to apply controls and defend himself against the anxiety that presumably accompanies the emergence of primary process material. Holt (1970) noted that it struck him in the mid-fifties that the Rorschach test was potentially a particularly suitable instrument for evaluating primary process. He listed three reasons for this. First, he pointed out that the test causes a subject to produce concrete visual images as the basis of his or her percepts; at the same time it discourages abstract thinking, which is unique to secondary process. Second, he asserted that the unfamiliar, ambiguous nature of the blots and the unstructured complexion of the task serve to "facilitate an imaginative, fantastic approach" (Holt, 1970, p 272). Finally, Holt felt that the reputation of the Rorschach as an "X-ray of the mind" that can penetrate one's conscious defenses and disclose deep secrets to the trained examiner gives it a mystique that arouses much anxiety and consequently stimulates primary process material.

ADMINISTRATION METHOD

No departure from a standard administration procedure is required for the spontaneous and inquiry phases of testing. A number of investigators using the Holt scale (Note 4) have employed the Klopfer system of conducting the inquiry after responses have been recorded to all 10 cards. There is nothing in the Holt approach, however, that would contraindicate an inquiry that takes place immediately after spontaneous associations to each card are obtained. What is demanded is a truly verbatim record so that wording nuances are available in evaluating responses. Furthermore the inquiry phase of the test is absolutely necessary, because Holt determined that a significant control category is associated with whether the primary process materials emerge in the spontaneous or inquiry phases of the Rorschach procedure.

After encountering some difficulties in assessing the affective component of responses even with good observational notes, Dr. Fred Pine, a colleague of Holt, suggested the administrative innovation of an affect inquiry. The affect inquiry simply involves asking the subject quite directly to describe what his emotional reaction was at the time of each percept. Holt cautions, however, that care must be taken to avoid establishing a set in the subject's mind that each of his responses ought to be charged with emotionality (Holt, 1970).

SCORING METHOD

Fundamentally, four types of scores are utilized in the Holt procedure for identifying those Rorschach responses manifesting primary process and for evaluating attendant defensive operations. These scores are
content scores, formal scores, control and defense scores, and ratings of
the total response. Because the major thrust of this book is a consideration
of Rorschach content scales, the content aspects of the Holt system will
be presented in some detail. The other components of his scoring will
be described more briefly.

Content Scores

Based on the premise that overt content of a libidinal or aggressive
type in an objectively neutral test situation reflects the drive domination
ostensibly characteristic of the primary process, Holt established seven
libidinal content categories and three types of aggressive content. Included under libidinal content are oral (receptive), oral-aggressive, anal,
sexual, exhibitionistic-voyeuristic, homosexual and miscellaneous. The
three aggressive categories are divided according to whether the reference
is to the subject or aggressor, the object or victim of the aggression, or
the results or aftermath of the aggression. Each of the seven types of
libidinal content and three types of aggressive content are subdivided
into the so-called levels. Level 1 applies to the more primitive, id-oriented,
blatantly unsocialized responses, whereas level 2 is designated for those
percepts that are more controlled and responsive to socialization factors.
In consonance with the previously mentioned notion of a primary process–secondary process continuum, level 1 and level 2 do not represent
a true dichotomy but rather what Holt terms "degrees of primariness."
Essentially, level 1 defines the type of response in which primary process
is evident to a very marked extent, in comparison to a level 2 type response, in which primary process is still clearly indicated but appears
to merge with secondary process material.

In keeping with the symbol approach employed in scoring Rorschach determinants, Holt has developed a shorthand of his own for
scoring type of content and the level. His notation scheme and examples
of responses falling into each of the categories at both levels are presented
below.

Content Scoring Examples

Libidinal level 1.

L 1 O (Oral): e.g., lips, mouths, breasts, nursing.

L 1 O–AG (Oral-Aggressive): e.g., female organs with teeth, bugs eating eyes out.

L 1 A (Anal): e.g., excretory organs, defecation or feces, buttocks.

L 1 S (Sexual): sexual acts, genitals.

L 1 E – V (Exhibitionistic-Voyeuristic): e.g., nudity.

L 1 H (Homosexual and sexually ambiguous): e.g., male and female sex characteristics seen on the same figure, homosexual acts.

L 1 M (Miscellaneous): e.g., birth, menstruation, urine.

Libidinal level 2.

L 2 O (Oral): e.g., kissing, eating food.

L 2 O (Oral-Aggressive): e.g., a sabertooth tiger, a man being chewed up.

L 2 A (Anal): e.g., rear views of persons, mud, sewer.

L 2 S (Sexual): e.g., brides and grooms, wedding rings.

L 2 E–V (Exhibitionistic–Voyeuristic): e.g., transparent clothing, eyes, masks.

L 2 H (Homosexual): e.g., uncertainty or ambiguity over sex of figures, transvestism.

L 2 M (Miscellaneous): e.g., internal sexual anatomy, embryos, self-admiring figures.

Aggressive level 1.

Ag 1 S (Subject): aggressor images, e.g., demons ripping a woman apart or a clawing tiger.

Ag 1 O (Object of Aggression): sadistic, castrative, or deadly images, e.g., a man being crushed or a male organ about to be chopped off.

Ag 1 R (Results): aftermath images, e.g., burnt flesh and rotting carcasses.

Aggressive level 2.

Ag 2 S (Subject): e.g., men fighting, charging bulls, pirates.

Ag 2 O (Object): e.g., frightened women, children being slapped.

Ag 2 R (Results): e.g., blood, broken branches, artificial limbs.

As can be readily determined from the above examples, the first letters in the symbol represent the libidinal or aggressive category, the number indicates level and the last letter(s) the category subtype. The designation weak (wk) denotes a situation in which a percept appears to deserve content scoring yet does not entirely fulfill the criteria.

Holt's scoring system has undergone many revisions, 10 at this writing. An early version (Holt & Havel, 1960) contained, for example, a third content category — anxiety and guilt — which was originally intended to capture responses projecting instinctual danger or superego punishment and conveying explicit or implied feelings of helplessness. Currently, percepts in this third category are generally scored as aggressive content, object type. It should be noted as well that the aggressive category as such has been scored on yet another dimension, namely, potential versus active aggression.

Formal Scores

This portion of the scoring deals with the perceptual organization of a particular response, the thought processes that contribute to it, and the language used to express it. Holt states that the attempt here is to measure deviations from the logical, reality-oriented thinking that characterize the secondary process. These specific categories utilized in this aspect of scoring include many forms of condensation, displacement, symbolism, contradiction, and autistic reasoning which Holt describes as largely stemming from Rapaport's work. The formal variables are also classified on a level 1- level 2 dimension, but unlike content a good many of the categories are scored only for a single level.

Control and Defense Scores

This part of Holt's system is designed to evaluate the subject's defensive organization, particularly with respect to the degree of control over his own regressive thinking. In essence this aspect of the scale focuses on the way primary process material is handled. Holt has identified a number of types of defenses and control operations, which are subdivided according to their degree of effectiveness. These include various types of remoteness, context (cultural, aesthetic, intellectual, and humorous), pathological defenses, types of overtness, sequence scores, adaptative transformation, and measures of delay and reflection. The scoring procedure involves both identifying the defensive operation being used and indicating by plus and minus signs whether the control and defense has enhanced or additionally impaired the percept, as evidenced not only by the content or the response, per se, but also by the manner in which it is offered.

Ratings of the Total Responses

Four scales compose this aspect of the scoring. Defense Demand (DD) and Defense Effectiveness (DE) are scored only when there is a content or formal score. The remaining two scales, form level and creativity, apply to all responses.

Defense demand.   Holt describes this scoring as that geared to assess the response's shock value as an interpersonal communication. It employs a 6-point scale which is an elaboration and refinement of the level 1 and level 2 differentiation. A DD of 1 implies minimal defensiveness in communicating in a socially acceptable manner, whereas a 6 reflects the maximum need for controls to dilute the inherent shock impact of both the content and formal deviations found in the percept.

Defensive effectiveness.   This score is also rated on a 6-point scale. At one extreme are fully acceptable percepts which reflect effective controls and defenses. At the other are poorly organized, fragmented percepts mirroring only pathological defensive efforts. The three major components of the DE score are a consideration of nature and appropriateness of the affect accompanying the response, the control and defense categories which were previously discussed, and the form level which will be described below.

Form level.   Holt bases his form level scoring on Mayman's 1960 unpublished scoring manual (Note 5) which presents an extension of the usual F+ and F– Rorschach measures. The categories in the Mayman system range from a well-delineated, clearly perceived, and accurate percept to one in which the response is markedly at variance with the inkblot area being utilized. The categories include a scoring that covers basically acceptable responses that have been spoiled by inappropriate elaboration.

Creativity.   Holt intends this 5-point creativity scale to replace the popular, unscored, and original classifications of Rorschach responses. The scale combines statistical infrequency with sensitivity in using determinants, imaginativeness, and expressiveness of language as measures of creativity. At one end of the scale are minimally elaborated popular or near-popular responses that occur with great frequency. At the other end are statistically rare percepts which are clearly original and creative and reflect a richness of associations.

Summary Scores

Holt has developed a series of summary scores that are not used for individual responses but for the record as a whole. These include computing content category, formal category, level 1 and level 2 percentages, and means for form level scores and for creativity, defense demand, and effectiveness ratings. Holt also proposes a total percentage of primary process (pripro) responses. He has additionally devised an adaptive regression score which can be calculated in several ways utilizing the DD and DE ratings. It should be noted that a number of the studies conducted utilizing the Holt primary process scale have focused principally on the summary scores.

RELIABILITY

In keeping with this book's focus on content, reliability data reported here, as well as the validity studies covered in the next section, will emphasize research in which the content categories of the Holt system are among the major variables being investigated. It should be noted, however, that content categories and formal aspects of the Holt scoring system are generally used conjointly in identifying primary process Rorschach responses as such.

Holt (1966/1975) stated that the degree of agreement between scores on specific categories in his system approximates that of traditional Rorschach determinants, about 65 percent. He indicated, however, that there is marked variability from category to category and that a much better level of agreement among independent judges is obtained for overall indices than for individual scores.

In an interscorer reliability check conducted by Holt (1966/1975) himself, he compared the drive content scoring of two graduate students working with him on the fourth edition of his primary process scoring manual. He found that the students made the same scoring decisions for 99.9 percent of 1089 Rorschach responses produced by 30 subjects and scored for 22 content categories. McMahon (1964), another of Holt's students working with a second experienced rater, found reliability coefficients of .94 for percent content and .85 for percent formal aspects in the Rorschach records of VA schizophrenic and medical inpatients. Rabkin (1967), also a Holt student, reported precisely the same r for content as McMahon and .90 for the formal categories in another interjudge reliability study of 25 randomly selected Rorschach protocols of patients.

In a study utilizing a sample of 40 college students and raters not trained by Holt, Benfari and Calogeras (1968) found reliability coefficients of .85 and .90 in scoring Rorschach records for formal aspects and total content respectively. Interjudge agreement for only the overall aggressive content category fell to .75. When there was an additional breakdown into aggressive subtypes (potential or active aggression; aggressor, victim, or aftermath of aggression), the level of interscorer agreement varied from .30 to .70. Benfari and Calogeras concluded that it is relatively easy to differentiate between content areas and to achieve agreement on this categorization. They cautioned, however, that a molecular analysis, that is, further classification of a content response in terms of its suggested components as the Holt manual describes them, is substantially more difficult.

All of the previously cited studies have been limited to the interscorer type of reliability. In a far more comprehensive reliability study, Gray (1967) administered both forms of the HIT a month apart to a group of 100 male undergraduates. On the basis of scores for almost 9000 HIT responses, interjudge content reliability was .95 and formal reliability .71. For total primary process scoring, the correlations were .70 for parallel form and .85 for test–retest. He also found split-half reliability coefficients of .83, .51, .78, and .78 for total, oral, libidinal, and aggressive content respectively and .88 for formal aspects. The lower agreement for the oral subscore was, according to Gray, based on the fact that a relatively small amount of data fell into this particular category.

As mentioned initially in this section, scoring reliability for individual categories varies considerably. Although the reliabilities for total primary process and overall content scores and formal variables are essentially satisfactory as indicated by the studies quoted above, there is evidence (Holt, 1970) to suggest that defense effectiveness and adaptive regression, for example, are somewhat less reliable indices.

VALIDITY

Among the most carefully designed and executed validity studies of the Holt system are those that endeavor to link measures in the Holt system with creativity. The theoretical foundation for such research is Kris's (1952) well-known notion of ego-controlled regression or what he termed "regression in the service of the ego." His lifelong studies of artists and their work convinced him that an aspect of the creative process entails an adaptive response on the part of the ego permitting greater access to primary process material. Kris carefully distinguished between creativity in which primary process is still very much under ego control and used in its service, and psychosis in which it succeeds in overwhelming the ego.

Turning first to Holt's own work in the creativity sphere, Pine and Holt (1960) were able to examine Kris's major hypothesis in a sample consisting of 13 male and 14 female college students. Creativity was evaluated by a composite of nine scores from a battery of procedures including Guilford's Brick Uses and Consequences tests, TAT stories scored for literary quality and a drawing task judged for artistic ability and originality. Individual Rorschachs were scored by the seventh edition of the primary process manual for three summary measures — amount of primary process, effectiveness of control, and adaptive regression. The amount of primary process was not significantly related to creativity in either the males or females. On the other hand the control effectiveness measure correlated at .80 ($p < .01$, one-tailed test) with creativity in the male group and at .52 ($p < .05$, one-tailed test) in the female sample; the adaptive regression score was a highly significant .90 for the men ($p < .01$, one-tailed test), but only an insignificant .28 for the women.

Pine (1962) conducted a very similar investigation with a group of 50 male unemployed actors using a slightly different battery of creativity tests and employing the same three Holt Rorschach summary scores. Contrary to the findings of the prior research with the male and female undergraduates, none of the tests of creativity, considered together or separately, bore a relationship to any of the three Rorschach scores.

Several years later Holt (1970) had a great deal of the available information about the group of actors punched onto IBM cards. These data included a large number of variables derived from his manual as well as the results of comprehensive personality evaluations. The latter included many scores from a variety of objective tests and also clinical ratings based on an autobiography, notes on several interviews, intelligence test results, and the TAT and the Rorschach (with traditional scoring only). A large correlational matrix was then derived with the help of a computer.

Holt's extended analysis confirmed Pine's finding that creativity measures were not related to adaptative regression or to the overall measures of the amount or control of primary process. Furthermore no indices of aggressive imagery and creativity were significantly correlated. He did discover, however, that three types of libidinal content were related to measures of creativity. In conjecturing about one of these libidinal content subtypes — level 1 orality as evident in Rorschach responses and its significant correlation with performance on several tests of creativity — Holt stated that the basis for the relationship "may entail first, an attitude of receptivity toward the world of sensory information and, second, a flexible mode of cognitive processing" (Holt, 1970, p 302).

In an independent study Von Holt and his associates (1960) found support for the meaning Holt attached to high libidinal orality in his primary process scale. These researchers examined the consistency between performance on the Hanfmann-Kasanin Concept Formation test and three Rorschach scores derived from the Holt manual. In three independent replications of their procedure, high libidinal orality successfully discriminated between those subjects who solved the Hanfmann-Kasanin test within 30 minutes and those who could not. The subjects were male and female college students whose primitive oral responses on the Rorschach, consistent with Holt's interpretation, seemed to reflect a passive open attitude to new ideas which helped them to succeed with the concept formation task. In a personal communication (reported in Holt, 1970) amplifying the findings of a 1968 study in which creativity in third graders was studied, Rogolsky noted that her artistically creative schoolboys gave more libidinal level 2 oral responses than the uncreative subjects. However no level 1 oral content was found in Rogolsky's entire sample.

In a doctoral study Gray (1967) also investigated the hypothesis that primary process thinking is associated with creativity. Primary process was once again measured by the Holt scoring system, this time applied to the HIT rather than the Rorschach. Creativity was assessed by a battery of tests of divergent thinking devised by Guilford. The sample studied was composed of 100 male college sophomores. Gray found a low but nevertheless significant correlation between creativity and formal manifestations of primary process ($r = 26, p < .05$). An oral primary process subscore also correlated at .22 ($p < .05$) with creativity. Gray (1969) then examined the impact of productivity on the relationship between primary process manifestations and creativity. Productivity on the HIT was represented as the total number of words used by each subject in describing and detailing his responses, whereas the productivity measure for the tests of creativity was the total number of responses. Gray found that productivity correlated at .77 and .81 with a total primary process score and a total creativity score respectively. When the productivity scores were partialed out, the primary process-creativity relationship was no longer found to be significant. Likewise, Gray reported that the highly significant correlations between formal primary process score and the aggressive and libidinal content categories scores were based to a large measure on the third variable of productivity. It must be recognized that Gray's productivity measure is, of course, very different from the total number of responses invariably used to tap this factor on the Rorschach.

Rogolsky (1968) also examined other variables in studying the relationship between artistic creativity and primary process. The study was done with a group of third graders, boys and girls, who were judged creative or noncreative by professional evaluation of their drawings. The Rorschach was scored for adaptive regression and form level. The adaptive regression scores as well as the form level score of the primary process responses failed to differentiate between the groups. However, when the non-primary process responses were scored for form level as well, the mean score for the creative boys was significantly higher than the mean score of the uncreative boys. In analyzing her data more extensively Rogolsky employed a composite measure of adaptive regression which consisted of the defense demand score, percentage of primary process responses, and two control variables — sum form level and number of Popular responses, which did differentiate between the creative and noncreative children. A multiple correlation indicated that the control measures were better discriminators than were primary process measures.

Because Holt's primary process scoring system was developed exclusively with adults, its application to the Rorschach protocols of children is open to question. Even more traditional Rorschach scoring variables may, of course, require special interpretation in children's records. As Holt (1970) points out, for example, the fact that the number of populars correlated with creativity in the Rogolsky study makes a good deal of sense, in that populars are defined by adult norms; therefore, in a group of third graders the high number of populars may be an indication of maturity rather than stereotyped thinking.

The type of design utilized in the above validity studies was basically correlational, focusing on possible relationships between two measures — the Holt primary process Rorschach scores and creativity test performance. In contrast the next group of studies entails the manipulation of drive-related stimuli, utilizing aspects of the Holt scoring system as criteria measures of the effects of such manipulations on thinking.

Silverman and his colleagues (Silverman, 1965; 1966; Silverman & Candell, 1970; Silverman & Goldweber, 1966) have developed an innovative methodology for assessing the effect that aggressive drive activation has on ideation. Their technique fundamentally consists of subliminal tachistoscopic presentation of pictorial stimuli to a variety of populations. The stimuli are either aggressive or neutral and the Rorschach and other projective measures are used to assess subsequent thinking.

In one of his initial investigations, Silverman (1966) studied a sample of 32 hospitalized male schizophrenics. Before the stimuli were presented he administered inkblots selected from the Rorschach, Harrower, and Zulliger sets to each subject in order to establish a baseline potential for engaging in deviant ideation. The subjects were then exposed to aggressive pictorial stimuli (e.g., a tiger chasing a monkey) on one occasion and to the neutral stimuli, serving as a control, at another time. Finally the inkblots were readministered. The Holt scoring system was used to evaluate pathological thinking. Both the formal and content categories of primary process were scored according to the Holt manual. As was predicted, there were significantly more formal manifestations of pathological thinking after the presentation of the aggressive stimuli. Contrary to what had been hypothesized, however, there were no increments in the aggressive and libidinal content scores under the experimental condition. In a further analysis Silverman subdivided the aggressive content category into subject-aggression and results of aggression. A significant difference was found between the experimental and control conditions for subject-aggression, but not for results of aggression.

Employing a parallel research design with normals, Silverman (1965) evaluated a group of 77 male nursing aides for their response to aggressive and control stimuli that were presented subliminally. In an initial phase of the investigation, Silverman primed 52 subjects participating in the study by reading them an aggressive and buffer passage represented as memory tasks. The results indicated that those subjects who were subject to prior external activation of aggressive ideas and who evidenced comparatively impaired ability to neutralize the expression of aggression — that is, subjects classed as high expressors of aggression on 42 related MMPI items — displayed increased manifestations of formal aspects of pathological thinking on the Rorschach in response to the experimental condition. Silverman pointed out that the results for this subgroup of nonschizophrenics were similar to the findings with the schizophrenic sample in the earlier study, except that prior external activation of aggression was not a necessary condition to produce formal primary process thinking in the schizophrenics. Aggressive content scores did not increase significantly under the experimental condition. But, in contrast to the schizophrenic group, the normals displayed a significantly greater amount of libidinal material. This result was interpreted as an attempt to combat the aggressive derivatives that had been triggered.

In a study representing a refinement of design with respect to the experimental conditions, Silverman and Goldweber (1966) attempted to replicate the 1965 research adding, however, a subliminal libidinal experimental condition and a supraliminal aggressive condition to the subliminal aggressive and neutral conditions of the prior investigation. The population studied was a group of male VA employees; 30 subjects were randomly assigned to each of the four experimental conditions. As before, each subject was initially read a highly charged passage designed to activate specific drive-related ideas. A baseline Rorschach performance was obtained once again prior to the tachistoscopic stimulus presentation, which was subsequently compared with a post-stimuli Rorschach. Consistent with the earlier study, the subliminal aggressive condition produced more of the primary process manifestations than did the subliminal neutral condition. Again an increase in pathological thinking subsequent to subliminal aggressive stimulation was displayed only by subjects whose capacity to neutralize aggression was comparatively impaired. The subliminal aggressive condition also yielded significantly more indications of primary process than the subliminal libidinal condition, which was equivalent to the neutral condition in its impact. Furthermore, the subliminal aggressive condition stimulated more pathological ideation than the supraliminal aggressive condition, but the difference was at a borderline level of significance.

Silverman and Candell (1970) were interested in determining whether it is necessary to contrast a subliminal with a supraliminal presentation of drive-related stimuli in order to elicit pathological thinking. They reasoned that when a subject is unaware of content, he cannot inhibit primary process ideation by ascribing the arousal of drive derivatives to an external source. A total of 60 relatively differentiated schizophrenics were seen individually for three sessions. A baseline assessment of the amount of manifest pathology and of the degree to which ego boundaries were intact was measured in each session. Subsequently, on different days and in counterbalanced order, one group of subjects were subliminally exposed to pictures containing aggressive content, content suggesting symbiotic merging, and a control condition of neutral content. The other group was presented with the same stimuli supraliminally. A critical assessment of manifest pathology using Holt's primary process system, and body boundary intactness employing Fisher and Cleveland's (1968) body Penetration and body Barrier Rorschach scoring, revealed that the subliminal subjects reacted to both the aggressive and symbiotic merging stimuli with changes in primary process thinking and body intactness, whereas the supraliminal group was unaffected by these two types of stimulation.

To sum up the studies by Silverman and his associates, their findings indicate that the content and, even more consistently, the formal aspects of the Holt scoring system provide a very satisfactory index of increases in primary process thinking subsequent to exposure to several types of drive-related stimuli. Evidence of primary process, as manifested on the Rorschach evaluated by the Holt procedures, is most apparent when the stimuli are aggressive rather than libidinal, and when they are presented at a subliminal level to schizophrenic subjects who experience difficulties in neutralizing aggressive expression.

In a last, very different type of study, which tapped aggression variables but did not depend upon experimental induction of aggressive stimuli, Benfari and Calogeras (1968) used the Holt primary process scoring to investigate types of conscience development, namely, integrated versus nonintegrated conscience. Their sample was 40 college students who were divided into two groups based on their performance on a conscience scale.

The nonintegrated conscience group was characterized by a propensity for adopting stringent moral principles and rigorous standards and prohibitions. These tendencies, however, are accompanied by rebellious feelings against the strict rules and regulations, and there are indications of ambivalent and conflictive feelings reflected in guilt and self-disparagement. The integrated conscience group, on the other hand, was characterized by high ethical and social principles whose acceptance was based on internalized standards and values and not on the fear of punitive environmental reactions. The nonintegrated group was found to be significantly higher in percentages of aggressive responses and primitive aggressive content, and in formal indications of primary process as scored on the Holt scale. Thus the Holt system was found useful in supporting the hypothesis that a less well developed ego is related to a more poorly integrated, conflict-ridden and punishing conscience.

Among other investigations that have contributed germane data to an assessment of the validity of the Holt method for scoring primary process on the Rorschach, studies by Goldberger (1961) and Wright and Zubek (1969) found the procedure useful in judging reactions to perceptual deprivation and isolation. More specifically, it was determined that the Holt Rorschach scale could serve as a meaningful indicator of effective control over the emergence of primary process thinking.

In a particularly interesting study with implications for the the previously discussed area of creativity, Feirstein (1967) investigated tolerance for unrealistic experience, which was broadly defined as an individual's ability to perceive in ways that contradict usual modes of perception. His hypothesis, based on psychoanalytic theory, held that the ability to indulge in both unrealistic and drive-related thinking that was integrated with more reality-bound, neutral, socialized thought should relate positively to tolerance for unrealistic experience. The subjects were 20 male graduate students who were administered the Rorschach, word association, and art preference tests, as well as four tests of tolerance for unrealistic experience. Amount and integration of unrealistic and drive-related thinking were measured by the Holt primary process scoring scheme for the Rorschach. Combined amount and integration scores for both unrealistic and drive-related ideation were significantly correlated with the measure of total tolerance for unusual experience. In the case of unrealistic thinking, an r of .49 ($p < .025$) was found whereas the correlation was .44 ($p < .05$) for drive-related material. Feirstein commented that tolerance for unusual experience may be an essential aspect of the creative process, which "seems to require an openness to new relationships and an ability to see beyond the constraints of conventional labels and anticipations" (Feirstein, 1967, p 394).

Aspects of the Holt system for evaluating primary process in the Rorschach have also succeeded in differentiating among diagnostic groups. Zimet and Fine (1965) examined the Rorschach responses of 36 process and 23 reactive schizophrenics utilizing the Holt scale for scoring oral, anal, sexual, aggressive, and anxiety content, as well as formal manifestations of primary process. They reported that the process schizophrenics evidenced more primary process than secondary process, whereas the reactive schizophrenics showed a reverse relationship. In addition a linear trend in the frequency of various kinds of content responses was noted in both groups. Anxiety occurred with the greatest frequency, followed by aggression, oral, sex, and anal content in decreasing order. Zimet and Fine observed that the oral content was invaded by primary process ideation to the least extent. It is pointed out by Holt (1975) that Zimet and Fine erred in identifying level 1 in his system with primary process and level 2 with secondary process thinking, and that instead level 2 should be perceived as an admixture of primary and secondary process features.

In another study in which Holt's scoring of the Rorschach was used to discriminate between diagnostic groups, Silverman, Lapkin, and Rosenbaum (1962) tested 20 schizophrenic adolescents and 20 psychoneurotics and patients with personality disorders. They found that the schizophrenic group revealed more of the formal characteristics of primary process in their ideation and were significantly less effective in dealing with manifestations of this kind of thinking. The notion that the schizophrenics would be more drive-dominated was not strongly supported, and then only for the aggressive content category.

Scores derived from the Holt procedure for assessing manifestations of primary process have been found useful in research within a psychotherapeutic context. Bachrach (1968) collected two tapes of a psychotherapy session and a Rorschach from each of 22 training psychotherapists. Therapist empathy was rated for each session on a scale he had developed. Scoring the Rorschach by the Holt method, Bachrach found significant rank-order correlations between ratings of conjunctive empathy in the therapy session and adaptive regression and defensive effectiveness on the Rorschach. Essentially, as empathy increased so did adaptive regression and defensive effectiveness.

In contrast to the Bachrach therapist research, Fishman (1971) studied the adaptative regression of 36 "typical" patients using the Rorschach and other measures. The study took place during the first 6 months of long-term outpatient psychoanalytic therapy, within a framework that viewed adaptative regression as an important "patienthood skill." By "patienthood skill" Fishman meant a characteristic of an individual that facilitates his successful functioning in psychoanalysis, namely, being able to engage in free associative exploration of his inner life to enhance self-understanding.

Three hypotheses were proposed by Fishman. The first stated that the patient's level of adaptative regression at the beginning of therapy was predictive of the therapy outcome 6 months later. The second proposed that a patient would enhance his skills in adaptative regression during treatment; therefore the level of adaptative regression the patient attained after 6 months would be more highly related than his initial level to therapy outcome at 6 months. The last hypothesis asserted that the Rorschach measure of adaptative regression would be positively related to other non-Rorschach measures of patienthood skills.

The Holt defense effectiveness score was used to assess adaptative regression. Initially this score correlated ($r = .28$, $p < .05$) with just one of four outcome measures employed, namely, the therapist's rating of overall success. Six months later this measure correlated at .32 ($p < .05$) with the therapist's success rating, at .57 ($p < .01$) with the patient's own success rating, and at .29 ($p < .05$) with a patient rating of decrease in experienced emotional distress. The measure of effectiveness of defense was found to be correlated with a number of non-Rorschach measures. The highest association of .43 ($p < .01$) was with the variable of how the patient perceives the cause of his problems. Fishman believes that his research clearly supports the use of the Holt scoring system as a valid indicator of adaptative regression.

GENERAL EVALUATION

Holt's primary process scoring system for the Rorschach is a comprehensive and often complex procedure, mirroring the exceptionally painstaking and reflective approach of its author. It is well grounded in theory and has been proved, for the most part, to have adequate reliability and validity. However reliability coefficients obtained for individual categories and subcategories tend to be substantially lower than the correlations for summary scores. It has been established that content scales within the system are among the most reliable components from the standpoint of both statistical robustness and psychological meaningfulness. But it is clear that content categories in combination with the formal aspects of the scoring procedure appear to represent the most effective approach to identifying and describing primary process thinking on the Rorschach.

The most striking and successful application of the Holt method of scoring primary process on the Rorschach has been in research designed to test a variety of hypotheses and conceptual formulations generated by psychoanalytic theory. It has also been shown to be a valuable criterion measure in a host of different types of studies, ranging from the assessment of change in psychotherapy to research entailing the experimental manipulation of stimuli potentially associated with aggressive drives. The Holt system has successfully differentiated between diagnostic groups as well as between normal populations categorized by other measures. It should be stressed that the method is principally intended as a research tool, not as a clinical instrument, and is regarded as far more applicable to groups than to individuals.

A prominent though not substantive difficulty of the Holt procedure is the multiplicity of scoring manuals — 10 at the present time. On the one hand, Holt's obvious willingness to revise his procedures is very commendable; it reflects his openness to new concepts and ideas, and his imagination and flexibility in incorporating them into his scoring system. At the same time the numerous versions of the manual present an unnecessary challenge to the psychologist who wishes to become familiar with an already intricate method.

The many manuals also seriously hamper studies that seek to establish more definitive reliability parameters for various aspects of the scoring system, and they make comparisons between such investigations substantially more formidable. It is hoped that Holt will resist what he describes as "tinkering with the system" and be content for a time with at least a "quasi-final draft" of his procedures.

As with the Rorschach ratios proper, a number of the scoring aspects of the Holt system are closely linked with the total number of responses, particularly the overall amount of primary process. Holt is very much aware of this factor, and has suggested dividing many of the summary scores by the total number of responses or, when indicated, statistically partialing out the effects of the total number of responses. Neither of these approaches is entirely satisfactory, however, and other solutions remain to be found.

Although the summary scores in the Holt procedure seem to have the highest degree of reliability, the very nature of dealing with totals, averages and global concepts sometimes obfuscates their fundamental meaning. On the other hand a number of his individual category scores are too unreliable to be used separately. It would therefore appear appropriate to encourage the development of combinations of category scores. Such combinations would avoid a meaningless lumping together of variables and numbers and possibly provide indices having greater reliability and lending themselves more readily to interpretation. To use Holt's (1970) own example, how reasonable is it to consider all manifestations of primary process taken together, and then to endeavor to arrive at an "average" measure of the effectiveness with which they are all controlled?

An aspect of the Holt scoring system that requires further clarification is the distinction between level 1 and level 2. Although Holt considered these levels to represent degrees of primariness, in effect they are sometimes used rather loosely; level 1 is sometimes seen as the equivalent of primary process, whereas level 2 is loosely interpreted as secondary process. The scoring of levels would benefit from some refinement aimed at delineating the secondary portion of the primary-secondary continuum in order to increase its representation in the Holt procedure.

Despite these insufficiencies the Holt primary process scoring system is an impressive accomplishment. In essence it represents the successful development of assessment procedures within a well-articulated, clinical and nonclinical theoretical framework. As a result these procedures are especially suited to the purpose of addressing an array of both basic and applied research issues.

8

Miscellaneous Content Scoring Categories

MEASURES OF "HOMOSEXUAL TRENDS"

The Wheeler Signs

A number of early Rorschach workers have suggested that content may be effectively used as an indicator of "homosexual trends" (Bergmann, 1945; Due & Wright, 1945; Harrower-Erickson & Steiner, 1945; Lindner, 1946). Drawing on the observations made by other workers in the field and on his own experience, Wheeler (1949) presented a list of 20 signs which he suggested as indicators of homosexuality. Wheeler's 20 signs are as follows:

1. *Card I (W or W^s): Mask or human or animal face.* Examples are a "theatrical mask" and a "fox leering." Wheeler's rationale for this sign lies in the theoretical link between homosexuality and paranoia. Responses such as these signify that the environment is perceived as "unreal and/or persecutory."

2. *Card I (lower center D): Male or muscular female torso.* Examples include a "Japanese man" and a "woman athlete." Wheeler believes these responses represent a confusion in the "body picture," confused concepts of male–female anatomy.

3. *Card II (lower center D): Crab or crablike animal.* Typical responses

are a "deep-sea crab" and a "cooked lobster." Wheeler holds that such responses symbolize the subject's perception that the female genital area is threatening and tactually unappealing.

4. *Card III (W or W*): Humans, with sex confused.* An example is the "image of a woman above, man below." These responses are thought to result from confusion about the "body picture" and male–female anatomy.

5. *Card III (W or W*): Humans with sex uncertain.* Common responses are "two sexless people" and "could be either [sex]." Wheeler sees the avoidance of sex in such responses, and the implication of underlying confusion.

6. *Card III (W or W*): Animals or animallike response (dehumanized).* Examples are "featherless chickens" and "ostrichlike natives." Wheeler includes this response category because such subjects may perceive people as "less than human" and consequently avoid sex.

7. *Card IV (W or W*): Contorted, monstrous, or threatening human or animal.* Two examples are a "man looking back through his legs" and a "horrid beast." Feminine, passive identification is seen in such responses while the male figure is seen as threatening.

8. *Card V (W, W, or center D): Human or humanized animal.* Examples include a "woman dressed as a bat" and "Bugs Bunny." Wheeler states that the rationale for the homosexual meaning of this response is not altogether clear — it may be partly that people are seen as less than human, a view that leads to avoidance of sex. A feminine, passive identification may also be involved.

9. *Card VI (center or top D): Object implying cleavage.* Two examples are a "ship with foaming wake" and an "oil well, drilling." Wheeler believes such responses suggest that the sexual act is perceived as aggressive or destructive.

10. *Card VII (W, W, or top D): Female figure with derogatory specification.* Common responses are "two old hags" and "women-yakety-yak." Such responses are thought to suggest a derogatory attitude toward women and hostile feminine identification.

11. *Card VIII (lateral D): Several incongruous animals or an animal with incongruous parts.* Two typical responses are a "rat or a lion or some-

thing" and a "bear with a rat's head." Wheeler's rationale for this category is that it involves confusion in the perception of anatomy, in this case animal anatomy.

12. *Card IX (upper lateral D): Dehumanized human figure.* Examples include a "witchlike creature" and a "monster with guns for arms." Such responses are thought to imply that people are viewed "as less than human." A derogatory attitude toward people is particularly evident when the image described is an anatomic monstrosity.

13. *Card X (top center D): An animal attacking or fighting over the central object.* Examples are "beavers gnawing a tree" and "ants arguing over this." Wheeler held that replies in this category represent symbolic destruction of the phallus; the phallus may be a sexual goal or the response may represent fear involving masturbation.

14. *Card X (all or upper half of pink plus center blue): Human figure with the blue region representing oral specification.* Two examples are an "ectoplasm coming from the mouth" and an "Irishman with growth on the lips." Such responses are viewed by Wheeler as signs of preoccupation with oral (pre-genital) stimulation.

15. *Human or animal oral detail on any card.* Typical images are "decayed teeth" and an "open mouth showing tonsils." A preoccupation with oral (pre-genital) areas is seen here.

16. *Human or animal anal detail on any card.* Responses typifying this category are a "woman with a huge ass" and "a bloody rectum." Preoccupation with anal areas is interpreted from such responses.

17. *Human or animals seen "back-to-back" on any card.* Examples include "two negroes with their backs pressed together" and "two sheep back-to-back." These responses are thought to represent "bizarre anatomical relationships" between people.

18. *Human object or architecture with a religious specification.* Two examples are "a priest's cross" and "two men praying." Wheeler interprets such responses as paranoid signs of preoccupation with religious and possibly guilt-laden objects or acts.

19. *Male or female genitalia on any card.* Responses in this category might be "part of a man — his nuts" or "a woman's private parts." Such

images are thought to represent a preoccupation with sex, which may indicate a lack of satisfaction.

20. *Feminine clothing on any card.* Examples are "a woman's fur jacket" and "panties." These responses are believed to suggest feminine identification, perhaps transvestism.

Several threads run through Wheeler's rationale for the signs. Four signs (2, 4, 5, and 11) suggest a confused body or sexual image. Preoccupation with pre-genital sexual gratification (oral and anal) is seen in signs 14, 15, 16, and possibly 17. Two signs (1 and 18) are included because of the theoretical link between paranoia and homosexuality. Derogatory views of people in general (signs 6, 8 and 12) and women in particular (sign 10) are also included. Other themes are the perception of women as threatening and unappealing (sign 3), castration threat (sign 7), sex seen as aggressive or destructive (sign 9), symbolic destruction of the phallus (sign 13), general sexual preoccupation (sign 19), and feminine identification (sign 20).

Two procedural rules for scoring that were set down by Wheeler (1949) have been altered by most subsequent researchers. Wheeler indicated that signs 15-20 should be scored only once for each subject. Reitzell (1949) and Davids, Joelson, and McArthur (1956) appear to have followed this precept. However Meketon, et al. (1962) indicate that in their own study and in those of Aronson (1952), Ferracuti and Rizzo (1956), Hooker (1958), and Yamahiro and Griffith (1960), these six signs are scored as many times as they occur in a single subject's test record. Stone and Shneider (1975) have also scored these responses as many times as they occurred and have further stated that they also scored Wheeler-relevant responses emerging in the inquiry.

The second such procedural point is the question of whether the raw number of Wheeler signs should simply be counted or whether they should be considered as a percentage of total responses. Wheeler opted for the former approach, stating that to compute percentages would complicate the clinical application of the test and would make the occurrence of signs during the "testing the limits" phase difficult to evaluate. Aronson (1952) has suggested that productivity on the Rorschach may in fact be a homosexual variable, thus necessitating a percentage measure. Davids et al. (1956) and Hooker (1958) have presented data that support Aronson's assertion. Yamahiro and Griffith (1960) strongly recommend the use of the percentage measure, and Meketon et al. (1962) note that it has become common practice to use the percentage measure.

RELIABILITY

There are very few data concerning the reliability of the Wheeler signs. Davids et al. (1956) had two investigators score the Wheeler signs for 10 homosexual and 10 normal test protocols. These authors found that the extent of interrater agreement on scoring was 83 percent. The correlation coefficient for the two sets of ratings was found to be .92. Davids et al. state that this result reflects the rather minimal ambiguity in the scoring of the Wheeler signs.

Stone and Schneider (1975) found a correlation of .98 between Wheeler scores assigned by two investigators; interscorer agreement for individual signs was 63 percent. Grauer (1954) has also indicated that the differences in scoring between two scorers were slight. However, both Hooker (1958) and Meketon et al. (1962) believe that the scoring of the Wheeler signs involves considerable subjectivity. There are no data reported in the literature on the test–retest or split-half reliability of the Wheeler signs.

VALIDITY

A number of research studies have dealt with the validity of the Wheeler signs. Wheeler (1949) worked with 100 male patients who had gone to eight or more sessions at an outpatient clinic. A distribution was made of the number of homosexual signs occurring in each of the protocols. Wheeler than divided his distribution between two and three homosexual signs; those test records having three or more signs were designated as being indicative of homosexual trends. The theraputic staff was asked to categorize each patient into one of four classifications of homosexuality: repressed, suppressed, overt, or absent. Wheeler then dichotomized the subjects into repressed–suppressed–overt and absent. The degree of correspondence between the Wheeler signs and the therapists' ratings was computed. Wheeler found that although most of the signs were not very successful, a fairly high positive relationship (Yule's coefficient of association = .42) was found between total Wheeler score and staff rating. Interestingly, the relationship was much higher for psychiatrists (.90) than for psychologists (.28) and social workers (.01).

Wheeler's is the only study on record in which degree of homosexual trends was used as the criterion. Only four of Wheeler's subjects were described as overt homosexuals. Most other validational studies have dealt with one of two issues: whether homosexual signs can distinguish between overt homosexual and nonhomosexuals, or whether the signs are prominent in the test records of paranoid patients.

Reitzell (1949) compared the Rorschach content of 26 hysterics (21 female, 5 male), 26 homosexuals (24 male, 2 female), and 26 alcoholics (20 male, 6 female). Most of the homosexual subjects were seen for testing as part of probation after their arrests for the commission of so-called homosexual acts. Reitzell made no attempt to equate the groups on relevant variables, most notably the variable of sex. She found that the Wheeler signs (plus two additional signs of her own) were able to discriminate significantly between the groups. The hysterics, homosexuals, and alcoholics scored "Wheeler signs" percents of 8.6, 14.1, and 9.0 respectively. Three items were found to be significant discriminators: items 7, 8, and 16.

Nitsche, Robinson, and Parsons (1956) compared 19 recently convicted homosexuals with 19 patients who had no known homosexual activity. All 38 subjects were white males who had been referred to a mental health clinic. The two groups were compared in 12 content categories: mythical distortion, qualifications toward the abnormal, dehumanization, double identification, uncertainty, evasiveness, projection of feminized behavior, preoccupation with feminine apparel, castration and phallic symbolism, sexual and anatomic responses, esoteric language and artistic references, and dislike of female genital symbols. Nitsche et al. found that although the homosexual group had more responses in 9 of the 12 categories, the differences were not significant. However these findings must be taken with a grain of salt because the categories used were somewhat different from those of Wheeler and there was apparently a total lack of effort to equate the two groups for demographic and/or other variables.

In a study that did attempt to control for relevant variables, Davids et al. (1956) compared 20 homosexual males with 20 neurotics and 20 normal subjects. All subjects were students attending large Eastern universities. The authors found that the homosexuals produced significantly more of the Wheeler signs than either of the two comparison groups. The differences held up when productivity was controlled. Four of the 20 signs discriminated significantly between the homosexuals and the other subjects: signs 7, 8, 10, and 19. Davids et al. found that sign 1 appeared to be invalid in their study. These authors suggested a further Rorschach sign of homosexuality based on their findings, namely, responses involving the rear view of human beings or animals. They also found that 4 of the 10 blots (Cards II, IV, V, and VII) were successful in differentiating between the homosexual and the control groups.

Davids et al. also correlated their subjects' Wheeler scores with their scores on a special homosexuality scale on the TAT. These investigators found a correlation of .52 ($p < .02$) between the two measures for their homosexual subjects, but correlations of only .05 and -.09 for their normal and neurotic subjects respectively. On the basis of their results, Davids et al. concluded that the Wheeler signs may be too crude to use in detecting varying degrees of latent homosexuality among nonhomosexual males. However the limited data on the TAT homosexuality scale made such a conclusion highly speculative.

In an Italian investigation reported by Ferracuti and Rizzo (1956), 20 prisoners classified as homosexual (although they had not been arrested for that reason) were compared with 20 prisoners who had never demonstrated homosexual behavior. They found that the 20 signs, if taken all together, did not differentiate the two groups. At the individual level the presence of one sign differentiated between the levels of .05 and the .02, and the presence of two signs differentiated at the .001 level. Eight of the signs (1, 3, 10, 13, 14, 16, 17, and 20) did not occur at all in the homosexual group and, with the exception of sign 19 (genitalia), the others occurred with such low frequency that the difference would not be significant.

In a very well controlled comparison of homosexual and heterosexual male subjects, Hooker (1957) compared 30 matched pairs of homosexuals and heterosexuals. Hooker's study is particularly interesting because the homosexual subjects were not a pathological or involuntary group — they were recruited through the Mattachine Society. Hooker had two experts attempt to distinguish between each pair of homosexual and heterosexual test records. The author noted that her two expert judges had considerable difficulty in doing so; neither judge was able to perform better than chance. Hooker reported that the judges were most successful when the homosexual test records contained strong emphasis on femininity and/or anality, that is, in about one-third of the homosexual group. On the basis of these and other findings, Hooker concluded that homosexuality does not exist as a clinical entity, that it may be a deviation in sexual pattern that is within the normal range.

In a later report on the same test protocols, Hooker (1958) applied the Wheeler signs to the task of discriminating between her homosexual and heterosexual subjects. The 60 protocols were scored for the Wheeler signs and were rescored a year later. Responses about which there was any question were typed and sent to Wheeler for blind scoring. Hooker determined that her homosexual subjects did indeed produce significantly more Wheeler signs (mean percent for homosexuals = 15.45; mean percent for heterosexuals = 8.80; $p < .001$ using the Signs Test). However this result was true only when matched pairs of individuals were compared with respect to the direction of the difference. Six of the individual signs (2, 5, 7, 9, 13, and 18) occurred most frequently in the heterosexual group. Sign 12 occurred with equal frequency in both groups. Three of the signs (1, 3, and 11) showed only a very small difference in frequencies between the two groups. The remaining 10 signs occurred so infrequently "as to make their value very dubious" (Hooker, 1958, p 39). The only two signs for which statistical computations were able to demonstrate significance at or close to the .05 level were signs 8 and 20.

Yamahiro and Griffith (1960) worked with a rather unique sample consisting of homosexuals who had been "rounded up" for possible hospitalization by a community outraged over sexual assaults on young children in Iowa. Twenty-three of these involuntary "patients" were tested with the Rorschach and the MMPI. Yamahiro and Griffith report the mean age of their subjects was 31.3 years, and that the mean IQ was 110. Unfortunately no control group as such was included in this study with respect to the Wheeler signs. Rather the authors compared their findings to those of Reitzell (1949) and Davids et al. (1956). No efforts were made to ensure comparability between the groups in demographic and other relevant variables. The results were found to be closely comparable to those of Reitzell (a mean of 2.3 Wheeler signs per record versus Reitzell's mean of 2.7) and different from those of Davids et al. (5.2 Wheeler signs per record). However, when the percentage of Wheeler signs per record was considered, the results were as follows; 12.1 percent in the Yamahiro study, 14.1 percent in the Reitzell study, and 9.3 percent in the Davids et al. investigation. Yamahiro and Griffith concluded that the percentage of signs rather than their absolute number would be the preferable measure of homosexuality. Unfortunately the conclusions that can be drawn from this study are limited by the absence of controls for many variables.

DeLuca (1966) noted that homosexuals are by no means a homogeneous group. This author posited the existence of at least 10 subgroups of homosexuals: passive, active, active and passive, sodomy, active and passive fellatio, active and passive fellatio and active and passive sodomy, passive fellatio, passive sodomy, active fellatio, and fellatio. DeLuca compared these 10 homosexual subgroups (42 subjects in all) with a control group of normals. Age, education and intelligence were controlled. All homosexual subjects were recent army inductees in the process of being discharged from the army because of their homosexuality. The 25 normal subjects were in the hospital for respiratory infections. DeLuca found that the Wheeler scale significantly differentiated between all 12 groups — the 10 specific homosexual groups, the homosexuals as a whole, and the normals ($p < .005$). However, no one sign taken by itself was able to discriminate significantly between groups. Wheeler signs, 2, 6, 8, 15, and 19 were found to be most promising. Signs 1, 3, and 7 actually loaded in the opposite direction.

Stone and Schneider (1975) investigated the ability of the Wheeler signs to discriminate between 9 male homosexuals, 8 sex-role disturbed men and 26 men judged to be adequately sexually adjusted. All subjects were seen in a university psychology clinic. The groups did not differ significantly in age, years of education, or intelligence. Stone and Schneider found that the percentage of Wheeler signs in the Rorschach test protocols of the subjects significantly discriminated the three groups (Kruskal Wallis H test, $p < .0001$). The mean Wheeler percentages were found to be 30 for the homosexuals, 12.38 for the sex-role disturbed subjects, and 7.38 for the adequately adjusted subjects. A cutoff of 15 percent correctly identified all homosexual subjects and incorrectly identified only 3 of the 34 nonhomosexuals. Stone and Schneider also presented anecdotal evidence which might suggest that these three incorrectly identified subjects may have significant latent homosexual conflicts. The impressive discriminatory power of the Wheeler signs in this study was the result of the exceedingly large percentage of such signs found in the homosexual group. Stone and Schneider have suggested two reasons for this phenomenon in their study: a more liberal scoring procedure for the Wheeler signs than that employed in previous investigations, and the lessened defensiveness that one might expect from individuals seeking psychotherapeutic help.

Three studies have specifically dealt with the question of whether paranoid patients are characterized by prominent homosexual content in their Rorschach protocols. Aronson (1952) began this line of investigation by focusing on the Freudian theory that paranoia involves unconscious homosexual conflicts. Consequently, Aronson hypothesized that paranoid subjects would be characterized by the prominence of Wheeler signs in their Rorschach protocols. This author tested the hypothesis by comparing the Rorschach records of 30 paranoid, 30 nonparanoid psychotic, and 30 normal subjects. All subjects were male. Aronson found that the paranoid group had a significantly higher mean percentage of homosexual signs than either of the other two groups. The nonparanoid psychotic subjects also had significantly higher homosexual content scores than did the normal subjects. This latter difference was largely due to a single sign, sign 19 (male or female genitalia). The paranoids exceeded both of the other groups in frequency of each of the Wheeler signs, except for signs, 1, 9 and 14. Aronson suggested that the Wheeler signs may prove to be useful aids in diagnosing paranoia clinically.

Grauer (1954) reinvestigated the problem posed by Aronson by altering the criteria for inclusion in the paranoid group. In the Aronson study 30 patients were selected for the paranoid group by the use of a delusional rating scale; only those subjects with very high ratings on this scale were included in the Aronson paranoid group. Grauer contended that Aronson's criterion for inclusion was too restrictive, and thus resulted in a sample that was not representative of the population of patients who are diagnosed as paranoid. Consequently, in Grauer's study, the criterion for inclusion in the paranoid group was a diagnosis agreed on by at least two psychiatrists after a total hospitalization period ranging from 3 months to over 2 years. Case records were also examined to determine the presence of unequivocal evidence of hallucinations and delusions. Grauer's 31 paranoid patients were then compared with Aronson's three groups. Grauer determined that the distinct differences between paranoid and nonparanoid subjects with respect to the Wheeler signs evaporated when the Grauer paranoid group was used in the comparisons. Grauer also found that the Wheeler signs were not significantly related to prognosis in his sample and concluded that "clear evidence of homosexual behavior is found in only a minority of paranoid patients" (Grauer, 1954, p 461).

Meketon et al. (1962) likewise compared Rorschach records of paranoid schizophrenic subjects to those of two other groups, alcoholics and neurotics. The subjects were 52 neurotics, 45 alcoholics, 50 paranoids, and 42 paranoid delusional patients. The groups were not matched for such variables as education, intelligence, and age because it was felt that the interest of the investigators was "in the paranoid as he comes to the hospital" (Meketon et al., 1962, p 282). Meketon et al. found no significant differences between the ratios of Wheeler signs in these groups. They also pointed out that two signs are included in the Wheeler list (signs 1 and 18) solely because of their paranoid significance. Thus, the dice are loaded in favor of finding Wheeler sign differences between paranoid and nonparanoid subjects.

Other Scales of Homosexual Trends

The literature includes several collections of homosexual signs other than those presented by Wheeler. One such set was presented by Ulett (1950), who listed seven homosexual signs: sexual and anatomic responses, castration and phallic symbols (e.g., broken bodies or poles sticking up), confusion of sexual identification, derealization and mythical distortion (e.g., witches and cartoon figures), feminine identification (e.g., female clothing,) dislike of female genital symbols, and esoteric and artistic language and references.

One study has evaluated the usefulness of the Ulett signs. Chapman and Reese (1953) compared the Rorschach scores of six patients in the process of developing schizophrenic psychosis with the scores of six normal subjects. The two sets of test records were scored for the seven homosexual signs listed by Ulett (1950). These authors found the mean number of homosexual signs to be 6.7 for the schizophrenics, and 1.8 for the normal control subjects. However no attempt was made to ensure comparability between the two groups, and no statistical tests were carried out.

Fein (1950) has also presented a list of 15 homosexual signs based on previous work in the field: derealization, confusion of sex identification, feminine identification, castration symbolism, phallic symbolism, sex anatomy – X-ray responses, esoteric remarks and art references, paranoid reactions, men with feminine attributes, anal responses, sex organs with signs of anxiety, movement responses with sexual or homosexual connotations, movement with sexual aversion, male and female in symmetrical areas, and activated sex organs.

To validate these signs, Fein determined the frequency of homosexual content responses in the Rorschach records of 43 male college students. Nine of these subjects were clinically diagnosed as homosexuals, 10 were diagnosed as anxiety neurotics, and the remaining subjects comprised the normal control group. The median ages of the three groups were 20, 19, and 17 years respectively. On the basis of percentage comparisons between the groups, Fein concluded that responses of feminine apparel and behavior, men with feminine attributes, M responses with sex connotations, male and female in symmetrical blot areas, and movement with sexual aversion are homosexual indicators. Esoteric language and art references were found to suggest homosexual tendencies. Sex organs, anatomy, and x-ray responses, qualifications toward the abnormal, and castration and phallic symbolism were indicators of homosexuality only when these responses piled up in a record. Feminine gender responses were not found to be indicators of homosexuality. Paranoid reactions and confusion of sex identification seemed to be more indicative of general insecurity than of homosexuality in the subjects studied. Although the percentages reported by Fein seem impressive, they are based on small numbers of subjects, no tests of significance were reported, and numerous potential covariables were left uncontrolled.

In an even less formal experiment, Coates (1962) set out to investigate whether what he designated as the three hallmarks of the typical male homosexual record were related to treatment outcome for 45 patients under treatment for their homosexuality. Coates listed the following three homosexual Rorschach characteristics. (1) Evidence of marked castration anxiety, which is frequently seen in catastrophic responses to Card II, such as "the vagina – a bloody mess" and "the effect of an explosion from the air." (2) Variation in form quality. (3) Excess of sexual responses. In analyzing his results, Coates determined that catastrophic responses to Card II were made by 22 (49 percent) of the cases investigated; sexual responses were present in 16 records (37 percent); and variation in form quality occurred in 18 records (40 percent). Unfortunately Coates did not present objective guidelines for the scoring of these characteristics, nor was a control group utilized. A strong positive relationship was seen between the presence of the catastrophic response in the test record and the patients' success rate in therapy. When patients had had heterosexual experience and also had the catastrophic response in their test record, they displayed even greater probability of being rated as improved following psychotherapy.

As mentioned in an earlier chapter, Schafer (1954) has also presented a thematic category of *fear and rejecting attitude toward masculine identity; feminine identification in men* — which is relevant to the measurement of homosexual trends. As noted in Chapter 3, the evidence for the validity of the Schafer scale with overt homosexuals is encouraging; several studies have indicated that the Schafer scale can discriminate between homosexuals and nonhomosexuals. Interestingly, one study (Raychaudhuri & Mukerji, 1971) directly compared the Schafer scale and the Wheeler signs in their capacity to discriminate between active homosexual, passive homosexual, sex-role disturbed, and heterosexual subjects. The Schafer scale was found to produce four significant discriminations between groups, whereas the Wheeler signs produced only two.

Evaluation of Measures of Homosexual Trends

A basic confusion characterizes this field of endeavor in Rorschach psychology. The distortions imposed by the "medical model" strike home here with a vengeance: homosexuality has been investigated as though it were a disease that one either "has" or "does not have," rather than as a multifaceted matter of sexual orientation, as it is increasingly regarded to be by social scientists. As was demonstrated by the recent decision of the American Psychiatric Association to remove homosexuality from the nomenclature of mental disorders, the meaning and value of establishing a "diagnosis" of homosexuality are becoming increasingly dubious.

A particularly unfortunate effect of the past regarding of homosexuality as a disease entity is the failure in most of the studies summarized above to distinguish between the homosexual individual and the individual with repressed homosexual drives that are striving for expression. It is only with the latter type of subject that measures of homosexual trends have some value in the clinical context. Such an individual would likely be unable to communicate openly about the existence of conflicts of which he is unaware; furthermore knowledge of the existence of such conflicts would be valuable to the therapist working with such a patient. In contrast a scale that could identify the overt homosexual would have little clinical relevance. If the clinician wishes to know whether a patient is overtly homosexual, in most cases, he has only to ask the patient. A judgment based on the patient's yes or no answer is likely to be both more reliable and more valid (a validity coefficient of 1.00?) than the same judgment based on inkblot responses.

Most of the studies discussed above do not make such a distinction between the overt and the latent homosexual, and the bulk of the research has been confined to the question of whether various scales can discriminate between overt homosexuals and heterosexuals. For a number of reasons, it would be a mistake to assume that measuring homosexual trends in latent homosexuals is equivalent to measuring homosexual trends in overt homosexuals. The subjects' attitudes toward homosexuality and heterosexuality, toward men and women, and toward the testing procedure may be entirely different in these two groups of subjects. Different patterns of physiological predisposition and/or environmental experience may also characterize these two subject populations.

Because most of the validation studies on homosexual signs have dealt with overt homosexuals, the results of these studies are of limited use to the clinician. The lack of controls in many of these investigations further limits the conclusions that can be drawn. Finally it should be noted that the subjects' motivations in the various validational studies were likely to have fluctuated considerably. The validational studies discussed above dealing with overt homosexuals included such diverse subject populations as an involuntary group of homosexuals rounded up by an irate community (Yamahiro & Griffith, 1960), homosexuals on probation (Reitzell, 1949), homosexuals in prison (Ferracuti & Rizzo, 1956), and homosexuals seeking help in a counseling center (Davids et al., 1956; Stone & Schneider, 1975). It would be naive to assume that the differing motivations of these diverse groups had no effect on their test protocols.

The findings in studies of paranoid subjects by means of the Wheeler signs are theoretically interesting but have little practical application. The fact that several of the Wheeler signs have paranoid origins makes Aronson's study something of a self-fulfilling prophecy. The failure to replicate his findings consistently (Grauer, 1954) further vitiates the meaning of this approach.

As a result of these problems, few conclusions can be reached at this time about the potential clinical usefulness of measures of homosexual trends. Only one study of the Wheeler sign has been carried out with nonovert homosexuals: that was Wheeler's own study (1949), which found the 20 signs to be considerably useful in measuring homosexual trends. This result is quite encouraging, given the direct relevance of Wheeler's subjects and experimental design. Later studies that compared overt homosexuals with other groups have likewise found the scale to be of some use, though the relationships noted were generally weaker than those seen by Wheeler. It is possible that this discrepancy is due to the above-noted difficulties in particular studies, as well as to the dubious assumption that the Wheeler signs are as useful with overt as with latent homosexuals. In short the Wheeler signs look promising, as they did in 1949. But after 25 years of research, this is about all that can be said.

The inappropriateness of most of the validational studies on specific Wheeler signs again makes it difficult to assess which of the signs is most likely to measure accurately the degree of homosexual trends in subjects who are not overtly homosexual. Wheeler's study on the validity of specific signs is again the only directly relevant investigation.

Wheeler (1949) carried out two analyses with his group of subjects to determine the usefulness of each specific item. He evaluated his 20 signs both in terms of internal consistency and in terms of validity. With respect to internal consistency, 14 of the items (signs 1, 6, 7, 8, 10, 11, 12, 13, 15, 16, 17, 18, 19, and 20) had coefficients of .62 or better. Four of the items (2, 3, 9, and 14) occurred so rarely that statements concerning consistency would be meaningless. Internal consistency was found to be low for items 4 and 5. Three of the items correlated quite well with the criterion of therapists' ratings; items 7, 8, and 17 yielded Yule coefficients of .62, .58, and .53 respectively. Four of the remaining items (1, 6, 10, and 16) had Qs of .30 and above. Again, four items occurred too rarely to be meaningfully evaluated statistically (items 2, 3, 9, and 14); but item 14 looked promising in terms of discriminating between the criterion groups.

Thus it presently appears that items 7, 8, and 17 are strongly supported in Wheeler's study as indicators of homosexual trends. Items 7 and 8 have also been supported by the studies of overt homosexual groups. In addition, items 1, 6, 10, 14, and 16 appear to be of at least some value in measuring homosexual trends. In the studies of overt homosexuals, there is some support (Davids et al., 1956; Hooker, 1958, Reitzell, 1949) for the validity of items 10 and 16. Item 20 has received some support in the studies of overt homosexuals, but Wheeler did not find it useful. This item must therefore be considered of doubtful validity for purposes of measuring homosexual trends in nonovert homosexuals.

Consequently, of the 20 Wheeler signs, it would seem that we can be most confident of the validity of items 7, 8, and 17, and fairly confident of the validity of items 10 and 16; but the validity of items 1, 6, 14, and

20 remains questionable. The validity of the remaining 11 signs also appears doubtful. It should be noted that these conclusions are based on only one investigation of direct relevance, and on several studies that may not be relevant at all. These conclusions should therefore be considered tentative until they can be corrected by further work in this area.

Little validity data are available for scales other than those of Wheeler. The Schafer scale appears promising in light of the research carried out to date. It is perhaps notable that in one study (Raychaudhuri & Mukerji, 1971) the Schafer scale outperformed the Wheeler signs in discriminating between groups differing in sexual orientation.

The Schafer scale's reliance on broad themes rather than on specific responses to delimited blot areas appears to the present authors to be an advantage over the Wheeler signs. Only six of the Wheeler signs (15 through 20) can be considered broadly thematic in nature. If such factors as derogatory views of people and confused body or sexual image are indeed associated with homosexual trends, it would make more theoretical sense to score all such responses on a homosexual trends scale, rather than only when they occur in response to certain blot areas. The Schafer scale's lesser reliance on specific Rorschach blot areas also makes the Schafer scale potentially applicable to other inkblot tests, such as the HIT, whereas the Wheeler signs must be considered largely Rorschach-bound.

Some very basic work remains to be done before these scales of homosexual trends can be used clinically. More studies must use nonovert or latent homosexuals as subjects, as in the initial Wheeler investigation. This recommendation is particularly important for the Schafer scale, because there are literally no data that concern the Schafer scale's applicability to latent homosexuals. If the scales should indeed prove useful in future research, further data on the reliability and differentiating precision must also be provided if the scales are to be beneficial to the practicing clinician.

ENDICOTT'S CONTENT MEASURES OF DEPRESSION AND SUSPICIOUSNESS

Two recently developed content categories that have been used with some success are those developed by Noble Endicott and his coworkers (Endicott, 1972; Endicott & Jortner, 1966; Endicott, Jortner & Abramoff, 1969). These scales measure depression and suspiciousness and are designed to be used with the HIT. Two scales are provided in both categories; the first has been found to correlate positively, and the second negatively, with the criterion.

Scoring — Depression Scale I

Blot described or referred to in terms frequently associated with depression. Examples of such descriptions are lonely, miserable, dejected, dismal, mournful, unloved, weary, and blackness when blackness denotes an emotional quality.

Dead or dying human beings. The subject must specifically describe the person as dead or dying, unless killing, being killed, or violence is the theme rather than death. Examples of responses scored for depression are "bodies in a morgue," or "they've been hung; they're performing an autopsy."

Dead or dying animals. These responses are scored with the same qualifications as those noted for the preceding category. If it is clear that the percept is food, it is not scored for depression. Thus "a dead deer, they're taking it home to cook" isn't scored for depression.

Remains of animals or human beings. This response is scored when the main connotation is a remnant of an organism that was once alive. The percept must have a clear connotation of death. Thus "skeleton" would not be scored for depression, but "Skeleton on the desert — the sand is shifting about it" would be scored. Other examples of scorable responses are "a fossil," a "pile of dried bones," and a "fossil of a butterfly." Examples of responses that are not scored are animal pelts, artifically preserved or frozen animals (when the emphasis is on a soiled object) and remains of objects destroyed by violence, such as a "burned house."

Scoring — Depression Scale II

Dark clouds. Images in this group include black clouds, storm clouds, rain clouds, and overcast skies. Clouds produced by explosions and such unmodified responses as storms, cloudy skies, and fog are not scored.

Dead or dying plants. This response is scored when plants are specifically referred to as dead or dying, for example: "It's green grass, the white would be dead grass." Dead leaves are not scored in this category.

Dead leaves. Typical responses in this category are "autumn leaves" or "autumn scene."

Damage due to the action of water.   Responses here involve erosion, rust, corrosion, and rotting due to water, for example: "A piece of driftwood on the beach — if you pick it up it breaks from being rotten."

Cold or coldness.   This response is scored when the subject describes the blot as cold or as giving a "feeling of coldness." Snow scenes, and the like are not scored unless cold is specifically described.

Bare trees.   Images in this group include such responses as "trees without leaves" or "barren trees."

Endicott noted that responses scorable under both Scale I and Scale II should only be scored under Scale I. No response should be scored more than once.

Reliability

The only reliability data reported for these scales concern interscorer reliability. Endicott and Jortner (1966) had 30 HIT protocols independently scored for depression by two psychologists. A reliability coefficient of .81 was found for Depression Scale I; for Depression Scale II, the coefficient was .90. There are no reported data regarding split-half or alternate form reliability.

Validity

On the basis of preliminary research, Endicott and his associates developed both a 5-point rating scale of depression and an inkblot content scale of depression. The rating scale ranged from minimal to extreme depression. Depression was defined as "a state characterized primarily by feelings of hopelessness, sadness, and being a failure" (Endicott & Jortner, 1966, p 250). The HIT and the MMPI were among the test measures administered to 90 hospitalized psychiatric patients (63 male, 27 female) and 40 outpatients (18 male, 22 female) who were being seen in private practice. All patients were also rated on the depression rating scale. Only 84 of the hospitalized patients were able to complete the MMPI. Based on a preliminary examination of the data on the hospitalized patients, the content categories were divided into the two scales listed above: those that correlated positively with the rating scale of depression (Depression Scale I), and those that correlated negatively with the rating scale (Depression Scale II).

Endicott and Jortner found that among the hospitalized patients, the rating scale of depression correlated at .51 ($p < .01$) with the MMPI *D* scale, at .32 ($p < .01$) with Depression Scale I, at -.22 ($p < .05$) with Depression Scale II, at .23 ($p < .05$) with HIT Anatomy responses, at .23 ($p < .05$) with HIT Rejections, and at -.23 ($p < .05$) with the HIT *CF* score. A multiple regression equation was developed for predicting rated depression using MMPI *D* scale score, Depression Scale I, Depression Scale II, HIT Rejections, and HIT Anatomy as the predictors. Endicott and Jortner found a multiple correlation coefficient of .61.

For cross-validation, the same correlations were computed on the outpatients. In this sample these investigators found that the rating scale correlated at .51 ($p < .01$) with the MMPI *D* scale, at .55 ($p < .01$) with Depression Scale I, and at -.28 with Depression Scale II. This last correlation was not significant. Using the same predictors as those used with the hospitalized subjects, Endicott and Jortner found a multiple correlation coefficient of .75.

Suspiciousness Scoring — Scale I

Potential threats with a personal or self-referential quality. Such threats are to be distinguished from overt expressions of hostility such as stabbing, or ongoing threatening situations such as storms. Examples are "A vampire looking for someone to get blood from"; and "two large-beaked vultures prepared to pounce."

Evil percepts. These are percepts described as "evil," "sinister," or "fiendish."

People or animals described as "sneaky, underhanded, crafty, dishonest, untrustworthy, cheating." This group includes percepts in which a person is engaged in a dishonest act such as robbing a store, but is not specifically described as "dishonest," or as "a crook."

People attempting to influence, control, manipulate, or exert power over others. An example is "two people sending messages — it's a form of thought control."

Miscellaneous masks. Masks other than religious, Halloween, party, or theatrical masks are scored in this category. The percept must be specifically labeled "a mask" to be scored. Masks given to HIT Cards 31A and 42A are excluded.

Percepts in which people or animals are being tortured or persecu-

ted.   An example is a "man being hounded by his enemies."

Devils or demons.   Monsters are not scored.

Human faces.   The percepts must be specifically labeled a "face" in order to be scored in this category. This category includes all face responses that are not specified as being "animal." Responses to HIT Cards 17A and 44A are excluded. An example is "some kind of face peering out of the fog."

Capes, cloaks, or cloaked figures.   Hooded figures to HIT Card 4A not scored.

Witches.

Costumed figures, costumes, disguised figures.   Costumed animals as well as people are scored in this category. An example is "two dancers, in costume as Spanish men."

People or fingers pointing.   Responses to HIT Card 34A are not scored.

Eyes.   Two types of responses are scored in this category: those in which "eye" or "eyes" were the only percepts mentioned, and those in which such a response was given initially, then followed by one or two other portions of the face.

Eyes emphasized.   These responses are ones in which special emphasis is placed on the eyes, but in which the eyes are only part of a larger percept, for example: "She has large eyes."

Clowns.

Animal faces.   The response must be specifically described as a "face" to be scored in this category.

Suspiciousness Scoring — Scale II

Concealed people or animals.   Typical responses in this category include people or animals "behind" something that would hide them, "hiding," or "looking out from bushes."

Shields.

Party masks.   Included here are masquerade masks or dance masks.

Theatrical masks.   Dramatic masks, comic masks, and tragic masks are included in this category.

Clothing or cloth hung or draped over objects.   This includes cloth designed for covering objects, such as "a bedspread," "a slipcover," or "curtains," but it does not include clothing unless the clothes are specifically described as being hung or draped over something.

Armor.   In addition to the two primary suspiciousness scales described above, Endicott also scores "suspicious popular" responses and adds these scores to either Scale I or Scale II scores. The three types of suspicious popular (SP) responses are (1) masks — other than religious, Halloween, party, or theatrical masks — in response to HIT Cards 31A and 42A; (2) human faces seen in HIT Cards 17A and 44A; and (3) people or fingers pointing in Card 34A.

The SP responses are added to Scale I scores when (1) the total Scale I score is 6 or more; (2) the total Scale I score is 4 or more and the Scale II score is 0; (3) there are three or more responses in the first five categories of Scale I, and the total Scale II score is less than 2; or (4) there are two or more responses in the first five categories of Scale I, and no Scale II responses.

The SP responses are added to Scale II when (1) the total Scale I score is 0; (2) the total Scale I score is 1 and the total Scale II score is 1 or more; or (3) the total Scale I score is less than 4 and the Scale II score is more than 2.

The order of precedence of these SP rules is that in which they are presented.

Reliability

The HIT Form A protocols of 90 subjects were scored by two persons (Endicott, Jortner & Abramoff, 1969). The product-moment reliability coefficients of the scales were .94 for Scale I, .85 for Scale II, and .88 for SP. No other information on the reliability of these scales is provided.

Validity

The validational design for the Suspiciousness scales was the same as for the Depression scales, that is, a 5-point rating of suspiciousness was used as the criterion, and both psychiatric inpatients ($N = 90$) and outpatients ($N = 40$) served as the subjects. Suspiciousness Scale I was found to correlate at .45 ($p < .01$) with rated suspiciousness among the inpatients (the group on which the scales were developed). It correlated at .58 ($p < .01$) among the outpatients (the cross-validation sample). Scale II correlated at -.38 ($p < .01$) with rated suspiciousness among the inpatients, and at -.23 among the outpatients. The latter finding was not significant. When SP was added to the HIT suspiciousness scores, the correlations among the outpatients changed to .58 ($p < .01$) for Scale I and -.46 ($p < .01$) for Scale II.

These authors also used the *Pa* scale of the MMPI and a specially designed MMPI scale of suspiciousness in predicting rated suspiciousness. The *Pa* scale did not correlate significantly with the ratings in either group, but the MMPI suspiciousness scale did correlate at .36 ($p < .01$) and at .44 ($p < .01$) among the inpatients and outpatients respectively. Combining the two HIT scales (with SP added) and the MMPI suspiciousness scale in multiple regression equations to predict rated suspiciousness, Endicott and coworkers found multiple correlations of .61 and .69 in the initial and the cross-validation groups respectively.

General Evaluation of the Endicott Scales

The Endicott scales of depression and suspiciousness represent a further successful attempt to develop valid inkblot content scales. It would appear that these measures hold considerable promise. They have been shown to hold up well when applied to groups of subjects different from those on whom the scales were initially developed. The outpatient group on which the scales were cross-validated differed from the inpatient subjects in a number of parameters, for example, socioeconomic status and diagnosis. Not only did the scales continue to predict effectively with this new group of subjects, but in most cases the correlations of the cross-validational group were actually greater than those found in the initial sample. That the scales were able to continue to operate effectively, even when applied to such a different group of subjects, suggests that they may have considerable value.

A particularly commendable feature of the Endicott research is the inclusion of the MMPI in an attempt to predict the criteria from both the HIT scales and the MMPI. Because psychological tests tend to be used in conjunction with other tests rather than in a vacuum, Endicott's approach makes good clinical sense. Thus in practice the question is not only one of whether inkblot content scales are valid, but also one of how much unique coverage of variance in criterion scores each test can provide. Endicott's results suggest that the HIT content scales do measure some aspects of depression and suspiciousness that are not measured by corresponding MMPI scales; thus his results point to the potential clinical usefulness of these inkblot scales. It is unfortunate that the combination of clinical instruments, especially in arriving at regression equations, is relatively rare in the Rorschach validational literature.

The major criticism of the Endicott scales is the lack of adequate reliability, validity, and normative data. It is hoped that such additional data will be forthcoming. Preliminary data on the interscorer reliability of the scales suggest some weakness in this area, particularly for Depression Scale I and Suspiciousness Scale II.

Finally, it should be noted that the division of the scales into those correlating positively versus those correlating negatively with the criterion is difficult to interpret. Some evidence presented by Endicott and Jortner (1966) and Endicott et al. (1969) suggest that the scales that correlate negatively with the criterion may measure mild degrees of the characteristics in question. In the hospitalized group of subjects, for example, a mildly depressed patient was six times more likely to give a Depression II response than was a markedly depressed patient. However such interpretations are based on a very small number of subjects. The meaning of Depression Scale II and the Suspiciousness Scale II must still be considered unclear.

Because of the paucity of data pertaining to these content scales, they are of little clinical use at this time. Reliability data, normative data, and further data on the validity of all the scales are necessary before the scales can be put to any clinical use. The meaning of Depression Scale II and Suspiciousness Scale II remains to be clarified.

Because so little work has been done in this area to date, the possibilities for research applications are numerous. For instance, it has not yet been determined whether the different diagnostic categories of depression (Involutional, Depressive Reaction, etc.) differ on the depression scales, or whether the suspiciousness scale scores are related to a diagnosis of Paranoia. Whether the scale scores change with amelioration in symptomatology is another unanswered question. Nor has it been determined whether any of the scales are related to prognosis. There are clearly many possibilities for the use of these scales, and much remains to be done.

RORSCHACH INDEX OF REPRESSIVE STYLE (RIRS)

Levine and Spivack (1964) noted that individuals differ in verbal development of their inkblot responses. These authors set out to quantify verbal Rorschach behavior as a measure of the strength of repression.

Scoring

In the RIRS system, responses are scored on seven scales, a brief summary of which follows. The interested reader is referred to Levine and Spivack (1964) for the full scoring criteria.

Specificity. Specificity refers to the extent to which the nouns in a response refer to a unique entity (e.g., "Fu Manchu") or to a vague concept (e.g., "a man"). High specificity indicates low repression.

Elaboration. This scale measures the extent to which the response is elaborated with adjectives and adverbs. These modifiers give affective qualities to the response and increase its personalization. "A tree" is unelaborated; "a dying tree with drooping branches" is elaborated. High elaboration indicates low repressive functioning.

Impulse responses. Direct references to sexuality, dependency, anality, or hostility indicate low repressive functioning.

Primary process thinking. Confabulations, contaminations, position responses, and abstract and symbolic responses indicate low levels of repressive functioning.

Self-references. Because such references reflect the presence in consciousness of personalized thought forms, these responses suggest low levels of repression. Self-references are usually manifested in associations to the percepts and the direct expression of affect.

Movement. Levine and Spivack consider M responses to be a "verbal derivative of affects and drives" indicating low repressive functioning. Only M responses indicated in the association phase of testing are scored; FM and m responses are also scored in this category.

Organization. This scale measures the extent to which the response is organized in terms of associational connections. High organization in a response is thought to indicate low repressive functioning.

The Rorschach Index of Repressive Style controls for total R in that a subject's total in these categories for his Rorschach record is divided by the number of responses to yield a total score. The polarity of the RIRS is such that a low score indicates high repression and a high score indicates low repression — a confusing convention.

Reliability

The interscorer reliability of the RIRS appears to be quite high. Levine and Spivack (1964) have reported four studies of interscorer reliability. These four studies varied in the scorers (the authors and interns), in the blots and administration used (Behn, Rorschach, group Rorschach), in the statistic reported (Pearson *r*, rho, Kendall *w*), and in the number of records (ranging from 7 to 20). All four coefficients, however, were .95 or better.

These authors report a number of coefficients with respect to test–retest and alternate form reliability. When the same form of inkblots was administered a short time after the first test, the resulting coefficients were high (median = .88). However such coefficients must be considered suspect, because the subject may merely be recalling percepts, and verbalizations surrounding the percepts.

When dealing with longer intervals between the two administrations, Levine and Spivack (1964) turned to the Ledwith (1959) and Paulsen (1954) longitudinal data. With the Ledwith protocols, these authors found that "for test-retest intervals ranging from four to ten years, the median reliability coefficient is .60" (Levine & Spivack, 1964, p 43). Reanalyzing Paulsen's (1954) longitudinal data, Levine and Spivack found substantially lower coefficients, blamed on very constricted Rorschach records. Although these investigators acknowledged the problem of memory effects on such data, they also argued that with the RIRS the subject would have to remember not only the percept, but also the contextual language in response to the test. They pointed as well to increases in the correlations with age. Although the present authors agree that the RIRS is less subject to the problem of memory effects than other Rorschach scores, it is felt that such coefficients should still be considered somewhat suspect. The increased magnitude of the correlations with age may also be affected by the subjects' greater ability to recall their responses after having been administered the test several times.

When different sets of inkblots were used (alternate form reliability), Levine and Spivack reported coefficients of .67 (Rorschach and Harrower blots, same-day administration) and .67 (Rorschach and Behn blots, 3 months or less between administrations). These results again suggest that the scale has a good deal of temporal stability, but the different test stimuli and subject groups used must temper this conclusion. Unfortunately, split-half coefficients are not reported for the RIRS. Although the scale should not be expected to have high split-half reliability (because it is heterogeneous), such coefficients would be useful in evaluating the alternate form coefficients reported above.

In short, the interscorer reliability of the RIRS appears satisfactory, and available evidence indicates that scale has less difficulty with temporal stability than many other content scales surveyed in this volume. However, further evidence in this area is required. It would be particularly useful to contrast the split-half reliability of the RIRS with delayed alternate form reliability, in order to be able to evaluate its temporal stability more effectively.

Validity

Levine and Spivack (1964) have presented substantial information regarding the validity of their scale. Much of this was obtained through reanalysis of data collected in prior studies, a technique similar to that of Fisher and Cleveland (1958/1968). Perhaps partially as a result of this strategy, few of the empirical results reported can be considered very direct tests of the validity of the RIRS.

In one study relevant to the construct validity of RIRS, Levine and Spivack reported that RIRS correlated at .44 (rho, $p < .05$) with rated degree of psychological as opposed to somatic orientation of 16 neurotic patients. However a similar replicative investigation found results of only borderline significance.

In a study of dreams these authors found that the number of dreams reported by 21 schizophrenic women correlated positively and significantly with RIRS (rho = .36, $p = .05$), as had been expected. Reanalyzing data collected on female college subjects, they found a significant positive correlation between the number of nights dreams were reported and the RIRS; however a negative correlation of borderline significance was determined for the male subjects in this study.

This pattern of inconsistent findings and sex differences continues in research that has related RIRS to anxiety. In an encouraging study Levine and Spivack reported a difference of borderline significance ($p = .10$) between high and low MAS female college subjects; the low anxiety students had higher RIRS scores, as might have been predicted. The introduction of self-esteem stress resulted in a significant drop (constricting) in RIRS scores, particularly for the low MAS group.

In an investigation on hypnotically induced anxiety, however, the results were precisely the opposite of what might have been expected. Medical and nursing student subjects in whom anxiety was hypnotically induced had significantly higher RIRS scores ($p < .01$) than they did when in the waking state or in a hypnotic state without special suggestion. Levine and Spivack suggested that the subjects may have had a set to reveal anxiety in the hypnotically induced anxiety state, and that this set resulted in higher RIRS scores. In a test of this hypothesis, these investigators found that college subjects asked to respond as though they were anxious did score significantly higher ($p < .01$) on the RIRS than they did under instructions to "be yourself" or under instructions to behave as though they were "trying to hide the fact" that they were anxious.

Using Cattell's IPAT, Levine and Spivack found no significant relationships between the RIRS and IPAT measurements of anxiety. RIRS was also determined to be unrelated to Sarason's test anxiety scale. On the MMPI, groups differing in RIRS did not differ significantly in Welsh anxiety (A) score regardless of sex. However the high RIRS males and the high RIRS females differed significantly in A ($p < .05$) because of the tendency of high RIRS scores to be associated with low A scores in males, but with high A scores in females. On the Pt scale, a similar trend in sex differences was noted: high RIRS males had lower Pt scores, whereas high RIRS females had higher Pt scores.

In a study related to the above anxiety investigations, Levine and Spivack also found that sex affected the relation of self-ideal discrepancy scores to the RIRS. High RIRS males tended to report low self-ideal discrepancies, whereas high RIRS females tended to report high discrepancies.

In investigations of interests, there was also a suggestion of sex differences. Whereas emotionally disturbed adolescent males with high RIRS had more differentiated Kuder profiles than low RIRS males ($p < .01$), the trend in females was of borderline significance in the opposite direction.

Studies of diagnostic groups might be expected to yield very direct evidence of the validity of the RIRS, because the patterns of defenses have long been thought to differ in subjects with certain psychiatric diagnoses (e.g., Fenichel, 1945). Unfortunately Levine and Spivack presented very little useful evidence in this regard. The test protocols of subjects of different diagnoses that had already been published in the clinical literature were used to score for RIRS, and the resulting scores seem consistent with what might have been expected. However this approach has major shortcomings. The subjects of differing diagnoses are by no means equated in terms of relevant control variables, and the diagnoses may have been established at least in part on the basis of Rorschach test performance.

In a study relevant to diagnostic issues, Levine and Spivack determined that schizophrenic women, whose ward behavior had been rated active or passive, differed significantly in RIRS ($p < .05$): the active patients had the higher RIRS scores. Length of hospitalization for these subjects was also related to RIRS scores, but only after three women were dropped from the subject pool.

These researchers also reported investigations in which psychosomatic patients scored significantly lower on the RIRS than did normal subjects ($p < .05$). In another experiment they found that adolescent subjects who acted out did not differ significantly from a control group. This latter finding was contrary to what had been predicted. However 5 boys who had committed sex offenses had high RIRS scores.

Irizarry (1971) contrasted male psychopaths with high versus low anxiety as part of a larger study. All subjects were inmates of a correctional institution. The groups were roughly equivalent in terms of race, age, intelligence, and socioeconomic level. The HIT was used as the inkblot measure. Although the RIRS scores of the two subject groups did not differ significantly, Irizarry found that the low anxiety subjects' RIRS correlated significantly with Holt's Defense-Denial Content of the Primary Process scoring system ($r = .84$, $p < .01$), and with a measure of deviations from common themes and moods in TAT stories ($r = .61$, $p < .05$). However, the correlations were not significant for the high anxiety subjects. Irizarry also reported that four of the six subjects who had extreme RIRS scores at either end of the continuum were characterized by impulsive crimes.

Levine and Spivack also briefly noted that RIRS did not prove to be significantly related to MMPI scales that were thought to measure the same dimension – Hanley's defensiveness scale, Welsh's repression scale, Welsh's internalization ratio, the K scale, and Byrne's repression-sensitization scale. There was, however, a significant relationship with Hy minus Pt among the male subjects, but the same was not true for the females.

RIRS has been found to be significantly related to verbal behavior occurring during sensory deprivation. Among 12 male college student subjects, RIRS correlated at .61, (rho $p < .05$) with Syndrome I ratings – a pattern of adaptive behavior to sensory deprivation; RIRS also correlated significantly with the subjects' imagery ratings during sensory deprivation and with their total verbal output and directed and logical thought. RIRS did not correlate significantly with Syndrome II (maladaptive) behavior.

The relationship of RIRS to verbal output has also been studied using the TAT. Although Levine and Spivack (1964) noted that no relationship has been found between RIRS and TAT total word output, significant relationships have been found on the TAT with so-called transcendence, that is, the extent to which the subjects' stories included material that goes beyond card description. As these authors explain, "the issue is *how* it is said, and not *how much* is said" (Levine & Spivack, 1964, p 68).

Several studies have related RIRS to field dependency (FD) since Witkin and coworkers (1954) theorized that field-dependent individuals have less awareness of inner life as well as fear of and poor control over their impulses. In an initial investigation, no relationship was found between RIRS and FD among 10-year-old-boys. Because the subjects were felt to be nonrepresentative, the procedure was repeated with a second sample of 10-year-old boys. The correlation was not statistically significant, but a t-test of extreme groups found that subjects with high field dependence had significantly lower RIRS scores than subjects with low field dependence, as had been predicted. Levine and Spivack (1964) also reported correlations between RIRS as measured by the HIT and three separate FD measures. The subjects were 48 male college students and 44 female college students. Of the six resulting correlations (RIRS correlated with the three FD measures for each of the two sexes), two were significant beyond the .05 level. In both cases low field dependence was associated with high RIRS score.

These investigators also noted a significant correlation between FD measured in a figure-drawing task and RIRS ($r = .34, p < .01$) and the correlation was in the expected direction. However, they reported another experiment in which a nonsignificant correlation was found between FD measured by figure drawings and RIRS.

Levine and Spivack related RIRS to performance on measures of "leveling-sharpening," measures previously shown on the Rorschach to be related to repression. Comparing extreme groups, these authors found a difference of borderline significance. RIRS correlated significantly with one of the two components of leveling-sharpening ($r = .44, p < .03$) but not with the second component.

RIRS has also been related to "scale checking style" on the Semantic Differential (Osgood, Suci, & Tannenbaum, 1957). Levine and Spivack considered two checking styles: positions 1, 4, and 7, which tend to be checked rapidly, and positions 2, 3, 5, and 6, which tend to be checked more slowly. The latter style is thought to be associated with a more cautious consideration of possibilities. There were 12 subjects in each of the four groups — high and low RIRS males, and high and low RIRS females. Subjects were asked to rate their art products and the meaning their art products had for them using the Semantic Differential. Significant differences were found between the groups. High RIRS females made extensive use of the 1–4–7 pattern, while high RIRS males used the 2–3–5–6 scheme extensively.

Levine and Spivack have also found RIRS to be related to other Rorschach scores; RIRS has been shown to be significantly related to such inkblot scores as M, m, C', and experience balance. As noted by these authors, "subjects who produce a rich record by the usual Rorschach scoring criteria, tend to produce high RIRS scores" (Levine & Spivack, 1964, p 62). Although the relationship with M may in part be an artifact of the scoring of movement responses as part of RIRS, Levine and Spivack have demonstrated that when this aspect of RIRS is not scored, a significant relationship remains between RIRS and M.

In other studies of the correlates of RIRS, these authors determined that there was no significant relationship with the status and sex of the examiner or with the F scale. A significant difference was found in a sleep deprivation experiment which revealed that a slight decrease in RIRS occurred following recovery from sleep deprivation.

As might be expected of an index of verbal behavior, RIRS has been found to be significantly related to intelligence in a variety of subject groups, with a variety of measures of intelligence. Levine and Spivack indicated a median correlation of .21 between RIRS and intelligence tests (.25 for females, .15 for males); the correlations were generally higher with verbal than with nonverbal intelligence measures. RIRS has also been shown to be related to tests of academic achievement, but only for male subjects. The pattern of relationships at different ages suggested to these authors that the correlations were highest in those areas in which achievement motivation was currently invested, for example, reading at age 8 and arithmetic among older adolescents. In line with this reasoning, they also found a significant relationship between RIRS and n Ach among male subjects as measured by the TAT ($r = .36, p < .05$). However there was no significant relationship between RIRS and n Ach as measured by the Edwards Personal Preference Schedule.

Levine and Spivack have presented developmental data on RIRS, using both cross-sectional and longitudinal studies. They found a trend toward higher RIRS scores with increasing age, particularly among female subjects. They attributed this trend to increased complexity of personality organization with age. Norms are unavailable for the RIRS, although in their book Levine and Spivack (1964) have presented the medians, interquartile ranges, and ranges for the RIRS of the various subject groups discussed above.

General Evaluation of RIRS

The reliability data on RIRS appear quite promising. Interscorer reliability is satisfactory, and available data on temporal stability suggest that this is less of a problem with RIRS than with many other systems discussed above. However temporal stability data must still be considered suggestive; further work must be done in this area.

Unfortunately conclusions about the validity of the scale are not as optimistic. As noted above, what might be considered very direct tests of the scale's validity have not yet been carried out. Two areas in particular have been little explored: the relationship of RIRS to therapists' ratings of strength of repression, and the relationship of RIRS to ego restitution in schizophrenia. Those validity studies that have been conducted have sometimes found relationships that were predicted, but sometimes they have not. Even when significant results are brought forth, it is not unusual for only a few of the obtained statistics to reach statistical significance, or for results to fail to be replicated (although the small numbers of subjects may in part be responsible). These facts suggest that the effect being measured is not particularly powerful. The failure of RIRS to correlate with MMPI measures of repression is particularly discouraging. Furthermore the meaning of RIRS is clearly mediated by sex, and thus the meaning of the validity data becomes even more clouded.

It is interesting to note that the most consistent and striking results were found in those studies that related the scale to expressive verbal behavior. RIRS has been shown to be associated with measures of subject's expressive verbal behavior in sensory deprivation, and has also been shown to be related to several measures of transcendence in TAT stories.

Although future research may indeed provide evidence that the RIRS is a valid measure of repressive defense, the validity of the system is by no means established at this time. One reason for the failure of the RIRS to demonstrate consistent validity may lie in the assumption on which the entire scoring system is based. Levine and Spivack assumed that the strength of repression could be reliably measured by an index depending heavily on verbal elaborations of inkblot responses and the inclusion of self-revealing material. That the system is basically measuring the subject's verbal expressiveness is demonstrated by the consistent relationships with other measures of expressive behavior noted above. Inasmuch as repression results in a constriction of verbal behavior, it is most likely true that the defense of repression will therefore affect RIRS scores. However constriction in verbal expressive behavior may be affected by numerous other factors, including the subject's conscious unwillingness to reveal himself to the examiner, the subject's intellectual endowment, transient situational factors, etc. This possibility may help explain the somewhat weak and inconsistent relationships with criteria that have been reported by Levine and Spivack (1964).

THE SCORING OF COMMUNICATION
DEFECTS AND DEVIANCES

In 1966, Singer and Wynne published an article (1966b) presenting a system for scoring communication deficiencies thought to be particularly characteristic of the parents of schizophrenic individuals. This scoring system developed out of previous work by these authors (e.g., Singer & Wynne; 1963, 1965a; 1965b; Wynne & Singer, 1963a; 1963b) in which communication deficiencies in the parents of schizophrenics were noted, and in which projective techniques were observed to be suitable vehicles for eliciting such verbal behavior. Singer and Wynne theorized that one of the factors leading to later decompensation into overt clinical schizophrenia is a child's early deficient orientation to "those aspects of speech, reasoning, behavior, and other events that will be important in his expectable life experiences" (Singer & Wynne, 1966b, p 262).

The scoring system developed by Singer and Wynne is to be used in the evaluation of Rorschach and TAT test performance. The verbal transactions between the examiner and the subject are analyzed for evidence of communication defects and deviances. This system is therefore another example of the development of a Rorschach scale to measure a contextual aspect of test performance, in this instance, some special characteristics of verbal behavior. The current presentation will not outline the system in detail; the interested reader is referred to the complete scoring manual (Singer & Wynne, 1966b).

Scoring

Singer and Wynne (1966b) score Rorschach responses in three main categories. [1]

Closure problems. This category is scored when the subject's verbalizations cause uncertainty about whether he has expressed closure over an idea, a response, or an exchange. Nine subcategories of closure problems are presented: speech fragments; unintelligible responses and comments; unstable percepts (i.e., the subject is unsure about what he

---

[1]In a later study (1966a), a fourth category, "negativism toward the testing task," was added.

is seeing); gross indefiniteness and tentativeness; responses in negative form (e.g., "It doesn't look like a sheep."); subjunctive "if" responses (e.g., "If I were sick and upset, I'd say it resembled a person."); question responses; contradictory information, inconsistent references, and incompatible alternatives; and disqualifications.

Disruptive behavior. The second category is scored when the subject's behavior disrupts the continuity of the test. Ten subcategories of disruptive behavior are described: interruption of the examiner's speeches; extraneous questions and remarks; odd, tangential, inappropriate responses to questions; nonverbal disruptive behavior; humor (including puns and playing with sounds); swearing; hopping around among responses; negativistic temporary card rejection followed by a response; concrete-set responses (in which the subject indicates he *is* recognizing or *has* to recognize the cards); references to "they" and to the intent of others.

Peculiar verbalizations. The final category is scored when the subject's words, syntax, and logic are used "in idiosyncratic ways that would ordinarily interfere with the sharing of meaning" (Singer & Wynne, 1966b, p 277). This category is similar to the responses that Rapaport et al. (1946) presented as those particularly associated with schizophrenia. (See Chapter 9.) Three subcategories of peculiar verbalizations are listed: peculiar word usages, constructions, and pronunciations; reiteration (e.g., "That's a pig — looks like a pig — yeah, a pig."); and peculiar logic.

Reliability and Validity Studies

Singer and Wynne (1966a) have reported on the interscorer reliability of their system. In this investigation the Rorschach protocols of 59 pairs of parents were utilized: 19 pairs of parents of schizophrenics, 20 pairs of parents of severe neurotics, and 20 pairs of parents of normal individuals. Two raters blindly scored each test record, initially scoring the first response to each blot, then scoring all the responses in a test record. Singer and Wynne reported their results in terms of percentage of agreement among the subject groups. For the schizophrenic group, 79 percent agreement was found; for the severe neurotic group, 87 percent; and for the normal group, 88 percent. These percentages represent the extent of agreement and disagreement on subcategory scores within the main headings. As noted by Jensen (1964), percentage of agreement is a poor substitute for reliability determined by a correlation coefficient. There are no further data relevant to the reliability of this scoring system.

Singer and Wynne (1965a; 1965b) carried out an extensive validity study with the families of 35 adolescents and young adults. Twenty of these families had a schizophrenic, nine a borderline schizophrenic, and six a severely neurotic offspring. Based on an evaluation of Rorschach and TAT protocols of the family members, four types of predictions about the offspring were made: global diagnosis (schizophrenic-borderline schizophrenic-nonschizophrenic), form of thinking (amorphous-mixed-fragmented-constricted), severity of ego disorganization (on a 6-point scale), and narrative descriptive predictions. In the same study a psychologist attempted to match blindly the test protocols of patients with those of their families. Singer and Wynne (1965b) found that all four classes of predictions were made with a very high degree of success. Of the 35 subjects, 28 were diagnosed correctly based on the family protocols ($p < .001$). Predictions of the subjects' form of thinking and severity of ego disorganization were likewise judged significantly better than chance ($p < .001$ in both cases). The accuracy of the narrative descriptions was also reported to be striking, but it was not evaluated statistically. Of 36 matchings, only 6 errors were made, a result that was again considerably better than chance ($p < .000002$).

Singer and Wynne (1966a) contrasted the Rorschach protocols of the parents of 19 schizophrenics, 20 neurotics, and 20 normals. The parents' protocols were scored according to the Singer and Wynne system and were contrasted as to total score and scores within the four categories (the three categories listed above and one additional category, negativism toward the testing task). The total score and all but one of the category scores (negativism) discriminated significantly between the parents of schizophrenics and the parents of nonschizophrenics. Interestingly, qualitative analysis of the category disruptive behavior revealed that the parents of schizophrenics tended to be covertly disruptive, whereas the parents of neurotics tended toward overt disruption.

General Evaluation

The scoring of communication defects and deviances is one of the few attempts to quantify contextual verbal behavior in an inkblot test. This system deals with a particularly novel Rorschach thrust, namely, the attempt to measure the specific defects in communication characteristic of the parents of schizophrenics. As such it is a highly original and theoretically interesting addition to the Rorschach literature.

The major criticism of the system is the dearth of adequate reliability data. It is strongly suggested that in the future collection of such data, correlation coefficients should be statistics of choice. The validity evidence presented for this system is quite convincing. Results thus far have been more than statistically significant: the precision of the scales in making discriminations seems quite impressive.

Although the system is a fascinating Rorschach application of work with schizophrenic families and therefore has considerable import in the understanding and treatment of schizophrenic illness, at this point the system has very limited application in the strictly psychodiagnostic domain. A possible future application of this system may be an investigation of the extent to which these defects in communication are generally characteristic of schizophrenic individuals. If such defects are found to be a general characteristic, the system or a modification thereof may prove to be a useful diagnostic adjunct to the approach discussed in the following chapter — that of pathological verbalizations.

9

Inkblot Measurement
of Pathological Verbalizations

The subject's general verbalizations during the test can be used as an indicator of pathological verbalization, which is particularly characteristic of, though not confined to, schizophrenic illness. Hermann Rorschach (1921/1942) first noted the occurrence of such responses in the test records of schizophrenics and mental defectives. Other Rorschachers (Levy & Beck, 1934; Piotrowski, 1937) have also noted the clinical significance of certain pathological verbalizations. It remained for Rapaport, Gill, and Schafer (1946), however, to put forward an extensive categorization of such responses. Although, as noted below, certain formal elements are sometimes intertwined in these categories, the verbalizations are the foremost element, and for that reason this inkblot category is included in the present volume.

As explained by Rapaport et al. (1946, 1968), this application of the Rorschach is an extension of the long-practiced psychiatric technique of using verbal interview behavior to elicit peculiarities of schizophrenic thought and speech (e.g., Bleuler, 1911/1950). The Rorschach test was seen by Rapaport as a vehicle that is even more sensitive than the psychiatric interview to this type of thinking. Many psychiatric authorities have also come to accept such evidence, gleaned from projective test data, as the most definitive evidence of schizophrenic illness (e.g., Knight, 1952).

In Holt's 1968 revised volume, Rapaport et al. listed 24 separate categories of pathological verbalizations as seen in the Rorschach test. Under the heading of *deviant verbalizations,* five categories were listed: fabulized responses, fabulized combinations, confabulations, contaminations, and autistic logic. Under the heading of *peculiar, queer, and related verbalizations,* five categories were given: peculiar verbalizations, queer verbalizations, vagueness, confusion, and incoherence. In a third *miscellaneous* group, there were 14 additional categories: symbolic responses, symmetry verbalization, relationship verbalization, verbalization of reference ideas, self-reference verbalizations, absurd responses, deterioration color responses, exactness verbalizations, criticism verbalizations, verbal aggression, aggression responses, self-depreciation verbalizations, affective verbalizations, and masturbation and castration verbalizations. The reader is referred to the revised Holt volume (1968) for a description of these scoring categories.

The Rapaport categories are clearly a heterogeneous lot, comprising as they do those that refer primarily to subjects' verbalizations (e.g., peculiar and queer verbalizations), others that involve a consideration of the thematic content of the responses (e.g., aggression responses), and still others that consider the perceptual characteristics of the response (e.g., the factors of location in the *confabulation* category and of color in the *deterioration color* response). Perhaps partly in response to the heterogeneity of the initial Rapaport presentation, much of the subsequent work in this area has striven to combine indications of pathological verbalizations into a single index; such work was stimulated by the early attempt of Watkins and Stauffacher (1952) to objectify the Rapaport categories. The reliance on single-index measures of pathological verbalizations has also been stimulated by the great infrequency of many of the individual categories.

Watkins and Stauffacher (1952) attempted to quantify some of the Rapaport categories of pathological verbalizations. Fifteen categories were selected for inclusion in the index. These authors arbitrarily assigned deviation or delta (Δ) values to these categories to weight them for the degree of disturbance indicated by each; higher values reflected greater pathology. The 15 categories and the assigned Δ values are listed below.

1. Fabulized responses .25
2. Fabulized combinations
   a. Spontaneously corrected or recognized .25
   b. Not corrected or recognized .50
3. Confabulations
   a. Extreme affect loading or specificity .50
   b. Farfetched elaboration 1.00
   c. DW 1.00
4. Contamination 1.00
5. Autistic logic 1.00

 6. Peculiar verbalizations   .25
 7. Queer verbalizations
    a. Usual   .50
    b. Extreme   1.00
 8. Vagueness   .25
 9. Confusion   .50
10. Incoherence   1.00
11. Overelaborate symbolism
    a. Moderate   .25
    b. Extreme   .50
12. Relationship verbalizations
    a. Between two percepts (same or different cards)   .25
    b. Within a series of cards
       (1) Corrected or recognized   .25
       (2) Not corrected or recognized   .50
13. Absurd responses   1.00
14. Deterioration color
    a. Pure color   1.00
    b. With form (CF)   .50
15. Mangled or distorted concepts   .25

Once a total score was derived for a subject, it was divided by the number of responses in the record. Two additional rules for scoring were provided by Watkins and Stauffacher: (1) If a response qualified for more than one of the items, it is scored only once, for the item with the highest weighting. (2) Scores are not given for additional responses.

Pope and Jensen (1957) suggested modifying the Δ scale to permit a 5-point rating of pathology for each response. These authors also prepared a detailed scoring manual with instructions and extensive lists of sample responses.

Holtzman et al. (1961) included the category *pathognomic verbalizations* (*V*) on the HIT, patterned after the Rapaport categories. Responses are scored for *V* on a 5-point scale ranging from 0 (no pathology present) to 4 (very bizarre verbalizations) to measure the degree of disordered thinking represented by fabulations, fabulized combinations, queer responses, incoherence, autistic logic, contaminations, self-references, deterioration color responses, and absurd responses. Holtzman allowed for one additional score independent of the main responses if there are side remarks or additional responses to the blot that have a pathognomic element. This addition results in a possible maximum score of 8 points on the *V*-scale for any one blot.

RELIABILITY AND VALIDITY OF THE SINGLE-INDEX
MEASURES OF PATHOLOGICAL THINKING

Reliability

Interscorer reliability. Watkins and Stauffacher (1952) had two examiners independently score the protocols of 25 normal, 25 neurotic, and 25 psychotic subjects. The resulting reliability coefficients were .04, .47, and .91 respectively. Very low frequencies and ranges of scores may have been factors in the low correlations found in the first two groups.

Powers and Hamlin (1955) also reported on the interscorer reliability for Δ. Two investigators independently scored 15 Rorschach protocols. A product–moment correlation of .88 was obtained. However the percentage of agreement was only 60 on specific responses. Powers and Hamlin also reported that the results of attempts to assign a response to a Δ category were even less satisfactory: "Seldom was a jointly scored response assigned to exactly the same category by both judges" (Power & Hamlin, (1955, p 122). They suggested that it may be largely impossible to score mildly deviant responses reliably.

Using 38 schizophrenic Rorschach protocols, Pope and Jensen (1957) found a rank order interscorer reliability coefficient of .85. These authors also noted poor consistency of response placements within Δ categories.

Holtzman et al. (1961) have reported on the interscorer reliability of the HIT *V* scale. With a sample of 40 schizophrenic protocols, two experienced scorers produced a coefficient of .96. The average coefficient for four less highly trained examiners with a college sample was .81. Whitaker (1965) has also found a coefficient of .81 for the HIT *V* scale.

Split-half reliability. Pope and Jensen (1957) explored the split-half reliability of the Δ scale using schizophrenic protocols. Their split was achieved by taking every other response throughout a test record. After correction with Spearman-Brown, the reliability coefficient was .52.

Holtzman et al. (1961) reported 15 split-half coefficients for their *V* scale. The coefficients ranged from .44 among housewives to .97 among schizophrenic subjects, with a median of .87.

Alternate form reliability. Holtzman et al. (1961) also explored the alternate form reliability of *V*, using Forms A and B of the HIT. On a college sample with a 1-week delay, they found a coefficient of .45; with a 1-year delay, the coefficient was .08. With a sample of eleventh graders and a 3-month delay, the coefficient was .43, and a coefficient of .24 was found among elementary school students with a 1-year delay. These four statistics are phi coefficients.

Validity

Watkins and Stauffacher (1952) explored the ability of their Δ index to differentiate between 25 normal, 25 neurotic, and 25 schizophrenic subjects. Unfortunately there is no indication that major demographic variables were controlled as part of the experimental design. In fact, the normal subjects were college students. Watkins and Stauffacher found that the Δ index significantly discriminated between the three groups $(p < .01)$.

Powers and Hamlin (1955) contrasted the Δ scores of 50 subjects who were equally divided among five clinical groups: socially adjusted subjects (normals), anxiety neurotics, latent schizophrenics, paranoid schizo-phrenics, and catatonic schizophrenics. The groups were chosen to repre-sent a continuum of schizophrenic disorganization, with the neurotics included because of the Watkins and Stauffacher (1952) findings on the elevated Δ scores of neurotics. These researchers apparently exercised great care in assigning diagnostic categories. Unfortunately they did not report the demographic characteristics of their groups and did not even indicate the sexes of their subjects. Powers and Hamlin found that the Δ values of the groups differed significantly $(p < .01)$. The following mean Δ scores were obtained: normals, -5.62; neurotics, -11.40; latent schizophrenics, -20.53; paranoid schizophrenics, -21.00; and catatonic schizophrenics, -33.50. The order of mean scores was exactly what Powers and Hamlin had predicted.

Pope and Jensen (1957) investigated the hypothesis that the Δ index could predict clinically observable changes in schizophrenic subjects over time. Fifteen subjects given insulin coma therapy, 14 given ECT, and 12 subjects who received routine hospital care were administered the Ror-schach test soon after hospital admission and approximately 3 months later. Psychiatric ratings of clinical change were carried out. Although the Δ score of the combined group of 41 patients did drop significantly after treatment $(p < .01)$, the three groups taken individually did not demonstrate declines in Δ that reached significance at the .05 level. Delta changes did not prove to be related to the ratings of clinical change. Pope and Jensen suggested that the notoriously poor reliability of psychiatric ratings may have been a causative factor in the latter findings. Finally these investigators reported that the Δ index correlated at -.46 $(p < .01)$ with $F + \%$ among the combined group of schizophrenics.

In the Kataguchi (1959) investigation discussed in an earlier chapter, the Δ index was also included in the differentiation between schizophrenic, neurotic, and normal subjects. Kataguchi modified the index by adding a category of perseveration, omitting the vagueness category, and combining several other categories. The author determined that Δ% significantly discriminated between the schizophrenic and the neurotic and normal groups. Kataguchi did not contrast the neurotics with the normals. The Δ% for schizophrenics was 17.70, for neurotics 5.15, and for normals 1.80.

Quirk and coworkers (1962) compared Δ% in 20 normal, 20 neurotic, 20 acute psychotic, and 20 chronic psychotic males. The four groups were matched on educational level. Although the authors stated that all subjects were between 20 and 40 years of age, the groups were apparently not equated on age. They found that Δ% significantly differentiated the normals and neurotics from the schizophrenic subjects ($p < .01$), but with a high degree of error. "There would be considerable error arising from the attempt to use this index for purposes of clinical prediction" (Quirk et al., 1962, p 435). These authors also remarked that the psychotic subjects differed from the other groups in total R, a fact that might have contributed to a spurious differentiation between the groups. Quirk et al. went on to suggest and to validate a list of 10 signs that might be useful in the diagnosis of schizophrenia.

The inclusion of the V scale on the HIT has resulted in a proliferation of empirical data on this scale. One study (Whitaker, 1965) investigated the relationship between the HIT V scale and V as scored on the Rorschach test. A scorer arrived at a correlation of .94 between the HIT and the Rorschach V scores of 45 psychiatric inpatients.

Several studies have found the HIT V scale to be related to various measures of psychopathology. First it should be noted that factor-analytic work with the HIT has linked V to pathology factors. Holtzman et al. (1961) found V to load heavily on Factor III, which these authors interpreted as an indication of "psychopathology of thought processes and emotional disturbances revealed in fantasy productions" (Holtzman et al., 1961, p 158). Moseley, Duffey, and Sherman (1963) submitted the HIT, the Inpatient Multidimensional Psychiatric Scale (IMPS), and the MMPI to factor analysis. The subjects were 82 neurotic depressive or psychotic depressive patients. The V scale had a significant loading on what was interpreted as a "withdrawal and disorientation" factor, along with IMPS disorientation and grandiose expansiveness, and HIT Sex responses and Form Appropriateness.

Megargee and Swartz (1968) correlated various HIT variables with the Extraversion (E) and the Neuroticism (N) scales of the Maudsley Personality Inventory. Among the 89 college subjects, Megargee and

Swartz found that V correlated at .23 ($p < .05$) with the Maudsley N scale.

Two studies have related V to measures of process-reactive schizophrenia. Steffy and Becker (1961) found V to correlate significantly with the Elgin scale; Ullmann and Eck (1965) determined that V also correlated significantly with the Ullmann-Giovannoni scale ($r = .39$, $p < .005$). In both cases the process schizophrenics were characterized by higher V scores.

Comparing the HIT scores of four clinic samples with the appropriate validational data reported by Holtzman et al. (1961), Morgan (1968) found that children being seen in a clinic had significantly higher V scores than Holtzman's elementary school subjects ($p < .05$). However, the comparability of Morgan's samples to those of Holtzman is open to some question.

In an investigation of the reading improvement of 24 elementary school students enrolled in a reading clinic (Krippner, 1967), V was found to correlate significantly with the degree of reading improvement ($r = -.96$, $p < .01$). However, because age was not controlled in this study, this correlation may be spuriously high.

Three studies using the V-scale suggest that in some cases elevated V may indicate creative rather than pathological processes, a suggestion reminiscent of Kris's (1952) concept of regression in the service of the ego. Using the Myers-Briggs Type Indicator, Richter and Winter (1966) compared 15 female college subjects with high creative potential to 15 with low potential. The subjects were matched for age and verbal ability. These investigators found that the subjects with high creative potential had significantly higher V scores ($p < .025$).

In the second study in this vein, Herron (1964) administered the HIT to 90 college subjects with the standard instructions, and to a second group of 90 with an instructional set that presented the HIT as a measure of intellectual ability. Under the latter instructional set, a significantly lower V was found ($p < .05$). Herron interpreted this and other results as evidence that the intelligence test condition constricted cognitive processes.

Hartung, McKenna, and Baxter (1969) tested the prediction that a loose and imaginative rather than a constrained and constricted test-taking attitude would result in higher V scores. Thirty-one college subjects were group administered the Rorschach test with "free-wheeling" instructions: subjects were told to "let their imagination go." A second group of 28 students was administered the test with an "up-tight" instructional set: subjects were admonished to observe the blots carefully. Unfortunately the subjects were self-selected by enrollment in the different classes — one a class in introductory psychology, the other in adolescent psychology. No contrasts were made to ensure comparability of the groups on relevant control variables. Three responses were obtained for each blot, and eight of the nine V categories were scored. (Absurd response was not scored because of the absence of location data.) Chi square tests revealed a significant difference in only the self-reference category ($p < .025$, one-tailed test) in the predicted direction.

This study and particularly the Richter and Winter (1966) and Herron (1964) investigations suggest that V cannot be viewed solely in terms of pathology. Holtzman et al. have remarked that the subject's awareness of the deviant character of the response must also be taken into account. "Generally when a normal subject gives an autistic response he shows some awareness of the liberties he is taking in letting his imagination run unfettered by ego control" (Holtzman et al., 1961, p 54).

Relationships of V with age and with IQ have been demonstrated in several studies. Thorpe and Swartz (1965) investigated the extent to which V and other HIT scores varied with increasing age. Five age groups were used, ranging from 5-year-old preschool children to college students from 18 to 22 years of age. The groups contained equal numbers of males and females (total N = 586). There were neither significant sex differences nor sex-by-age interactions for V. However V did significantly decline and then rise again with age.

A follow-up study by Thorpe and Swartz (1966) used three age groups whose respective ages were 6.7, 9.7, and 12.7 years. Each group contained 60 males and 60 females. V scores were found to decrease monotonically and significantly with age. It should be noted that the later rise in V observed by Thorpe and Swartz (1965) would not have been expected in the 1966 study, because 12.7 was the oldest age group sampled by Thorpe and Swartz (1966). However, in a study carried out with Mexican subjects, Swartz, Tapia, and Thorpe (1967) did not find V to vary significantly with age. The subjects of this investigation were 300 school children in Mexico City at three age levels: 6 years and 8 months, 9 years and 8 months, and 12 years and 8 months.

Swartz, and associates (1971) investigated the relationship of several HIT categories to IQ level. The protocols of 96 subjects were selected from the HIT standardization samples. Three groups of 24 mentally retarded subjects were included. Each group had a different IQ range. Twenty-four normal subjects were also included. The groups were matched for sex and chronological age. No sex differences were found with respect to V, but V was determined to decrease significantly with increasing intelligence ($p < .001$).

THE MEANING OF PARTICULAR CATEGORIES
OF PATHOLOGICAL VERBALIZATION

In recent years a perceptible shift has taken place in interest in the inkblot measurement of pathological verbalization. Recent investigations have dealt to a greater extent with the specific meaning and usefulness of each particular category rather than with a composite measure derived by summing up heterogeneous categories. This shift seems to reflect a recognition that the various categories may differ in their implications, and information may therefore be lost because of reliance on a summary index. Investigators have also constructed additional categories not posited by Rapaport et al. (1946).

Rapaport et al. (1946) reported on differences between various clinical groups in their delineated categories of response. Their presentation, however, was quite inadequate from the standpoint of research: Holt deleted the research portions of the text in his 1968 revision. Numbered among its shortcomings are the small sample groups, some of which were so minimal that no inferences can legitimately be drawn from them. Furthermore there was no real effort to control a number of potential co-variables, such as intelligence, education, socioeconomic status, or even sex and age. The research is also seriously flawed because the investigators failed to recognize that the number of responses is a major contributing variable to some of the results obtained. Rapaport et al. did endeavor to assess their populations very thoroughly in an attempt to undercut the marked heterogeneity that is typically subsumed by the label of schizophrenia. Their shotgun method of statistical testing, however, casts considerable doubt on some of the statistically significant differences they report; a number of their findings could have resulted from chance factors alone. Given all these considerations, the present authors have decided not to resurrect the Rapaport findings in the current presentation.

In a later investigation of individual categories, Jortner (1966) studied nine separate thought process categories to determine their validity in the diagnosis of schizophrenia. Six of the nine categories were invented by Jortner: impossible, supernatural, ancient, combining realms arbitrarily, inside and outside, and symbol responses. Three HIT thought process categories were adopted from the research literature: abstract, self-reference, and contaminations. These nine HIT categories were contrasted with two interview ratings (poor reality testing and disturbances in thought processes) in a group of 90 psychiatric patients. Jortner also explored the ability of the various categories to differentiate between 25 schizophrenics (13 males, 12 females), 24 nonschizophrenics (20 males, 4 females), and 23 possible schizophrenics (10 males, 13 females). The three groups were equated for age, education, race, religion, vocational background, marital status, IQ, and number of responses to the HIT. Sex was determined to be unrelated to the scoring categories used in this study.

The HIT scores were also related to HIT factor scores, to one another, and to other scales including those of the MMPI. Three of the HIT categories — impossible, abstract, and combining realms arbitrarily — appeared to be consistently good measures of mental illness. Each of these correlated significantly with the Sc scale of the MMPI and correlated to a very high degree (.75 or higher) with the psychopathology factor of the HIT. All three of these scales also had high scoring reliability (.93, .94, and .93 respectively). Six of the nine HIT scales, including the three scales mentioned above, differentiated significantly between the schizophrenic and nonschizophrenic subjects. All nine of Jortner's HIT scales correlated significantly with the HIT V scale; the highest correlations were again found with the three highly successful scales. Eight of the nine HIT scales correlated significantly with the interview ratings of poor reality testing, whereas seven of the scales correlated significantly with the ratings of thought disturbance. By specifying cutoffs using the HIT scales, these investigators were able to diagnose 21 of the 25 schizophrenics correctly. All of the 24 nonschizophrenics were diagnosed correctly.

Using the categories comprising the HIT V scale, Swartz (1969) contrasted normal, schizophrenic, depressed, and mentally retarded subjects. The subject pool in this study included 550 normal subjects (school children, firemen and adult women), 106 paranoid schizophrenic subjects, 90 depressed patients, and 148 retarded individuals. From this subject pool Swartz drew six matched samples that contrasted all six possible combinations of these groups. Contrast groups were equated as closely as possible for sex, age, number of rejections, and total V score. Swartz found that significantly more normal subjects gave fabulation and fabulized combination responses than the schizophrenics, whereas significantly more schizophrenics gave contamination responses. When normals were contrasted with retardates, significantly more normals gave fabulation, fabulized combination, and queer responses, and significantly fewer normals gave absurd responses. Significantly more schizophrenics gave self-reference responses and significantly fewer gave absurd responses than the retarded group. Significantly more depressives gave self-reference responses than normals. Swartz also found that significantly more depressives produced fabulation and significantly fewer produced autistic logic responses than the schizophrenics. In contrast to retarded subjects, depressives gave significantly more fabulation, fabulized combination, and self-reference responses and significantly fewer gave autistic logic and absurd responses.

Swartz (1969) concluded that the significance of the divers V categories varied, and that the meaning of the categories was often not in accord with expectations set forth by Rapaport and other clinical workers. Although the chronicity of the schizophrenic group in this study (the average length of hospitalization was 10.5 years) might have limited the usefulness of these categories in the diagnosis of schizophrenia (see Dudek, 1969), what is particularly disturbing in Swartz's findings is the high percentage with which certain of these categories occurred in the normal samples. Ninety-eight percent of the normals who were contrasted with the mental retardates gave at least one fabulized combination re-response. Sixty percent of those normals who were contrasted with schizophrenics gave at least one queer response. Although these percentages do not take into account the number of such responses occurring in a test record or the degree of deviance of the verbalization, they do suggest that the clinician must exercise particular care in regarding such responses as pathognomonic of schizophrenia or other serious mental disorder.

Blatt and Ritzler (1974) selected groups of patients with instances of contamination, confabulation, and fabulized combination in their Rorschach test protocols. Additional groups were included with both contaminations and confabulations, with both confabulations and fabulized combinations, and with combination responses. Many of the test protocols were chosen from Rapaport's (1946) reported data. Level of boundary disruption was theorized as a continuum from the most severe (contamination) to the least severe (combination). A chi square analysis proved this classification of the patients to be significantly related to judgment of psychotic versus nonpsychotic disturbance, as indicated in hospital records. Severity of boundary disturbance, indicated by the type of pathological Rorschach response, was also found to be significantly related to impairment in complex cognitive functions (as measured by WAIS subtests and the Object Sorting test), degree of contact with conventional reality (as measured by Rorschach $F\%$, $F+\%$, D, P, and rare detail responses), degree of affective control (as measured by Rorschach determinants), involvement in disruptive behavior and interpersonal relationships (as rated by nurses and a scoring of intact versus disrupted Rorschach human responses), and responsiveness to therapeutic intervention.

Quinlan and associates (1972) assessed 71 schizophrenic and non-schizophrenic hospitalized patients on three Rorschach scales of thought disorder: disruption of logical thought (TQ), irrelevant or personalized associations (AE), and elaboration in affective terms (OS). In an initial study of reliability using 38 protocols, the respective reliability coefficients for the three scales were .65, .67, and .58. (Reliability was computed for the TQ scale after minor deviations were excluded.) On a subsequent sample of 20 protocols, the interscorer reliability coefficients were found to improve, with practice, to .79, .92, and .90 respectively. All three scales were found to discriminate significantly between schizophrenics and neurotic depressives ($p < .05$). All three scales proved to be significantly related to other Rorschach indices of thought disturbance (form level, fabulized combinations, and the Holt and Havel [1960] scale of drive content). Two of the three scales (TQ and OS) also correlated significantly with clinical ratings of bizarre behavior.

Quinlan and Harrow (1974) investigated primitive thought indicators from a boundary perspective, focusing on four such thought indices: contaminations, fabulized combinations, and the Fisher and Cleveland Barrier and Penetration scores discussed in an earlier chapter. The subjects of this study were 171 psychiatric patients, of whom 48 were schizophrenics, 35 latent schizophrenics, 38 subjects with personality and character disorders, 38 depressives, and 12 subjects with other diagnoses. Quinlan and Harrow found that contaminations and fabulized combinations were more consistently related to other Rorschach measures of thought disturbance (thought quality, affect elaboration, overspecificity, form level, and Holt's drive content index) than were the Barrier and Penetration scales. Contaminations and fabulized combinations were also sporadically related to questionnaire and therapist ratings of psychopathology and patients' length of hospitalization. (Seven of 14 correlations were significant.) Barrier and Penetration were not significantly related to any of these pathology measures.

The thought process indicators also proved useful in diagnosis, with contaminations markedly different across diagnostic groups. The schizophrenics gave significantly more contamination responses than any other group. Fabulized combinations were also highly different across groups, with schizophrenics and latent schizophrenics giving significantly more of these responses than depressive subjects. In the Penetration category, depressives were significantly lower than schizophrenics, latent schizophrenics, and subjects with personality disorders. The Barrier scores of the groups did not differ. Quinlan and Harrow concluded that the contamination and the fabulized combination responses were particularly useful measures of psychopathology, and that contaminations were strongly associated with schizophrenia. However these authors warn against assuming that contaminations and contamination tendencies are found solely among schizophrenics, because 25 percent of their nonschizophrenic patients gave this reponse one or more times.

As part of a larger study, Dudek (1969) contrasted 54 ambulatory schizophrenics and 54 matched neurotic subjects. Among the Rorschach indices used were a pathological reasoning category (including position responses, confabulations, and peculiar logic) and perseveration. The schizophrenics manifested significantly more of both types of responses ($p < .01$). Dudek also found that the pathological reasoning type of response occured exclusively in the schizophrenic sample, among 70 percent of the schizophrenic subjects. None of the nonschizophrenics manifested this type of response. The greatest incidence of this sign was among the schizophrenic subjects with high IQs. Dudek also noted that few pathological reasoning responses were seen among a group of 28 chronic schizophrenics. Thus she concluded, in accordance with a suggestion in a personal communication from Piotrowski, that this sign may be present only in early schizophrenia.

In a study by Bower, Testin, and Roberts (1960), two measures of the thought processes were investigated for diagnostic effectiveness: a disorganization scale, and an arbitrary tightening scale. Items classified as disorganized included poor form quality, generalized conclusions about the similarity of two perceptions when the blot areas did not support such inferences, and loss of a logical progression of ideas, as shown by rambling, flighty, or peculiar verbalizations. Items classified on the arbitrary tightening scale were those involving farfetched relationships between objects, absurdly overspecific, concrete, or literal perception of objects, defensiveness evidenced in accusatory, hypercritical, or rejecting statements, and unsolicited, semi-pertinent discussion about the process of arriving at an association to a blot. The thought process scoring was found to differentiate catatonics from other groups; the catatonics scored high on disorganization. Obsessives scored low on disorganization, whereas paranoids scored high on arbitrary tightening. The thought process scales were not effective overall in differentiating depressive subjects.

Although the nature of most studies of pathological verbalizations can be easily classified as either molar or molecular — that is, as dealing either with a summary index measure or with the differing meanings of the various categories of responses — one study has actually taken an intermediate approach. Powers and Hamlin (1958) noted the poor intracategory scoring reliability of the Δ index and suggested reordering the Rapaport (1946) categories under four general rubrics: intellectual organization, deviant content, inappropriate increase or loss of distance, and affective responses.

Using 75 subjects (25 normals, 25 neurotics, and 25 schizophrenics) and controlling for race and sex while "roughly" controlling for age, IQ, education, and Rorschach R, these authors contrasted the three groups on their four categories of response. Of the 12 possible group contrasts, 6 were statistically significant, 5 in the predicted direction. When a total score was applied, all three groups were significantly differentiated from one another. The most effective tool for differentiating the groups proved to be a combination of the categories of intellectual organization and inappropriate increase or loss of distance: a particular cutoff score correctly identified 19 of the 25 schizophrenics and misidentified only 1 normal subject and 2 neurotics. The interscorer reliability coefficients for the four broad categories were determined to be .57, .68, .81, and .89, respectively.

GENERAL EVALUATION

The reliability data on the single indices of pathological verbalizations Δ and V) are difficult to evaluate because of the infrequency of such responses in nonpathological populations, thus resulting in truncated ranges of these scores. Among schizophrenic subjects the interscorer reliability of the scales has certainly been shown to be satisfactory. As with other scales discussed earlier in this volume, it is questionable whether Δ and V should be expected to have high split-half reliability. However the substantial gap between the split-half and delayed alternate form coefficients reported for the V scale of the HIT suggests that the temporal stability of this scale may be a problem. If such is the case, these scales may be too unreliable for most clinical use.

The validity data on these scales are encouraging; it has been demonstrated that they differentiate significantly between clinical groups, though with a high degree of overlap, and that they are associated with psychopathological factors, neuroticism, and type of schizophrenic illness. The scales do thus appear to be associated with pathological thinking, though there are some indications that the V scale may also be indicative of creative processes and of a lessening of constrictive mechanisms (Hartung et al., 1969; Herron, 1964; Richter & Winter, 1966).

As noted above, recent studies on pathological verbalizations have moved in the direction of investigating the differential diagnostic meaningfulness of the various categories. As admirably demonstrated by Jortner (1966), Swartz (1969), and others, the diagnostic meanings of the various categories appear to differ considerably. Some categories seem to be associated most closely with schizophrenic illness (notably contaminations and autistic logic responses), whereas other categories (especially fabulations and fabulized combinations) are apparently not uncommon among normal subjects. Queer responses (Swartz, 1969) have been shown to be particularly associated with mental retardation. The fact that the categories of primitive thinking do so differ in their clinical implications is a strong justification for the shift in emphasis from single-index studies. The use of a summary statistic such as V or Δ may thus muddy the diagnostic waters instead of helping to clear them.

In a clinical context, the psychologist is typically faced with the problem of differential diagnosis, that is, with a decision between two alternate diagnoses or the simultaneous presence of two or more diagnoses. Thus the psychologist may have to determine whether a thought disorder is present in addition to observed mental retardation. In reaching such day-to-day diagnostic decisions, the single-scale measures of pathological verbalizations are likely to be of little help, as demonstrated by the fairly high degree of overlap found between diagnostic groups. Further study of the diagnostic implications of each category seems likely to yield the most useful information for future clinical purposes, although the infrequency with which many of the categories occur is likely to prove a hindrance. As noted by Dudek (1969), future studies in this area should not overlook the influence of intelligence and chronicity in mediating the diagnostic meaningfulness of the categories. Dudek's (1969) extraordinary findings indicate that although this area of Rorschach analysis is still largely experimental, it seems to hold more strictly diagnostic promise than any other scoring approach discussed in this volume.

Rapaport (1946) initially conceived of these categories in terms of the distance the subject is able to maintain from the blots. "We may profitably conceive of the reality of the testing situation in terms of the distance maintained by the subject between himself and the inkblot" (Rapaport et al., 1946, p 329). As was mentioned by Holt (1968), this theoretical conceptualization has not withstood the test of time: it does not appear to adequately account for and link the diverse categories of deviant verbalizations.

An alternative theoretical viewpoint has been put forward by Blatt and Ritzler (1974), whose theory seems to show a greater capacity for forging a link between the many observed categories of pathological verbalizations. These authors theorized that many characteristics of thought disorder can be understood as aspects of a general disturbance in the ability to establish boundaries and to maintain distinctions between discrete events and objects, including self versus non-self. Such a conceptualization is consistent with much that is already known of schizophrenic thought processes, for example, the deficiencies in ego boundaries in schizophrenics (Bellak & Loeb, 1969). In addition this conceptualization logically links such diverse categories of pathological verbalizations as self-reference responses, contaminations, and perseverations. Self-reference responses may then be understood as the inability to separate the personal domain from the objective; contaminations may be conceptualized as the result of the blurring of boundaries between discrete percepts; and perseverations may be viewed as the result of the loss of distinction between diverse blots or blot areas.

This theoretical viewpoint is also consistent with the psychological theory of Werner (1948), which sees increasing capacity in the ability to differentiate and integrate stimuli as a major element in cognitive ontogenesis. Werner viewed conscious experience as initially syncretic, then as increasingly sorted into discrete categories with the progressive differentiation in thinking that occurs with maturation. Werner compared the thinking of psychotics with that of children in this regard. Conceptualizing the pathological implications of deviant verbalizations in terms of a breakdown in the ability to discriminate between discrete objects, percepts, etc., thus seems to be valuable both because such a concept convincingly links the diverse manifestations of pathological verbalizations, and because it ties in with general theoretical conceptions in psychology.

10

The Interpretation of Individual Psychodynamics

As was seen in the preceding chapters, scoring Rorschach content in terms of certain categories of responses can result in valid judgments about test subjects. In addition to this psychometric approach to content, however, there is another approach to the understanding of Rorschach content which, if not as well represented in the research literature, is more often practiced by the clinician. This other technique of content interpretation focuses on the individual dynamic meaning of Rorschach responses. What is of interest here is the patient's unique self-concept, his idiosyncratic view of the world, his unique perceptions of important figures in his environment, and his major personality conflicts as evidenced in his Rorschach protocol. Particularly in the area of unique self-concept, the Rorschach often evokes symbols that are interpretable by an examiner trained in psychoanalytic theory.

An example of this alternate technique of content interpretation is seen in the following response, and in associations to the response garnered through a procedure discussed in Chapter 12. The subject was a 45-year-old divorced female with complaints of depression who was seeking outpatient psychotherapy.

Response to Card II: It looks like a . . . a black orchid.

Associations: It reminds me of a . . . beautiful orchid that a gentleman friend gave me many years ago . . . But this one is black . . . and . . . it looks like it's wilting around the edges.

In only a few words, this woman has managed to convey her image of herself as decaying, depressed, and no longer attractive, as well as her strong narcissistic needs.

The extent to which self-concept responses predominate among the psychodynamically meaningful responses on the Rorschach was demonstrated by Hertzman and Pearce (1947). These authors classified the idiosyncratic human responses of a group of 12 patients into seven categories. The patients had been seen in psychotherapy, and the interpretable Rorschach responses were classified in seven categories based on information about the patients derived from the therapy. Fifty-three percent of the dynamically interpretable responses were in the category of self-identification. A further 23 percent were responses in which the self-concept was partially involved. Thus these investigators found that 76 percent of the interpretable responses involved the patients' self-concepts.

Many psychologists have lauded the ability of the Rorschach to reveal these unique aspects of the individual personality. For example, Schafer has noted that "the Rorschach test is so often . . . dramatically revealing of the adaptive and defensive strengths and weaknesses of the patient, his pathological trends, his conscious and unconscious values, yearnings, fears, wrath, guilt and joy, and the overall color and tone of his personality" (Schafer, 1954, p 113). McArthur remarked that

> The Rorschach and the TAT . . . are the only techniques in all of psychology . . . that take as their goal to discover what, in fact, the relevant dimensions for understanding John Jones may be, given the common sense assumption that John Jones does not obey the laws that govern Abel Harriman. The Rorschach is unique among psychological techniques in that it takes seriously the mission of entering John Jones' and Abel Harriman's worlds. (McArthur, 1972, p 443)

The distinction between the psychometric approach to content and the individual psychodynamic approach is similar to Allport's distinction (1937; 1961) between the nomothetic and the idiographic study of personality. Nomothetic methods have as their aim the discovery of general laws. Idiographic methods pertain to the thorough study of a particular event or individual. Bellak (1954) pointed out that projective techniques in general, and the Rorschach test in particular, can be used in these two ways, nomothetically and idiographically. When the test is used nomothetically, "the goal — extremely valuable in part, and in part carried over from the brass-instrument laboratory concepts of the 'average' person, and from statistically oriented psychometrics — is to arrive at criteria which are applicable to groups of people or to syndromes" (Bellak, 1954, p 280). When it is used idiographically, "one would be satisfied to describe Mr. Jones as a unique specimen who perceives configurations in a certain way and tends to control his impulses under given circumstances, generally constituting a uniqueness of functioning which will not be exactly duplicated by any other individual" (Bellak, 1954, p 280).

The contrasting types of information yielded by these two approaches can be seen very graphically in the following two Rorschach percepts.

1.   A withdrawn young male psychiatric inpatient who lives with a domineering wife and mother-in-law gives the following as one of his responses to Card V: "It looks like a rabbit in the middle, with two big heavy women leaning on him."

2.   A child who is being considered for placement in a foster home in order to remove him from a chaotic and destructive home environment sees the following scene in Card X: "Two monsters separated by a little boy. He doesn't know he's doing it, but once he's gone the monsters may kill each other."

Both of these responses may be scored for various content themes, themes such as anxiety, hostility, and dependency. With summary scores, the subjects could be compared with other test subjects in the extent to which such content themes are present in their Rorschach protocols. The objective of the idiographic approach is quite different. It focuses on intensive understanding of the individual case and what is revealed of the subject's self-concept and his unique pattern of viewing himself and his surroundings. Such an approach would concern itself with the first subject's view of himself as a weak and helpless creature being overwhelmed by his interactions at home, and with the second subject's secret fear of what might happen were he to leave his home.

Clearly, this approach to the interpretation of content leans heavily on psychoanalytic theory with its emphasis on unconscious personality dynamics and the intensive investigation of the individual case. As noted by Schafer (1954), the Rorschach response process is then viewed as simply a special instance of thought processes in general. Similar to dreams, Rorschach percepts may be used as a port of direct entry into the psychodynamics of the test subject, though the technique of symbol interpretation. "Dreams and Rorschach responses are or may be microcosmic expressions of the macrocosmic trends and conflicts in the personality" (Schafer, 1954, p 105).

The range of possible dynamic elements that can be revealed in inkblot responses runs the gamut of human personality. In general, however, we have observed five broad classes of responses that predominate.

1. Responses that reveal the self-concept
2. Responses that reveal the subject's attitudes toward significant others (parents, spouses, etc.) in the environment
3. Responses that reflect the subject's perceptions of his environment, both social and otherwise
4. Major concerns of the subject as revealed in test responses
5. Conflicts that the subject is experiencing

Typically, when the latter four types of responses occur, the patient's self-concept is intertwined with these other dynamic elements. It is also very common for combinations of these elements to be presented simultaneously as a gestalt in a test response, as the subject actually experiences them in his life. The following are some examples of Rorschach responses in which one of these five elements is dominant. As in the response presented earlier, the associations were elicited by a procedure discussed in Chapter 12.

SELF-CONCEPT RESPONSES

These are the most common dynamically meaningful responses we have found in Rorschach protocols. Perhaps because of the population with which we have worked (patients seeking help), negative aspects of the self-concept seem to predominate, although responses characterized by grandiose self-concept are also sometimes seen. Hertzman and Pearce (1947) have similarly commented on the tendency of the Rorschach to elicit negative aspects of the self-concept.

The following response to Card VII was elicited from a 30-year-old artist.

Response: It looks like melted snow patches . . . with that city grit in it.

Associations: It makes me remember glaciers, from where I used to live . . . It doesn't melt in the summer, because of the grit in it. It's like an unresolved thing. It hasn't been digested . . . it exists after it should have melted. [What does that have to do with your life?] My inability to get over my protected childhood and my relationship with my brother . . . to free myself from past memories and disappointments.

In this response, the patient vividly presents himself as someone who has not gotten over what he should have by now — his strong dependency, hostility to his brother, etc. Seeing himself as immutably cold is also implied in this response.

The following percept and associations were made in response to Card VI by a 25-year-old patient hospitalized for depression.

Response: A flower . . . not the ordinary type . . . an odd flower . . . It has a device for capturing insects.

Associations: Documentaries that I've seen on TV showing a flower capturing an insect. [What might that reflect in your life?] Sometimes . . . my feeling of . . . I capture people sometimes . . . I make them get involved with me . . . and either I end up regretting it, if I don't dig them, or I end up being alone. Yet I treat them good.

In this response the patient describes his tendency to trap people into relationships with him, and the unfortunate results of such interpersonal relationships.

The response to Card III that follows was seen in the test record of a 28-year-old depressed female patient.

Response: The head of a man, looking down.

Associations: He's ashamed. [Makes you think of?] He's thinking that he hurt others. [What does that make you think of in your own life?] I feel guilty every time I get into arguments with someone . . . I feel like I'm the whole cause of the thing.

In this response the patient's abashed self-concept is foremost; it is possible that suppressed hostility (desire to hurt others) is the basis of this difficulty.

The Greenwich Village sample that provided the protocols discussed in this volume has a disproportionate number of responses indicating confused sexual identification, a special type of self-concept response. The following response to Card III was made by a 26-year-old bisexual male anxiety neurotic.

Response: Two little drunk clowns with pudgy noses. It's funny because . . . the two people seem to have their sexes confused . . . they have breasts but they also have penises.

Associations: It makes me think of some bisexual tendencies I've done. I went to bed with men . . . used to get blow jobs from men. But I wasn't confused — I always played the male part.

This response highlights both sexual confusion and the patient's denial of it.

Responses indicating a grandiose self-concept are also sometimes seen. The following was a response to Card IV by a 29-year-old schizophrenic lawyer.

Response: Someone sitting sort of grandly . . . though the head is kind of freaky.

Associations: It's frightening . . . the head is frightening. It doesn't resemble anything that I know . . . just a freaky head. [What does sitting grandly make you think of?] Presumptiousness — but not necessarily the negative connotation. [What does it remind you of?] Myself. [But not in a negative sense?] Assumption rather than presumption. I like myself.

This response illustrates both the patient's grandiose self-concept and his awareness of mental disorder.

ATTITUDES TOWARD SIGNIFICANT OTHERS

Most commonly attitudes toward parents, particularly the mother, fall into this category. The following is a response to Card I elicited from a 29-year-old male homosexual patient with complaints of depression and disorganization.

Response: It looks like a devil kind of thing . . . but not a real devil . . . something superficial . . . like a woman . . with her hands up in the air . . . having a lot of power over something . . . maybe over me . . . or some person.

Associations: It reminds me of somebody always telling me something to do . . . a lot of tension and yelling. [What does that call to mind?] It calls to mind a lot of things that happened in my past . . . [?] Like my mother, telling me what to do . . . but in a nice way . . . trying to help me.

In this response the patient projects his malevolent image of women in general and his mother in particular. The patient is also defending against his hostility toward his mother.

The following percept was elicited on Card VII from a 22-year-old male subject complaining of difficulty controlling his anger.

Response: Here, I'm looking at another vagina . . . and this one is sealed [laughs].

Associations: Makes me think of a virgin or something you can't get into — a tight cunt. [What does that make you think of?] A bitch. [What do you think of then?] Something that I hate. [What does that remind you of?] [pause] Something stupid . . . something that believes they're born to be subordinate. [who?] Anybody . . . could even be my own mother . . . she was subordinate. But I didn't hate my mother . . . my hatred only came after a number of experiences with women.

In this thread of associations, the patient displays his anger at his mother (despite his denial) and at women in general, for what he perceives as their inaccessibility. The patients also displays resentment toward his mother for her self-assumed subservient role.

The response that follows is a Card II percept from a 24-year-old black male office worker whose musical ambitions were thwarted by his mother.

Response: It looks like an old lady who might have fallen from a great height . . . she's splattered on the sidewalk [laughs].

Associations: It reminds me of accidents, mostly. Also, old age and death. You can't avoid accidents . . . and you can't avoid getting old.

This response points to considerable hostility toward the mother (note the laughter), hostility that does not appear to be acknowledged consciously.

The following responses to Card II were given by a 28-year-old female patient hospitalized following a histrionic suicide gesture.

Response: Two old women having a coffee klatch . . . Dogs looking out of a window and seeing two people fighting outside.

Associations: When I was a little girl . . . my mother was born in Germany . . . she and her friend would go in the kitchen and talk in German . . . I'd never know what they would talk about. [What does that make you think of?] Mixed feelings . . . glad she wasn't bothering me . . . but she wasn't there when I wanted to bother her. My sister and I watching my mother and her friend in the kitchen . . . feeling closed out . . . window represents the fact that they were speaking German.

These responses demonstrate the patient's alienation from her mother as well as her ambivalent attitudes toward her (she wants more closeness but is afraid of what that might entail.)

**RESPONSES REFLECTIVE OF THE SUBJECT'S
PERCEPTIONS OF HIS ENVIRONMENT,
BOTH SOCIAL AND OTHERWISE**

The following Rorschach percepts were elicited from a 19-year-old anorexic girl in response to Cards IV and VII.

Response to Card IV: It looks like the bottom of a scarecrow ... and the post that it's leaning on.

Associations: A farm ... a farmer. [Reminds you of?] Fields with corn ... it's nice. [What do crows make you think of?] All the crows pecked away so much at the top that they destroyed it. [What do you think of then?] Crows are just like people ... they kill them just like people do to people. [What do you mean?] People take advantage of people, use them, to see what they can get out of them.

Response to Card VII: Two lambs standing on icebergs ... their heads are turned around the wrong way ... they're twisted.

Associations: Reminds me of something soft, nice. [What do icebergs make you think of?] Icebergs shouldn't be there ... something cold against a nice thing. The iceberg will break, they'll go off in different directions ... but lambs should be in a flock.

In these two responses the patient's perceptions of her environment are strongly fused with her self-concept. She expresses distrust of people who are perceived as out to use her and possibly destroy her. She expresses her sense of innocence and helplessness, her growing isolation from others, and yet her wish for closeness with others.

What follows is a response to Card I made by a 43-year-old male patient complaining of depression, social isolation, and apathy.

Response: It's a large beetle being attacked by killer moths.

Associations: It reminds me of the life-and-death struggle of the animal and insect world. [What does that make you think of?] The turbulence and danger that nature imposes on life. [What does it make you think of in your own life?] I've spent as much time with animals in my life as I have with people.

In this percept and associations the subject expresses his isolation from people and his view of life and social relations as a vicious struggle.

MAJOR CONCERNS OF THE SUBJECT

This highly heterogeneous category includes health concerns, major fears, and the like.

The following responses were made by a 38-year-old white homosexual who was convinced (incorrectly) that he was becoming prematurely senile.

Response to Card I: Two haughty D.A.R.-type matrons . . . arguing over something . . . trying to take the thing in the middle away from each other. Their feathers are molting.

Associations: I think I've been . . . intimidated by certain women . . . at business. I don't know how to react maturely to certain women. [What does molting remind you of?] Reminds me of a pillow losing its down. [What do pillows make you think of?] Also, maybe the loss of youth. [What do you think of then?] Loss of looks and virility . . . growing old.

Response 1 to Card VII: It looks like two Martha Mitchells turning around to stare at each other.

Associations: Vanity. [What does vanity make you think of?] Myself. [What do you mean?] I sometimes think that I'm too self-centered.

Response 2 to Card VII: Or it could be a young girl looking at herself in the mirror — primping.

Associations: Vanity . . . this whole card is just very vain. [What does that make you think of?] I think that I'm putting too much stock into my youth . . . what youth I have left . . . sex appeal . . . physique . . . whatever is still left.

In these responses the subject reveals the cause of his present symptom — his fears of growing old and his losing his attractiveness in homosexual circles. Strong narcissism and hostile undertones toward women are also evident.

The next response was present in the test record of a 30-year-old man who sought help because of murderous feelings towards his wife.

Response to Card X: Whirling dervishes of some sort . . . connected to these baby heads.

Associations: Lack of control. [What does that make you think of?] Makes me think of murder. [What do baby heads make you think of?] The baby heads are in anguish because of their immaturity.

In this response the patient vents his fears of losing control and also indicates that his marked infantilism is linked with his homicidal wishes.

Acute situational concerns are often seen when the ego is coping with stress that it is unable or barely able to handle.

The response that follows appeared in the test record of a 33-year-old male patient who suffered brain damage after an operation:

> *Response to Card IX:* Two airplanes.
> *Associations:* It's just flying kind of crooked . . . like something is wrong. [What does that make you think of?] I used to be so organized, and now I can barely do anything.

This response has a strong component of self-concept and demonstrates the patient's concern about his present predicament.

The next response was seen on Card IX by a 34-year-old unemployed homosexual male.

> *Response:* It looks like some kind of acid is eating into the magic of two magicians.
> *Associations:* The acid is eating away from the inside, destroying their power. [What does that make you think of?] I'm self-destructive in many ways . . . I once felt that I had the power to function . . . I had the help from a supernatural source. I sometimes wish for something to happen, and it does . . . it scares me.

This response indicates the patient's feelings of being destroyed, his magical thinking, yet also his capacity for some insight. Self-concept elements are prominent.

The breakup of relationships is also sometimes vividly displayed in Rorschach percepts. The next responses to Cards I and V were elicited from a 30-year-old male musician after his wife left him.

> *Response to Card I:* Parts of the wing . . . look like a state . . . part of it is falling apart . . . pieces are falling off here.
> *Associations:* Just vaguely, it reminds me of the situation that I'm in now . . . I don't read newspapers . . . I don't like being in New York . . . everything fell apart before . . . it's falling apart again. [What does the state make you think of?] It looks like Michigan. [Michigan?] That's where my wife and kids are.

> *Response to Card V:* It also looks like a vagina . . . but if it is, it's in flight [laughs].
> *Associations:* Sex. [What does sex make you think of?] Nothing in particular . . . I have no unpleasant feelings about it. [What does the whole picture call to mind?] It . . . looks like it's flying away. [What does it make you think of?] Every pleasant situation I've ever been in seems to run itself out.

The patient's first response contains a play on words: "state" refers both to his present feelings of disintegration and to the "state" in which his family now lives — an interesting example of symbol condensation in the test. (See Palm, 1956.) This response reflects the patient's preoccupation with the loss of his family, his depression, and threat to the ego ("falling apart"). The latter response indicates the perception of the limited duration of gratifications in his life, specifically the present loss of his wife and sexual gratification.

CONFLICTS OF THE SUBJECT

A sense of division, of intrapsychic conflict, is sometimes demonstrated in inkblot percepts.

The following response to Card I was made by a 25-year-old female subject who was crippled in a suicide attempt.

Response: Those are hands.
Associations: These hands are angry . . . they're grasping and open. [What does that make you think of?] Conflicting emotions . . . they're reaching out . . . yet they're angry . . . pushing away.

This response clearly illustrates the patient's conflicted relationships with others: she wants to be close with others, yet her anger pushes her to avoid intimacy.

The next response to Card I was seen in the Rorschach record of a 21-year-old cabdriver.

Response: This part in the middle looks like a body that's torn . . . divided in half.
Associations: It's like . . . being very confused . . . not knowing which way to go. [What do you mean?] I'd like to . . . try to make myself adjusted and not suppress everything . . . The other side makes me suppress things . . . I want to say that I feel things . . . but I don't want people to see me when I'm not at my best.

This response demonstrates the patient's conflict over expressing emotions and his fear that he will demean himself and drive others away by an expression of what he really feels.

The following response to Card II was elicited from a 43-year-old male patient complaining of depression, apathy, and social isolation.

Response: Two masked and concealed figures toasting something. If you look at it upside down, they're not toasting anymore, they're drawing away from each other.
Associations: Reminds me of the kind of people I know . . . surreptitious . . . illegal . . . relations are more fragile and endangered than

the average relationship. [What does that make you think of?] The difficulty of maintaining constancy.

In this response the patient expresses his feelings about interpersonal relations — both attraction and repulsion — and the resultant fluctuating and inconsistent quality of his relationships.

The clinical literature on the Rorschach test is replete with psychodynamic interpretations of inkblot percepts. Unfortunately, although many authors have utilized Rorschach content to gather psychodynamic information, few have specified broad ground rules or techniques for doing so. Hertzman and Pearce (1947), Schafer (1954), and Mindess (1970) are notable exceptions.

Hertzman and Pearce have stated that the dynamic meaning of percepts on the Rorschach test may be revealed through the figure that is seen, the nature of the action taking place, and any commentary or verbalization that is included in the response. These authors suggest that "departures . . . from conventional modes of perception or expression" (Hertzman & Pearce, 1947, p. 419), particularly completely original responses, are likely to reveal dynamic factors in the subject.

Although these authors are generally optimistic about such interpretation, they also point to a major difficulty: the meaning of such responses often is not entirely obvious without clarifying data elicited from the subject through therapy contact or through associations to the percepts. Because the Rorschach is typically administered before the onset of psychotherapy, supporting data are rarely available from this source. Hertzman and Pearce also describe the conditions under which the test is administered as "not conductive to a fruitful exploration of responses through associations" (Hertzman & Pearce, 1947, p. 419). The examiner thus usually has little information that can help to clarify the meaning of responses. However, based on their study of 12 subjects and confirmatory information derived from psychotherapy, Hertzman and Pearce concluded that in 75 percent of the interpretable responses, interpretations in the correct direction could be made without data other than the Rorschach.

These same authors note that a major problem in such interpretation is knowing when *not* to interpret. They caution against interpreting historical, literary, or mythological figures unless they are accompanied by revealing remarks. They also observe that symbolically-toned responses and responses that may have multiple identities can be particularly misleading.

Schafer (1954) has discussed the similarities and differences between the dream and the Rorschach perceptual process. The Rorschach percept, like the dream, allows subconscious events to surface in the context of symbols. The Rorschach percept is, however, fundamentally different from the dream in that there is an external stimulus and reference point in the Rorschach percept, namely, the inkblot. Consequently "the physical properties of the test stimulus tend to limit the variety of content in Rorschach responses in a way not true for the dream" (Schafer, 1954, p. 95). Although this limitation could be seen as a shortcoming of the Rorschach, Schafer points out that it is actually a strong point of the test. Because the subject can tell himself that he is only describing what is on the blots, much psychodynamic material can be allowed to surface without triggering excess anxiety.

Schafer also notes that Rorschach protocols are considerably more difficult to interpret than are dreams because Rorschach protocols provide the interpreter with considerably less information. In addition to the symbols themselves, dreams also contain what Schafer terms "narrative continuity" and "autobiographical specificity." The narrative content and sequence of the dream are seen only in a truncated form in the Rorschach response process. In addition dreams often deal with objects and persons from the patient's life experience. Because this information is absent from the Rorschach, "it follows that insofar as the Rorschach response expresses unconscious, infantile tendencies, it is ordinarily a guidepost to these tendencies and not a highly articulated map of the unconscious terrain" (Schafer, 1954, p. 96).

Schafer cautions against wild analysis of Rorschach symbolism, which he asserts can be even more misleading than wild analysis of dreams because it is based on less information. He presents a number of suggested guidelines for valid psychodynamic interpretation of inkblot percepts. Six major criteria for judging the adequacy of inkblot interpretations are listed.

Schafer's first such criterion is that there should be sufficient evidence for the interpretation. Dynamic trends in the subject will likely manifest themselves in a number of inkblot images, test attitudes and behavior, and, Schafer asserts, formal scores. In addition there should be a confluence of similar indications from other tests in the battery. Only if the available information seems to converge on the interpretation can the psychologist be reasonably confident that the interpretation is correct. He cautions against symbol interpretation from isolated inkblot responses that is not otherwise confirmed.

The second criterion discussed by Schafer is that the depth of the interpretation should be appropriate to the material on which it is based. Thus those test records that contain unelaborated, popular, and vague responses are less revealing than test records containing highly elaborated thematic content. This concept is similar to the comment of Hertzman and Pearce on the dynamically revealing nature of unconventional and original responses. Schafer cautions psychologists to avoid arbitrarily attempting to force interpretations from unrevealing test records based on such factors as the assumed symbolic meaning of the cards. Even in such constricted records, however, he holds that the defensive system of the patient is often revealed, although the deeper instinctual trends are not.

Schafer's third point is that whenever possible the *manifest form* of the interpreted tendency should be specified. Thus psychologists are urged not only to state the underlying dynamic trends in the patient, but also to predict manifest behavior from test material. Although Schafer recognizes the difficulties in doing so, he declares that the attempt must be made. Interpretation of defensive operations is held to be a great boon to the prediction of overt behavior, because patterns of behavior are associated with defenses such as "the meticulousness, conscientiousness and pedantry associated with compulsive defenses, and the guardedness, suspiciousness and implicit arrogance associated with paranoid defenses" (Schafer, 1954, p. 152). Again, linking Rorschach content interpretation with an analysis of test attitudes and other test data is held to improve the chances of making adequate and useful interpretations in this area. However Schafer cautions the psychologist not to overestimate his ability to predict overt behavior, because the patient's positive and adaptive responses are difficult to estimate and because behavior may also be determined by outside forces over which the patient has little control.

A fourth criterion for psychodynamic Rorschach interpretation is that the intensity of the interpreted trend should be estimated. To state that hostility or orality or anality is present in a patient is in fact a non-statement, because such is the case for everyone alive. Useful interpretations must deal with the intensity of the trend. Schafer suggests that descriptions of dynamic tendencies in patients be placed on a 5-point rating scale: extreme, strong, moderate, weak, negligible.

Schafer's fifth suggestion for enhancing the usefulness of interpretations is that the interpreted tendency be given a hierarchic position in the total personality picture. He maintains that personality trends are interrelated in a hierarchic fashion. Wishes, fears, and other personality constituents do not merely coexist; they are interrelated. Thus a subject may have strong hostile impulses which he tries to control with compulsive defenses. The defenses may be weak and thus cause intense anxiety. Simply to state that the subject is anxious and hostile and uses compulsive defenses does not provide the three-dimensional picture of personality functioning that specifies the cause-and-effect relationships existing between the trends. Because Freudian theory is usually the basis of such hierarchial interpretations, Schafer contends that the background and

training of the examiner are important variables in adequate psychodynamic inkblot interpretation.

The sixth and final suggestion of Schafer is that the examiner specify
both the adaptive and pathological aspects of the interpreted tendencies.
Too often the pathology is stressed and the healthy, adaptive aspects of
the patient are not given enough emphasis. Schafer points out that a
particular personality trend may have both adaptive and pathological
facets. For example, schizoid withdrawal into fantasy often results in a
deep distrust of human relationships on the one hand, and a cultivation
of artistic creativity on the other. Schafer proposes that viewing personality trends in terms of identity problems and solutions is helpful in
perceiving their adaptive aspects.

A third author who has attempted to establish ground rules for the
interpretation of individual psychodynamics is Mindess (1970). Mindess
focuses on what he calls the symbolic Rorschach response — "the
dramatic, poetic image — the symbol which portrays its referent with
striking, immediate impact" (Mindess, 1970, p. 84). Such responses are
characterized not by how much they can be generalized to other patients
and other situations, but by their unique nature, their ability to reveal
the subject's feelings and his self-concept. Mindess notes four criteria by
which the symbolic response may be recognized.

The first of these criteria is originality: "the more unusual an idea
is, the more justified are we in considering it symbolic" (Mindess, 1970,
p. 84). This idea is again similar to the Hertzman and Pearce unconventional response and to Schafer's elaborated, thematically meaningful response. Thus "a bat seen" on Card I is unlikely to have symbolic connotations, but "the Greek winged victory, a statue of a woman representing
freedom," is likely to contain important symbolism.

The second criterion of a symbolic response is the emotional cathexis
attached to the percept. "The more imbued it is with feeling or portent,
the more it can be considered symbolic" (Mindess, 1970, p. 85). Thus
seeing two people on the sides on Card I has less emotional coloring than
seeing two people tearing a child apart.

The third aspect distinguishing the symbolic response is what Mindess refers to as the imaginativeness of the percept. He presents an example of a highly imaginative response given to Card IX: "Vapor shooting
up into the air and in the background there are mountains, pure white,
and golden gates, carved perfectly, and way back in the distance is a
tower and that tower is the capitol of the world and it's so beautiful that
it makes everything look bright" (Mindess, 1970, p. 85).

The fourth and last criterion of a symbolic response is, according
to Mindess, repetition. Thus seeing "slashing knives" may be symbolically

significant, but the recurrence of this percept several times in the test record strongly suggests symbolic referents.

In his discussion of how symbolic responses are interpreted, Mindess opts for an anecdotal approach. He presents several examples of highly charged symbolic responses and their likely meanings. One such example involves the case of a devout Catholic doctor accused by his wife of being sadistic. His revealing Rorschach percept was "a royal scepter covered with dirty ice. It has a cross on top and a sword blade on the bottom." Mindess interprets this response as signifying that the subject's sexual feelings "are anything but warm and loving" (Mindess, 1970, p. 90). A second example is a response of a female college professor who suffered a nervous breakdown several months after being tested: "Everything seems to be held together, but the foundation is not solid" (Mindess, 1970, p. 90).

Mindess asserts that the process of symbolic interpretation is largely intuitive. "It is aided by openness to poetic levels of thought and hampered by insistence on logical chains of deduction" (Mindess, 1970, p. 88). He sees the psychologist's traditional reliance on statistics and verifiable data as a hindrance to the learning of effective symbolic interpretation of inkblot percepts.

In a different approach to the psychodynamic applications of content, Phillips and Smith (1953) have presented major content categories and their interpretations. Prominent in their discussion is a list of common animal responses and what they interpret to be the symbolic meaning of the animal. They contend that five major aspects of personality are revealed by specific animal content: relations with the mother, relations with the father, immaturity, hostility, and passivity. An alphabetical list of 55 animals describes the personality implications of each. The types of interpretations offered are exemplified by those presented for *ape:* "a) Suggests an unresolved relationship with a strong patriarchal father figure and implies that subject in the present tends to assign to authority figures a role comparable to that of this father; b) Implies that his father figure was seen as threatening or potentially destructive" (Phillips & Smith, 1953, p. 120).

Phillips and Smith assert that the listed relationships between specific animal content and personality variables have all been observed empirically rather than derived on a priori grounds. They also state that often these empirically derived relationships correspond to what might be hypothesized on the basis of psychoanalytic theory. However no data are presented in support of the interpretations.

Phillips and Smith also focus on what is revealed of the subject's "life thema" by expressive test behavior exclusive of the test response per se. Life thema are seen by these authors as patterns of behavior that are so dominant that they epitomize an individual's social behavior. They compare their concept of life thema to Murray's unity thema and Allport's cardinal trait. "Life thema deal with the central problems of adjustment in our culture: sexuality, hostility, and dependence. Each life thema represents a solution to one or more of these problems ... it provides a key to understanding the personality" (Phillips & Smith, 1953, p. 164). Examples of life thema presented are "I must devote myself to mother — until she dies," and "How could little weak me do any harm?"

Such life thema are viewed by Phillips and Smith as they are revealed by stylistic analysis of Rorschach performance, both verbal and nonverbal. Because the Rorschach test is in part an interaction between the subject and the examiner, the subject's pattern of interaction with the examiner can be viewed as constituting useful information, as do the subject's nonscorable verbalizations and other behavior during the test. Phillips and Smith present numerous categories of style that may be interpreted on the Rorschach test, such as head shaking (implying an inability to cope), manually demarcating the boundaries of percepts (suggesting immaturity and passivity), and remarks that structure the test situation (e.g., "Can I turn the cards?"), which indicate attempts to master the situation by setting rules or limits.

Schafer (1954) takes Phillips and Smith to task for their approach to content and expressive behavior. He voices skepticism about their statement that the content interpretations presented were empirically derived. The fixed significance of the meaning of classes of content is held by Schafer to be close to wild analysis. Phillips and Smith's analysis of expressive behavior in the test situation is also criticized by Schafer on the grounds that such an analysis "gives little or no recognition to external reality, the ordinary requirements of verbal communication, and the existence of relatively autonomous, conflict-free thought" (Schafer, 1954, p 143).

Brown (1953/1960) published a controversial article in which he discussed the interpretation of psychodynamics based on Rorschach responses. He states that the greater the distance of the percept from popular and borderline popular responses, the more revealing it is of "the invisible segments of the spectrum of mental life" (Brown, 1953/1960, p 361). The cards are thought to present the subject with symbolically suggestive stimuli. The subject's responses to the stimuli are affected by censorship similar to that observed in free association and resistance in psychotherapy. Brown further contends that an analysis of Rorschach content will reveal the "struggles of the individual with reference to psychosexual stages of development" (Brown, 1953/1960, p 362). Genetic reconstructions and inferences with respect to psychosexual development can thus be made.

Brown presents a breakdown of the areas of each card and the feelings that are easily evoked by them. Aspects of the self-concept revealed by certain types of responses are also discussed. For example, the center figure of Card I is held to have "the ambiguous quality of solid matronliness and . . . 'Prussian officer' bulkiness" (Brown, 1953/1960, p 363). The lower "bell" area "arouses unconscious associations of softness, yieldingness and acceptance" (Brown, 1953/1960, p 363). If the figure is described as a statue, Brown suggests that the mother was perceived as rigid, cold, and unattainable; an alternate interpretation is a wish to immobilize and dehumanize the figure so as to avoid its erotic seductiveness. Seeing the figure as a soldier suggests that the mother was a strict disciplinarian. Feelings of inner emptiness are said to be expressed by perception of the figure as clothing or a tailor's dummy. On each of the 10 Rorschach cards, Brown similarly remarks on the evocative aspects of blot areas and the dynamic meaning of certain responses.

Although no statistical or experimental evidence is marshalled in support of his interpretations, Brown notes that "validative support comes from approximately 600 cases for which detailed clinical material was available" (Brown, 1953/1960, p 362). Over 1500 subjects in all were involved. Thus clinical experience is presented as the validational evidence of the suggested interpretations.

Brown's work in this area has received criticism on several grounds. Charen (1953) has called attention to the lack of quantitative treatment in Brown's speculations about content. Charen cited a number of studies that have applied statistics to Rorschach content. In a rejoinder Brown (1953) emphasized the fact that his approach to content was idiographic in nature, with the stress on dynamic factors. "With all due respect to statistical studies of the Rorschach content factor, these have been categorical rather than dynamic" (Brown, 1953, p 463).

Schafer has also been critical of Brown's work, though for different reasons. Although many of Brown's clinical formulations are viewed by Schafer as valuable, his approach to the study of dynamic content is seen as an extension of the errors of Phillips and Smith. Schafer notes that, whereas in Phillips and Smith only narrow classes of content are assigned invariant meaning, Brown proceeds to assign such meaning to single responses to specific card areas.

Schafer's warning against assigning invariant meaning to certain Rorschach symbols echoes the observations of psychoanalysts about the idiosyncratic meaning of symbols occurring in dreams. Fromm-Reichmann's (1950) caution is typical.

Their [symbols'] significance definitely varies with the personality, the life-circumstances, and the problems of the dreamer. In one person's dream, for instance, a snake may appear as a male symbol, while another dreamer may use a snake to express female shrewdness and seductiveness. Again a snake may be used by an archaeologist to express the attributes of one or another of the multitude of male and female gods or goddesses whose total or partial embodiment is that of a snake. (Fromm-Reichmann, 1950, p. 165)

Palm (1956) has written briefly on the similarities between the dream and the Rorschach percept: both are seen as expressions of unconscious thoughts and wishes. Palm holds that the actual form of the blots is analogous to the "day residues" (i.e., recent memory images), in that the subject incorporates elements of each in the "sign language" of the dream and Rorschach percept, respectively. The Rorschach blots, Palm maintains, are conducive to the expression of unconscious symbols because of their indefinite structure. "To the extent that [the subject] . . . abandons his dependence on the real object, he regresses from conceptual thinking to visual perception and from visual perception to imaginative creation, and, briefly, from the reality principle to the laws of the pleasure principle" (Palm, 1956, p. 248). The subject is forced to relax his powers of mental integration, and the result is regression from reality testing to wishful thought.

GENERAL EVALUATION

There seems little question that the Rorschach test can be utilized to yield a vivid picture of the individual psychodynamics, particularly the self-concept, of test subjects. On the basis of the views of authors in this field, the most fertile grounds for such interpretations lie in those Rorschach percepts that evidence: (1) a unique and original character, (2) great emotional cathexis, (3) remarks that clarify the meaning of the response, and (4) a repetition of themes seen elsewhere in the test record. It is interesting to note that the first and the third of these characteristics resemble the RIRS categories of specificity and elaboration in Levine and Spivack's *index of repressive style,* which was discussed in Chapter 8. Although, as mentioned there, the validity data on RIRS has been less than totally satisfactory, the intriguing possibility is raised that the self-revealing character of Rorschach percepts can be quantified through a procedure that emphasizes the verbal content of responses, as does the RIRS. It will be recalled from Chapter 8 that RIRS has been most successful in predicting verbal expressiveness of subjects.

It is likewise apparent that the interpretation of individual psychodynamics with inkblot tests is beset by several problems. Firstly, the inherently intuitive nature of the interpretations being made renders it extremely difficult to establish objective standards for the psychodynamic interpretation of content. Although the proposed standards for interpretations have certainly helped to clarify the nature of the interpretative process, it is nevertheless true, as Mindess states, that symbol interpretation remains more of an art than a science. Thus there is no substitute for the skill, training, and good judgment of the clinician.

Strauss (1967) has described this state of affairs as a problem by no means confined to the Rorschach test.

> The criticism has been made, especially of the Rorschach, that it is only as good as the examiner. There is no doubt about it. But one can also point out that surgery is only as satisfactory as the surgeon, that therapy is not likely to surpass the ability of the therapist, and that the drive to eliminate man, his feelings, his empathy in arriving at an understanding of another individual is a deplorable and regressive symptom. (Strauss, 1967, p 255)

A further and related difficulty is the lack of statistical application in the area. As rightly pointed out by Schafer (1954), traditional psychometric techniques are not appropriate for the idiographic interpretations arrived at by this method. Q-methodology, as expounded by Stephenson (1953), is designed for use with idiographic data. But this type of technique is also rejected by Schafer as inappropriate to psychodynamic formulations, because Q-technique does not take into account the hierarchic organization of personality characteristics.

Although recent years have witnessed an increasing sophistication in dealing statistically with the individual case (e.g., Chassan, 1960; 1961; 1967), the present authors are not aware of any studies, other than the quasi-experimental investigation of Hertzman and Pearce (1947), that have applied rigorous research methods to study the idiosyncratic uses of Rorschach content. Until this area proves amenable to research methods, psychologists are left in the unfortunate position of being unable to determine empirically how the test can be validly used as an idiographic measure, and in what way such use of the test yields misleading results. One factor that has likely hindered the statistical applications in this field is the differing temperaments of researchers and Rorschach clinicians. As noted by Mindess (1970), clinicians attracted by this application of the test are likely to be uninterested in rigorous research methods and esoteric statistical techniques. Likewise, competent researchers are equally likely to be repelled by the ambiguity and lack of structure in the psychodynamic interpretation of Rorschach content. The application of statistical methods to this area has suffered as a result.

A third difficulty is the tendency toward wild analysis warned against by Schafer. Although wild analysis can be a general problem in psychoanalysis, it is particularly acute in interpretation of the Rorschach test and projective tests in general (e.g., McMahon, 1969). Just why this is so can be seen by contrasting Rorschach interpretation with the interpretation of the dreams of a psychoanalytic patient. Schafer (1954) has stated that symbolization is central to both types of interpretations. However, as Schafer goes on to note, the dream and the Rorschach percept are not equivalent in their revealing qualities. The narrative continuity and autobiographical specificity of the dream are rarely found in the inkblot percept. The Rorschach percept is also partly stimulated by the properties of the stimulus cards.

It should also be recognized that there are differences between the contexts in which dreams and Rorschach percepts are interpreted. In general, a psychotherapist is intimately familiar with the patient whose dream is to be interpreted and is thus in a favorable position to understand symbol usage that is idiosyncratic to that patient. In contrast, the Rorschach examiner often knows very little beforehand of the testee's background, personality, and idiosyncratic views of the world. Furthermore a psychotherapist usually has the subject associate to various aspects of the manifest dream. Interpretations are thus also made on the basis of the patient's waking associations to the dream. It is not common testing practice, however, to garner free associations to the Rorschach percepts. And because testers often do not receive feedback on the accuracy of their interpretations, a potential corrective for wild analysis is eliminated. The psychoanalytic patient, on the other hand, can and does correct the therapist's erroneous symbol interpretations.

In short, the Rorschach examiner typically has a good deal less information on which to base his interpretations than does the psychotherapist interpreting a dream, although it should be noted that the tester also has available information from other tests included in the clinical battery. The result is that the tester often feels unable to make meaningful interpretations from a test record. Because the tester's salary and self-esteem depend on the making of such interpretations, resort to wild analysis and to tables of fixed interpretations of content categories is not infrequent.

The Rorschach test is thus typically far less dependable than the dream in understanding the psychodynamics of test subjects. Therefore the examiner should exercise considerable caution in arriving at interpretations. As noted by Hertzman and Pearce (1947), knowing when *not* to interpret a response is an important skill for the clinician. The psychologist should certainly refrain from attaching dynamic significance to common individual responses to the blots; of course the practice of such forbearance requires a knowledge of typical percepts on the test.[1] The clinician should also avoid fixed interpretations for certain responses (e.g., the Phillips and Smith animal list), because such "dream book" interpretation is likely to lead to a very high degree of error. Finally, it is also necessary to be familiar with the stimulus characteristics of the blots, in order to be able to take them into account and to eliminate them as a source of error in interpreting responses. The stimulus characteristics of the blots are discussed in the following chapter.

The present authors believe that there is a further solution to the problem of wild analysis and insufficient data in Rorschach interpretation. The current method of test administration is largely determinant-based, with the time-consuming inquiry period focusing on an aspect of test performance that has limited validity and is little used for interpretative purposes by many modern clinicians. Principally through more productive use of the inquiry period, the test situation can be altered so as to gather a maximum amount of dynamically relevant associational information from the patient. Schafer (1954) has also pointed out that it is possible to elicit associations to or reflections on Rorschach responses, associations that reveal otherwise unverbalized autobiographical and narrative information and provide the Rorschach examiner with further valuable input. These content-oriented methods of test administration are discussed in Chapter 12.

Despite the difficulties inherent in dynamic content interpretation, it seems likely that this approach will continue to be one of the major uses of the Rorschach test. The information provided to the examiner is highly valuable, and furthermore it is relatively unique. Objective tests of personality have been and can be constructed to measure such personality variables as hostility and anxiety. Such instruments are psychometrically sounder than the Rorschach, but they are largely useless in providing information on the unique patterning of psychodynamics in test subjects. In imparting structure to the test stimuli, the subject often reveals much of his idiosyncratic inner feelings. This is the unique advantage of the Rorschach, the TAT, and other projective instruments over strictly objective tests.

[1]The sequencing of common responses in the test record may, of course, have considerable dynamic significance.

11

Stimulus Characteristics
of the Rorschach Blots

One aspect of Rorschach interpretation that has long fascinated clinicians is the analysis of card "pull," that is, the tendency of the cards to evoke affective responses and certain classes of responses from the subject. Schafer (1954) and others, have noted that the Rorschach percept differs fundamentally from the dream image in this respect: the inkblot percept is partially determined by a stimulus in the real world (the blot), whereas the dream is not.

Zubin (1956) has highlighted the dual nature of the Rorschach response in his distinction between the projective and nonprojective aspects of the response. "Some responses reflect more heavily the stimulus properties; others reflect these to a lesser degree, and the latter are . . . called 'projective'" (Zubin, 1956, p 183). Rorschach clinicians must thus take into account the card pull in order to disentangle the projective from the nonprojective aspects of inkblot responses.

The literature on the evocative characteristics of the cards is, like much general Rorschach literature, divided between largely clinical and intuitive excursions on the one hand, and empirical studies on the other. The following is a brief review of the relevant research literature. This review focuses primarily on what Baughman (1958) refers to as the "total impact" of the blot on the subject, inasmuch as subjects' typical reactions to the blots are likely to be of high interpretative relevance to the content-oriented clinician. The relative influence of the various stimulus dimensions (e.g., color and shading) are considered only secondarily. For this reason Baughman's admirable work on the effect of stimulus variations on test performance (Baughman, 1954, 1959) is only summarily presented, and many of the studies analyzing the effects of color and other stimulus dimensions on "shock" and other indices are also excluded.

SEMANTIC DIFFERENTIAL STUDIES

Many empirical investigations of blot characteristics have used the Semantic Differential (Osgood, Suci & Tannenbaum, 1957) as the measuring instrument. Osgood's well-known Semantic Differential (SD) consists of 50 scales defined by two adjectives with opposite meanings. These opposing adjectives are separated by seven spaces, one of which must be checked to indicate how the subject perceives the concept in relation to the pair of adjectives. Factor analytic studies have indicated three major SD factors: evaluation (e.g., good–bad, valuable–worthless), potency (e.g., strong–weak, large–small), and activity (e.g., active–passive, fast–slow).

Most semantic differential Rorschach research has used college students as subjects. In one such study Rabin (1959) asked 66 college students (28 males and 38 females) to apply 20 SD scales to the 10 Rorschach blots. In no instance were the SD ratings of males and females significantly in opposite directions. The most positive evaluations were given to Cards VII, III, and IX, and the most negative to Cards IV and I. Cards IV and I were judged the most potent, and Cards VII, III, and V the least potent. Cards IX and X were judged the most active, and Cards VII, VI, and II the least active. Rabin also noted that the SD profile for Card VII was almost a perfect mirror image of that for Card IV.

Little (1959) similarly asked 40 college students (20 males and 20 females) to rate the blots and concepts on nine SD scales. He reported his results as factor scores. Cards VII and X (and Card III for women) were seen most positively in terms of the evaluation factor. Cards I and IV were evaluated negatively. Cards IV and IX were seen as the most potent by males, whereas females viewed II and IX as the most potent. Both sexes saw Cards V and VII as the least potent. Cards III and IX were seen by men, and Cards III, IX, and X by women, as the most active. Men rated Cards V, VI, and VII, and women rated Cards VI and VII as the least active. In comparing SD ratings of the cards to those of the concepts, Little determined that the concept "mother" was most similar in connotation to Card VII, and least to Card IV. The connotations of "father" were most similar to Card VI and least similar to Card I.

Zax and Loiselle (1960a) used 40 male and 40 female undergraduate subjects who rated the blots on 21 SD scales. These investigators reported what adjectives were significantly associated with each blot.

Hays and Boardman (1975) worked with 60 male and 60 female college subjects. A regular and an achromatic series of blots were administered, and 12 sets of adjectives were taken from the Semantic Differential. These authors found that the presence of color on the chromatic Rorschach blots increased the degree of positive evaluation for four of the five chromatic blots (not for Card II), decreased potency for four of the five blots (not for Card VIII), and increased activity for all five blots. Hays and Boardman's finding that three of the five chromatic blots had the least connotative meaning of the Rorschach inkblots contradicts traditional Rorschach views on the overriding effect of color.

Rosen (1960) used the SD with two groups of subjects: 57 college students (28 males and 29 females), and 36 clinicians (29 males and 7 females). Subjects were asked to rate the blots, percepts, and determinants on 15 SD scales. Rosen noted that Cards I and IV tended to be disliked, Card IV "so strongly that the term 'shock reaction' comes to mind" (Rosen, 1960, p 417). Rosen also found that Card VII was seen as extremely feminine, and that the data warranted describing Card IV as a "bad father" and Card VII as a "good mother." Although considerable agreement was found between the students' and the clinicians' SD ratings of the blots, there was a tendency for clinicians to overvalue the blots, attributing more force to them.

In another investigation using college students, Loiselle and Kleinschmidt (1963) had 40 female undergraduates rate the Rorschach blots on 21 SD scales, while 40 other subjects used the SD to rate percepts they had given in response to the blots. Loiselle and Kleinschmidt determined that there was a great deal of similarity between meanings assigned to the blots and those assigned to the percepts.

A study by Otten and Van de Castle (1963) is notable in that Set A of the HIT inkblots was included in the research. Fifty-two college students (26 males and 26 females) rated the 10 Rorschach blots and the 45 HIT blots on the same set of 14 SD scales. These investigatiors found the number of adjectives considered descriptive of the blots was proportionately equivalent between the Rorschach and the HIT. Sex differences in the attribution of meaning were more pronounced on the HIT. Some HIT cards, particularly those with high factor scores, seemed to tap patterns of meaning not found in the 10 Rorschach blots. Rorschach Cards II, III, and VII had the most positive evaluations, and Cards I, IV, and V had the most negative evaluations. Cards I, II, and IV were judged the most potent, and Cards III, VII, and X the least potent. Cards III, IX, and X were rated the most active, and Cards II, IV, and VI the least active.

Zax and Loiselle (1960b) reported an SD study of the blots in which the order of blot presentation was altered. Two groups of 40 subjects each (all female undergraduates) responded to blots on 21 SD scales. Cards were presented to one group in the standard order. But to the second group the cards were presented in 10 different orders, following a Latin Square design. Order effects were found on Cards I, VII, and VIII, with significant differences in the distributions of ratings on six, seven, and seven SD scales respectively. Card I, when not the first in the test, tended to be viewed more benignly. Card VIII was also felt to be more benign when not seen in the standard order (the first chromatic after several achromatic blots). Card VII was viewed as a more attractive stimulus when it was presented in the standard order.

Several investigations have used the SD to describe blot characteristics with children, noncollege adults, or psychiatric patients as subjects. In one such study, Zax and Benham (1961) worked with fifth- and sixth-grade students (40 males and 40 females) who rated the Rorschach blots on 21 SD scales. Zax and Benham observed that Cards I and IV were perceived negatively and as potent by males and females; Card I also suggested activity to the subjects. Cards V, VIII, and X were seen as positive, and indicative of activity. Of these three, V was the least potent. Females tended to view blots as more positive and less potent than did the males.

Hafner and Rosen (1964) worked with 161 boys and girls in the third, sixth, and ninth grades. The subjects were asked to rate the 10 blots, 9 common Rorschach responses, and 2 determinants not embodied in responses; 15 SD scales were used. Hafner and Rosen found that the older groups tended to give more extreme connotations; girls differentiated the blots at an earlier age than boys.

Loiselle, Fisher, and Parrish (1968) used the SD with 40 fifth- and sixth-grade girls and 40 female schizophrenic inpatients. Twenty-one SD scales were used in rating inkblots and percepts. In contrasting these two groups with previously collected data on the SD ratings of college students, these authors noted that the school girls had just about as many significant ratings as the college subjects, and that both of these groups had far more significant ratings than the schizophrenic subjects. The school girls tended to view the cards — especially I, II, and IX — as more active and more potent than did the college students. The schizophrenics tended to view Cards I and IV more positively then did the other two groups.

Zax, Loiselle, and Karras (1960) had their subjects rate the Rorschach blots on 21 SD scales. The subjects were 40 male schizophrenic inpatients and 40 male hospitalized nonpsychiatric patients who were matched with the schizophrenics on age and education. On the whole, fewer significant ratings were found for these subjects than has been the case for college students. The authors noted that Cards I and IV conveyed the strongest impression — both cards were evaluated negatively and were seen as highly potent. Both groups also agreed that Card V was active and low in potency. None of the blots was perceived as masculine or feminine.

SPECIAL MEANINGS ASSIGNED TO BLOTS

A surprisingly large number of studies have focused on the question of whether certain blots are particularly evocative of feelings toward the father, the mother, the family, the male sex organ, and other such concepts. This line of research stems from the assertions made by several clinical workers (e.g., Bochner & Halpern, 1945; Brown, 1953/1960; Phillips & Smith, 1953) about the evocative characteristics of certain cards, particularly Cards IV and VII. Bochner and Halpern stated that Card IV "embodies something sinister . . . [It] may suggest the father in general. . . . [Card VI] is weighted for sexual implications. . . . It is generally . . . the most difficult card to interpret. . . . [Card VII has] . . . a feminine quality, frequently with maternal implications" (Bochner and Halpern, 1945, pp 81–82). Brown (1953/1960) also spoke of Card IV as a father card and Card VII as the mother card. Halpern (1953) wrote of Card IV as the authority card, Card VI as the sex card, and Card VII as the mother card. Phillips and Smith (1953) saw IV as the father card, Card VI as male sexuality, and Card VII as the mother figure.

Semantic Differential Studies

In a Semantic Differential study relevant to the so-called parental cards (IV and VII), Smith (cited in Osgood et al., 1957) had 20 college students rate the 10 blots on 10 SD scales; they also rated 10 verbal concepts, including "my mother," "my father," and "sex." The parental SD ratings were not similar to the SD ratings of Cards IV and VII, and the ratings of the concept of sex did not prove similar to the ratings for Card VI.

In another SD study in this vein, Kamano (1960) used SD scales in trying to test the hypothesis that Cards IV and VII represent father and mother symbols. In this investigation 80 undergraduate subjects (40 males and 40 females) rated Cards IV and VII and the concepts mother and father on seven SD scales that particularly stressed the potency factor. It was predicted that Card IV would show greater semantic similarity to father than to mother while Card VII would be more similar to mother than to father. The hypothesis was confirmed: Card IV (like father) was harder, larger, stronger, stricter, more masculine, and more aggressive than Card VII. Card VII (like mother) was soft, small, weak, permissive, feminine, and retiring. No significant differences were found between the SD ratings of the male and the female subjects. Kamano viewed these results as support for the parental interpretations of Cards IV and VII.

Sines (1960) similarly used the SD to investigate the similarity between the connotative meanings attached to Cards IV and VII on the one hand, and those attached to various concepts, including father and mother. The subjects were 20 college students (16 males and 4 females). Sixteen SD scales were used; 20 concepts were rated. Sines found that the SD ratings of Cards IV and VII were not similar to the SD ratings of the concepts father and mother. The concepts that were rated similar to Card IV were rather frightening and unpleasant: monster, ape, fighting, witch, and iceberg. Concepts rated similar to the ratings for Card VII were people, woman, mask, hide, and dancing.

Conceptual Meaning of the Blots

A number of studies have investigated the so-called special meanings of the blots by having subjects label or match the blots with certain concepts. In an early study of the extent to which concepts would be associated with the blots, Rosen (1951) worked with three groups of college subjects (193 subjects in all), who were asked to choose the blots that represented certain concepts or symbols, including male sex organ, masculine aggression, authority, father symbol, mother symbol, and family symbol. Rosen found that specific cards were significantly associated with the following concepts in at least one of the three subject groups.

Card I: nighttime (2 groups); masculine aggression (1 group); X-ray (1 group); feeling of authority (2 groups); family symbol (1 group)
Card II: human beings (1 group); animals (1 group); emotional security (2 groups)
Card III: human beings (3 groups); ornamental design (1 group)
Card IV: male sex organ (1 group); nighttime (3 groups); masculine aggression (2 groups); X-ray (1 group); feeling of authority (2 groups); father symbol (3 groups); animal skin (3 groups)
Card V: bat (3 groups)
Card VI: male sex organ (3 groups); female sex organ (2 groups); feeling of authority (1 group); animal skin (3 groups)
Card VII: human beings (1 group); clouds (3 groups); mother symbol (2 groups)
Card VIII: house (1 group); animals (1 group); human internal

organs (2 groups); X-ray (1 group); ornamental design (1 group)
Card IX: animals (2 groups); female sex organ (1 group); human internal organs (3 groups); landscape (1 group)
Card X: house (2 groups); human internal organs (2 groups); emotional insecurity (3 groups); family symbol (1 group); ornamental design (3 groups); landscape (2 groups)

Rosen concluded that, in general, the father association to Card IV, the mother to Card VII, and male sexuality to Card VI were borne out by the data. However Rosen also noted that "no one card approaches identity in meaning for a great number of subjects. Different subjects can perceive a father figure in various cards, and the same card has various connotations for different subjects" (Rosen, 1951, p 243).

Meer and Singer (1950) instructed 49 members of a college fraternity to select which Rorschach cards represented father and which mother, and to state their reasons. Card IV was most often chosen for father; Card II was in second place. Cards VII and X were the most frequently chosen as the mother card.

Engel (1959) administered the Rorschach test to 30 boys in grades 5 through 7 and then asked them to choose the cards that reminded them of their mother and father, and to explain the reasons for their choices. Engel found little consistency in the choices made by the children: Card III was chosen most often for mother, by 8 of the 30 children. Only 6 children chose Card VII as mother. Cards III and IV were chosen by 6 students each as the father card. Engel concluded that blind interpretation of reactions to Card IV and VII as reactions to parents could lead to "gross errors of interpretation" (Engel, 1959, p 313).

Hafner (1961) asked 80 children (48 boys and 32 girls, mean age: 10.5) to select the cards that reminded them of their mother, their father, and to specify which they liked best, which they liked least, and which was the most frightening. Hafner determined the children chose Card III most frequently as both mother and father. However Card IV was least frequently chosen as the mother card. Card X was liked best, and Card IV was most frequently chosen as the least liked and the most frightening.

Magnussen and Cole (1967) attempted to replicate Hafner's results. They asked 93 children (50 boys and 43 girls, mean age 10.7) in a child guidance center to say which blot reminded them or made them think of their mother or their father, which blot they liked best, which they liked least and which was the most scary or frightening. These investigators found that Card VII was the most frequent choice for the mother card. For the father card, boys chose IV most often (Card III ran a close second), whereas girls chose III most frequently. The children liked Card X best and Card IV the least. Boys chose Card IV as the most frightening (followed by Card I); girls chose VI as the most frightening (followed by IV). Magnussen and Cole noted, however, that these were only group trends: "Without additional corroborative information, the symbolic meaning of a card for a child will more likely be different from the significant results for his group than the chance that it will correspond to the group finding" (Magnussen & Cole, 1967, p 46).

Cole and Williams (1968) used subjects from five different grade levels: 67 first-graders, 75 fourth-graders, 76 eighth-graders, 59 twelfth-graders, and 260 college students. Subjects were asked to choose the blots that reminded them most of father and mother. Cole and Williams found that Cards VIII and X were significantly associated with mother, whereas Card IV was associated with father by the college students and the male precollege subjects. (The latter subjects also chose III for the father card). The female precollege subjects tended to choose VI and X for father. These authors suggested that the choice of VI for father by the females might represent Oedipal feelings or penis envy.

Beck and Herron (1969) reported a study in which 516 children in grades one through six had to select from every pair of Rorschach cards the card reminding them most of mother, father, family, and self, as well as the card they liked best and the one they liked least. These authors found that Cards II and III were most frequently chosen as mother cards, and that Card IV was most often selected as the father card (with Card I coming in second). Cards X, III, IX, and II were chosen as family cards. Card X was best liked by girls, whereas boys liked Cards X, I, and V. Girls disliked Card IV, boys disliked Cards IV, VI, and VII. Most boys selected Card I as the card that reminded them of themselves, whereas the girls most often chose Cards II and III.

In an investigation carried out in Japan, Taniguchi et al. (1958) instructed 50 delinquents and 50 nondelinquents who were equally divided as to sex, to decide which blots reminded them of father and of mother, and to state the reason why. The comparison groups were not matched on intelligence; the nondelinquents were, in fact, college students. It was determined that among the college subjects, Card IV was most frequently chosen for father (24 subjects of 50); Card VII was most frequently chosen for mother (11 subjects of 50). Among the delinquents, Card III was most frequently selected for father (13 of 50) and Cards VIII and X for mother (10 subjects each).

In a study using doll figures rather than verbal labels, Levy (1958) asked 27 children (13 girls and 14 boys between 7 and 8 years old) to match dolls representing a man, woman, boy, girl, and baby to each card.

Card IV was matched as a male card beyond the .05 level and Card IX was matched as a female card beyond the .05 level. Card VI approached maleness, but the association was not significant. In addition Levy found that both Cards IV and VI were associated with the "man" doll at the .01 level. "[Card] VII as a 'mother' card did not receive support in this study" (Levy, 1958, p 296).

Direct Studies of Card Effectiveness

Six reported studies directly investigated the effectiveness of Cards IV and VII in eliciting feelings toward the parents, and the effectiveness of Card VI as the sex card. On the assumption that attitudes towards authority can be judged from responses to Card IV, Dana studied the usefulness of responses to that card in predicting improvement in long- and short-term therapy. The subjects were 44 patients who had gone to fewer than 20 therapy sessions, and 46 patients who had had 20 or more sessions. Card IV responses for these patients were separated into three categories: adequate, inadequate, and negative. Three hypotheses were made, namely, that adequate responses to Card IV would predict good prognosis, that inadequate responses would predict poor prognosis, and that negative responses would suggest poor prognosis in short-term therapy but good prognosis in long-term therapy. Adequate response on Card IV was found to predict a favorable prognosis, although the relationship was only significant for the short-term therapy patients. Inadequate responses were associated with poor prognosis in short-term ($p < .01$) but not in long-term therapy. Negative responses on Card IV significantly predicted improvement in long-term ($p < .01$) but not in short-term therapy.

In general the three hypotheses were confirmed. However the relevance of this study to an understanding of Card IV may be less than meets the eye. Whereas Dana initially described Card IV responses as reactions to authority, the Card IV categories — adequate, inadequate, and negative — have no direct reference to feelings toward authority; instead they involve such questions as adequacy of form, bizarreness of content, and the like. In addition, as noted by Zelin and Sechrest (1963), responses to cards other than IV were not included as a control in the study. These is no evidence that it was an attitude toward authority projected onto Card IV that resulted in the significant relationships found, and in fact it seems likely that other factors, such as the intactness of the thought processes, may have been the effective predictors.

Hirschstein and Rabin (1955) compared 20 male juvenile delinquents from family backgrounds with 20 delinquents from nonfamily backgrounds. These authors predicted that the former group would experience greater difficulty with the two parental cards. The two groups were compared for $F+\%$, R, and RT on Cards IV and VII. No significant differences were found on the first two Rorschach scores, but the groups did differ in the expected direction on RT. Interestingly, these were the only two cards on which the groups differed in RT. However it should be noted that only one of the three Rorschach variables discriminated as expected between the groups. Furthermore the theoretical rationale of the expected differences seems somewhat shaky; one could construct an equally convincing rationale for expecting results in the opposite direction.

In a very well designed study, Zelin and Sechrest (1963) carried out two separate experiments to test directly the effectiveness of Cards IV and VII in eliciting attitudes toward parents. In the first experiment four therapists rated 17 patients' relationships with their parents; judges carried out the same ratings based on the patients' Rorschach responses to Cards I, III, IV, and VII. (Cards I and III were included as control cards.) Ratings of responses to Card IV proved to be more closely related to rated attitudes toward the father than responses to the other blots; Card VII came in a close second. However none of the obtained correlations was significant at the .05 level. Ratings on Card I and III proved to be the most closely related to ratings of attitude toward the mother. Card VII ratings were found to be negatively related to mother attitude. Again, however, none of the statistics was significant.

In their second experiment, Zelin and Sechrest related a questionnaire on attitudes toward parents to rated relationships with parents as judged from Rorschach percepts on Cards I, III, IV, and VII. Thirty college students were the subjects. The Rorschach ratings of attitudes toward parents were not significantly related to the questionnaire; neither were there significant differences between the cards.

Lingren (1968) also directly tested assumptions about Cards III, IV, and VII by relating the negative content in responses to these blots to subjects' performances on the Family Relations test (FRT). The subjects of this study were 30 children with reading difficulty. Lingren found no significant differences in attitudes toward parents expressed on the FRT between children who gave popular versus those who gave negative responses to the three blots.

In a study focused on Card VI, Guertin and Trembath (1953) attempted to determine the extent to which habitual sex offenders would show greater psychosexual disturbance on this blot than a group of normal control subjects. These authors contrasted 63 hospitalized "sexual deviates" with a control group of state hospital employees. The only variable controlled was age. Furthermore the "sexual deviates" appear to have been a very mixed group, including individuals convicted of indecent exposure, oral perversions, and homosexuality. An attempt by a clinician to sort the protocols based on Card VI disturbance proved to be unsuccessful. Various Rorschach quantitative indices and ratios also failed to differentiate the two groups' performances on Card VI.

Charen (1957) warned of the pitfalls of blindly interpreting parental symbolism in responses to Cards IV and VII. This author reported having asked over 50 test subjects, following the administration proper, to pick out the cards most like their parents. Charen indicated that most subjects interpreted these instructions to mean that they should choose the *response* that reminded them of their parents. The subjects were found to pick a variety of areas on the various Rorschach blots. "They tended to use all 10 cards in such manner that no distinction between Cards IV and VII and the other eight cards could be made" (Charen, 1957, p 56).

BLOT PREFERENCE STUDIES

Several investigations have focused on the blot preferences of diverse subject groups. In two such studies, the Hafner (1961) and the Magnussen and Cole (1967) investigations discussed above, child subjects were asked to state which cards were liked best and least. Both studies found that Card X was liked best, and Card IV least. Mitchell (1952) worked with 200 adult mental hygiene clinic patients, 28 psychiatric inpatients, and 42 nonpatient adults; all were male. They were asked to choose the cards liked best and least, and to state their reasons. Card X was liked best by all three groups, primarily because of its colors. However the neurotic group also liked this card least because of its scattered quality. Card IX was not liked as much by the neurotics as it was by the psychotics and normals. Card VII was disliked more frequently by the normals than by the patients. Card V was disliked by the psychotics, who described the content as disturbing, but it was preferred by the less intelligent neurotics because of its easy percept. Card IV was among the least preferred in all three groups.

Hershenson (1949) asked 30 high school juniors (15 males and 15 females) to arrange the cards in order of preference. They were also asked their reasons for selecting the two most preferred cards and the two least preferred. This author found that Cards VIII, IX, and X were preferred by both boys and girls, that Cards I and II were preferred least by the girls, and that Cards V and VI were preferred least by the boys. Color was often given as the reason for preference.

Wallen (1948) asked 419 subjects ("stable" and "unstable" males at a military training station) to indicate whether they liked or did not like the blots. Some of the subjects saw the blots in the usual order, some in reverse order, some in the usual order except that Card X was presented first, and some in the usual order with the cards inverted. The "stable" subjects who saw the cards in the usual order liked Cards VIII, IX, and X best, and Cards I, II, III, and VII least. However, the preferences given were drastically altered when the order of the cards was changed. Whereas 69 percent reported liking Card X in the usual order, only 23 percent liked it in the reverse order. Wallen compared this tendency to prefer later cards and to dislike the first cards to the warm-up effect in interviews, in which the client becomes progressively more relaxed as the session progresses. Other findings of Wallen that merit interest in the present discussion include his observation that inverting the cards had little effect on expressed liking. Cards II, VI, and IX elicited more reactions of dislike among the unstable than among the stable subjects, but color appeared to be a factor only for Card II. Unstable subjects frequently disliked color cards because the red reminded them of blood.

In the Ames et al. (1974) normative study of children, the subjects were asked to indicate the cards liked best and least, and to state the reasons for their preferences. At almost every age level from ages 2 through 10, Card X was preferred by both boys and girls. Cards I, II, and VIII were sometimes the most frequently chosen as best liked at some age levels under age 5. Girls most often chose VI, IV, and II as the least liked, while boys most often chose I, VI, and IV.

George (1955) reported previously unpublished data on the expressed card preferences of 60 college subjects, each of whom had been asked to pick his favorite card. The cards were then ranked according to frequency of choice. As in the Hershenson study, Cards VIII and X were highly preferred. Cards IV, I, and V were the least preferred blots. George also correlated the results of various studies on card preference with one another and with data on the sexual suggestiveness of blots, with data on card productivity and card complexity, and with the order of card presentation. Card preference in the Wallen (1948) investigation was found to correlate significantly with the sexual suggestiveness of the blots. Card complexity (as determined by Beck's data on the difficulty of producing whole responses) correlated significantly with the card preferences of high school and college students, who favored the more complex blots.

As part of a larger study on the effects of color on test responses, Crumpton (1956) had subjects choose the blots they preferred most and least. The standard blots were administered to 10 psychotic, 10 neurotic, and 10 organic subjects. A comparable group of subjects was administered an achromatic version of the Rorschach blots. Crumpton found that when subjects were given a free choice, the normally colored cards and the normally achromatic cards were preferred about equally.

Crumpton also offered a qualitative report on reasons given by the subjects for preferring the achromatic versions of Cards II and VIII. Subjects had apparently reacted negatively to the color-form incongruity of Card VIII and to the emotional associations called forth by Card II (e.g., a bloody bear). A final interesting finding of this study was that there were significantly more aggressive and submissive responses, and significantly fewer neutral responses to the chromatic blots.

Greyson (1956) also studied card preference as part of a larger investigation on the effects of color and shading. This investigation employed the standard Rorschach blots plus nine experimental blot series: three achromatic series differing in degree of blackness, and six monochromatic sets (blue, green, yellow, orange-tan, brick, and red). The standard blot sequence was used, but each blot in a particular administration came from a different one of the 10 series. A Latin Square design was used, with the subjects being 30 nurses in a psychology course. All subjects assigned ratings of pleasantness to the blots on a 5-point scale. Card X elicited the greatest number of responses irrespective of color. Cards III and IX were tied for second place in terms of productivity. Card VII elicited the least number of responses. When the pleasantness ratings were averaged across all 10 series (a technique which Grayson used to neutralize the effects of color), Grayson found the following order of pleasantness, ranked from highest to lowest: Card II, Card V, Card III, Cards I and IX, Cards VII and VIII, Card X, Card VI, and Card IV.

MISCELLANEOUS STUDIES

Some of the investigations on the stimulus characteristics of the blots are not classifiable under the above rubrics. A few studies have looked at the ability of the blots and blot locations to elicit sexual responses. Shaw (1948) instructed 50 college males first to locate the Beck populars, then to indicate the sexual areas of the blots by labeling them male, female, or either. Almost twice as many female as male sexual responses were elicited. Female percepts were preponderant on Cards I, II, III, IV, VII, VIII, and IX. Card VI was the only card on which more male than female responses were found. On Cards V and X, an almost equal number of male and female responses appeared. Shaw presented a list of 13 sex populars — responses in which 10 or more of the subjects agreed about the area and the sex.

Using subjects of both sexes, Pascal, Ruesch, Devine, and Suttell (1950) devised a Rorschach administration procedure which they called "Testing the Limits for Sex" (TLS), in which subjects were asked to point out sexual areas in the blots. The subjects were 190 male and 47 female college students and psychiatric patients. The mean number of sexual responses on the blots was 4.4, and there were no significant differences between the sexes, diagnostic groups, examiners, or for marital status. Male subjects gave significantly more vagina responses than penis responses. Female subjects gave an equal number of vagina and penis responses. Card VI elicited the most sexual responses, particularly male sexual responses. Cards I, IV, VII, VIII, and IX evoked primarily female sexual responses; on VI and X, more male than female sexual responses were brought forth. On Cards II and III, the gender of the sexual responses depended on the sex of the subjects. Pascal et al. listed 14 areas as the most common in which sexual responses appeared.

Pascal and Herzberg (1952) tested the ability of the TLS procedure to discriminate between control subjects and groups of sex offenders. The subjects were 78 male penitentiary prisoners: 19 controls, 19 rapists, 20 pedophiliacs, and 20 homosexuals. They were matched for age, IQ, and length of imprisonment. The control subjects and the rapists gave more of the sex populars (Pascal et al., 1950) and fewer sexual responses to other blot areas than either the pedophiliacs or homosexuals.

George (1953) correlated the sexual suggestibility of the blots as determined by Shaw (1948) with blot preferences as determined by Wallen (1948). A rho correlation of .65 ($p < .05$), found using Wallen's stable group, indicated that the more sexually suggestive blots were the less preferred. For Wallen's unstable subjects, the correlation was .70 ($p < .03$).

Sappenfield (1965) asked 161 college subjects (68 males and 93 females) to indicate whether each of the blots and each of their responses was attractive or repelling. Cards II, III, VI, and VII were significantly seen as attractive. Cards I and IV were significantly seen as repelling. Card VII was the most attractive and least repelling blot, and Cards I and IV were very close in their perceived repellent qualities. There were no significant sex differences in card perception.

Sappenfield (1961) asked 104 undergraduates (53 males and 51 females) to indicate whether each Rorschach blot and each of their percepts seemed masculine or feminine. In this study the author found that five of the blots were significantly ascribed masculine stimulus values (I, IV, VI, VIII, and IX), while three of the blots were ascribed feminine characteristics (III, V, and VII). There were no significant sex differences in perception of gender characteristics in the blots.

In a different type of study on the stimulus properties of the blots, Bakan and Brown (1967) measured the free looking time (FLT) accorded to the blots by 100 college students; the subjects were also asked to rate the complexity of the blots. Bakan and Brown found correlations of .78 ($p < .01$) between FLT and complexity, .72 ($p < .05$) between FLT and card productivity, and .70 ($p < .05$) between productivity and complexity. Cards VIII, IX, and X were seen as the most complex and were accorded the greatest amounts of FLT. Cards V and VII were viewed as the least complex, while I and V had the smallest FLT.

Meer (1955) formulated seven hypotheses with respect to the difficulty level of the blots: differences among the cards in RT will be greater than would be expected on a chance basis; the rank of the cards on RT will be relatively constant in a variety of clinical groups; differences among the blots in form-level will be greater than expected by chance; form-level and RT to the blots will correlate significantly; judgments of difficulty among the cards will differ significantly and will be related to both RT and form-level. Data on RT, form-level, and judgments of card difficulty were obtained from 50 male college subjects; the order of card presentation was varied according to a Latin Square design. Data from previous research on RT were also included in the analysis. All seven of the hypotheses were confirmed.

Mensh and Matarazzo (1954) presented data on card rejection among 201 hospitalized patients. Card IX was found to result in the largest number of rejections, followed by Cards IV, VI, VII, and X. Rejections for these five cards accounted for 83 percent of card rejections among this sample.

Beck and associates (1950) reported on a variety of Rorschach indices among 154 normal subjects. Two of Beck's indices are relevant to the present presentation. With respect to mean RT, Cards V, VIII, and I were found to be the fastest, Cards IX, X, and IV the slowest. Card X appeared to have the highest productivity, and Cards VIII, IX, V, and IV were also relatively high in productivity for various occupational groups. Card II was the lowest in terms of productivity, while Card V was also fairly low among certain socioeconomic groups.

Levy (1950) investigated changes in palmar skin conductance accompanying each of the Rorschach cards, using 50 male college subjects. Change in conductance among the cards was not found to be significantly different. Card V had the lowest reaction from the subjects, Card VIII the highest. Position in the series was found to have a significant effect on change in conductance; conductance was high for the first card in a series and dropped off for the next two cards. Conductance increased with the last three cards presented, possibly because of anticipation of the end of the test.

In an elaborate study of the stimulus properties of the blots, Ewert and Wiggins (1973) collected similarity judgments of the blots from 20 clinical psychologists and 49 state hospital psychiatric patients. Using a multidimensional scaling analysis, Ewert and Wiggins found four dimensions for each group. These dimensions were in turn related to independently obtained preferences for the 10 blots by a variety of subject groups and also to various stimulus calibrations of the blots (e.g., evaluation and meaningfulness). Both subject groups perceived a dimension of the blots labeled "cognitive integration," which contrasts those blots that tend to elicit integrated responses from those that do not. The psychologists perceived a second dimension that correlated with preference ratings made by both a psychotic and a neurotic group, whereas the patients split this aspect into two dimensions: psychotic versus neurotic preference. The psychologists included a further dimension not seen among the patients, namely, difficulty in eliciting a response.

Baughman (1954; 1959) has conducted two well-known studies on the effect of stimulus modifications on Rorschach response categories. Baughman (1954) first used five series of blots designed to differ in terms of their stimulus properties. The five series were the standard blots, an entirely achromatic series, a series showing only the peripheral forms, a silhouette series, and an internal form series. The subjects were 100 neurotic male veterans, who were equally divided between the five series. The subject groups were equated for age, intelligence, and educational background. The most relevant findings of Baughman with respect to the impact of the standard Rorschach blots were the following: despite the prevalence of blood responses to Card II in the standard series, there was not a resulting drop in card preference; there was an increased preference for Card VIII in the standard chromatic form; negative effects due to color were not apparent in preferences assigned to the other chromatic blots.

In a later study Baughman (1959) used modifications of the standard Rorschach blots to investigate the effects of such modifications on Rorschach response categories. Six series of blots were presented to subjects: achromatic blots, complex silhouette blots, silhouette blots, white blots, complex form blots, and form blots. A total of 648 subjects participated in the experiment. Six groups of 81 subjects each were administered one of the six modified series of blots. Two groups were administered the standard Rorschach blots; one of these groups received the standard inquiry, while the other group received a paired comparison inquiry.

The most relevant of Baughman's findings in this latter study include the following observations: Card II rejections were more frequent with the chromatic version of the blot; Card VI was difficult for subjects because of its basic form; color on Card VIII did not contribute to an inability to respond; form is the primary factor in Card IX rejection.

THE TEN BLOTS

The empirical work presented above makes it possible to draw some reasonable conclusions about the stimulus qualities of the blots, particularly with reference to assertions that have been made by clinicians. The following is a blot-by-blot presentation of the stimulus qualities.

Card I

Clinicians rather consistently interpret reactions to Card I in terms of reactions to a new situation, that of the test administration (Alcock, 1963, Allen, 1966; Brown, 1953/1960; Halpern, 1953). Allen is most explicit in describing some of the characteristic ways of responding to such a new situation.

The possibilities are many but these four loom largest: (1) an immediate good response; (2) an immediate poor response; (3) a delayed good response; and (4) a delayed poor response. The inferences respectively are: (1) A healthy constructive approach to new problems ... (2) This characterizes the impulsive doer; ... a need to comply as quickly as possible regardless of the quality of compliance ... (3) The ability to demur may reflect either the thinker, the person who prefers to examine a situation ... or one who is habitually slow in responding ... or the person whose ... processes are being interfered with ... (4) ... usually seen in the markedly disturbed and deficient testee. (Allen, 1966, p 168)

There is some disagreement among clinicians as to the extent to which Card I in and of itself is likely to provoke negative reactions from subjects. On the one hand Halpern has stated that "from the formal point of view, Card I had been considered an 'ice breaker,' something to set the subject at ease. For adult subjects it is therefore generally an easy card, and only rarely produces 'shock' reactions" (Halpern, 1953, p 45). On the other hand Alcock (1963) and Allen (1966) state that Card I is indeed disturbing. "Card I invites disturbance, both because it is the beginning of a task strange to the subject, and on account of its inherent qualities" (Alcock, 1963, p 7).

A few of the empirical studies are relevant to the first clinical assertion about Card I, namely, that the card tends to elicit from the examinee his typical manner of relating to a new problem. Wallen's study (1948) showed a strong effect of stress in the decreased liking of cards that appear earliest in the series. Zax and Loiselle (1960b) found that subjects respond more negatively to Card I when it appears first in the series. Levy (1950) found skin conductance to be high for the first inkblot in a series. Levine and Spivack (1964) found that Card I elicits verbalizations scored at the repressive end of the spectrum, and they interpreted this finding as an indication of the subject's reaction to a new task. These studies generally support the clinical view of Card I as a stressful new situation to which the subject must respond. This view is also one of the more common sense interpretations in the Rorschach literature.

Research evidence on the second clinical hypothesis is clear-cut: Card I is perceived quite negatively by the typical examinee. Most Semantic Differential studies have found Card I to be among the highly negative blots on the evaluation factor; it is typically second only to Card IV in negative evaluation. A perusal of the adjectives significantly associated with Card I bolsters this negative impression. Adjectives such as ugly, dirty, cruel, and bad, occur repeatedly. Card I is also observed as a very potent card in terms of the SD, again second only to Card IV. In activity, Card I tends to be one of the intermediate blots. The data on card preference are likewise consistent with a generally negative view of Card I: in the studies on normal subjects by Hershenson (1949), George (1955), and Wallen (1948), Card I was among the least preferred blots.

The strong negative valence of this blot is consistent with the clinical view that it is a disturbing stimulus to many subjects; thus negative responses to this blot should be clinically interpreted with a great deal of caution. Responses such as "a rather ugly bat" or "a sinister-looking moth" may simply be appropriate reactions to the stimulus properties of Card I. It is the impression of the present authors that over-interpretation of negatively toned responses to this blot and to Card IV is one of the more common errors made by naive examiners.

Card II

This blot, the first of the chromatic blots, is held by clinicians to be disturbing to many subjects. Halpern (1953) has stated that the implications of this card can be disturbing to adults, although this is not the case with children. Alcock has described the tendency of this blot "to elicit percepts with dysphoric content" (Alcock, 1963, p 8). The color (red, reminiscent of blood) has been remarked on as one of the foci of disturbance. "There seems no doubt that the color is the chief focus of disturbance . . . for many it has associations to damage, including menstrual blood" (Alcock, 1963, pp 8 – 9).

The sexual implications of this blot are also described as among its upsetting aspects (Allen, 1966; Brown, 1953/1960; Halpern, 1953). "The plate is highly charged for both male and female sexuality . . . so that the person who is sensitive to this type of conflict would give some sign or signs of this feeling" (Allen, 1966, p 170). Finally, Brown has commented on the tendency of Card II to evoke childhood experiences and feelings.

The implications of the research literature on Card II must be considered mixed. On the one hand, in the Semantic Differential studies, this blot has not often been found to have strong connotative meaning. Hays and Boardman (1975) have found it to be one of the three least connotative Rorschach blots on the SD; Hafner and Rosen (1964) found no adjective associated with this blot by their subject groups. Card II seems relatively intermediate in factor scores of both evaluation and potency, and low in activity. Hershenson (1949) and George (1955) found that Card II is one of the intermediate blots in terms of card preference for normal subjects.

On the other hand, there is also some evidence of this card's negative impact on certain classes of subjects. There seems to be a tendency toward sex differences in perceptions on this blot. Little (1959) found that Card II was rated as the second highest in potency by the women, while male subjects assigned relatively low potency ratings to this card. Hershenson (1949) noted that female high school students listed Card II as among the least liked blots, while males disliked other blots. Ames et al. (1974) likewise found girls to dislike Card II more than boys did. As suggested by Hershenson, these differences may tie in with the association of this card to menstrual blood. It is perhaps notable in this regard that Card II was the only one of the chromatic blots for which Hays and Broadman (1975) did not find color to increase positive evaluation. Baughman (1959) found that rejections of Card II were more frequent when the blot contained color. As noted above, Crumpton (1956) reported that subjects preferring the achromatic version of Card II were responding out of aversion to emotional associations called forth by the mixture of color and form. Additional evidence for the negative effects of the color factor on this card is found in Grayson's 1956 study, in which Card II catapulted to the position of the most pleasant blot when the color factor was neutralized. Furthermore, in the Wallen (1948) investigation, Card II aroused more reactions of dislike among unstable than among stable men, particularly because of the color factor. (Card II was the least preferred blot among Wallen's unstable subjects.)

There is some corroboration of the sexually evocative characteristics of Card II in the study of Pascal et al. (1950). These investigators found that Card II was the second most evocative blot for sexual responses.

In conclusion the general clinical view that Card II tends to be upsetting to subjects seems to be supported for certain female and unstable subjects, although many subjects have a blander reaction to this blot. As suggested by clinicians, the card does appear to be one of the most prone to elicit sexual responses.

Card III

Clinical views on Card III have centered on the very popular human figures. Interpretations have revolved around whether the people are seen at all, what they are doing, and the sex of the figures.

Allen (1966) held that the absence of human association on this card should be considered pathological. In data presented by Molish (1951), the human percept on Card III was reported significantly more frequently by normals than by schizophrenics or neurotics; such a result tends to bolster Allen's contention. In the Meer (1955) data on judgments of difficulty in interpreting blots, Card III was judged by subjects to be the easiest blot to interpret, this finding constituting further evidence of the pathological implications of failure to recognize the popular human percept. However Hammer (1966) reported that surprisingly large percentages of normal control subjects (23 percent of normal females and 27 percent of normal males) perceived no human figure on Card III.

Clinicians have suggested that the type of action in which the people are engaged may reveal the subject's attitudes toward people and relationships with others. Brown (1953/1960) has stated that Card III has a particular tendency to elicit themes of cooperation–competition. Halpern (1953) noted that responses to this blot tend to indicate how people are perceived by the subject. Richards (1958) described responses to Card III in terms of the subject's concept of early parental interaction. An interpretation of the testee's views of interpersonal relationships would thus depend on whether he saw the figure engaged, on the one hand, in a cooperative action, or, on the other, in a battle or in the act of tearing something apart, etc.

Unfortunately the empirical literature on the blots is not relevant to this particular assertion about Card III. This situation is particularly regrettable because, in the experience of the present authors, many clinicians place great stock in responses to Card III as indicative of the pattern of social interactions.

The sexes of the figures perceived on this blot has also been a concern of clinicians (Alcock, 1963; Allen, 1966; Brown, 1953/1960; Klopfer & Davidson, 1962). Brown (1953/1960) has discussed the implications of males who describe the figures as women, and of subjects who see the figures as a man and a woman. Allen (1966) has said that attribution of both male and female characteristics to the figures may indicate sexual confusion.

Brown (1971) has reported a study of the gender of human figures perceived on Card III. There were three subject groups: private patients referred for psychological examination, and two groups of neuropsychiatric patients. Brown found a significant trend over time toward perception of female rather than male figures on Card III, and he discussed the implications of this finding in terms of changes in sexual identification in our culture. Two prior studies in this area (Hammer, (1966; Nelson, Wolfson & Lo Cascio, 1959) appear to support Brown's contention in that a pronounced shift toward perceiving the Card III figures as female on the part of both male and female normal subjects is seen from the earlier to the later of these investigations.

In an extensive normative study, Ames (1975) has presented data that tend to temper Brown's conclusions. Ames indicated that, although there was indeed a jump in the percentage of males in their twenties who saw two women on Card III (from 36 percent in 1958 – 1961 to 76 percent in 1972 – 1973), this change seemed to be accounted for by the fact that young men in the latter period merged the categories of two women and two people into simply two women. Ames conjectured that this result may merely reflect a greater willingness of male subjects today to *name* women when they are perceived on Card III.

Ames's data also indicated that the age of the subject was a factor in whether he or she perceived his or her own sex, or the opposite sex, in the blot figures. In addition Ames demonstrated that among young subjects (20-year-olds and 30- to 40-year-olds), more male subjects perceived females on Card III, and more female subjects perceived males. These findings clearly indicate that the mere sex of the figures perceived cannot be clinically used as an index of sexual identification.

It is evident from the Semantic Differential studies that Card III is generally perceived positively; it is also one of the lowest blots in terms of potency. Zax and Loiselle (1960a) found that male college students perceived Card III as the most feminine of all the blots. Card III has often been chosen as the mother or father card by child subjects (Hafner, 1961; Magnussen & Cole, 1967), but that may merely be due to the ease with which humans can be seen on this card. Sappenfield (1961, 1965) found that Card III was seen as feminine and as attractive by college subjects.

In view of the Ames data (1975) on the tendency of young subjects to perceive figures of the opposite sex on Card III, it is clearly unwise to interpret subjects' perceptions of figures of the opposite sex in terms of sexual identification. In our experience the gender characteristics of Card III, especially in combination with the nature of the activity of the figures, does constitute highly useful clinical material, largely in cases in which the subject is perplexed and disturbed over the possible sex of the figures, and is either unable to reach a decision or describes the figures as having both male and female sexual parts. We believe that such responses indicate confused sexual identification. However there is not yet any empirical data to support such an interpretation.

Because interpretations regarding the manner in which social relations are perceived are commonly interpreted from Card III, it is unfortunate that there is not yet a basis for evaluating the validity of such interpretations. Research in this area — possibly patterned after the type of study conducted by Zelin and Sechrest (1963) — would probably prove to be less sterile than the proliferating studies on the father and mother cards of the Rorschach.

Card IV

As noted earlier in this chapter, clinicians have long interpreted reactions to Card IV in terms of reactions to male authority; Card IV is described as the father card. Alcock has qualified this interpretation by explaining that "the 'father' as projected has no tenderness. Rather he typifies the terrible sexual male of Oedipal phantasies" (Alcock, 1963, p 11).

Empirical studies on Card IV reveal that this blot projects a highly consistent image. Semantic Differential studies indicate that Card IV is seen very high in potency, very low in evaluation, and somewhat low in activity. Hafner (1961) and Magnussen and Cole (1967) found that children tended to choose this blot as least liked and as the most frightening. Card IV was often described in the Ames et al. (1974) study as the least liked of the blots. In the George (1955) investigation, Card IV was the least preferred blot. Sappenfield (1965) found it to be described as repelling, and in another study (1961) found it to be classified as masculine. It will be recalled that in the Grayson (1956) research in which color effects were neutralized, Card IV was still assigned the lowest pleasantness ratings, a result indicating that the basic form of the blot is responsible for subjects' negative reactions to Card IV.

As might be expected of investigations varying so much in methodology and populations studied, the empirical literature on the subject of Card IV as the father card has yielded equivocal results. Although Kamano (1960) found SD ratings of "father" to be closer to Card IV than to Card VIII, Smith (cited in Osgood et al., 1957) and Sines (1960) found that the SD ratings of the concepts of "my father" and "father" were not close to the SD ratings of Card IV. Rosen (1951), however, found that such concepts as masculine aggression, feeling of authority, father symbol, and male sex organ were significantly assigned to this blot.

In studies in which subjects had to pick a father card (Beck & Herron, 1969; Cole & Williams, 1968; Engel, 1959; Hafner, 1961; Levy, 1958; Magnussen & Cole, 1967; Meer & Singer, 1950; Taniguchi et al., 1958) the evidence is generally positive. Card IV is often the most frequently chosen father card, particularly among male subjects (Cole & Williams, 1968; Magnussen & Cole, 1967).

In the four studies that directly researched the effectiveness of Card IV in eliciting feelings toward the father (Dana, 1954; Hirschstein & Rabin, 1955; Lingren, 1968; Zelin & Sechrest, 1963), the results cannot be described as encouraging. As noted above, it is questionable whether the significant results found by Dana can be attributed to the father characteristics of Card IV, and the investigation of Hirschstein and Rabin did not include a control blot and was based on questionable theoretical grounds. In the well-designed Zelin and Sechrest study (1963), judgments of attitudes toward the father, as evaluated from responses to Card IV, did not prove to be significantly related to rated attitudes toward the father, although the correlation for Card IV was higher than those for the other blots. The Lingren study also failed to support the hypothesis that Card IV evokes feelings toward the father.

It is clear that Card IV is perceived quite negatively by many subjects. Negatively toned responses to this blot should therefore be interpreted with care. Without additional evidence, it is inappropriate to interpret such responses as "a frightening gorilla" or "a large ugly animal" as indicative of fear of the father and Oedipal difficulties. (Of course such an interpretation is valid to the extent that all subjects may be assumed to have some difficulties in this regard, but then the interpretation would be totally nonspecific to the subject.)

The present authors believe that the stimulus characteristics of Card IV may make it particularly conducive to the eliciting of Oedipal feelings and feelings toward authority. (See, for example, the responses of subject No. 1 in Chapter 12.) However, by no means does Card IV always elicit Oedipal responses, and it should not be blindly assumed that a subject's responses to Card IV mirror such attitudes unless sufficient evidence supports that interpretation.

An example of the type of error that can be made by assuming that responses to Card IV always reflect attitudes toward the father can be seen in a contrast between the responses of subjects No. 1 and No. 2 in Chapter 12. In both cases the female patients reported seeing an abominable snowman. Their associations revealed that the first patient was describing feelings toward her father, whereas the second patient was expressing feelings about her mother. A clinician assuming that Card IV is invariably the father card would grossly misinterpret the response of the latter patient.

It is our impression that the labeling of Card IV as the father card has had two unfortunate effects. First, this label misleads many naive clinicians into inappropriately interpreting troubled attitudes toward male authority when there is merely an appropriate response to the stimulus characteristics of Card IV. Zimmerman, Lambert, and Class state that "the strongly negative quality typically ascribed to [Card] IV . . . suggest[s] an implicit bias . . . which might lead a naive examiner to find all his subjects obsessed with . . . negative attitudes toward authority" (Zimmerman, Lambert, & Class, 1966, p 259).

The second unfortunate effect of the father label on Card IV is that clinicians may overlook the extent to which attitudes toward the father can be projected on each and every one of the Rorschach blots, as has been pointed out by Charen (1957).

In summary, Card IV is generally a negative and frightening stimulus. It may be particularly conducive to negative feelings toward the father and male authority, but such interpretations should not be made without sufficient evidence. Clinicians should particularly guard against interpreting negative feelings toward male authority in what may be an appropriate reaction to the negative stimulus characteristics of this blot. Clinicians should also keep in mind that attitudes toward the father may be projected on any of the blots.

Card V

Clinical views of Card V largely agree that this blot is very easy for the subject, is relatively undisturbing, and provides a breathing spell after the disturbing character of earlier cards. Alcock (1963) has stated that responses to this card rarely have a negative tone, and when they do, it is in response to the darkness of the blot.

Brown (1953/1960) has referred to Card V as the "reality card," because of the ease with which this blot elicits the popular winged object. Alcock (1963) and Halpern (1953) agree that failure to perceive this popular image is a pathological indication.

Semantic Differential ratings of Card V have not displayed much consistency. In the Hays and Boardman (1975) investigation, Card V was rated most positively in evaluation. This study is the exception, however.

Most SD studies have found Card V to be fairly neutral or somewhat negative in the evaluation factor. This blot is generally rated low in potency, and somewhat active.

The research literature seems to support the clinical view that Card V does not usually evoke extreme reactions from subjects and may serve to spell the typical subject after more disturbing earlier cards. Meer (1955) reported that this blot ranks second in terms of the ease with which percepts can be distinguished. Meer also reported this blot to be the easiest on which to obtain a high form-level response, and among the blots with the shortest reaction time. Levy (1950) found that Card V elicited the smallest galvanic skin response of the 10 blots. Rosen (1951) remarked that Card V appears to lack extreme connotations for most subjects. Only one concept, bat, was found to be significantly associated with Card V. Bakan and Brown (1967) found Card V to have the lowest complexity ratings of the 10 inkblots, and also the lowest free looking time. Card V was seen as neither attractive nor repelling in the Sappenfield (1965) study. Pascal et al. (1950) and Shaw (1948) found that the blot elicited the fewest number of sexual responses from subjects. Card V is rarely rejected and has been reported to be the lowest of the blots in productivity (George, 1955; Richards 1958).

The ease with which a percept can be distinguished on Card V appears to evoke a differential response from subjects of varying intellectual capacity. Mitchell (1952) found that those preferring Card V had lower mean educational levels and IQs than those who preferred other blots. While above average intelligence subject groups (George, 1955; Hershenson, 1949) rate this card low in preference, subjects of average intelligence (Wallen, 1948) rate it high in preference.

Although the flying animal on Card V is the most popular percept, evidence of the pathological implications of not seeing this popular response is not supported in the Molish (1951) investigation: Molish found that this response did not differentiate between normal, neurotic, and schizophrenic groups.

Few studies are relevant to the connection between negative responses on this blot and the color factor. Rosen (1951) found that the concept of nighttime was significantly associated with Card V by the female subjects in only one of three clinical groups. Card V was disliked by many psychotics in the Mitchell (1952) investigation, but the most frequent reason given was its disturbing content.

Card VI

This blot has been referred to as the sex card because of a phallic symbol at the top and a vaginal symbol below. Halpern (1953) has stated that this blot is likely to be quite disturbing to adults with unresolved sexual problems. Allen (1966), Alcock (1963), Brown (1960), Klopfer and Davidson (1962), and Richards (1958) all agree about the strong sexual connotations of this blot and about its tendency to be upsetting to subjects.

Semantic Differential studies of Card VI have found somewhat negative evaluations of this blot, either neutral or somewhat potent ratings on the potency factor, and low ratings on the activity factor. Card VI is one of the less meaningful blots on the SD; in the investigations of Hafner and Rosen (1964), Otten and Van de Castle (1963), and Rosen (1960), none of the adjectives were significantly associated with this blot by the subject groups. Meer (1955) has reported that Card VI has one of the slowest reaction times, and Richards (1958) has indicated that it is one of the most frequently rejected. Baughman (1959) has described this blot as difficult because of its basic form.

The findings of Pascal et al. (1950) were consistent with the assumed sexual significance of this blot: they found that Card VI was the blot most frequently responded to with sexual percepts. Shaw found this to be the only blot on which male gender responses were more numerous than female gender responses. Rosen (1951) found that the concepts of male sex organ and female sex organ were among those associated with Card VI, although Smith (cited in Osgood et al., 1957) did not find the SD ratings for this blot to be similar to ratings of the concept of sex. Levy (1958) found that Card VI was significantly associated with a man or father doll. Sappenfield (1961) found that patients ascribed this blot masculine stimulus values. Cole and Williams (1968) found that Card VI was significantly chosen by female precollege subjects as reminding them of father. Card VI has been described in several studies as the most disliked by subjects; however Sappenfield (1965) found that Card VI was described as attractive by college subjects. Wallen (1948) found that, in terms of card preference, this blot differentiated stable from unstable subjects more effectively than any other blot. However Guertin and Trembath (1953) did not find that responses to this blot differentiated habitual sex offenders from normal control subjects.

On the whole the evidence does indicate that Card VI is sexually suggestive, particularly of male sexuality, and that it tends to elicit negative reactions. The clinician should be aware of and sensitive to these blot characteristics. However, as discussed in the section on Card IV, blanket interpretations should not be made on the assumption that this card is the so-called sex card. The clinician should also be aware that information relevant to sexual functioning can of course be brought forth by other blots. Furthermore the difficulty in distinguishing percepts on Card VI must be recognized as another factor affecting subjects' reactions to it.

Card VII

In several ways Card VII is viewed by many psychologists as the reverse of Card IV. Clinicians often refer to Card VII as the mother card because, as Brown explains, it suggests "predominantly feminine figures in conjunction with a soft textural pervasiveness" (Brown, 1953/1960, p 383). Alcock (1963) also noted that Card VII tends to evoke concepts appropriate to a mother – child relationship. Halpern is the most specific: "The child's reaction to the whole blot reflects his perception of the mother" (Halpern, 1953, p 51).

Other factors cited by clinicians as important factors in Card VII's pull are the presence of sexual organs in the blot and the lack of solid form. Klopfer and Davidson (1962) have referred to the presence of a female sex organ on Card VII, while Alcock (1963) has noted both a penis and a vaginal entrance. Allen (1966) reported that subjects seeing this blot can be upset by a feeling of not being able to take hold. On the other hand, Klopfer and Davidson (1962) described the light and airy qualities of this card.

Semantic Differential studies with Card VII indicate a marked contrast with Card IV. Card VII has typically been rated quite high in evaluation, very low in potency, and low in activity. There is some evidence (Zax & Loiselle, 1960b) that the positive response of subjects to Card VII is in part an effect of card sequence. Rejections on Card VII are relatively rare (Richards, 1958). Sappenfield (1965) found that Card VII was described as the most attractive and the least repellent of the blots.

In those studies that have specifically investigated this blot's connotations of mother, the results have been mixed. Whereas Kamano (1960) found that the SD ratings for Card VII were closer to the concept of mother than to that of father, Smith (cited in Osgood et al., 1957) and Sines (1960) did not find that the SD ratings for Card VII were close to the ratings for mother. Rosen (1951) found that the concept of a mother symbol was significantly associated with Card VII; this concept was not significantly associated with any other card. Rosen (1960) also found that this card was rated as extremely feminine.

In investigations in which subjects had to choose a mother card, results have likewise been equivocal. Meer and Singer (1950) found that college males chose Cards VII and X most frequently for mother. Magnussen and Cole (1967) found that Card VII was most frequently chosen as the mother card by children. Taniguchi et al. (1958) found that Japanese college students most frequently chose VII for mother. However Beck and Herron (1969), Cole and Williams (1968), Engel (1959), and Hafner (1961) did not find that Card VII was the most frequent choice for mother and in the Taniguchi study the noncollege subjects did not most often associate Card VII with mother. Nor did Levy's study with doll figures (1958) support the association of Card VII with mother.

In direct investigations of the effectiveness of Card VII in eliciting feelings relevant to mother, Hirschstein and Rabin (1955) did find some support for their hypothesis. But the studies of Zelin and Sechrest (1963) and Lingren (1968) did not support the hypothesis. In fact the Zelin and Sechrest investigation found a nonsignificant negative relationship between Card VII and attitudes toward the mother.

In studying the sexually evocative character of Card VII, Shaw (1948) found more female than male sexual percepts on this card. Pascal et al. (1950) found that of all the cards, Card VII had the largest preponderance of female over male sexual percepts. Sappenfield (1961) determined that Card VII was significantly designated as female by his subjects.

Meer's data (1955) on the quality of form-level for the various blots include an interesting finding about Card VII: it was the third most difficult blot on which to produce responses of good form-level.

In summary, this blot is perceived as high in evaluation, low in potency, and low in activity. It often elicits a positive response. However the evidence on this card's particular ability to evoke attitudes toward the mother is not encouraging. The findings of Zelin and Sechrest (1963) suggest that interpreting responses to VII in terms of feeling toward the mother, without sufficient evidence for such an interpretation, can be quite misleading. Card VII is also one of the most difficult blots in terms of producing responses of good form-level.

Clinicians should be aware that attitudes toward the mother can be projected onto any card, and should be wary of categorically interpreting Card VII responses in terms of the mother without sufficient evidence. In view of the predominantly female gender of sexual responses to this card, it also seems likely that, at least in some cases, subjects can be expected to react to the female genitals on the blot.

Card VIII

Alcock (1963) has stated that Card VIII can generally be considered a mild stimulus — the pastel coloring is soft, and it is easy to discern the shapes of animals in Card VIII. Because of this mild stimulus, Alcock noted that "disturbed reactions to the color in Card VIII should . . . be taken more seriously than those to the more emotionally provocative red in Cards II and III, or to the mixed-up colors of Card IX" (Alcock, 1963, p 17).

Allen (1966) remarked that because the animals seen at the side of this blot are the second most popular percept on the Rorschach blots, failure to recognize the animals should be considered indicative of serious disturbance. Clinicians also stress the importance of the type of animal that is seen. Halpern (1953) felt this point to be important, particularly among children. Alcock (1963) has also stressed the importance of the type of animal. Brown (1953/1960) has suggested that the side animals project the "expression of animal impulses" as felt by the subject. For example, "salamanders and chameleons express the need to be compliantly passive and excessively adaptable" (Brown, 1953/1960, p 368).

On the Semantic Differential, Card VIII has been found to be one of the least connotative in meaning. Hafner and Rosen (1964), Hays and Boardman (1975), and Otten and Van de Castle (1963) found that none of the SD adjectives was significantly associated with this blot. Card VIII is usually determined to be intermediate in the SD factor of evaluation, somewhat high in potency, and somewhat low in activity. Consistent with Card VIII's more or less neutral ratings on the SD scales, Sappenfield (1965) found that this blot was perceived as neither attractive nor repellent by college subjects.

There is some evidence that the perception of Card VIII is affected by the sequence in which it is presented. Zax and Loiselle (1960b) found that this card was perceived as less benign when presented in the standard order, that is, as the first chromatic after several achromatic blots. Levy (1950) found that the eighth card in a 10-blot series elicited high GSR reactivity, perhaps as a response to the impending end of the series.

Card VIII has generally fared well in the investigations on card preference. In data summarized by George (1955) and Richards (1958), Card VIII was among the best liked of the blots. Alcock's (1963) views on the benign character of this blot have been generally confirmed: investigations incorporating altered achromatic blots as part of the experimental design (e.g., Baughman, 1954; Crumpton, 1956; Grayson, 1956) have indicated that the colors of this card add to the generally positive response. However Crumpton (1956) also indicated that subjects who preferred the achromatic version of this card were reacting to the incongruity between form and colors.

Unfortunately there are few empirical data that bear directly on the common interpretations of the type of animal seen on Card VIII. Although Gill (1967) has found that specific ego qualities are associated by subjects with certain animals, this is rather indirect evidence for such interpretations. It is certainly recommended that clinicians refrain from interpreting the very popular animals (bears, rodents) that are often seen in response to the blot in the absence of evidence that the specific animal has some dynamic meaning for the subject. It is also advisable that clinicians investigate the testee's associations to the specific types of animals seen, because although the choice of animal may indeed have dynamic significance, the meaning may be idiosyncratic to the test subject. (See Chapter 10.)

The Molish (1951) study on Popular responses in schizophrenics, normals, and neurotics found that the popular animal response was given significantly more frequently by normals than by schizophrenics. This result tends to confirm the clinical view that the inability to perceive the popular animals is a pathological sign.

Card IX

Clinical authorities agree that Card IX has an unstructured quality which makes discerning percepts quite difficult. Consequently, clinicians note that this blot is rejected more frequently than any other. However Brown (1953/1960) has cautioned that the common rejection of this blot cannot be considered "wholly neutral" because the forms and colors of the blot also lend themselves to some disturbing associations. Brown noted that the muddy colors in the center may evoke anal associations. Eyes and the mystical qualities of the blot were also cited by Brown. Allen (1966) too has pointed to Beck's D10 area as a sexual popular that may be disturbing to subjects. Klopfer and Davidson (1962) have noted that this blot elicits a great variety of responses, and therefore that it is one of the more valuable blots.

In Semantic Differential studies, Card IX has been accorded fairly high evaluation and potency ratings and high activity ratings. In the investigations of Rosen (1960) and Hafner and Rosen (1964), none of the subject groups associated SD adjectives with Card IX. Hays and Boardman (1975) found this blot to be one of the least connotative in meaning.

Card IX is the most difficult of the blots on which to produce percepts of good form-level (Meer, 1955). Meer also found that subjects judged Card IX the most difficult blot on which to perceive responses, and Meer's data summary on *RT* indicates that Card IX is usually the slowest of the 10 blots. Bakan and Brown (1967) found that Card IX was rated as one of the three most complex Rorschach blots: it elicited a long free looking time from most subjects. Rejections are also most frequent for Card IX (Richards, 1958). Baughman's 1959 study indicated that the basic form of this blot is responsible for rejections, and that color is largely irrelevant.

Empirical data on Card IX suggest some liking in studies of card preference. Perhaps because of the difficulty in perceiving percepts, this blot apparently elicits more dislike from neurotic subjects than from normals. Mitchell (1952) found that neurotics liked this blot significantly less than did psychotics and normals. Wallen (1948) noted that this blot differentiated stable from unstable subjects, arousing more dislike among the former. Wallen's finding that the color of the blot is irrelevant to the reaction of dislike tends to discredit the traditional notion of the so-called color shock associated with this blot. Preference for this blot appears to be augmented by the coloring (Baughman, 1954; Grayson, 1956).

Card X

Alcock (1963) has stated that, because of its several popular percepts, Card X can be considered easy for the subject. The pleasantness of the colors is also cited by clinicians. But both Brown (1953/1960) and Halpern (1953) have pointed to the tendency for subjects to feel pulled in many directions by this blot, to be disorganized by the chaotic stimuli. Lindner (1946) has said that content analysis is less successful on this blot than on others, but Brown disagreed. Both Alcock and Halpern felt that key responses are often elicited on Card X because it is the last in the series. Halpern stated that "the note on which the subject is willing to let the matter rest is of great importance, frequently representing a composite picture of his problems and conflicts" (Halpern, 1953, p 52).

In Semantic Differential investigations, Card X is usually given positive evaluations, fairly low potency ratings, and a high activity score. In studies of blot preference, Card X is often the best liked blot. Preference for this blot appears to be significantly affected by the coloring (e.g., Baughman, 1954; Crumpton, 1956; Grayson, 1956).

The clinical view that Card X tends to be difficult because of its somewhat disorganized quality is likewise validated by empirical data. Bakan and Brown (1967) found Card X to be rated the most complex of the blots. In the Mitchell (1952) study, Card X was both best and least liked by the neurotic group; patients not liking the blot cited its scattered quality. Grayson noted "when stripped of the advantage of its multiple colorfulness . . . [Card X] fared not too well, with a pleasantness ranking of third from last. The disparateness or lack of cohesiveness of the card design is the likely reason for this low ranking" (Grayson, 1956, p 293). Rosen (1951) determined emotional insecurity to be one of the concepts significantly associated with this blot. Card X has been judged the second most difficult blot on which to distinguish percepts, and it is one of the slowest in RT (Meer, 1955). It should also be noted that Meer's data (1955) indicated that Card X is second only to Card IX in difficulty of producing high form-level responses.

In short, Card X appears to evoke positive responses from most subjects, though it also has an inherent disorganizing quality that may be disturbing. It should be noted as well that Meer and Singer (1950) found mother qualities ascribed to this blot. Halpern (1953) has suggested that the common sea scene and flower garden perceived in this blot may reflect such qualities, and that maternally related responses are elicited by this blot. Reiterating an opinion expressed earlier, the present authors believe it unwise to interpret Card X responses as mother-related percepts unless sufficient evidence supports such an interpretation.

CONCLUSION

It is clear from all of the above findings that the 10 Rorschach blots cannot be considered totally unstructured stimuli to which the subject contributes structure; each of the 10 blots has distinct stimulus characteristics which influence responses. In the process of test interpretation, the examiner must strive to untangle the stimulus elements from the dynamic elements in each subject's responses, as well as possible interactions between the two. In thus interpreting Rorschach protocols, the present authors suggest the following rule of thumb: The examiner should be most reluctant to accord dynamic meaning to those responses that are in keeping with the stimulus qualities of the blot, for example, negative responses to I and IV and positive responses to VII. Conversely, the examiner should give greater weight to those responses that seem to be out of step with the stimulus characteristics of the blots.

Because the dynamic referents of Rorschach responses are often obscure, it would be of great practical help to the Rorschach clinician if blanket assumptions could be made concerning the meaning of responses to particular cards. Thus if Card IV could be assumed to be the father card, Card VI the sex card, and Card VII the mother card, clarity and focus would be brought to the meaning of many otherwise uninterpretable test responses. The extent to which such assumptions could help to clarify blot interpretation is evidenced in the great amount of research interest devoted to such assumptions. However it is important to recognize the inherent dangers of this type of technique, as has been demonstrated by studies such as the incisive investigation of Zelin and Sechrest (1963). In the considered judgment of the present writers, the clinician faced with obscure responses and symbols in the patient's test record would do better to try to clarify the dynamic meaning of the response through the techniques presented in Chapter 12, than to make what are likely to be highly questionable assumptions about the inherent meaning of particular Rorschach blots.

12

Content-Oriented Methods of Test Administration: the Content Rorschach

Over the years the technique of Rorschach test administration has come to assume a standard form. The cards are first presented to the subject and his percepts are recorded. Following this first phase, the cards are again presented and an inquiry about the location and the determinants of the response is conducted. In general the inquiry phase of administration takes longer than the first phase, and thus the Rorschach test is one of the longer tests in a standard clinical battery.

A number of workers (e.g., Aronow & Reznikoff, 1973; Kessel, Harris, & Slagle, 1969; Zubin et al., 1965) have pointed out the lack of flexibility and innovation in the Rorschach field; the test and its standard method of administration have achieved quasi-religious status. Rorschach's interpretations and technique often seem to be defended as dogma, and attempts to alter or extend them are rejected as heresy. Nowhere is the need for flexibility greater than in the technique of test administration. Because the research literature appears to indicate that determinant interpretation is clearly not the most productive approach to the test, the need for the traditional inquiry seems moot. On the other hand, because content provides the major validity for the test, it seems reasonable that the inquiry period could best be utilized in enriching the clarity and detail of content, particularly the idiosyncratic meaningfulness of the responses. As noted in Chapter 10, such an altered emphasis in the inquiry could do much toward providing the Rorschach examiner with information that is vital to the interpretation of psychodynamics.

A number of attempts to alter the traditional Rorschach administration procedure are reported in the literature. All of these previously suggested techniques are proposed as additions to the traditional procedure. In an early proposed administration technique, Janis and Janis (1946/1965) suggested the use of a free association method that utilized the subject's own responses as the stimuli for spontaneous associations, They reported that "the rich symbolic data provided by free associations to Rorschach responses tends to supplement in a variety of ways the information about personality structure gained from the Rorschach technique" (Janis & Janis, 1946/1965, p 126).

In the Janis procedure, either immediately after the standard test administration or soon thereafter, each subject's response is read to him; the exact words that the subject used are repeated. Elaborations of the responses are included, except for common form details (e.g., eyes, nose, legs). Inquiry material relating to perceptual aspects of the response is not included. These authors felt it useful to follow this procedure, whenever possible, for every one of the test responses.

The instructions for this novel phase of the test involve informing the subjects that they would be read their phrases from the previous administration of the test, and asking them to say the first thing that comes to mind. Janis and Janis attempted to get a chain of three or four associations to each response; they achieved this by getting subjects to associate to their associations. Thus, if a subject replies that a response reminds him of going to the dentist, he is then asked what going to the dentist reminds him of. Prodding questions are usually dropped after the first few responses, because subjects usually learn what is expected of them.

Janis and Janis presented several examples of the types of material elicited by their procedure, as well as a Rorschach protocol in toto. They observed wide variability in the manner in which subjects responded to their method. Some subjects simply elaborated on their original concepts, whereas others gave much more meaningful associations. They also noted the tendency of some subjects to refer to past events in their lives, particularly events that were highly charged. Fantasy material was said to be quite common, including the recall of dreams. Janis and Janis regarded their technique as appropriate for use with both children and adults, although they suggested modifying the instructions with child subjects.

Arthur (1965) published suggestions for a supplemental inquiry designed to elicit more complete data from children. She suggested that her method, dubbed the "forced confabulation technique," is best suited for use with children who produce barren or constricted records.

Arthur's technique, like the method of Janis and Janis, is a means of obtaining more complete information from subjects after the standard Rorschach administration: the child is asked to give further associations to his original responses. If the child blocks after the first such association, specific questions are asked about the response or association so that the child will construct a story, that is, confabulate the response.

Thus a 10-year-old girl who gives very terse responses during the administration proper leads Arthur to utilize her technique. In one percept the child saw a fly. Arthur therefore asks the subject to use her imagination and make up a story about the fly. Arthur asks such questions as "How does he look to you?" "Why is he flying?" and "What do you think will happen?" Gradually a story takes shape about a fly that people want to kill and discard.

As is demonstrated by examples, Arthur's technique is highly flexible; the examiner is free to ask any and all questions that seem relevant. Thus, in one example presented, the child is asked what two hands that were perceived in the association phase might be doing, because the examiner felt it was a useful question in light of the prior test record. Arthur presented a number of clinical examples in which the examiner interacts with the child to elicit thematic material that highlights affect and conflict areas by use of this method.

Appelbaum (1959/1965) proposed a novel technique designed primarily to change the atmosphere in which the test is administered. In his procedure, which follows the standard Rorschach administration, the examiner implies by his behavior that the test session is over; papers are shuffled together and the examiner informally leans back and speaks in a conversational tone. The subject is asked to go through the cards again and say whether he sees anything else. With this informal presentation of the cards, Appelbaum asserted that it is possible for the subject to relax considerably and to make responses that would otherwise not be given. "What each patient does with the opportunity to relax becomes a prime source of diagnostic information" (Appelbaum, 1959/1965, p. 13).

Appelbaum presented several examples in which this altered atmosphere resulted in information of considerable diagnostic and dynamic import. In one such example, the author presented the case of a depressed, suicidal woman with a relatively unrevealing Rorschach record. In the revised administration, however, new responses emerged in which cooperation between figures is highlighted, optimism is expressed, and insight is revealed. Appelbaum makes the point that testers usually want to know how people are likely to behave in a wide variety of life situations, and that varying the atmosphere during the test is thus likely to yield meaningful results.

A technique similar to that of Appelbaum (1959/1965) was presented by Kornrich (1965), who stated that many tests are often used in a test battery because of dissatisfaction with results obtained by standard instruction procedures. Kornrich gives the following supplemental Rorschach instructions: "I would like you to go over these once again. You need not spend more than 30 or 40 seconds on each card, but the idea is to come up with something new, something that you did not see before" (Kornrich, 1965, p 214). Kornrich, like Appelbaum, becomes more informal during this stage of the test. Additions to previous responses are discouraged, while rejections are accepted. This author also presented examples of revealing responses that result from the use of this technique.

Halpern (1957/1965) stated that the technique of Janis and Janis (1946/1965) and other methods of clarifying the meaning of perceived Rorschach content do not validate the examiner's interpretations. Consequently, Halpern developed a technique whereby the examiner makes interpretations based on the initial Rorschach content, and then in a second session asks the subject questions designed to confirm or to cast doubt on the interpretative hypotheses which were formulated in the interim.

Halpern suggests the following instructions: "I am going to be asking you some questions of a rather personal nature. It is very important that you cooperate by answering them as frankly and as honestly as you can. At times, I may cut your response short. This is because I know there will be another question about it later. Are you ready?" (Halpern, 1957/1965, p 69).

Halpern suggests that, by using this procedure, the examiner may give his hunches full reign, because they will be checked before any conclusions about their validity are reached. Several examples of this procedure are presented, as are the first five cards of two test protocols. In one such example, color naming was observed in response to the last three cards. In a later session, the examiner asked if "your emotions sometimes get the better of you." The subject responded with, "Yea, they override my reasoning power and push me very hard. Normally I use reasoning, but after a while I don't give a damn anymore. I smash things apart, etc." (Halpern, 1957/1965, p 68). Halpern also proposed asking questions in the most easily acceptable form — blunt or harsh wording should be avoided. Thus a patient of whom grandiosity was suspected was tactfully asked, "Do you have secret thoughts of wanting to be in the spotlight?" (Halpern, 1957/1965, p 69).

Halpern acknowledged criticism of his technique on the basis that the inquiries are general and could be asked of most people. However he stated that in practice he has found the questions asked to vary widely. He further presented two types of evidence in support of the ability of the technique to "strike home" with patients. First, he noted that patients tend to respond to the questions with metaphors similar to the percept.

Second, he found that patients are strongly stimulated by the questions.

Leventhal and coworkers (1962) also suggested a more flexible use of the Rorschach and other tests. They pointed out that psychologists have long recognized that in guarded records there is little material that is useful in understanding the subject's personality. They went on to propose that the examiner can elicit a more useful test record through "the active handling of the patient-psychologist relationship" (Leventhal et al., 1962, p 77). The major goal of their procedure is to motivate the patient to participate actively in the testing process. They accomplish this goal primarily through an extensive pre-test interview in which the subject is encouraged to collaborate with the examiner to produce a useful test record. The subject is thus encouraged to discuss his problems in some depth, including his feelings about them and what he sees as possible solutions. The subject's feelings toward testing are also explored. In the testing proper, the therapeutic relationship with the examiner is assumed to continue; if the subject is giving guarded test responses, the examiner may consequently point out his defensiveness and explore it.

Leventhal et al. presented several examples of the use of their type of testing procedure. They appear to use a technique similar to that of Halpern (1957/1965), although it seems that their aim is more to provide the subject with a stimulus that can lead to productive interview information. Thus in one example these authors noted a percept involving a lonely animal. The subject was asked if she felt lonely, and she then began to speak of deep feelings of loneliness in relation to her family. Leventhal et al. asserted that their interweaving of the test situation with a clinical interview actually results in a more standardized test situation, because the patient's set toward testing can be expected to be more uniform.

Rosner (1960) is another author who feels that the inquiry procedure of the Rorschach test could be used more productively to enhance the test's ability to yield information about the subject's idiosyncratic feelings and dynamics. Rosner presented two examples of the expanded use of the inquiry. In one of the examples the subject perceived a butterfly and was asked during the inquiry what the butterfly brought to mind. She responded that "it looks like a butterfly that is falling apart, jagged." The examiner then asked how it had happened and the subject gave the following answer: "Like it got caught in something and was fighting and got torn. It looks like it was trying to fly away, to get away" (Rosner, 1960, p 50).

Kessel et al. (1969) drew attention to the fact that in actual clinical practice scoring is often ignored, and that much emphasis is placed on content as analyzed by the examiner. They hold that the content is often sparse and that the examiner is thus often forced to engage in wild analysis. As an alternative, it is suggested that the examiner should encourage associations to some Rorschach responses in order to have more information on which to base interpretations. As an example, these authors discuss a response to Card I: "A peasant woman dancing." In the traditional inquiry, she was described as whirling around and wearing a big crinoline dress through which one could see her legs. Following the administration proper, the subject was asked what peasants made him think of. The subject then went through a series of associations including his mother, his mother's aunt, and girls with whom he had had intercourse. Kessel et al. (1969) interpreted these associations as signifying a wish for sexual intercourse with the mother. These authors further asserted that once the meaning of the initial theme is established, sequence analysis is more useful.

All of these attempts to alter the Rorschach administration procedure have in common the desire to enrich the idiosyncratic, dynamic character of content and thereby to facilitate the psychologist's interpretations of test productions. The Leventhal et al. technique of interweaving the test with the psychotherapeutic process has the further intent of enlisting the subject's constructive help in the testing procedure.

Despite the perceived difficulties with traditional test administration, these suggested modifications of the Rorschach procedure have not been adopted to any great extent. We believe there are two major reasons for this. First, as noted above, there is an inherent conservatism in the Rorschach field — a tendency to treat the test's administration as a sacrosanct procedure that should not be tampered with. However there is an even more important practical basis for the failure to adopt extensively any of the proposed modifications in testing procedure: all of these modifications would require more testing time than is now necessary for Rorschach test administration. Because the Rorschach is already one of the longest tests, if not *the* longest test in a clinical battery, psychologists have been understandably reluctant to extend its time demands. To do so would likely result in a decrease in the time available for the administration of other tests in the battery.

Consequently, the present authors have concentrated on developing a Rorschach administration technique that would enhance the interpretative value of content but would not extend the time requirements of the test. We have done this by drastically modifying the standard inquiry procedure, as was suggested in the Burt monograph (Note 1), in order to inquire into the dynamic meaning of percepts rather than their determinants.

THE CONTENT RORSCHACH —
AN INTERVIEW PROCEDURE

Several lines of thought converge in the administration technique that is described below. First, several Rorschach workers in recent years (e.g., Reznikoff, 1972; Zubin et al., 1965) have suggested that the Rorschach test could best be conceptualized as a type of standard interview; the present authors agree with this view. Second, as noted in Chapter 10, the Rorschach can be an incredibly rich source of material for the interpretation of individual psychodynamics. But it suffers from the fact that the dynamic referents of symbols are often obscure, and the tester usually lacks associations to the percepts that can clarify the meaning of responses. Although some authors believe that the Rorschach is not conducive to associations (e.g., Hertzman & Pearce, 1947), other clinicians maintain that associations to inkblot percepts are highly valuable clinical data (e.g., Janis and Janis, 1946/1965). A third influence on our administration procedure was Burt's suggestion of the value of looking for the influence of the subject's *past experiences* on his test responses. Janis and Janis (1946/1965) have similarly remarked on the presence of crucial memories in associations to inkblot responses.

Consequently, the present authors have constructed an inquiry procedure that greatly enlarges the interview characteristics of the Rorschach by asking for the subject's associations to percepts; the features of our procedure are similar to a "patterned" interview. The aim of the associative procedure is to clarify the dynamic referents of the responses and to elicit more dynamically relevant information from the testee. We have also included a reference to memories in our instructions, in order to encourage their expression.

According to the proposal of Burt (Note 1), our procedure eschews the traditional inquiry. We have found that the traditional inquiry is an arbitrary and time-consuming procedure that yields little valid information about test subjects. At the same time, we have tried to preserve aspects of traditional Rorschach categories that seem to have validity in order to avoid throwing out the Rorschach baby with the bathwater.

The inquiry instructions that we have used follow.

There's one more part to this test. Sometimes, what people see in the cards brings to mind something that they remember, either recently or a long time ago, or makes them think of something. When I read back your responses to you, I'd like you to tell me the first thing that comes to mind.

Following the subject's first association to these instructions, further associations may be elicited if the data warrant it. The subject may be asked to associate to his associations, as in the Janis and Janis (1946/1965) procedure, or the subject may be asked to associate to a particular part of the percept or previous association. Paralleling the Arthur (1965) technique discussed above, the procedure is flexible enough to permit the examiner to direct associations into areas that are clinically useful. As in a patterned interview (e.g., McMurry, 1947), there is thus a standard procedure to initiate an area of inquiry; but once this inquiry begins, the examiner is free to pursue leads that are clinically valuable.

In order to avoid stereotyped repetition, the examiner's phrasing in asking for associations is varied. He or she alternates such phrases as "What does ――― make you think of?" "What does ――― remind you of?" "What does that bring to mind?" "What does ――― call to mind?" and "What do you think of then?" Other examiners will doubtless find other ways to initiate the subject's associations. Our technique is not presented as a rigid and stereotyped pattern, but rather as a flexible means to an end — the garnering of dynamically relevant information. Thinking of the inquiry period as akin to an interview will help the examiner establish the proper mental set for this procedure.

At times the Rorschach testing may actually develop into a full-fledged interview. An example occurred during the examining of a 20-year-old male art student, who was referred for testing because of leg pains. A neurological basis for the pain had been ruled out. On Card IV, the patient saw "a monster on the late movie . . . big feet, a tail . . . it looks like it came out of a science fiction movie." The patient's associations during the inquiry period began as follows: "It makes me think of horrible dreams I had when I was a kid . . . fat and thin people — when I was a kid I used to see them in the closet . . . they were being either stretched or pulled. [What do these dreams remind you of?] I haven't had them since I was a kid, until recently . . . until I came to New York. [What does that call to mind?] The change of the moving. [And what does moving make you think of?] Well . . . I guess I may as well tell you . . . I've been much more bisexual since coming to New York."

At this point the patient began speaking of a long history of bisexual experiences, which were becoming increasingly homosexual since his arrival in New York. He spoke of a male dancer who was particularly aggressive in seeking his attentions. He was asked what dancers made him think of and he said, "Male dancers are very . . . feminine . . . very sweet . . . I don't know how they can consider themselves men . . . the way they talk — everything." He then spoke of his own inability to participate in his school's dance program because of his leg pains. The information acquired on this response suggested a possible etiology for the patient's leg pains. This departure from the test proper took approximately 20 minutes. The administration of the balance of the test then resumed with associations to the percepts of Card V.

If the Rorschach test is conceptualized as a patterned interview, one might well ask why one needs to bother with the blots at all. Why not simply interview the patients? In our experience there are two primary reasons why the Content Rorschach is superior to an interview per se: First, the Rorschach test evokes symbols that express the patient's unconscious dynamics, and the associations to the percepts can cast further light on their dynamic meaning. Often patients will give almost transparently obvious symbols and associations, and yet be unaware of the meaning of their responses. It is highly unlikely that an interview per se would yield such information. Second, the Content Rorschach often results in patients discussing some of their most private conscious thoughts and feelings after knowing the examiner for only a few minutes. Patients might also reveal such information in an interview setting — particularly in the context of psychotherapy — but it is likely that far more time would have to be invested in encouraging the patients to talk of their deeper feelings in a traditional interview. The Content Rorschach thus has a facilitative function: it yields a great deal of highly personal information in a short amount of time.

A further convention that we have introduced is to ask the patient from time to time what a particular percept or association might "reflect in your life." Answers to this question give the examiner relevant information about the subject's degree of insight and psychological-mindedness, and in many instances yield very dynamically relevant information. When subjects are guarded and unreflective, they will typically deny any self-referential aspects of their responses. We have not found this procedure to increase their guardedness, however. Furthermore this aspect of the technique often helps to establish the type of partnership between the testee and tester described by Leventhal et al. (1962), in which both work at making the test situation as productive as possible. This convention clearly violates the traditional Rorschach dictum that the subject is not to be told that his inkblot responses are revealing of his personality. In our experience, this admonition is of little relevance: the great majority of subjects in our patient population are well aware of the purpose of the test, and those who do not wish to know what is being revealed will manage to remain unaware.

Another change we have made in the standard administration procedure involves ascertaining locations in the association phase of the testing, rather than during the inquiry period, by use of a standard location sheet.

Asking for locations in the first phase of testing has the primary advantage of not requiring the subject to change his set during the inquiry from free association and openness to concentration on objective blot properties. In addition, in some instances subjects have difficulty recalling the location of the percept; this alteration of the administration procedure generally circumvents that difficulty. It is not our impression that inquiring as to locations in the first phase of testing has a biasing effect on subjects' test productions. It remains to be established by research in this area, however, whether existing Rorschach norms can be considered applicable to protocols obtained by means of our modified technique.

The use of associations to clarify and extend the interpretation of Rorschach symbols is consistent with the psychoanalytic use of associations in dream interpretation. Freud cautioned against interpreting symbols occurring in dreams without the supplementary use of associations.

> I should like to utter an express warning against over-estimating the importance of symbols in dream-interpretation, against restricting the work of translating dreams merely to translating symbols and against abandoning the technique of making use of the dreamer's associations. The two techniques of dream-interpretation must be complementary to each other; but both in practice and in theory the first place continues to be held by the procedure which I began by describing and which attributes a decisive significance to the comments made by the dreamer, while the translation of symbols, as I have explained it, is also at our disposal as an auxiliary method. (Freud, 1900/1965, p 395)

The advantages of the Content Rorschach technique are many. We have found that the administration time is approximately the same as for the traditional Rorschach procedure — about 45 minutes to 1 hour. The richness of the content for purposes of dynamic interpretation, however, is usually immeasurably greater. The procedure allows for the scoring of RT, P, locations, content — in fact, most of the Rorschach categories with the exception of determinants. Because the determinant scores are unavailable, it is not possible to compute the standard $F+\%$. However it is usually possible to compute an approximation of $R+\%$, the extended version of form-level which includes all form-dominated responses. As noted by Weiner, $R+\%$ "provides an alternate and sometimes more reliable index of perceptual inaccuracy than . . . $F+\%$" (Weiner, 1966, p 114). This approximation of $R+\%$ is accomplished by scoring for form-level all responses except those in which form is clearly secondary to another determinant, for example "drops of blood" on Card

II, and "a jumble of colors." In addition this technique can be used flexibly: if testing time is minimal, the examiner may wish to use the inquiry procedure on only the most promising of the subject's test responses.

The only disadvantage that we have found in the Content Rorschach is the lessened possibilities for assessing instances of "autistic logic," which is particularly characteristic of schizophrenic subjects. (See Chapter 9.) Because in the traditional inquiry the subject must reason aloud in response to the examiner's questions, the tester is provided with a favorable opportunity to observe defects in the patient's reasoning ability. This unintentional by-product of the traditional inquiry suggested by Hermann Rorschach is largely lost in our revised administration technique. However other instances of pathological verbalizations presented in Chapter 9, including confabulations and contaminations, are evoked by our type of test administration. Furthermore, because in the Content Rorschach subjects are required to associate rather than to present sources for their responses, our procedure appears to provide the examiner with a novel additional source of diagnostic information, namely, evidence of disturbances in the associative processes. Although there is as yet no empirical evidence in this regard, it is our impression that characteristically schizophrenic disturbances are indeed sometimes evident in patients' associations. (For example, see the last association of Case No. 3, response I-4 in this chapter.)

Associations to the percepts elicited by our technique often clarify what would otherwise be an undecipherable use of a symbol idiosyncratic to the patient. An example is the following response to Card VIII by a 26-year-old male outpatient with complaints of anxiety and depression.

> *Response:* The general shape reminds me of a sugar bowl . . . Upside down, it looks like a chandelier.
> *Associations:* My girl friend bought me a sugar bowl 9 months ago. [What does that make you think of?] It was a time when our relationship . . . I didn't think about her relationship with her fiancé. [What does that call to mind?] Just a very good time . . . I spent most of my time with her. I enjoyed being with her. [What do chandeliers make you think of?] My parents have one like this hanging in their dining room, and that makes me think of their house, how much I like it, how comfortable it is. [What does that call to mind?] Where me and my girlfriend live now is kind of bare . . . We have very little furniture.

In these associations the patient enables us to interpret the sugar bowl and chandelier symbols in terms of his past gratifications from his girl friend (who is engaged to someone else) and his present dissatisfaction

with their relationship, as well as his longing to return to his relationship
with his parents.

The contrasting types of information yielded by the traditional versus
our modified technique can best be demonstrated by another example.
On Card IX of the Rorschach test, a 29-year-old woman saw four pink
geese in the lower red D. A traditional inquiry would have tried to determine what it was about the blot that suggested geese; our procedure
focused on the dynamic meaning of the percept for the patient. When
asked what geese made her think of, the patient said,

> My uncle's farm. [What does that remind you of?] Good and bad.
> I spent lots of time there as a child . . . but I remembered recently
> that my uncle molested me as a child. Now I'm reluctant to acknowl-
> edge that the pink geese are nice. [Four geese, what do they remind
> you of?] Funny . . . my uncle had four daughters. [What does pink
> remind you of?] I saw my uncle slaughtering geese . . . The blood
> runs down their neck, and the white becomes pink.

By means of this altered inquiry, the examiner gathers far more material
with which to puzzle out the dynamic meaning of the four pink geese.

To date, this Content Rorschach procedure has been used with
approximately 100 adult patients. It has not been tried with children. We
have found the technique to be highly useful when the subject is reasonably cooperative, and also when the subject is of at least average intelligence. If the subject is extremely guarded or below average in intelligence,
this procedure can result in as unrevealing a test record as the traditional
administration technique.

Subjects respond to this sort of procedure in a variety of ways, as
has been noted by Janis and Janis (1946/1965). Some subjects focus
primarily on memories, some talk of their personality as revealed by their
responses, and some delve into fantasy material. There is often a bit of
initial puzzlement on the subject's part about what is expected of him.
We have found it helpful to encourage a relaxation of defenses by a
statement such as, "Just let yourself hang loose a bit, and tell me the
first thing that ——— makes you think of."

SAMPLE PROTOCOLS

Following are three complete Rorschach protocols arrived at by the
Content Rorschach technique. The first two test records were elicited from
fairly bright, verbal subjects; they have considerable psychodynamic
relevance. The latter test record was evoked from a subject who was

neither particularly insightful nor verbal. The Full Scale WAIS IQ of the third patient was 101. The degree of extra interpretative material seen in the test inquiries of the third test record thus lies midway between the constricted test protocols of dull or uncooperative patients on the one hand, and the rich, elaborated inquiry of the other two test records. Other examples of responses evoked by this associative procedure are presented in Chapter 10.

Case 1

The following is the Rorschach test record of a 26-year-old female graduate student in psychology. Her Full Scale WAIS IQ was 128. This individual had been hospitalized 6 months prior to the test session for 1 month. Her reported symptomatology at that time included catatonic symptoms and a delusion that the president was going to kill himself and that she had to stop him. At the time of the testing, she had sought outpatient psychotherapy. Her therapist found her to be unusually insightful.

Responses	*Associations*
I. 5″ 1. Two witches over a brewing pot.	I. 1. Here and here.
2. I also see a headless woman crying out for help.	2. She's wearing a dress — I can see the shape of the body under the dress.
3. Right figure looks like a devil — left looks like a king.	3. The devil was always a figure that I feared . . . it entered into my episode in January . . . I felt I was somehow in confrontation with the devil. [What does that make you think of?] A man I met. I had strange communications with him . . . I thought he was diabolical. [What does the king figure remind you of?] This king reminds me of the little king in the pictures the other day. [What does that make you think of?] When I was deciding on whether they were different . . . I could easily have been confused.

II.   15″   1. A butterfly with thorns.

2. I see two dogs' heads here.

3. Two lambs without front feet.

4. Middle part looks like some kind of urn. That's all.

II.   1. Like thorns on an animal or life in the sea, with thorns to protect itself. [How do you see it?] Looks like it's trying to get away. [What does it remind you of?] Looks like there's something destructive about these two figures.

2. Ears are back. [How do you see them?] They look blind. [How did they become blind?] I think they were in lots of fights with other dogs.

3. Victims. [Victims of what?] Of anyone who might want to hurt them. [What do you think of then?] Someone who is overwhelmed by circumstances beyond that person's control.

4. Genie's urn. [What does an urn make you think of?] Incense. [What does incense remind you of?] Reminds me of when I was young — I went to church with my mother. They would have incense in the church. [What do you think of then?] I never liked the smell of it. Supposed to have a magical quality — put people in a trance. I felt it was phony.

III.   21″   1. Two cannibals over a brewing pot. With horses' hooves for legs.
        2. A butterfly being torn apart.

III.   1. They're getting ready to cook somebody.

2. Wings are . . . being spread out from the bottom. [By what?] Cannibals have something to do with it . . . maybe heat from the pot.

3. Profiles of two unhappy children.

3. These are mouths . . . forehead, hair, chin, mouths. [What do they make you think of?] Children being ostracized by their parents. [What does that remind you of?] Reminds me of feelings I had when I was young — when I felt that my parents hated me. If I did something wrong — would be as if I was banned.

IV.   35″   1. Giant monster towering over someone very small. His arms look like . . .

IV.   1. Big furry monster. [What does that remind you of?] Reminds me of an abominable snowman. [What does that make you think of?] I think of a ruthless and insane monster who goes completely out of control and destroys people. [What do you think of then?] My father [laughs]. Because he used to go out of control when I was young, out of anger. Very quickly and without warning.

2. Eagles' heads.

2. [What does that remind you of?] Eagle to me is a symbol of power and leadership . . . I guess it's supposed to be a symbol of strength . . . but not for me . . . are fearful, ruthless birds.

3. Two small lambs looking up at him.

3. They seem insignificant and helpless — again, like victims. [What do they remind you of?] The way I felt in relation to my father when I was younger.

V. 25″ 1. A big bat with antennas.

V. 1. Reminded me of butterfly antennas when I first looked at it. [What does it make you think of?] Something very sneaky, very isolated. [What does that remind you of?] Reminds me of my father, too — though I hate to keep saying my father. I always had a feeling he was a sneaky person . . . I remember him laying little traps for my mother . . . makes me feel he was a very alone person.

2. Two crocodiles.

2. Looks like they're about to die. [Why?] Because they're exhausted . . . spent all their lives eating people up.

3. Two old men sleeping.

3. Features look very big and sagged out.

4. Underneath them are two younger men who're sleeping.

4. At first, the older figure — he was an older version of this one. But also reminds me of feelings I have towards my father and someone I went out with, similar to my father. Both are dead to me. [What do you mean?] I want to forget about them — not to let them be part of my life.

VI. 35″ 1. A cat reaching out.

VI. 1. In some ways, looks like all four legs are spread out. When I first looked at it, it looked like a cat's head. Extended fur is reaching out in some way. [What does it make you think of?] Like tentacles reaching out for food — fur is reaching out for something from the atmosphere.

2. Two middle-aged men
with big noses.

2. [How do you see them?]
Miserable. [What do you
mean?] Very dissatisfied with
their lives.

VII. 28″ 1. Two little rabbits who
just jumped on rocks.

VII. 1. Reminds me of a fantasy —
happy, playful rabbits. [What
does that make you think
of?] Like a fantasy I'd have
in childhood . . . Rabbits are
happy, little perky creatures.

2. An anal thermometer.
Should I keep the cards
like this, or can I turn
them around?

2. Goes all the way up . . . this
whole area looks very
irritated and sore. [What
does it remind you of?]
When I was younger, my
mother used an anal
thermometer to take my
temperature. I felt it was
very humiliating. [What does
that make you think of?]
When I was younger my
father used to spank me. I
was really very disgusted and
completely humiliated.

3. Two dancing ladies —
each is missing a leg, an
arm, and a head.

3. Dancing ladies are here.
[What do they make you
think of?] Makes me think of
ballerinas who I think are
really beautiful women. Also
— these ladies look like
French dancing ladies.
[What does that remind you
of?] Very happy and joyful,
uninhibited women.

VIII. 24″ 1. Two ground hogs
walking up a mountain.

VIII. 1. [What does that make you
think of?] A very hard climb
up . . . a difficult mountain to
climb.

2. A very square butterfly
being torn apart.

2. Because it's too rigid . . . not
a beautiful butterfly . . .
supposed to be smooth and
round. [What does it make

3. Seems to be a prettier
butterfly underneath
him. Looks like he's
sucking the other one
in.

you think of?] Something
that breaks very easily, that's
inflexible.

3. Wants to devour the other
one, because it isn't pretty.
[What does that remind you
of?] Reminds me of myself,
trying to do myself over, so
I'm a prettier person. [What
does that make you think
of?] I feel like I'm a very
bitter person — the square
butterfly looks like a bitter
butterfly.

4. Images of Don
Quixote.

4. Profiles. [What do profiles
make you think of?] Don
Quixote was very idealistic
. . . These images remind me
of him, especially because
they're white. They seem
very . . . don't seem very
solid to me . . . seem very
shallow, very tenuous. [What
does that remind you of?]
Reminds me of myself.
[Why?] I feel like . . . I used
to feel stronger in my
idealism than right now. I
feel like it could be
disintegrated or blown away.
[Idealism?] Faith in other
people, I think.

IX.   8″   1. Two witches again.

IX.   1. Someone very mean. [What
does that remind you
of?] [long pause] Reminds
me of when I was young, my
parents took me to
StoryLand. There was a big
witch's pot outside, bones
inside supposed to be bones
of children. . . . They said to
me, "The witch can get you,"

or something like that
[laughs].

2. Now they look like
   lions.
3. Two women's
   half-breasts.

3. Makes me think of myself. .
   . . when I was growing up,
   entering puberty, my breasts
   weren't developing. . . . I felt
   insecure about it . . . even up
   until recently, I felt I wasn't
   completely a woman.

4. Two newborn babies.
   Looks like umbilical
   cords coming out of the
   babies' mouths — only
   one has eyes open,
   other has eyes closed.

4. Makes me think of myself
   right now. Sometimes I feel
   I'm still tied to the umbilical
   cord . . . I haven't broken ties
   to my parents I should have
   by now. [What do the opened
   eyes and closed eyes remind
   you of?] Sometimes I see it,
   sometimes I don't let myself
   see it.

5. Two old washerwomen
   working very hard.

5. Old washerwomen have
   always evoked pity in me
   because I feel sorry they
   have to work so hard —
   they're getting older, still
   have to do that work. [What
   does that remind you of?]
   Reminds me of peasants who
   came to this country. [What
   do peasants make you think
   of?] Reminds me of my
   mother's family. [What do
   you think of then?] My
   mother reminds me of a
   washerwoman — she's very
   subservient, simple — she
   works very hard and doesn't
   get anything from it — just
   enough to sustain herself.

X.   32″ 1. A wishbone in the
            center.

X.   1. We used to pick wishbones. .
            . . My mother would say,

"Make a wish." [What does that make you think of?] Wishes never came true, but it was fun to pretend.

2. Two beetles arguing with one another.

2. [What do they remind you of?] I don't know . . . bitter beetles. Each one is defending himself. [How?] Not physically — like defending his ego.

3. Two big spiders coming at them from the outside.

3. [What do they make you think of?] Beetles are so busy arguing with one another, they don't see something bigger coming at them. [What does that remind you of?] Reminds me of my parents fighting with one another . . . were actually destroying the family.

4. Two little woodpeckers trying to eat two big green worms.

4. [What does that make you think of?] I think woodpeckers are very silly. They're very unrealistic about eating worms — you can see they'll never be able to do it. [What does that remind you of?] Reminds me of me . . . thinking someday I'll just be able to overcome all the bad feelings I have.

5. Two little bats without wings.

5. Sort of helpless. As if the wings made them look as though . . . they should be feared. Without them, they're helpless little creatures. [What does that make you think of?] All creatures need covering and defenses to protect themselves.

6. A devil's mask.

6. [What does it remind you

of?] Looks like a mask my
father used to have — a red
rubber mask. It fit over his
head . . . would wear it to
frighten us . . . he was
kidding around.

The strongest impression that one gets from this record is the subject's extraordinary insight into her problems and her openness to introspection. In many cases this patient not only gives associations that can aid interpretation, but actually provides the interpretations; the interpretations have a convincing ring to them. This general impression serves to validate her therapist's view that she is unusually insightful.

A major problem for this patient, as she puts it herself, is her inability to tear herself away from the destructive dynamics of her family: "I haven't broken ties to my parents that I should have by now" (IX-4). An intense preoccupation with her feelings toward her father is seen in many responses (e.g., IV-1, IV-2, IV-3, V-1, V-4, VII-2, X-6). She evidently harbors feelings of hatred against her father, an "abominable snowman" who is cold and sadistic (e.g., X-6). The patient rejects her bitterness and says she is "trying to do myself over, so I'm a prettier person . . . I'm a very bitter person" (VIII-3). At the same time she displays some evidence of admiration and envy for her father's power, strength, and leadership (I-3, IV-2). The interesting alternation of responses on Card IV brings out this ambivalence ("abominable snowman," "eagles' heads," "small lambs") and is also a good example of the use of content sequence analysis in the elucidation of personality dynamics.

It is interesting to speculate about the connection between her excessive preoccupation with and hatred for her father, her admiration of his power, and her rejection of her bitterness on the one hand, and her delusion on the other hand. Her belief that the president was going to kill himself and that she had to stop it may thus represent a fusion of wish and defense: her death wish against her father, and her defense against the wish. However there is no direct evidence of this connection in her test record.

The patient's view of her mother is also strongly ambivalent. Although the mother is seen as an evil person who humiliated the patient (e.g., I-1, VII-2, IX-1), she also pities her mother as subservient and a fellow victim of her father (V-1, IX-5).

The patient feels highly vulnerable and in intense conflict (e.g., II-3, III-2, IV-3, X-5). It should be noted that there is, in addition, some evidence of primitive thought processes (e.g. "butterfly with thorns" [II-1], and the causal connection between responses III-1 and III-2). Paranoid ideation is evident as well (I-3).

Some weeks after the test session, the patient was briefly hospitalized with a repetition of her previous symptoms. Her breakdown at that time occurred after an altercation with her parents.

Case 2

The Rorschach record that follows was obtained from a 25-year-old single white female inpatient with a Full Scale IQ of 122. This patient was admitted to the hospital because of a suicide gesture following an injury to a family member. There were numerous past suicide gestures. The patient had also been hospitalized on occasion for anorexia nervosa. She reported having had sexual relations with various male members of her family during adolescence.

Responses

I.   10″ 1. It looks like two people with their wings against each other . . . hooded figures waving to each other.

[Some people see more than one thing. Do you see anything else?]

2. Yeah — a crab. An existential crab.

3. A woman with two heads . . . reaching out for help.

4. Also . . . a man trying to fly . . . a flying machine on his back . . . But it isn't working very well.

Associations

I.   1. The story of Passover . . . angel of death flying over. [What does that call to mind?] Lambs' blood over the door. [What does that make you think of?] I just generally think of the story — they were OK . . . because they were passed over.

2. It doesn't have any philosophical meaning, it just is . . . it just exists. [What does it bring to mind?] Jean-Paul Sartre . . . hell is other people.

3. She knows what she thinks, but she doesn't know what she feels . . . She needs help coordinating the two.

4. He's pretty stupid . . . he could work on more important things than trying to fly. [What might that reflect in your life?] I don't know why she swallowed the

fly ... perhaps she'll die.
[What's the connection?] Just
the word *fly*.

II.   5″   1. It looks like two witches   II.   1. Black Sabbath [What do you
            − praying by putting   think of then?] Instead of
            their hands up against   looking inward, look
            each other instead of   outward at each other ... an
            putting their hands   evil thing to do ... they're
            together.   looking at each other's
                                                    actions so they can operate.
                                                    They're watching each other
                                                    ... to see what they can get
                                                    out of each other.

         2. Looks like a goose   2. Silly person is a goose ... I
            looking in the mirror.   also think of ducks and
                                                    swans ... the story of the
                                                    ugly duckling ... ducks that
                                                    laughed were the geese ...
                                                    they were silly. [What might
                                                    that reflect in your life?]
                                                    When I look in the mirror −
                                                    I don't see anything. [What
                                                    do you mean?] I don't think
                                                    anything about what I see.

         3. Head of an Indian   3. Reminds me of a cigar store
            carved out of rock.   Indian ... I was on the street
                                                    once ... I looked at a
                                                    dummy in a window ... it
                                                    looked like a real person.

III.   7″   1. Two monkeys   III.   1. My parents. [In what way?]
            −warming their hands   Just the word *monkeys*. The
            over a fire.   stupidest thing they ever did
                                                    was to get married ... Fire
                                                    they're warming their hands
                                                    over is their children
                                                    burning.

         2. Two people falling   2. Chagall. I've read in his
            through the air.   pictures ... people flying ...
                                                    looks to me like they're
                                                    falling ... falling towards

3. Big red butterfly in middle.

3. Also looks like a red bow tie ... makes me think of my father's wild ties ... that's something I like about him. [Is there anything else you like about him?] Yes — his sense of humor, ability to care about others sometimes, his idealism ... mixed with cynicism.

IV. 5″ 1. Definitely the abominable snowman ... walking on glass ... looking at him through the glass ... makes his head look far away.

IV. 1. Just when I was in elementary school ... wishing there really was one. [What does that make you think of?] [pause] Wishing I really had a mother ... I don't ... I never did. [What do you mean?] Always just so into herself ... partly because she just drank so much ... into another world ... gave herself in some ways ... took care of us ... but didn't give emotionally ... didn't care about us.

V. 55″ 1. Only thing I see is an old man with a staff ... bent over from age.

V. 1. Story of Moses wandering in the wilderness ... wandering, looking for the promised land. I don't think he ever reached it.

2. These look a little like arms.

2. Being slapped or being hugged. [What does that make you think of?] A lot of times you don't know what to expect.

3. Back of the head of a rabbit ... that's all.

3. Stories of Peter Rabbit and Uncle Wiggly. A summer cottage we used to go to ... the atmosphere of the

cottage bothered me. I had earaches, eye infections. [What does the cottage make you think of?] Very old and . . . once, my mother had to put stuff in my eyes . . . I couldn't see. I slept by myself . . . I was afraid. I couldn't see . . . that made it even more frightening.

VI.   10″ 1. I see an exotic flower.

VI.   1. Tropical climates and . . . just a wish I used to have . . . to live on a tropical island by myself . . . but not anymore . . . I don't like to be by myself anymore. [What does that make you think of?] Just . . . I'm not as different as I thought I was . . . I can relate to people better than I used to.

2. An X-ray of somebody's spinal cord.

2. A spinal tap . . . my brother had one years ago . . . he was in a new part of the hospital . . . he was frightened and lonely . . . He wanted me to visit him . . . but I didn't feel I was enough support to him. [What does that call to mind?] My parents not being enough support to him now . . . and I'm not now . . . in a way that's my fault, in a way, not.

3. A handcarved statue inside some container.

3. [What does it remind you of?] [pause] Statue of a native . . . basket on its head . . . container takes away from its beauty . . . supposed to preserve it. If it was mine, I wouldn't keep it in a container. [What does that

mean in your life?] Really nothing.

VII. 3″ 1. Two little girls having an argument . . . each pointing in a different direction . . . I think maybe they're Indians . . . wearing feathers . . . I don't see anything else.

VII. 1. I used to play a game in which I was an Indian . . . I remember telling my mother about the game . . . it was like giving my inner self to her . . . she just didn't react. Respond is a better word. [What does pointing in different directions make you think of?] Just conflict in general. [What does that remind you of?] That's when I get angry . . . when there's a conflict inside of me. [What do you mean?] Wanting to refuse to do something . . . but knowing I have to do it.

VIII. 50″ 1. A polar bear . . . must be climbing up a sheer cliff . . . he must have glue on his feet.

VIII. 1. [Pause] Story of a 14-year-old boy . . . he lived in my town . . . he died sniffing glue. [What does that bring to mind?] Not such a bad way to die . . . just suffocated. [What do animals climbing up sheer cliffs make you think of?] If it's that difficult — why bother?

IX. 28″ 1. A magic candle sends off different colors of light.

IX. 1. Just . . . I like lights . . . and I like color . . . I like a flame . . . because it looks like it has so much life . . . a mysterious thing. [What does that remind you of?] People. [What do you mean?] You never really get to know anyone . . . there's always a mysterious part of them.

X.   8″   1. An underwater sea   X.
                scene.
            2. Two crabs and coral.
            3. Fishes.
            4. Sea urchins.
            5. An eel.
            6. And two jellyfish.
            7. Head of a man   7. My older brother. He smokes
                smoking a pipe.   a pipe. [What does that make
                                              you think of?] I don't
                                              understand him anymore . . .
                                              he doesn't show things like
                                              he used to . . . he talks about
                                              very intellectual things.
                                              [What comes to mind when
                                              you think of understanding
                                              him?] Makes me very sad
                                              because I used to feel that I
                                              understood him.

Perhaps the most striking feature of this patient's Rorschach record is the great hostility toward her parents, who are seen as the cause of her and her brother's misfortunes (III-1, VI-2). The patient's anger is particularly focused on her mother whom she sees as a cold, distant, indifferent, and threatening figure (IV-1, V-3, VII-1). More positive feelings are associated with the father; the patient identifies with him (III-3). Response IV-1 is particularly interesting because it closely resembles the first response of Case 1 described above ["abominable snowman"]. In this instance, however, the associations reveal that it is the mother the patient is describing. This example underscores the danger inherent in making blanket interpretations based on assumed card meaning.

A perception of human relationships as negative, unpredictable, and exploitative is also evident (I-2, II-1, V-2), although the patient seems to have shown some improvement in terms of her ability to relate to people (VI-1). An erratic, labile quality is implied in her response to conflict (V-2, VII-2). The patient is preoccupied with thoughts of death (I-1, association on I-4; VIII-1). There is also a futile, hopeless quality in several responses (I-4, V-1, VIII-1), and a blasé reaction to this state of affairs (III-2, VIII-1). As the patient states in her associations to Card VIII, "If it's that difficult — why bother?" Feelings of emptiness are also present (II-3), and an intellectualized quality is seen as well (I-2).

Several of this patient's responses indicate pathological thought processes. One of her responses (II-2) is a confabulation: "Actually, just the beak reminded me of a goose." An autistic association is present in response I-4. The existential crab in I-2 is an overly abstract and intellectualized response. It should also be noted that although the patient responded with seven Beck populars, she did not make two of three highly popular responses (on Card III and Card V).

Although many of this patient's test responses were clearly interpretable through her associations, others remain largely undecipherable. Her first response on the test and her associations to it, the Passover story, suggest an idiosyncratic meaning that is only partly interpretable: they imply a sense of threat and preoccupation with death. The patient's associations to response VI-3 suggest penis envy, but again the full meaning of this response remains unclear.

Case 3

The third case is that of a 38-year-old white fireman who had been admitted with complaints of visual and auditory hallucinations. The oldest of three children, he described a history of considerable neglect by both parents. He is married to a woman he described as quiet and simple, and he has seven children. Erratic behavior on the job had been noticed, and he had periodically been assigned to easier, less demanding work.

Responses	*Associations*
I. 3″ 1. Looks like a bat. [Some people see more than one thing. Do you see anything else?]	I. 1. Once when I was painting a house . . . there was a bat stuck behind the shutter . . . when the bat came out I was scared shit. [What does that make you think of?] Fear . . . uncertainty. [What do you think of then?] I have a tendency to think I'll get screwed . . . I'll always end up with the short end of the stick.
2. Looks like a spider. I can't think of anything else.	2. I watched spiders at work . . . they would catch a fly, tie him up and . . . I watched him with a praying mantis

... we let him loose. [What does that make you think of?] Caution, uncertainty. You try to allow for everything, but something unexpected comes up — things don't go your way. [For example?] I try to do what I can at work ... Everyone tells me that I do a good job ... but others don't care ... and they end up with better deals ... Why do I always get the shit end of the stick?

II. 8″ 1. Red things look like seals.

II. 1. Seeing seals jumping around and playing in the park ... I like to watch the seals. [What does that make you think of?] I always wanted to play, but I worked since I was 13. I've always been resentful that I wasn't playing.

2. Looks like the entrance to a castle, and the red things look like something symbolic.

2. A castle ... like in a movie ... that's hidden away. [What does it make you think of?] Peace, quiet, no conflict. [What does that remind you of?] People ... other people create situations where there's conflict. I want to be left alone. [You mentioned seeing something symbolic. What did you mean?] Like ... smoke comes up, like in the movies ... to guard it ... makes the area safe. But guys get in and loot the temple ... steal the diamond eyes.

3. The red thing looks like a butterfly on the bottom.

3. Nothing ... butterflies just look nice.

III. 3″ 1. This looks like two women . . . holding a bowl . . . trying to lift a big bowl.

2. Looks like a bow tie in the middle.

IV. 11″ 1. All these seem to have . . . looks like a uterus. I guess you could call it that. The rest of the card leaves me blank.

2. Oh . . . and a tree . . . a dead tree.

V. 1″ 1. This looks like a better bat.

2. I guess it could also be an insect . . . has claws to grab.

III. 1. Nothing at all. [What does it make you think of?] I'd like to see two women do anything together [laughs]. I don't think of them as a teamwork, you know?

2. When I was a kid, sissies always wore bow ties. I don't like them. [What do sissies remind you of?] Just people that I don't like.

IV. 1. Just that it's part of a female. [What does that make you think of?] Sex . . . enjoyment . . . that's all.

2. I've seen dead trees . . . that's the way they look . . . their branches droop . . . everything is sloping towards the ground. [What does that remind you of?] Nothing.

V. 1. I seem to associate bats with some kind of terror. [What does that make you think of?] Need to get away from them. They're blind, they can't see what they're doing. [What do you think of then?] You might get attacked . . . They get stuck in your head — I mean your hair.

2. Ants taking little pieces of food. [What does that remind you of?] Insects grabbing other insects and devouring them. [What do you think of then?] The difficulty of living 24 hours a day . . . you never have it made . . . it's always a struggle.

3. Could be a leaf ... part
   of a leaf.

3. Nothing ... just a dead leaf,
   part of it decaying. The
   natural course of events.

VI.   8″   1. They all look like they
            have that sex symbol
            ... a uterus ... I don't
            understand it.
         2. This looks like a
            wooden totem pole that
            the Indians have ...
            with faces on them.

VI.   1. Pleasure and enjoyment.
         [What does that make you
         think of?] It ain't always easy
         to come by.
      2. I've seen them on the side of
         the road. [What do they
         remind you of?] That's all
         they have left ... They were
         wiped out at the Little
         Bighorn. Their whole way of
         life is gone.

VII. 3″   1. Two faces in the
            middle, on either side.

         2. On top, a little animal
            with pieces missing ...
            head missing ... looks
            like it's sitting down but
            the head is missing.

         3. Bottom part looks like
            that same sex symbol
            again — Jesus.

VII. 1. Nothing. It looks like a mask
         — a horror mask. [What does
         it make you think of?] Being
         afraid.
      2. A dog looking for a favor ...
         a biscuit. [What does it
         remind you of?] I guess he's
         not very friendly, if someone
         took his head off. Why
         would anyone want to do
         that to a dog?
      3. Same things — sex, pleasure,
         enjoyment.

VIII. 4″   1. Again, the sex thing on
            the bottom.
         2. Two rats at each side
            ... they're going up to
            the top of something.

VIII. 1. ———

      2. We always had rats in the
         house when I was a kid. I'm
         afraid of them. I used to be
         afraid to go to bed ... they'd
         bite me on the throat. They
         hurt my dog one time.
         They'd always be fighting
         with the cat. [What does that
         make you think of?] I hated
         that cat ... I tried to flush
         him down the toilet ... I

once threw him out a four
story window . . . he landed
on someone's face, and the
guy came up to our
apartment all bloody. I got a
beating for it . . . I was
jealous of the cat getting
more attention than I did.
The dog got kicked around
the house too — but the cat
didn't get hurt too bad.

3. Could be the skull of a
person — or an animal.

3. When I drink, I get
hallucinations of rats going
around in a circle, with me in
the middle. [What does that
make you think of?] They're
finishing off a decaying body
left in the weeds.

IX.   3″   1. The top . . . some type
of witch . . . ghost.

IX.   1. I was always afraid of ghosts,
bogeyman, etc. I thought I
saw them at night. [What
does that remind you of?]
Recently, I've been thinking
I see burglars . . . I'd get my
gun and chase them. Real
crazy [laughs].

2. Again, the sex symbol.

2. ———

X.   7″   1. Spiders . . . on the
outside.

X.   1. I saw a movie with a black
widow spider biting a guy . . .
he died. [What does that
make you think of?] They
bite indiscriminately . . .
anybody . . . might bite me.

2. A pole, with rats
standing up.

2. Nothing in particular . . . you
find rats all over.

3. Green things look like
menacing ghosts.

3. They scared the hell out of
me. But ghosts I'm not afraid
of . . . it's the spiders and rats
[laughs].

4. Two gold things, statues
of a lion.

4. Old movies . . . this is where
the gold is. They'd be
standing guard outside the

	temple.
5. That sex symbol again	5. Same thing — female, sex,
— it's crazy.	pleasure.

The narrative response provided for each association by this patient gives the examiner a much expanded base from which to draw conclusions. What is especially interesting about this test record is the extent to which common, popular responses also yield associations rich in meaning: note the responses to populars on Card III, Card V, and Card VIII.

A number of dynamic trends are apparent in the patient's Rorschach record: considerable bitterness about his lot in life, particularly with respect to his job (I-1, I-2); the struggle that life has become for him (V-2); resentment at being deprived of much of his childhood (II-1), a feeling that has implications with respect to his pressing for an early retirement; his experience of other people as noxious aspects of his environment (II-2); his derogation of women (III-1) and doubts about his masculinity (III-2), both suggestive of latent homosexuality. Feelings of torpidity and devestation are also evident (IV-2, VI-2). The patient's deprived childhood is graphically portrayed in several of his responses (II-1, VIII-2). In addition the arbitrary and perseverant sexual responses suggest a disorder of psychotic proportions, an impression supported by the patient's MMPI profile. A paranoid orientation suffuses the test record.

13

The Use of Content in the Consensus Rorschach

Previously it was mentioned that Leventhal et al. (1962) utilized a lengthy pre-test interview in which an attempt was made to develop a collaborative relationship between the subject and the examiner in producing a meaningful Rorschach record. The Consensus Rorschach represents a dramatically different type of cooperative effort reflecting the burgeoning interest in the variety of groups in which the individual functions.

Essentially, Consensus Rorschach is the designation given to a protocol obtained from two or more individuals who, through some form of negotiation, have arrived at a single set of agreed upon percepts. Major emphasis is placed on content in the interpretive approach employed by some clinicians and researchers working with the Consensus Rorschach, whereas others are primarily concerned with group process and with the formal perceptual aspects of the record. However, although it is innovative and promising, the technique currently lacks genuine standardization both in procedures for assessing responses and in its administration per se. It may now be viewed more as a collection of idiosyncratic methodologies than as a standard test.

LACK OF STANDARDIZATION

The Consensus Rorschach is ordinarily given in conjunction with the individual Rorschach. As Wynne (1968) observes, there is much variability in the order of test administrations and in the time interval between testing sessions. Furthermore the number of cards actually presented varies from a single blot to 10, and the number of percepts expected per card can be restricted to one or may have no specified limits. Wynne points out that the degree of participation by the examiner is another grossly unstandardized factor. The examiner may or may not be in the room when a Consensus Rorschach is administered. He may elect to use a tape recorder and/or to utilize one-way mirrors and other observers.

At the very core of this inadequate standardization, however, is the absence of uniform criteria for determining when consensus has actually been achieved. In some procedures the examiner makes the judgment that the group has reached consensus, whereas in others he assigns specific responsibility to the group to indicate when they have agreed. Whether or not he subsequently elects to conduct an inquiry and how he goes about it are additional elements in the current variability of the Consensus Rorschach procedure.

ORIGIN OF THE CONSENSUS RORSCHACH

The Consensus Rorschach in its basic form can be traced to Blanchard (1959) who, while showing several Rorschach cards to some social worker colleagues, serendipitously observed that the blots stimulated much group interaction and discussion about what the shapes and colors might represent. Convinced that the group situation enhanced the spontaneity of response, Blanchard administered the Rorschach to groups of juvenile offenders with very successful results. When taking the Consensus Rorschach, these youths were far less defensive, and produced records that had significantly richer content and improved form-level. Describing a Consensus Rorschach administered to a group of youths involved in a gang rape, Blanchard (1968) characterized it as "a reenactment of the gang rape experience" with respect to the patterns of interaction among the gang members.

Blanchard appears to have relied largely upon his clinical impressions and experience rather than on any well-standardized interpretive procedures in working with the Consensus Rorschach as such, and in contrasting individual and Consensus Rorschach protocols. However, in order to assess Consensus Rorschach, several investigators have developed reasonably systematic methods in which content plays a significant role.

THE CONSENSUS RORSCHACH: CONTENT ANALYSIS

Bauman and Roman (1968) label their procedure "interaction testing." They assert that group products may be treated conceptually as though they had been produced by individuals, and that group process scores can be derived inferentially from test products. These process scores, they feel, are "reliably characteristic" of groups and useful in understanding them in terms of such clinical factors as potential and efficiency.

They outline their scoring system utilizing data from a Consensus Wechsler-Bellevue scale, but they state that the same analytic principles would apply to a Consensus Rorschach. The system is based on testing subjects individually, then as a group, with the identical items. The interaction test response and individual percepts are subsequently contrasted and classified under four process categories. Dominance is scored when the interaction response contains only one member's individual response. A combination is recorded when components of all members' individual percepts are present in the interaction response. Emergence is scored when a new idea occurs in the interaction response. Lastly, reinforcement is recorded when the same response is given by each individual and by the group. Bauman and Roman found that their scoring procedure enabled them to differentiate between normal couples and couples with an emotionally disturbed spouse on the basis of the efficiency with which individual resources were pooled in consensual testing.

Cutter (1968) and Cutter and Farberow (1970) make the most explicit use of content in their interesting but sometimes recondite system for analyzing Consensus Rorschachs. They have named it the method of "content polarities." The rationale for this method stems from their efforts to conceptualize the individual Rorschachs of symbiotic partners: they observe complementary meanings in each partner's reactions to the same inkblots, reactions that can be regarded as polar opposites of a dimension describing a range of behavioral or role expectations. Within the context of the Consensus Rorschach, a parallel complementary polarity is said to exist in the controversies in which members of the group engage as they attempt to reach agreement in deciding what the inkblots denote.

According to Cutter and Farberow, the actual process of identifying content polarities consists of examining a record for disagreement in whatever affective degree it is present and regardless of the source from which the disagreement arose. Nonverbal behavior, exclamations, and verbal asides are also taken into account in this process. The linking of the two contents that express the relevant extremes within the group as it defines each blot forms the array of content polarities for a particular Consensus Rorschach record.

An illustration of how a content polarity can be used clinically is the consensus percept reported by Cutter and Farberow of "two something." This percept was made by a family in response to Card VII and was accompanied by a content polarity of "wild gyrations–kissing." Cutter and Farberow interpreted the response as an indication of considerable family disagreement about the content which, in light of the content polarity, reflects a conflict over the appropriate expression of heterosexual feelings and impulses.

Cutter and Farberow explain that the general notion of consensus and content polarities subsumes group-imposed agreements as well as conflicts in expectation. A group member's willingness to accept these expectations and the degree of resolution when conflicts occur can be gleaned from an examination of the member's individual Rorschach record and by evaluating his contribution to the consensus process. The extent to which individual content and the consensus record overlap determines how identified the member is with the group and how susceptible he is to its influence.

Cutter and Farberow (1968) actually endeavored to study the impact of disparate groups on the Consensus Rorschach by a serial administration of the technique to an alcoholic, three of his friends, three of his roommates, his wife (on two occasions separated by 6 months), and a high-low status pair. An individual Rorschach was also administered before and after the series. Striking differences were apparent in the consensus contents, the content polarities, and in other aspects of the protocols, in keeping with the diverse social contexts in which the tests were administered.

In a brief paper, W. Klopfer (1969) notes that problems that interfere with learning in school children may involve interpersonal as well as intrapsychic problems. The Consensus Rorschach is presented as a procedure that can be used in the school context to clarify both of these areas. Klopfer reports having administered the test to two grades of children, first requiring individual responses to the blot and then a group consensus. The order in which subjects responded was staggered in order to minimize the parroting of responses. The data are presented in subject-by-blot tables that include brief summaries of the interactions occurring in reaching consensus on each blot. Klopfer proposes that this technique may be particularly useful at the beginning of the school year.

THE CONSENSUS RORSCHACH:
RELIANCE ON VERBAL AND NONVERBAL CONTEXT

It might be mentioned here, by way of establishing a general perspective, that content per se plays a largely subordinate role in the manner in which some psychologists use the Consensus Rorschach. Several clinicians who have worked in this area have focused mainly on the complex of verbal and nonverbal interactions that occur during testing rather than on the content itself.

Loveland (1967), for example, has developed a scoring system that focuses on transactional components such as the clarity of each individual's communication, his comprehension of the communications of others, and the affective posture participants assume toward each other and toward the task. Loveland's system is, in fact, an analysis of the content of behavioral interactions. She labels her procedure the "relation Rorschach." Utilizing only one or two Rorschach cards, Loveland tape records the group members' interactions without the tester in the room for as long as 10 minutes as they strive to reach consensus. A final step in the procedure is individually asking each member to indicate in writing all the things that he thought were agreed upon so that the extent of the consensus, as it was verbally reported, can be better evaluated.

Levy and Epstein (1964), also deemphasizing content, focus on utilizing the Consensus Rorschach to disclose how a family endeavors to attain equilibrium. They maintain that this striving for equilibrium is reflected in the process of each family member's attempt to modify his individual Rorschach percepts so that they are more congruous with the developing family consensus.

Willi (1967), however, skillfully interweaves noncontent and content variables. He believes that the basic method in his use of the Consensus Rorschach — or what he labels "joint Rorschach procedure" — is essentially similar to that of Loveland (1967) and Levy and Epstein (1964). However Willi notes that his system is quite different in its aims and mode of interpretation. In describing his approach, Willi explains that he endeavors to answer two basic questions. First, what is the comparative strength of the individuals taking the test and the nature of their interactions? Second, what personality changes take place in one individual in the course of a discussion with another?

Willi administers the Rorschach to each person individually in the usual manner. Immediately thereafter, before they have had the opportunity to discuss their responses, he asks them to look at the inkblots once more and to attempt to arrive at a single joint solution. The examiner remains in the room, recording the discussion verbatim but allowing the pair to proceed at their own pace without interruption. If the subjects attempt to go on to the next card without reaching consensus during the first five cards, the examiner repeats the instructions. Otherwise the subjects are permitted to set a card aside if they cannot achieve agreement, and this is designated as a "failure to respond."

In keeping with the thrust of his two questions, Willi's analyses of the protocols incorporate what he characterizes as quantitative and qualitative aspects. The quantitative analysis is concerned primarily with partner interactions as they reflect efforts at domination. Conceptually, this is not unlike the dominance scoring utilized in the previously discussed system of Bauman and Roman (1968), but it essentially taps behavior content rather than Rorschach content per se, much in the manner of Loveland's (1967) approach. More specifically, Willi proposes four aspects to his quantitative analysis. These aspects are concerned with: (1) the number of proposals a subject makes during consensual testing relative to the number offered by his partner; (2) the way subjects endeavor to gain acceptance of, or to implement their proposals; (3) which subject assumes a leadership role in formally deciding that a joint response has been achieved or that agreement is not possible; and (4) who holds the card.

The qualitative evaluation portion of Willi's approach is essentially directed toward interactional influences on the Rorschach responses; these influences are revealed in both content and standard determinant comparisons of individual and Consensus Rorschachs for altered, omitted, and new percepts.

CURRENT STATUS

Presently the content analysis of Consensus Rorschach records appears to be especially valuable in the diagnostic evaluation of family constellations, especially when the family is experiencing stress because of an emotionally ill member. It has also proved its worth as a method for studying an individual's role and interpersonal transactions in sundry other types of group settings. A particularly novel application is its direct use within the framework of treatment rather than that of diagnosis. Loveland (1967) has administered consensus procedures to clinicians conducting groups, family therapy, and individual therapy, and to their patients. Walter Klopfer (reported in Cutter & Farberow, 1970) is reported to have used the Consensus Rorschach as a way of sensitizing patients to the disparities between their private behavior (individual Rorschach) and their actions in a family group (Consensus).

Basically, employing and evaluating consensus productions seems to be an approach which efficaciously mirrors current interest in studying the individual's behavior in social situations through very direct observational methods. The various content assessment techniques now available, although somewhat lacking in uniformity and at times rather unsystematic and markedly imprecise, appear to be moving in the direction of greater sophistication and more rigorous standardization.

Indicative of such movement is work currently in progress at the Payne Whitney Psychiatric Clinic of the New York Hospital–Cornell Medical Center. A family therapy research group composed of Philip M. Bromberg, John F. Clarkin, Charlotte G. Kallum, Michael Rothenberg, and Stephen H. Wells is pursuing a comprehensive and multifaceted exploration of the Consensus Rorschach technique with married couples. This investigation incorporates standardization in administration, scoring, and clinical interpretation of content. Its fundamental approach is an exploration of the interrelationship between concurrently sampled intrapsychic processes and interpersonal behavior.

The guiding assumption for the technique is that an individual brings to a marital relationship his unique personality organization, which is both expressed and modified in the relationship with the other partner. From a theoretical standpoint, the attempt has been made to design a procedure which as far as possible creates the natural demand that a marital situation imposes upon members. Specifically, the procedure tries to simulate the need to relinquish a certain amount of freedom in order to achieve conjoint goals. It is regarded as essential that the individual members of the marriage have some degree of experienced personal investment and commitment to their individual Rorschach responses in order for the subsequent consensus procedure to mirror authentically the way in which they deal with the state of conflict between personal needs and marital demands.

Administration of the Payne Whitney Clinic (PWC) conjoint Rorschach procedure is strictly controlled in terms of sequence, timing, and examiner participation. Married couples are tested during the period between outpatient department intake and commencement of family treatment. The subjects first take the Rorschach individually. Seated separately, they go through the 10 cards at their own pace, writing down one response for each plate and outlining a location sheet. Each then ranks his or her 10 responses in order of preference; this ranking is interpretatively regarded as an ordering in terms of degree of commitment as well.

In the immediately following second phase, the couple is brought together in a marital therapy seating arrangement. The examiner reads each member's individual response to the particular card, following which the couple works unassisted toward a conjoint product. The criterion for true consensus is that each subject must declare explicit agreement. The couple then separates once more and evaluates, again by ranking, the conjoint responses.

The protocols are scored systematically from taped transcripts. In all, some 10 variables, a number of which are derived from Willi (1969), are evaluated. They include changes in content themes and in form level from individual to conjoint phase. Commitment to individual and conjoint responses is assessed from the rankings and provides a basis for the scoring of a variable denoted "prepotency." This variable is defined as the relative degree of power, representation, or embodiment of each of the members in the dyadic system. It is derived from each subject's ranking of his or her individual response and from a measure of the degree to which that response is carried through or survives in the conjoint product. Other scores relating to the interpersonal power balance include card holding during the conjoint phase, origin of the accepted response, and origin of the consensus decision (Willi, 1969). In addition the consensus process is assessed in terms of the extent to which the partners offer new proposals or modify each other's by way of negotiation, the judgments they make of each other's percepts, the quality of their consensual agreement, and its affective accompaniments.

An example of the clinical uses of the PWC conjoint Rorschach procedure is the following brief case history of a couple encountering marital difficulties, including selections from their conjoint session transcript and discussion, all presented verbatim.[1]

CASE HISTORY

Mr. G is a 24-year-old advanced graduate student in anatomy. Mrs. G is 23, is employed as a secretary, and attends evening classes. She withdrew from her graduate studies shortly after the marriage 5 years before in order to support them financially. They have no children. The couple sought family therapy in the face of impending marital dissolution.

The history of their relationship portrays a pattern of interaction characterized by a growing state of mutual frustration, defensiveness, use of interpersonal power operations, and an overall deterioration of goodwill. In the early

[1]The case history, test protocols, and interpretations presented here have been provided through the courtesy of the PWC group.

stages of the relationship, each member reported viewing the complementary personality style of the other as gratifying and supportive. Over the period of 5 years, their idealizations were gradually replaced by disillusionment, and the same qualities that each formerly valued in the other became increasingly experienced as burdensome and intruding upon striving for personal growth and security.

The general state of defensiveness and disharmony is exemplified in their presenting complaint, by the respective descriptions of their sex life. Mr. G cannot openly acknowledge a sexual problem as such. He attributes his wife's complaint to her unreasonableness and demandingness, that is, to her inability to understand that he is a man highly interested in his work who does not need intense sexual involvement. Mrs. G, in contrast, reported that her husband had closed himself off to her sexually and that he responded to any sexual overture from her by either withdrawing into sleep or by covertly hostile mechanical performances including premature ejaculation.

The task of the psychologists was to assess from the conjoint testing procedure the basic personality dimensions of each partner, the manner in which their interaction has led to the present state of their marriage, and the sources of potential leverage in clarifying the patterns of mutual distortion.

RECORD FROM A PWC CONSENSUS RORSCHACH SESSION

Card I

Examiner: On this card you, Mrs. X, saw two monkeys with wings . . .
F: It looks like the monkeys in *The Wizard of Oz,* the bad monkeys with wings that fly around. I guess I assumed you saw *The Wizard of Oz.*
E: And You, Mr. X, saw a . . .
M: Cross-section of lower medulla. It could be a monkey's tail. It could be that.
F: I don't know if that's it — you see I saw these as wings. Okay, we'll go for a monkey with a wizard.

On the initial plate, the issue of personal identity is joined immediately. The couple offers in two strikingly different self-perceptions a revealing consensus perception of the relationship.

Mr. G's sense of self is pre-eminently cognitive and intellectualized (note that his response of "cross-section of lower medulla" is followed by "cross-section of upper medulla" and by "cross-section of the pons" on Cards II and III) to the exclusion of other aspects, such as affect and human relationships.

Mrs. G's self-perception is the polar opposite of her husband's self-contained isolation. She presents an image ("the monkeys in *The Wizard of Oz*") whose source content involves captive slaves in the service of a cruel master who is, however, needed for survival. She thus expresses as a component of her identity a need for a supportive figure with extraordinary powers. The consensus product proposed by Mrs. G "a monkey with a wizard," is a direct manifestation of this need, as is her projection onto Mr. G of the wizard perception itself, a wizard being an outwardly powerful but fraudulent figure.

Interactionally, it can be seen on another level that, although Mrs. G has offered a highly creative response, when confronted with her husband's lack of responsiveness she becomes notably insecure and threatened and must attempt to justify her response. Her dissatisfaction with this sacrificing of personal creativity and self-expression in order to maintain security is evidenced by the lower rank she assigns to the consensus as opposed to her own individual response. He shows no such need in his responses. On the contrary, in making no effort to elaborate his response in any way for her, he highlights the fact that he has a private domain into which she cannot enter. Mr. G ultimately surrenders his neuroanatomic response, but he can retain the gratification provided by his wife's ignorance of his specialized knowledge.

Card VI

E: On Card number VI you, Mr. X, saw . . .

M: That's a statue of the crucifix at Rio de Janeiro, when you go over it on a plane. You know what I'm talking about?

F: Yeah, that's just a San Cristobal.

M: Something like that, yeah.

F: It's nothing except a little statue.

M: Statue, a statue of Christ where his arms are out.

F: Yes.

E: You say, Mrs. X, a pussycat . . .

F: This is a pussycat and it's flattened out and this is his paws, this is his head, and these are his whiskers. Do you see that? [Laughs] This could be on the mountain. I just saw this pussycat and this is his nose, or a bear rug flattened on the floor. I'll go with a statue.

E: So your response is . . .?

M: A statue, crucifix.

F: San Cristobal in . . .

M: . . . in Brazil.

F: Yeah, in Brazil.

Card VI provides indications of the extent to which the differing narcissistic needs of the partners are no longer gratified mutually, in contrast to what may well have been the case earlier in the marriage. The speculation is offered that an earlier narcissistic bargain has been broken, particularly by Mrs. G's increasing commitment to her own autonomy and her reluctance to play the good audience to her husband. It is suggested that his need is to be seen as a god, in the sense of an all-powerful, omniscient male. In the relationship, this need has required her to be in the role of constantly looking up to him. This is graphically depicted in his percept ("a statue of the crucifix at Rio de Janeiro") which embodies a number of psychodynamic expressions. These include themes of interpersonal distance, of elevated standing, of male martyrdom and crucified potency (parts of his present experience in the relationship), and of grandiose self-expression.

Viewed interactionally, the form of Mr. G's expression of his percept is an ostentatious display of knowledge. (Note that he comments, "You know what I'm talking about?") She manifests her unwillingness to attribute extraordinary qualities to his response in her own emasculating comments: "That's *just* a San Cristobal . . . nothing except a *little* statue" (emphasis added).

For her part, Mrs. G's parallel need has been to achieve gratification for an early self-representation as a beloved, sweet child or, as in her own percept, as a "pussycat." That she presents her pussycat as "flattened out" indicates feelings of rejection and *her* lack of continuing gratification in this self-image. Moving to define herself in newer and more autonomous ways, she is breaking an unspoken former marital bargain by claiming more for herself then subservience and infantilization.

The implicit balance of pressing needs affecting the evolution and direction of this marital system can be noted. As indicated by the almost equal PWC conjoint Rorschach prepotency scores obtained by the partners, they appear to contribute to and to influence the relationship fairly equally. This might suggest a positive prognosis for marital therapy, insofar as it sought to assist the couple to realize an overt relationship of equality comparable to their covert standing.

Card IX

E: On Card number IX you, Mr. X, saw two witches facing each other and you, Mrs. X, saw . . .

F: Maybe I can read my handwriting. Shall I tell you what I saw?

E: Yes, please.

F: I saw not anything real. I saw fire at the top, setting sun in the middle. This was forest and greenery. This was cold or like ice base. I couldn't make anything out of it so it sort of looked like hot, medium, and cold. The green was kind of in the middle and this was cold and this was hot.

M: I saw two witches.

F: What's all this?

M: I don't know. Sitting on a ball.

F: [Laughs] All right, either one. I didn't see anything from the beginning.

M: I neither.

F: I don't know that I can't think of another thing, so let's take the witches unless you see something else.

M: Well I can't. I can't see anything in there.

F: I didn't either. This could look like eggs or apples. Just sitting there. Or upside down, that could be an apple tree.

M: Yeah.

F: This is upside down.

M: Yeah, it may be an apple tree upside down. Would that do upside down?

E: You're free to turn the card upside down if you want.

M: Well, OK.

F: Let's do that. An apple tree upside down, that does make sense. Yeah, we should have realized we could turn it upside down. We should have turned some of the others upside down. It might have made more sense.

This next-to-final card in the sequence rounds out the developing picture of the dynamics of the relationship by revealing the extent to which it has been comfortably organized around his support of her fear that she will lose emotional control.

That fear on her part appears to derive from a most fragile sense of controlling rapidly shifting and markedly contrasting affective states. She craves the structure embodied in her husband, appealing to him ("What's all this?") while denying ownership of her affectively diffuse original response. This affirmation of her inadequacy potentiates a supportive atmosphere interactionally. His response, that he is unable to "see anything in there" either, serves to confirm and maintain her perception of flux, but also to reestablish, by virtue of his presence and involvement, her security. This in turn permits her to draw upon potential resources in order to work toward a new response.

This schema depicts a system of relating which, unfortunate as some of the consequences may be for Mrs. G, allows for some openness and freedom. The card provides a picture very different from the one that emerges as characteristic throughout the rest of the record. In other responses the picture is one of system rigidity and construction in that extremely few efforts to modify each other's proposals or to present new proposals are observed. Mrs. G's comment is very much to the point:

"We should have realized we could . . . have turned some of the others upside down." The particular problem evidenced here is, however, that while productive resources are apparently available (the consensus product, "an apple tree upside down," directly embodies this possibility of fruitful cooperativeness), they are manifested in the context of a retreat to a pattern of support that has elements of defeatism and immutability ("upside down") as well.

In summary, a clinical picture emerges which the researchers feel has the following implications for therapy: Two individuals struggling with personal growth are trapped by their unawareness of core aspects of their personality. Each has depended upon the other to provide gratification of childlike needs for security and self-esteem. To the degree that each member is developing more complex roles and working toward more clearly defined separate identities, they are unable to offer the same quality of mutual support. In order for the feelings of rejection, betrayal, and desertion to be productively understood with compassion, Mr. and Mrs. G will have to begin to acknowledge these needs in themselves as acceptable and worthy of open expression. Only then can they see their pattern of retaliation as a direct consequence of their injured feelings. Since their personality organizations and cognitive styles are almost polar opposites, marital therapy might help to establish a channel of communication based on the development of a common language.

Conclusions

HIGH BAND WIDTH AND LOW FIDELITY

The primary conclusion that can be reached from the evidence presented above is that various content approaches to Rorschach interpretation are consistently related to relevant criteria. Rorschach content scales can serve as valid measures of such diverse characteristics as anxiety, hostility, dependency, somatic preoccupation, ego boundaries, sex role identity, depression, and suspiciousness. This high versatility of inkblot-based scales is reminiscent of what Cronbach and Gleser (1965) have referred to as the "wide band" characteristic of projective techniques. The Rorschach test thus can simultaneously measure a host of personality characteristics in a relatively short period of time.

Unfortunately there is a second half to the equation of Cronbach and Gleser which may be equally applicable to the Rorschach test. These authors have contended that the price paid for high band width is low fidelity; in other words, the personality characteristics are likely to be measured with a relatively low degree of precision. Given the rather low reliability coefficients generally reported for the inkblot scales, this expectation of a low degree of precision appears to be borne out. As noted by Jensen, "few other tests provide so many opportunities for the multiplication of error variance as does the Rorschach" (Jensen, 1964, p 65).

Although reliability data on the content scales are still sparse and are often entirely based on the HIT, the coefficients are rather consistently lower than is required for satisfactory individual prediction, except in the case of the Anxiety scale, the Rorschach Index of Repressive Style, and certain of Zubin's contextual scales. Furthermore, in those instances in which specifically Rorschach-based reliability data are available, the coefficients are not demonstrably higher than the corresponding HIT coefficients. Given the greater length of HIT protocols, one would indeed not expect greater reliability for the Rorschach than for HIT scales. It must therefore be concluded that, by and large, the content scales discussed in this volume can be of little use to the clinician at this time, other than for very rough screening (Cronbach & Gleser, 1965). The dearth of Rorschach norms for most content approaches, and the unavailability of measures of group overlap also militate against clinical use of the scales at this time. Even those scales for which the reliability data are generally positive cannot be recommended for clinical use because of the dearth of norms and evidence on group overlap. In addition validity for Zubin's scales data are sparse, and the validity evidence for the RIRS is not very favorable. The primary present use of the scales discussed in Chapters 2 through 8 appears to be in the areas of clinical and general research.

CONTEXTUAL SCALES

As noted in the introduction to this book, four approaches to the quantification of the verbal and nonverbal contextual aspects of Rorschach performance are discussed: Zubin's contextual scales, the Rorschach Index of Repressive Style, the quantification of pathological verbalizations, and communications defects and deviances. The present authors believe it is notable that of the three Rorschach approaches demonstrating satisfactory reliability in studies carried out to date, two of these — Zubin's contextual scales and the RIRS — are based on the contextual aspects of test performance. It will be recalled from Chapter 4 that the Zubin contextual scales demonstrated very high split-half reliability, even by the standards of objective tests; as noted in Chapter 8, the reliability evidence on RIRS is also quite favorable. The reliability evidence concerning pathological verbalizations is difficult to evaluate because of specific methodological problems, most notably the infrequency of occurrence of such responses outside of psychotic samples. The reliability evidence on the communications defects and deviances system is simply too sparse to interpret.

That the contextual approaches to test performance have fared so well in reliability testing suggests to the present authors that the future search for inkblot scales that are sufficiently reliable for clinical use would do well to explore further the possible use of scales which thus tap the subject's verbal and nonverbal behavior during testing. It is unfortunate that although substantial inroads have been made in the development and validation of inkblot content scales, the study of subjects' verbal and non-verbal contextual test behavior has failed to make comparable progress.

NONOVERLAP WITH OBJECTIVE TESTS

A fascinating though elusive thread running through the body of literature on Rorschach content scales involves the extent to which the scales can be said to measure aspects of personality traits that are not measured by objective tests. As noted earlier, Endicott and Jortner (1966; 1967) and Endicott, Jortner, and Abramoff (1969) applied multiple regression equations and found the inkblot content scales of depression, somatic preoccupation, and suspiciousness to add significantly (and substantially) to the prediction of these characteristics by objective scales. Endicott and Endicott (1963) have commented impressionistically on the tendency of *At* to measure aspects of somatic concern left untapped by the *Hs* scale of the MMPI. One study (Mogar, 1962) is reported in which the anxiety content scale was found to correlate with anxiety indicators of another projective test (the DAP), and yet neither of the projective tests correlated significantly with the MAS.

If inkblot content scales do generally measure aspects of variance in personality traits that are not measured by common objective tests, this might help to explain the often observed nonsignificant or inconsistent pattern of correlations between content scales and objective tests of the same characteristics, despite the fact that the content scales seem to be valid in terms of other criteria. (See Chapter 5 in particular.) However the imperfect validity of both the inkblot scales and the objective measures and the poor reliability of many of the content scales cannot be overlooked as at least partial explanations for many of the nonsignificant correlations. Furthermore, what unique aspects of variance in personality traits the content scales may be tapping is by no means clear. Several researchers (e.g., Endicott & Endicott, 1963; Nichols & Tursky, 1967) have described the Rorschach as contributing to the measurement of unconscious aspects of the particular traits. A further possibility is that inkblot-based measures may be less prone to conscious distortion and falsification than are objective tests. This question of the unique measurement potential of content scales is one that must be answered by future research.

THE TWO APPROACHES TO CONTENT INTERPRETATION

As mentioned several times in this book, the present authors contend that there are essentially two approaches to Rorschach interpretation, one of which is normative, the other idiographic. Many modern clinicians utilize both sources of information for purposes of interpretation: the clinician scores responses in various content and formal categories and compares the resulting scores to normative tables, and the clinician also uses the subject's responses and verbalizations to analyze his unique, idiosyncratic view of himself and his world.

We believe that this simultaneous use of normative and idiographic information in Rorschach analysis has led to some confusion about what should be expected from the test in terms of general psychometric requirements. If the test is applied normatively, that is, with the responses scored and the resulting totals, ratios, and averages evaluated against an external standard (presumably empirically derived), the Rorschach test cannot be considered exempt from the standard psychometric requirements of reliability, validity, and freedom from response set that all normatively based tests must meet. The fact that idiographic information is also provided by the test does not allow the suspension of these requirements when the test is normatively applied. It is our impression that clincial usage of the Rorschach test too often combines the idiographic approach with a very crude, inaccurate, and often invalid normative approach. As noted above, there is not yet enough of a basis for the clinical application of Rorschach content scales. Such clinical application of these scales, or of the formal Rorschach indices for which the psychometric justification is considerably poorer, is likely to lead to a very high degree of error in measurement and prediction.

Should further accumulation of data on the reliability and validity of content and contextual scales prove favorable, a major effort must be mounted to collect norms. In the survey of MMY book reviews carried out by the present authors (Aronow & Reznikoff, 1973), it was noted that many of the early reviews decried the absence of normative data for the formal scoring categories. In the later reviews the absence of such comments suggested that norms provided by Ames, Ford, Hertz, and others had met this deficiency. There is presently a need for similar norms for major content and contextual categories. Traditionally, Rorschach norms have been provided in terms of age and sex. Other relevant variables, such as social class, race, and intellectual level, have often been overlooked. If content and contextual norms are indeed to be collected, it is suggested that such variables be taken into account.

The present authors would also like to suggest that in future normative applications of the test, expectancy charts be used to provide clinicians with a measure of the degree of accuracy to be expected from Rorschach scales. Such charts, of long-recognized usefulness with objective tests of aptitude in particular, would provide the clinician with a very concrete indication of the expected degree of error. If, for example, the anxiety scale were to be validated against therapists' ratings for a large sample of subjects, and the data were presented in a two-dimensional expectancy chart, a clinician could easily determine the likelihood that subjects with given Rorschach anxiety scores would be rated low, or medium, or high in anxiety, as the case may be. Goldfield et al. (1971) have similarly suggested providing norms for rated levels of content variables.

CLINICAL UTILITY

At the present time the normatively based content and contextual scales provide for wide band measurement of many aspects of personality, and the reliability of a few of these approaches appears to be satisfactory. There is also some suggestion that the content scales may measure aspects of personality traits that are not measured by objective tests.

While the normative approach thus demonstrates potential uses to researchers and clinicians, it is our opinion that the greatest usefulness of the Rorschach test lies in the assessment of individual personality dynamics. Inasmuch as psychoanalytic theory and derivatives of psychoanalysis remain major schools of thought in clinical psychology, the information provided by such idiographic use of the Rorschach is likely to be highly useful to the clinician, particularly in the context of psychotherapy. Furthermore, it should be recognized that in this respect the Rorschach and other projective tests serve a unique function which is not duplicated by objective tests. To the extent that the analytically based approach remains a major force in clinical psychology, the Rorschach test's future place in personality assessment appears assured.

Although we thus see the idiographic approach as the most valuable source of information provided by the Rorschach test, we also recognize numerous limitations and hazards in this approach. As discussed in Chapter 10, the Rorschach test often provides only a rough and unsteady vehicle for the interpretation of individual psychodynamics. Although Rorschach interpretation bears some similarity to the interpretation of dreams, the nature of the Rorschach percept as opposed to the dream and the interpretive context of inkblot testing render Rorschach interpretation intrinsically less dependable than the interpretation of dreams. The present authors therefore suggest that clinicians be conservative in such interpretive work, relying on ground rules set forth in Chapter 10.

An important clinical skill that has often been underemphasized is knowing when *not* to interpret a response. We recommend the avoidance of inkblot interpretation that is based on rigid rules of correspondence between certain classes of responses and dynamic meaning. The clinician must also be able to take into account aspects of the test stimuli in the process of interpretation. Finally, techniques for enhancing the revealing quality of the subject's content and verbalizations on the test were presented in Chapter 12. We believe that a consistent application of these principles and procedures is likely to decrease significantly the prevalence of wild analysis in Rorschach work and correspondingly increase the probability of accurate assessment.

As discussed in Chapter 12, an unfortunate fact of life in idiographic Rorschach work is the difficulty of applying statistical techniques. However the present authors believe that research techniques have far more applicability to this field than has been realized to date. For example, it should be possible to establish by empirical procedures: the aspects of Rorschach responses that cue in the examiner to the fact that something significant about the subject is being revealed; the relationship between insight as verbalized in associations to responses and degree of insight as rated by psychotherapists; the extent to which the self-concept as revealed in Rorschach responses relates to the patient's unique self-concept as evident in psychotherapy; the types of changes in idiosyncratic content that accompany psychotherapeutic change, as observed through serial Rorschach administrations, to name just a few possibilities. While the investigation of such questions presents some thorny problems of experimental design and methodology, the results of such studies would have a high degree of clinical relevance. Until significant inroads can be made in the application of empirical techniques in this area, idiographic Rorschach interpretation is likely to remain a quasi-artistic practice bearing little resemblance to a science.

THE RORSCHACH AND THE HIT

In surveying the literature on inkblot content interpretation, the increasing research importance of the HIT was noted. Our impression is that the research and clinical trends in inkblot test usage are in one respect moving in opposite directions: inkblot research relies increasingly on the HIT, while similar widespread use of the HIT in the clinical domain has not been evident. The HIT is clearly the technique of choice for most research purposes; there is control over the total number of responses, the administration and scoring procedures are well standardized, and there is in addition an available alternate form. However it would also appear that in clinical applications in which the elucidation of idiosyncratic personality dynamics is a major goal, the Rorschach test is superior. The Rorschach procedure allows for more than one response per blot and thus encourages the emergence of dynamic sequences; and the generally lower number of total responses permits more in-depth exploration of each response. In terms of the above-mentioned dichotomy between normatively and idiographically-based approaches, it is clear that the HIT is more appropriate to the normative approach while the Rorschach is more appropriate to the idiographic form of test interpretation.

It would appear that we are moving in the direction of eventually having two clinically useful inkblot instruments: a relatively precise test that can be scored on various content scales (the HIT), and an instrument used solely for the assessment of individual personality dynamics (the Rorschach). Although this trend is understandable, it may present future problems for psychologists who wish a simultaneous combination of normative and idiographic interpretation. A single instrument integrating the advantages of both would be theoretically what is needed. Whether such an instrument is a practical possibility is by no means clear.

In a review of the Rorschach test published in the *Fifth Mental Measurements Yearbook,* Laurance Shaffer (1959) questioned how long a diagnostic test should be permitted to be considered "promising," a term used to describe the Rorschach since the test's introduction to this country. Shaffer argued that there must come a time when one decides that a promising instrument did not fulfill its early promise. It is unfortunate, but Shaffer is indeed correct in asserting that the test still must be described as merely promising for many clinical purposes. It is our contention that this is so largely because clinical psychology has been led down a blind alley in electing to approach the Rorschach test primarily from a perceptual standpoint. It is our hope that with the emphasis placed primarily on content and the analysis of verbalizations, the Rorschach test will indeed fulfill its promise as a significant and valid assessment instrument.

References

Abrams, S. A refutation of Eriksen's sensitization-defense hypotheses. *Journal of Projective Techniques,* 1962, **26,** 259–265.

Ackerman, M. J. Alcoholism and the Rorschach. *Journal of Personality Assessment,* 1971, **35,** 224–228.

Alcock, T. *The Rorschach in practice.* Philadelphia: J. P. Lippincott, 1963.

Allardice, B. S., & Dole, A. A. Body image in Hansen's disease patients. *Journal of Projective Techniques and Personality Assessment,* 1966, **30,** 356–358.

Allen, R. M. *Elements of Rorschach interpretation.* New York: International Universities Press, 1954.

Allen, R. M. *Student's Rorschach manual.* New York: International Universities Press, 1966.

Allport, G. W. *Personality: A psychological interpretation.* New York: Henry Holt & Company, 1937.

Allport, G. W. *Pattern and growth in personality.* New York: Holt, Rinehart, & Winston, 1961.

Ames, L. B. Further check on the diagnostic validity of the Ames danger signals. *Journal of Projective Techniques,* 1959, **23,** 291–298.

Ames, L. B. Are Rorschach responses influenced by society's change? *Journal of Personality Assessment,* 1975, **39,** 439–452.

Ames, L. B., Métraux, R. W., Rodell, J. L., & Walker, R. N. *Rorschach responses in old age* (Rev. ed.). New York: Brunner-Mazel, 1973.

Ames, L. B., Métraux, R. W., Rodell, J. L., & Walker, R. N. *Child Rorschach responses* (Rev. ed.). New York: Brunner-Mazel, 1974.

Ames, L. B., Métraux, R. W., & Walker, R. N. *Adolescent Rorschach responses* (Rev. ed.). New York: Brunner-Mazel, 1971.

Anastasi, A. *Psychological testing* (4th ed.). New York: Macmillan, 1976.

317

Andersen, D. O., & Seitz, F. C. Rorschach diagnosis of homosexuality: Schafer's content analysis. *Journal of Projective Techniques and Personality Assessment,* 1969, **33,** 406-408.

Appelbaum, S. A. The effect of altered psychological atmosphere on Rorschach responses: A new supplementary procedure. In M. Kornrich (Ed.), *Psychological test modifications.* Springfield, Ill.: Charles C. Thomas, 1965. (Reprinted from *Bulletin of the Menninger Clinic,* 1959, **23,** 179-189.)

Armitage, S. G., & Pearl, D. Unsuccessful differential diagnosis from the Rorschach. *Journal of Consulting Psychology,* 1957, **21,** 479-484.

Armon, V. Some personality variables in overt female homosexuality. *Journal of Projective Techniques,* 1960, **24,** 292-309.

Arnaud, S. H. A system for deriving quantitative Rorschach measures of certain psychological variables, for group comparisons. *Journal of Projective Techniques,* 1959, **23,** 403-411.

Aronow, E., & Reznikoff, M. Attitudes toward the Rorschach test expressed in book reviews: A historical perspective. *Journal of Personality Assessment,* 1973, **37,** 309-315.

Aronow, E., Reznikoff, M., & Tryon, W. The interpersonal distance of process and reactive schizophrenics. *Journal of Consulting and Clinical Psychology,* 1975, **43,** 94.

Aronson, M. L. A study of the Freudian theory of paranoia by means of the Rorschach test. *Journal of Projective Techniques,* 1952, **16,** 397-411.

Arthur, B. The forced confabulation technique: An extension of the Rorschach method for use with children. In M. Kornrich (Ed.), *Psychological test modifications.* Springfield, Ill.: Charles C. Thomas, 1965.

Auerbach, S. M., & Spielberger, C. D. The assessment of state and trait anxiety with the Rorschach test. *Journal of Personality Assessment,* 1972, **36,** 314-335.

Bachrach, H. Adaptive regression, empathy, and psychotherapy: Theory and research study. *Psychotherapy: Theory, Research, and Practice,* 1968, **5,** 203-209.

Bakan, P., & Brown, R. A. On the attention-demand value of Rorschach stimuli. *Journal of Projective Techniques and Personality Assessment,* 1967, **31** (3), 3-6.

Bartlett, F. C. An experimental study of some problems of perceiving and imaging. *British Journal of Psychology,* 1916, **8,** 222-266.

Baughman, E. E. A comparative analysis of Rorschach forms with altered stimulus characteristics. *Journal of Projective Techniques,* 1954, **18,** 151-164.

Baughman, E. E. The role of the stimulus in Rorschach responses. *Psychological Bulletin,* 1958, **55,** 121-147.

Baughman, E. E. An experimental analysis of the relationship between stimulus structure and behavior on the Rorschach. *Journal of Projective Techniques,* 1959, **23,** 134-183.

Bauman, G., & Roman, M. Interaction product analysis in group and family diagnosis. *Journal of Projective Techniques and Personality Assessment,* 1968, **32,** 331-337.

Beck, N., & Herron, W. G. The meaning of the Rorschach cards for children. *Journal of Projective Techniques and Personality Assessment,* 1969, **33,** 150-153.

Beck, S. J. Personality diagnosis by means of the Rorschach test. *American Journal of Orthopsychiatry,* 1930, **1,** 81–88.

Beck, S. J. *Personality structures in schizophrenia.* New York: Nervous and Mental Disease Monograph No. 63, 1938.

Beck, S. J. *The six schizophrenias.* New York: American Orthopsychiatric Association Research Monograph No. 6, 1954.

Beck, S. J. *Rorschach's Test: II. A variety of personality pictures* (2nd ed.). New York: Grune & Stratton, 1967.

Beck, S. J., Beck, A. C., Levitt, E. E., & Molish, H. B. *Rorschach's test I. Basic processes* (3rd ed.). New York: Grune & Stratton, 1961.

Beck, S. J., Rabin, A. I., Thiesin, W. G., Molish, H., & Thetford, W. N. The normal personality as projected in the Rorschach test. *Journal of Psychology,* 1950, **30,** 241-298.

Bellak, L. A study of limitations and "failures": Toward an ego psychology of projective techniques. *Journal of Projective Techniques,* 1954, **18,** 279–293.

Bellak, L., & Loeb, L. (Eds.). *The schizophrenic syndrome.* New York: Grune & Stratton, 1969.

Benfari, R. C., & Calogeras, R. C. Levels of cognition and conscience typologies. *Journal of Projective Techniques and Personality Assessment,* 1968, **32,** 466–474.

Bergmann, M. S. Homosexuality on the Rorschach test. *Bulletin of the Menninger Clinic,* 1945, **9,** 78–83.

Berkowitz, M., & Levine, J. Rorschach scoring categories as diagnostic "signs." *Journal of Consulting Psychology,* 1953, **17,** 110–112.

Bertrand, S., & Masling, J. Oral imagery and alcoholism. *Journal of Abnormal Psychology,* 1969, **74,** 50–53.

Biederman, L., & Cerbus, G. Changes in Rorschach teaching. *Journal of Personality Assessment,* 1971, **35,** 524-526.

Binet, A., & Henri, V. La psychologie individuelle. *Année Psychologique,* 1896, **2,** 411-465.

Blanchard, W. H. The group process in gang rape. *Journal of Social Psychology,* 1959, **49,** 259–266.

Blanchard, W. H. The consensus Rorschach: Background and development. *Journal of Projective Techniques and Personality Assessment,* 1968, **32,** 327–330.

Blatt, S. J., & Ritzler, B. A. Thought disorder and boundary disturbances in psychosis. *Journal of Consulting and Clinical Psychology,* 1974, **42,** 370–381.

Bleuler, E. Dementia praecox; Or, the group of schizophrenias (J. Zinkin, trans.). New York: International Universities Press, 1950. (Originally published, 1911.)

Bloom, B. L. Prognostic significance of the underproductive Rorschach. *Journal of Projective Techniques,* 1956, **20,** 366–371.

Bloom, B. L. The Rorschach popular response among Hawaiian schizophrenics. *Journal of Projective Techniques,* 1962, **26,** 173–181.

Bochner, R., & Halpern, F. *The clinical application of the Rorschach test.* New York: Grune & Stratton, 1945.

Bolgar, H. Consistency of affect and symbolic expression: A comparison between dreams and Rorschach responses. *American Journal of Orthopsychiatry,* 1954, **24,** 538–545.

Booth, G. Organ function and form perception: Use of the Rorschach method with cases of chronic arthritis, parkinsonism, and arterial hypertension. *Psychosomatic Medicine,* 1946, **8,** 367–385.

Bower, P. A., Testin, R., & Roberts, A. Rorschach diagnosis by a systematic combining of content, thought process, and determinant scales. *Genetic Psychology Monographs,* 1960, **62,** 105–183.

Bradway, K., & Heisler, V. The relation between diagnoses and certain types of extreme deviations and content on the Rorschach. *Journal of Projective Techniques,* 1953, **17,** 70–74.

Brown, F. Reply (to critique of S. Charen). *Journal of Projective Techniques,* 1953, **17,** 462–464.

Brown, F. An exploratory study of dynamic factors in the content of the Rorschach protocol. In M. H. Sherman (Ed.), *A Rorschach reader.* New York: International Universities Press, 1960. (Reprinted from *Journal of Projective Techniques,* 1953, **17,** 251–279.)

Brown, F. Changes in sexual identification and role over a decade and their implications. *Journal of Psychology,* 1971, **77,** 229–251.

Burnham, C. A. A study of the degree of relationship between Rorschach *H*% and Wechsler-Bellevue Picture Arrangement scores. *Rorschach Research Exchange and Journal of Projective Techniques,* 1949, **13,** 206–209.

Buros, O. K. (Ed.). *Personality tests and reviews.* Highland Park, N. J. Gryphon Press, 1970.

Buss, A. H., Fischer, H., & Simmons, A. J. Aggression and hostility in psychiatric patients. *Journal of Consulting Psychology,* 1962, **26,** 84–89.

Cameron, N. A. *The psychology of behavior disorders.* Boston: Houghton Mifflin, 1947.

Carnes, G. D., & Bates, R. E. Rorschach anatomy response correlates in rehabilitation failure subjects. *Journal of Personality Assessment,* 1971, **35,** 527–537.

Cassell, W. A. A projective index of body-interior awareness. *Psychosomatic Medicine,* 1964, **26,** 172–177.

Cassell, W. A. A tachistoscopic index of body perception. I. Body boundary and body interior awareness. *Journal of Projective Techniques and Personality Assessment,* 1966, **30,** 31–36.

Chapman, A. H., & Reese, D. G. Homosexual signs in Rorschachs of early schizophrenics. *Journal of Clinical Psychology,* 1953, **9,** 30–32.

Charen, S. A critique of "An exploratory study of dynamic factors in the content of the Rorschach protocol." *Journal of Projective Techniques,* 1953, **17,** 460–462.

Charen, S. Pitfalls in interpretation of parental symbolism in Rorschach cards IV and VII. *Journal of Consulting Psychology,* 1957, **21,** 52–56.

Chasey, W. C., Swartz, J. D., & Chasey, C. G. Effect of motor development on body image scores for institutionalized mentally retarded children. *American Journal of Mental Deficiency,* 1974, **78,** 440–445.

Chassan, J. B. Statistical inference and the single case in clinical design. *Psychiatry,* 1960, **23,** 173–184.

Chassan, J. B. Stochastic models of the single case as the basis of clinical research design. *Behavioral Science,* 1961, **6,** 42–50.

Chassan, J. B. *Research design in clinical psychology and psychiatry.* New York: Appleton-Century-Crofts, 1967.

Cleveland, S. E. Body image changes associated with personality reorganization. *Journal of Consulting Psychology,* 1960, **24,** 256–261.

Cleveland, S. E., & Fisher, S. A comparison of psychological characteristics and physiological reactivity in ulcer and rheumatoid arthritis groups: I. Psychological measures. *Psychosomatic Medicine,* 1960, **22,** 283–289.

Cleveland, S. E., & Johnson, D. L. Personality patterns in young males with coronary disease. *Psychosomatic Medicine,* 1962, **24,** 600–610.

Cleveland, S. E., & Morton, R. B. Group behavior and body image: A follow-up study. *Human Relations,* 1962, **15,** 77–85.

Cleveland, S. E., Snyder, R., & Williams, R. L. Body image and site of psychosomatic symptoms. *Psychological Reports,* 1965, **16,** 851–852.

Cleveland, S. E., & Sikes, M. P. Body image in chronic alcoholics and non-alcoholic psychiatric patients. *Journal of Projective Techniques and Personality Assessment,* 1966, **30,** 265–269.

Coan, R. W. Review of the Holtzman Inkblot Technique. In O. K. Buros (Ed.), *The sixth mental measurements yearbook.* Highland Park, N. J.: Gryphon Press, 1965.

Coates, S. Homosexuality and the Rorschach test. *British Journal of Medical Psychology,* 1962, **35,** 177–190.

Cohen, D. Rorschach scores, prognosis, and course of illness in pulmonary tuberculosis. *Journal of Consulting Psychology,* 1954, **18,** 405–408.

Cole, S., & Williams, R. L. Age as a determinant of parental interpretation of Rorschach cards IV and VII. *Perceptual and Motor Skills,* 1968, **26,** 55–58.

Compton, N. H. Body-image boundaries in relation to clothing fabric and design preferences of a group of hospitalized psychotic women. *Journal of Home Economics,* 1964, **56,** 40–45.

Consalvi, C., & Canter, A. Rorschach scores as a function of four factors. *Journal of Consulting Psychology,* 1957, **21,** 47–51.

Cook, P. E., Iacino, L. W., Murray, J., & Auerbach, S. M. Holtzman inkblot anxiety and shading scores related to state and trait anxiety. *Journal of Personality Assessment,* 1973, **37,** 337–339.

Cronbach, L. J., & Gleser, G. C. *Psychological tests and personnel decisions* (2nd ed.). Urbana, Ill.: University of Illinois Press, 1965.

Crumpton, E. The influence of color on the Rorschach test. *Journal of Projective Techniques,* 1956, **20,** 150–158.

Cutter, F. Role complements and changes in consensus Rorschachs. *Journal of Projective Techniques and Personality Assessment,* 1968, **32,** 338–347.

Cutter, F., & Farberow, N. L. Serial administration of consensus Rorschachs to one patient. *Journal of Projective Techniques and Personality Assessment,* 1968, **32,** 358–374.

Cutter, F., & Farberow, N. L. The consensus Rorschach. In B. Klopfer, M. M. Meyer, F. B. Brawer, & W. G. Klopfer (Eds.), *Developments in the Rorschach technique* (Vol. 3). New York: Harcourt Brace Jovanovich, 1970.

Dana, R. H. The effects of attitudes towards authority on psychotherapy. *Journal of Clinical Psychology,* 1954, **10,** 350-353.

Darby, J. A. Alteration of some body image indexes in schizophrenics. *Journal of Consulting and Clinical Psychology,* 1970, **35,** 116-121.

Daston, P. G., & McConnell, O. L. Stability of Rorschach penetration and barrier scores over time. *Journal of Consulting Psychology,* 1962, **26,** 104.

Davids, A., Joelson, M., & McArthur, C. Rorschach and TAT indices of homosexuality in overt homosexuals, neurotics, and normal males. *Journal of Abnormal and Social Psychology,* 1956, **53,** 161-172.

Davids, A., & Talmadge, M. Utility of the Rorschach in predicting movement in psychiatric casework. *Journal of Consulting Psychology,* 1964, **28,** 311-316.

Davis, A. D. Some physiological correlates of Rorschach body image productions. *Journal of Abnormal and Social Psychology,* 1960, **60,** 432-436.

Davis, R. W. Comment on H. S. Brar: Rorschach content responses of East Indian psychiatric patients. *Journal of Projective Techniques and Personality Assessment,* 1970, **34,** 95-97.

Dearborn, G. V. Blots of ink in experimental psychology. *Psychological Review,* 1897, **4,** 390-391.

Dearborn, G. V. A study of imaginations. *American Journal of Psychology,* 1898, **9,** 183-190.

De Luca, J. N. The structure of homosexuality. *Journal of Projective Techniques and Personality Assessment,* 1966, **30,** 187-191.

De Vos, G. A quantitive approach to affective symbolism in Rorschach responses. *Journal of Projective Techniques,* 1952, **16,** 133-150.

Dörken, H., Jr. A psychometric evaluation of 68 medical interns. *Canadian Medical Association Journal,* 1954, **70,** 41-45.

Dosey, M. A., & Meisels, M. Personal space and self-protection. *Journal of Personality and Social Psychology,* 1969, **11,** 93-97.

Draguns, J. G., Haley, E. M., & Phillips, L. Studies of Rorschach content: A review of the research literature. Part 1: Traditional content categories. *Journal of Projective Techniques and Personality Assessment,* 1967, **31** (1), 3-32.

Dudek, S. Z. Intelligence, psychopathology and primary thinking disorder in early schizophrenia. *Journal of Nervous and Mental Disease,* 1969, **148,** 515-527.

Due, F. O., & Wright, M. E. The use of content analysis in Rorschach interpretation: I. Differential characteristics of male homosexuals. *Rorschach Research Exchange,* 1945, **9,** 169-177.

Eichler, R. M. A comparison of the Rorschach and Behn-Rorschach inkblot tests. *Journal of Consulting Psychology,* 1951, **15,** 185-189.

Eichler, R. M. Experimental stress and alleged Rorschach indices of anxiety. *Journal of Abnormal and Social Psychology,* 1951, **46,** 344-355.

Eigenbrode, C. R., & Shipman, W. G. The body image barrier concept. *Journal of Abnormal and Social Psychology,* 1960, **60,** 450-452.

Elizur, A. Content analysis of the Rorschach with regard to anxiety and hostility. *Rorschach Research Exchange and Journal of Projective Techniques,* 1949, **13,** 247-284.

Ellenberger, H. The life and work of Hermann Rorschach (1884-1922). *Bulletin of the Menninger Clinic,* 1954, **18,** 173-219.

Endicott, N. A. The Holtzman Inkblot Technique content measures of depression and suspiciousness. *Journal of Personality Assessment,* 1972, **36,** 424-426.

Endicott, N. A., & Endicott, J. Objective measures of somatic preoccupation. *Journal of Nervous and Mental Disease,* 1963, **137,** 427-437.

Endicott, N. A., & Jortner, S. Objective measures of depression. *Archives of General Psychiatry,* 1966, **15,** 249-255.

Endicott, N. A., & Jortner, S. Correlates of somatic concern derived from psychological tests. *Journal of Nervous and Mental Disease,* 1967, **144,** 133-138.

Endicott, N. A., Jortner, S., & Abramoff, E. Objective measures of suspiciousness. *Journal of Abnormal Psychology,* 1969, **74,** 26-32.

Engel, C. The relationship between Rorschach responses and attitudes toward parents. *Journal of Projective Techniques,* 1959, **23,** 311-314.

Epstein, S., Nelson, J. V., & Tanofsky, R. Responses to inkblots as measures of individual differences. *Journal of Consulting Psychology,* 1957, **21,** 211-215.

Eron, L. D. Review of the Rorschach. In O. K. Buros (Ed.), *The sixth mental measurements yearbook.* Highland Park, N.J.: Gryphon Press, 1965.

Ewert, L. D., & Wiggins, N. Dimensions of the Rorschach: A matter of preference. *Journal of Consulting and Clinical Psychology,* 1973, **40,** 394-403.

Exner, J. E. *The Rorschach systems.* New York: Grune & Stratton, 1969.

Federn, P. *Ego psychology and the psychoses.* New York: Basic Books, 1952.

Fein, L. G. Rorschach signs of homosexuality in male college students. *Journal of Clinical Psychology,* 1950, **6,** 248-253.

Feirstein, A. Personality correlates of tolerance for unrealistic experiences. *Journal of Consulting Psychology,* 1967, **31,** 387-395.

Fenichel, O. *The psychoanalytic theory of neurosis.* New York: Norton, 1945.

Fernald, P. S., & Linden, J. D. The human content response in the Holtzman Inkblot Technique. *Journal of Projective Techniques and Personality Assessment,* 1966, **30,** 441-446.

Ferracuti, F., & Rizzo, G. B. Analisi del valore discriminativo di alcuni segni di omopessualita silevabili attraverso techniche proittive. *Bolletino di Psicologia e Sociologia Applicato,* 1956, **13-16,** 128-134.

Finney, B. C. Rorschach test correlates of assaultive behavior. *Journal of Projective Techniques,* 1955, **19,** 6-16.

Fisher, S. Patterns of personality rigidity and some of their determinants. *Psychological Monographs,* 1950, **64**(1, Whole No. 307).

Fisher, S. Prediction of body exterior vs. body interior reactivity from a body image schema. *Journal of Personality,* 1959, **27,** 56-62.

Fisher, S. Right-left gradients in body image, body reactivity, and perception. *Genetic Psychology Monographs,* 1960, **61,** 197-228.

Fisher, S. Relationship of Rorschach human percepts to projective description with self-reference. *Journal of Projective Techniques,* 1962, **26,** 231-233.

Fisher, S. The body boundary and judged behavioral patterns in an interview situation. *Journal of Projective Techniques and Personality Assessment,* 1964, **28,** 181-184. (a)

Fisher, S. Sex differences in body perception. *Psychological Monographs,* 1964, **78**(14, Whole No. 591). (b)

Fisher, S. Body image in neurotic and schizophrenic patients. *Archives of General Psychiatry,* 1966, **15**, 90–101.

Fisher, S. *Body experience in fantasy and behavior.* New York: Appleton-Century-Crofts, 1970.

Fisher, S., & Cleveland, S. E. Body-image boundaries and style of life. *Journal of Abnormal and Social Psychology,* 1956, **52**, 373–379.

Fisher, S., & Cleveland, S. E. *Body image and personality.* Princeton, N. J.: Van Nostrand, 1958.

Fisher, S., & Cleveland, S. E. *Body image and personality* (2nd ed.). New York: Dover, 1968.

Fisher, S., & Fisher, R. L. A developmental analysis of some body image and body reactivity dimensions. *Child Development,* 1959, **30**, 389–402.

Fisher, S., & Fisher, R. L. Body image boundaries and patterns of body perception. *Journal of Abnormal and Social Psychology,* 1964, **68**, 255–262.

Fisher, S., & Hinds, E. The organization of hostility controls in various personality structures. *Genetic Psychology Monographs,* 1951, **44**, 3–68.

Fisher, S., & Renik, O. D. Induction of body image boundary changes. *Journal of Projective Techniques and Personality Assessment,* 1966, **30**, 429–434.

Fishman, D. B. Rorschach adaptive regression and change in psychotherapy. *Journal of Personality Assessment,* 1973, **37**, 218–224.

Forsyth, R. P. The influences of color, shading, and Welsh anxiety level on Elizur Rorschach content test analyses of anxiety and hostility. *Journal of Projective Techniques,* 1959, **23**, 207–213.

Frede, M. C., Gautney, D. B., & Baxter, J. C. Relationships between body image boundary and interaction patterns on the MAPS test. *Journal of Consulting and Clinical Psychology,* 1968, **32**, 575–578.

Freud, S. [*The interpretation of dreams*] (J. Strachey, Ed. and trans.). New York: Avon Books, 1965. (Originally published, 1900.)

Friedman, H. A comparison of a group of hebephrenic and catatonic schizophrenics with two groups of normal adults by means of certain variables of the Rorschach test. *Journal of Projective Techniques,* 1952, **16**, 352–360.

Fromm-Reichmann, F. *Principles of intensive psychotherapy.* Chicago: University of Chicago Press, 1950.

Gallagher, J. J. Test indicators for therapy prognosis. *Journal of Consulting Psychology,* 1954, **18**, 409–413.

Gamble, K. R. The Holtzman Inkblot Technique: A review. *Psychological Bulletin,* 1972, **77**, 172–194.

Gardner, R. W. Impulsivity as indicated by Rorschach test factors. *Journal of Consulting Psychology,* 1951, **15**, 464–468.

Geil, G. W. The similarity in Rorschach patterns of adult criminal psychopaths and pre-adolescent boys. *Rorschach Research Exchange,* 1945, **9**, 201–206.

George, C. E. Some unforeseen correlates between the studies of Shaw and Wallen. *Journal of Abnormal and Social Psychology,* 1953, **48**, 150.

George, C. E. Stimulus value of the Rorschach cards: A composite study. *Journal of Projective Techniques,* 1955, **19**, 17–20.

Gibby, R. G., Stotsky, B.A., Miller, D. R., & Hiler, E. W. Prediction of duration of therapy from the Rorschach test. *Journal of Consulting Psychology,* 1953, **17,** 348–354.

Gill, W. S. Animal content in the Rorschach. *Journal of Projective Techniques and Personality Assessment,* 1967, **31** (2), 49–56.

Gluck, M. R. Rorschach content and hostile behavior. *Journal of Consulting Psychology,* 1955, **19,** 475–478.

Goldberger, L. Reactions to perceptual isolation and Rorschach manifestations of the primary process. *Journal of Projective Techniques,* 1961, **25,** 287–302.

Goldfried, M. R. The assessment of anxiety by means of the Rorschach. *Journal of Projective Techniques and Personality Assessment,* 1966, **30,** 364–380.

Goldfried, M. R., Stricker, G., & Weiner, I. B. *Rorschach handbook of clinical and research applications.* Englewood Cliffs, N.J.: Prentice-Hall, 1971.

Goldman, R. Changes in Rorschach performance and clinical improvement in schizophrenia. *Journal of Consulting Psychology,* 1960, **24,** 403–407.

Goodstein, L.D. Interrelationships among several measures of anxiety and hostility. *Journal of Consulting Psychology,* 1954, **18,** 35–39.

Goodstein, L. D., & Goldberger, L. Manifest anxiety and Rorschach performance in a chronic patient. *Journal of Consulting Psychology,* 1955, **19,** 339–344.

Gorlow, L., Zimet, C. N., & Fine, H. J. The validity of anxiety and hostility Rorschach content scores among adolescents. *Journal of Consulting Psychology,* 1952, **16,** 73–75.

Grauer, D. Prognosis in paranoid schizophrenia on the basis of the Rorschach. *Journal of Consulting Psychology,* 1953, **17,** 199–205.

Grauer, D. Homosexuality in paranoid schizophrenia as revealed by the Rorschach test. *Journal of Consulting Psychology,* 1954, **18,** 459–462.

Gray, J. J. An investigation of the relationship between primary process thinking and creativity (Doctoral dissertation, Fordham University, 1967). *Dissertation Abstracts,* 1968, **28,** 5206–B. (University Microfilms No. 68-3692)

Gray, J. J. The effect of productivity on primary process and creativity. *Journal of Projective Techniques and Personality Assessment,* 1969, **33,** 213–218.

Grayson, H. M. Rorschach productivity and card preferences as influenced by experimental variation of color and shading. *Journal of Projective Techniques,* 1956, **20,** 288–296.

Guertin, W. H., & Trembath, W. E. Card VI disturbance on the Rorschachs of sex offenders. *Journal of General Psychology,* 1953, **49,** 221–227.

Haan, N. An investigation of the relationships of Rorschach scores, patterns, and behavior to coping and defense mechanisms. *Journal of Projective Techniques and Personality Assessment,* 1964, **28,** 429–441.

Hafner, A. J. Rorschach card stimulus values for children. *Journal of Projective Techniques,* 1961, **25,** 166–169.

Hafner, A. J., & Kaplan, A. M. Hostility content analysis of the Rorschach and TAT. *Journal of Projective Techniques,* 1960, **24,** 137–143.

Hafner, A. J., & Rosen, E. The meaning of Rorschach inkblots, responses, and determinants as perceived by children. *Journal of Projective Techniques and Personality Assessment,* 1964, **28,** 192–200.

Halpern, F. Rorschach interpretation of the personality structure of schizophrenics who benefit from insulin therapy. *Psychiatric Quarterly*, 1940, **14**, 826–833.

Halpern, F. *A clinical approach to children's Rorschachs.* New York: Grune & Stratton, 1953.

Halpern, H. M. A Rorschach interview technique: Clinical validation of the examiner's hypotheses. In M. Kornrich (Ed.), *Psychological test modifications.* Springfield, Ill.: Charles C. Thomas, 1965. (Reprinted from *Journal of Projective Techniques,* 1957, **21**, 10–17.)

Hammer, M. A comparison of responses by clinic and normal adults to Rorschach card III human figure area. *Journal of Projective Techniques and Personality Assessment,* 1966, **30**, 161–162.

Harris, J. G., Jr. Validity: The search for a constant in a universe of variables. In M. A. Rickers-Ovsiankina (Ed.)., *Rorschach psychology.* New York: John Wiley & Sons, 1960.

Harrower-Erickson, M. R., & Steiner, M. E. *Large scale Rorschach techniques: A manual for the group Rorschach and multiple choice test.* Springfield, Ill.: Charles C Thomas, 1945.

Hartley, R. B. The barrier variable as measured by homonyms. *Journal of Clinical Psychology,* 1967, **23**, 196–203.

Hartung, J. R., McKenna, S. A., & Baxter, J. C. Test-taking attitudes and Rorschach pathognomic verbalization. *Journal of Projective Techniques and Personality Assessment,* 1969, **33**, 146–153.

Hartung, J. R., McKenna, S. A., & Baxter, J. C. Body image and defensiveness in an LSD-taking subculture. *Journal of Projective Techniques and Personality Assessment,* 1970, **34**, 316–323.

Haskell, R. J., Jr. Relationship between aggressive behavior and psychological tests. *Journal of Projective Techniques,* 1961, **25**, 431–440.

Hays, J. R., & Boardman, W. K. An analysis of the function of color in the Rorschach. *Journal of Personality Assessment,* 1975, **39**, 19–24.

Hayslip, B., Jr., & Darbes, A. Intra-subject response consistency of the Holtzman Inkblot Technique. *Journal of Personality Assessment,* 1974, **38**, 149–153.

Herron, E. W. Changes in inkblot perception with presentation of the Holtzman Inkblot Technique as an "intelligence test." *Journal of Projective Techniques and Personality Assessment,* 1964, **28**, 442–447.

Hershenson, J. R. Preferences of adolescents for Rorschach figures. *Child Development,* 1949, **20**, 101–118.

Hertz, M. R. The reliability of the Rorschach inkblot test. *Journal of Applied Psychology,* 1934, **18**, 461–477.

Hertzman, M., & Pearce, J. The personal meaning of the human figure in the Rorschach. *Psychiatry,* 1947, **10**, 413–422.

Higgins, J. Process-reactive schizophrenia and environmental orientation. *Journal of Schizophrenia,* 1968, **2**, 72–80.

Higgins, J. Process-reactive schizophrenia. *Journal of Nervous and Mental Disease,* 1969, **149**, 450–472.

Hirschstein, R., & Rabin, A. I. Reactions to Rorschach cards IV and VII as a function of parental availability in childhood. *Journal of Consulting Psychology,* 1955, **19**, 473–474.

Holt, R. R. Editor's foreword. In D. Rapaport, M. M. Gill, & R. Schafer, *Diagnostic psychological testing* (Rev. ed.). New York: International Universities Press, 1968.

Holt, R. R. Artistic creativity and Rorschach measures of adaptive regression. In B. Klopfer, M. M. Meyer, F. B. Brawer, & W. G. Klopfer (Eds.), *Developments in the Rorschach technique* (Vol. 3). New York: Harcourt Brace Jovanovich, 1970.

Holt, R. R. Measuring libidinal and aggressive motives and their controls by means of the Rorschach. In P. M. Lerner (Ed.), *Handbook of Rorschach scales.* New York: International Universities Press, 1975. (Reprinted from Nebraska symposium on motivation (Vol. 14). Lincoln, University of Nebraska Press, 1966.)

Holt, R. R., & Havel, J. A method for assessing primary and secondary process in the Rorschach. In M. A. Rickers-Ovsiankina (Ed.), *Rorschach psychology.* New York: John Wiley & Sons, 1960.

Holtzman, W. H. Holtzman inkblot technique. In A. I. Rabin (Ed.), *Projective techniques in personality assessment.* New York: Springer Publishing, 1968.

Holtzman, W. H., Thorpe, J. S., Swartz, J. D., & Herron, E. W. *Inkblot perception and personality.* Austin, Texas: University of Texas Press, 1961.

Holzberg, J. D., & Wexler, M. The predictability of schizophrenic performance on the Rorschach test. *Journal of Consulting Psychology,* 1950, **14,** 395–399.

Hooker, E. The adjustment of the male overt homosexual. *Journal of Projective Techniques,* 1957, **21,** 18–31.

Hooker, E. Male homosexuality in the Rorschach. *Journal of Projective Techniques,* 1958, **22,** 33–54.

Howard, J. W. The Howard Ink Blot Test: A descriptive manual. *Journal of Clinical Psychology,* 1953, **9,** 209–254.

Iacino, L. W., & Cook, P. E. Threat of shock, state anxiety, and the Holtzman Inkblot Technique. *Journal of Personality Assessment.* 1974, **38,** 450–458.

Irizarry, R. Anxiety, repression, and varieties of anti-social behavior in psychopaths. *Journal of Personality Assessment,* 1971, **35,** 56–61.

Janis, M. G., & Janis, I. L. A supplementary test based on free association to Rorschach responses. In M. Kornrich (Ed.), *Psychological test modifications.* Springfield, Ill.: Charles C Thomas, 1965. (Reprinted from *Rorschach Research Exchange,* 1946, **10,** 1–19.)

Jaskar, R. O., & Reed, M. R. Assessment of body image organization of hospitalized and non-hospitalized subjects. *Journal of Projective Techniques and Personality Assessment,* 1963, **27,** 185–190.

Jensen, A. R. The Rorschach technique: A re-evaluation. *Acta Psychologica,* 1964, **22,** 60–77.

Jensen, A. R. Review of the Rorschach. In O. K. Buros (Ed.)., *The sixth mental measurements yearbook.* Highland Park, N. J.: Gryphon Press, 1965.

Jortner, S. An investigation of certain cognitive aspects of schizophrenia. *Journal of Projective Techniques and Personality Assessment,* 1966, **30,** 559–568.

Kagan, J. The long term stability of selected Rorschach responses. *Journal of Consulting Psychology,* 1960, **24,** 67–73.

Kagan, J., & Moss, H. A. The availability of conflictful ideas: A neglected parameter in assessing projective test responses. *Journal of Personality*, 1961, **29**, 217–234.

Kagan, J., Sontag, L. W., Baker, C. T., & Nelson, V. L. Personality and I.Q. change. *Journal of Abnormal and Social Psychology*, 1958, **56**, 261–266.

Kamano, D. K. Symbolic significance of Rorschach cards IV and VII. *Journal of Clinical Psychology*, 1960, **16**, 50–52.

Kantor, R. E., & Herron, W. G. *Reactive and process schizophrenia*. Palo Alto, Calif.: Science & Behavior Books, 1966.

Kataguchi, Y. Rorschach schizophrenic score (RSS). *Journal of Projective Techniques*, 1959, **23**, 214–222.

Kates, S. L., & Schwartz, F. Stress, anxiety and response complexity on the Rorschach test. *Journal of Projective Techniques*, 1958, **22**, 64–69.

Kessel, P., Harris, J. E., & Slagle, S. J. An associative technique for analyzing the content of Rorschach test responses. *Perceptual and Motor Skills*, 1969, **29**, 535–540.

Kirkpatrick, E. A. Individual tests of school children. *Psychological Review*, 1900, **7**, 274–280.

Klopfer, B., Ainsworth, M. D., Klopfer, W. G., & Holt, R. R. *Developments in the Rorschach technique, Vol. I: Technique and theory*. New York: Harcourt, Brace & World, 1954.

Klopfer, B., & Davidson, H. H. *The Rorschach technique: An introductory manual*. New York: Harcourt, Brace & World, 1962.

Klopfer, W. G. Current status of the Rorschach test. In P. McReynolds (Ed.), *Advances in psychological assessment* (Vol 1). Palo Alto, Calif.: Science & Behavior Books, 1968.

Klopfer, W. G. Consensus Rorschach in the primary classroom. *Journal of Projective Techniques and Personality Assessment*, 1969, **33**, 549–552.

Knight, R. P. Introduction. In E. B. Brody & F. C. Redlich (Eds.), *Psychotherapy with schizophrenics*. New York: International Universities Press, 1952.

Knopf, I. J. Rorschach summary scores in differential diagnosis. *Journal of Consulting Psychology*, 1956, **20**, 99–104.

Knutson, J. F. Review of the Rorschach. In O. K. Buros (Ed.), *The seventh mental measurements yearbook*. Highland Park, N. J.: Gryphon Press, 1972.

Kobler, F. J., & Stiel, A. The use of the Rorschach in involutional melancholia. *Journal of Consulting Psychology*, 1953, **17**, 365–370.

Kornrich, M. Eliciting "new" Rorschach responses. In M. Kornrich (Ed.), *Psychological test modifications*. Springfield, Ill.: Charles C Thomas, 1965.

Krippner, S. The relationship of reading improvement to scores on the Holtzman Inkblot Technique. *Journal of Clinical Psychology*, 1967, **23**, 114–115.

Kris, E. *Psychoanalytic explorations in art*. New York: International Universities Press, 1952.

Lebo, D., Toal, R., & Brick, H. Rorschach performance in the amelioration and continuation of observable anxiety. *Journal of General Psychology*, 1960, **63**, 75–80.

Ledwith, N. H. *Rorschach responses of elementary school children: A normative study*. Pittsburgh: University of Pittsburgh Press, 1959.

Leventhal, T., Slepian, H. J., Gluck, M. R., & Rosenblatt, B. P. The utilization of the psychologist-patient relationship in diagnostic testing. *Journal of Projective Techniques,* 1962, **26,** 66–79.

Levi, J. Rorschach patterns as a tool in predicting success or failure in the rehabilitation of the physically handicapped. *American Psychologist,* 1950, **5,** 320–321. (Abstract)

Levi, J. Rorschach patterns predicting success or failure in the rehabilitation of the physically handicapped. *Journal of Abnormal and Social Psychology,* 1951, **46,** 240–244.

Levine, M., & Spivack, G. *The Rorschach index of repressive style.* Springfield, Ill.: Charles C Thomas, 1964.

Levitt, E. E., Lubin, B., & Zuckerman, M. A simplified method for scoring Rorschach content for dependency. *Journal of Projective Techniques,* 1962, **26,** 234–236.

Levitt, E. E., & Truumaa, A. *The Rorschach technique with children and adolescents.* New York: Grune & Stratton, 1972.

Levy, D. M., & Beck, S. J. The Rorschach test in manic-depressive psychosis. *American Journal of Orthopsychiatry,* 1934, **4,** 31–42.

Levy, E. Stimulus-values of Rorschach cards for children. *Journal of Projective Techniques,* 1958, **22,** 293–296.

Levy, J. R. Changes in the galvanic skin response accompanying the Rorschach test. *Journal of Consulting Psychology,* 1950, **14,** 128–133.

Levy, J., & Epstein, N. B. An application of the Rorschach test in family investigation. *Family Process,* 1964, **3,** 344–376.

Lindner, R. M. The Rorschach test and the diagnosis of psychopathic personality. *Journal of Criminal Psychopathology,* 1943, **5,** 69–93.

Lindner, R. M. Content analysis in Rorschach work. *Rorschach Research Exchange,* 1946, **10,** 121–129.

Lingren, R. H. Child-parent attitudes: A comparison of the Family Relations test and perceptions on Rorschach cards III, IV, and VII. *Psychology in the Schools,* 1968, **5,** 81–84.

Little, K. B. Connotations of the Rorschach inkblots. *Journal of Personality,* 1959, **27,** 397–406.

Loiselle, R. H., Fisher, V., & Parrish, C. E. Stimulus value of Rorschach inkblots and percepts as perceived by children and schizophrenics. *Journal of Projective Techniques and Personality Assessment,* 1968, **32,** 238–245.

Loiselle, R. H. & Kleinschmidt, A. A comparison of the stimulus value of Rorschach inkblots and their percepts. *Journal of Projective Techniques,* 1963, **27,** 191–194.

Loveland, N. The relation Rorschach: A technique for studying interaction. *Journal of Nervous and Mental Disease,* 1967, **145,** 93–105.

Lubin, B., Wallis, R. R., & Paine, C. Patterns of psychological test usage in the United States: 1935–1969. *Professional Psychology,* 1971, **2,** 70–74.

Lucas, W. B. The effects of frustration on the Rorschach responses of nine year old children. *Journal of Projective Techniques,* 1961, **25,** 199–204.

Magnussen, M. G., & Cole, J. K. Further evidence of the Rorschach card stimulus values for children: A partial replication (and generalizations). *Journal of Projective Techniques and Personality Assessment,* 1967, **31,** 44–47.

Malev, J. S. Body image, body symptoms and body reactivity in children. *Journal of Psychosomatic Research,* 1966, **10,** 281–289.

Margulies, H. Rorschach responses of successful and unsuccessful students. *Archives of Psychology,* 1942, **38** (Whole No. 271).

Martin, D. G. Test reviews. *Journal of Counseling Psychology,* 1968, **15,** 481–484.

Masling, J., Rabie, L., & Blondheim, S. H. Obesity, level of aspiration, and Rorschach and TAT measures of oral dependence. *Journal of Consulting Psychology,* 1967, **31,** 233–239.

Masling, J., Weiss, L., & Rothschild, B. Relationships of oral imagery to yielding behavior and birth order. *Journal of Consulting and Clinical Psychology,* 1968, **32,** 89–91.

McArthur, C. C. Review of the Rorschach. In O. K. Buros (Ed.), *The seventh mental measurements yearbook.* Highland Park, N. J.: Gryphon Press, 1972.

McConnell, O. L., & Daston, P. G. Body image changes in pregnancy. *Journal of Projective Techniques,* 1961, **25,** 451–456.

McMahon, F. B., Jr. Psychological testing — A smoke screen against logic. *Psychology Today,* 1969, **2** (8), 54–59.

McMahon, J. M. The relationship between "overinclusive" and primary process thought in a normal and a schizophrenic population (Doctoral dissertation, New York University, 1964). *Dissertation Abstracts,* 1965, **25,** 6062–6063. (University Microfilms No. 65-1650)

McMurry, R. N. Validating the patterned interview. *Personnel,* 1947, **23,** 263–272.

Meer, B. The relative difficulty of the Rorschach cards. *Journal of Projective Techniques,* 1955, **19,** 43–53.

Meer, B., & Singer, J. L. A note on the "father" and "mother" cards in the Rorschach inkblots. *Journal of Consulting Psychology,* 1950, **14,** 482–484.

Megargee, E. I. Relation between barrier scores and aggressive behavior. *Journal of Abnormal Psychology,* 1965, **70,** 307–311.

Megargee, E. I., & Swartz, J. D. Extraversion, neuroticism, and scores on the Holtzman Inkblot Technique. *Journal of Projective Techniques and Personality Assessment,* 1968, **32,** 262–265.

Meketon, B. W., Griffith, R. M., Taylor, V. H., & Wiedeman, J. S. Rorschach homosexual signs in paranoid schizophrenics. *Journal of Abnormal and Social Psychology,* 1962, **65,** 280–284.

Mensh, I. N., & Matarazzo, J. D. Rorschach card rejection in psychodiagnosis. *Journal of Consulting Psychology,* 1954, **18,** 271–275.

Mindess, H. The symbolic dimension. In B. Klopfer, M. M. Meyer, F. B. Brawer, & W. G. Klopfer (Eds.), *Developments in the Rorschach technique* (Vol. 3). New York: Harcourt Brace Jovanovich, 1970.

Mitchell, M. B. Preferences for Rorschach cards. *Journal of Projective Techniques,* 1952, **16,** 203–211.

Mogar, R. E. Anxiety indices in human figure drawings: A replication and extension. *Journal of Consulting Psychology,* 1962, **26,** 108.

Molish, H. B. The popular response in Rorschach records of normals, neurotics, and schizophrenics. *American Journal of Orthopsychiatry,* 1951, **21,** 523–531.

Molish, H. B., Molish, E. E., & Thomas, C. B. A Rorschach study of a group of medical students. *Psychiatric Quarterly,* 1950, **24,** 744–774.

Morgan, A. B. Some age norms obtained for the Holtzman Inkblot Technique administered in a clinical setting. *Journal of Projective Techniques and Personality Assessment,* 1968, **32,** 165–172.

Morris, W. W. Rorschach estimates of personality attributes in the Michigan assessment project. *Psychological Monographs,* 1952, **66** (6, Whole No. 338).

Moseley, E. C., Duffey, R. F., & Sherman, L. J. An extension of the construct validity of the Holtzman Inkblot Technique. *Journal of Clinical Psychology,* 1963, **19,** 186–192.

Moylan, J. J., Shaw, J., & Appleman, W. Passive and aggressive responses to the Rorschach by passive-aggressive personalities and paranoid schizophrenics. *Journal of Projective Techniques,* 1960, **24,** 17–20.

Murstein, B. I. The projection of hostility on the Rorschach, and as a result of ego-threat. *Journal of Projective Techniques,* 1956, **20,** 418–428.

Murstein, B. I., & Wheeler, J. I. The projection of hostility on the Rorschach and Thematic Stories test. *Journal of Clinical Psychology,* 1959, **15,** 316–319.

Nelson, M. O., Wolfson, W., & Lo Cascio, R. Sexual identification in responses to Rorschach card III. *Journal of Projective Techniques,* 1959, **23,** 354–356.

Neuringer, C. Suicide and the Rorschach: A rueful postscript. *Journal of Personality Assessment,* 1974, **38,** 535–539.

Nichols, D. C., & Tursky, B. Body image, anxiety, and tolerance for experimental pain. *Psychosomatic Medicine,* 1967, **29,** 103–110.

Nitsche, C. J., Robinson, J. F., & Parsons, E. T. Homosexuality and the Rorschach. *Journal of Consulting Psychology,* 1956, **20,** 196.

Ogdon, D. P. *Psychodiagnostics and personality assessment: A handbook* (2nd ed.). Los Angeles: Western Psychological Services, 1975.

Orbach, C. E., & Tallent, N. Modification of perceived body and of body concepts. *Archives of General Psychiatry,* 1965, **12,** 126–135.

Osgood, C. E., Suci, G. J., & Tannenbaum, P. H. *The measurement of meaning.* Urbana, Ill.: University of Illinois Press, 1957.

Otten, M. W., & Van de Castle, R. L. A comparison of set "A" of the Holtzman inkblots with the Rorschach by means of the semantic differential. *Journal of Projective Techniques,* 1963, **27,** 452–460.

Page, H. A. Studies in fantasy-daydreaming frequency and Rorschach scoring categories. *Journal of Consulting Psychology,* 1957, **21,** 111–114.

Palm, R. A comparative study of symbol formation in the Rorschach test and the dream. *Psychoanalytic Review,* 1956, **43,** 246–251.

Parsons, C. J. Children's interpretations of inkblots. *British Journal of Psychology,* 1917, **9,** 74–92.

Pascal, G. R., & Herzberg, F. I. The detection of deviant sexual practice from performance on the Rorschach test. *Journal of Projective Techniques,* 1952, **16,** 366–373.

Pascal, G. R., Ruesch, H. A., Devine, C. A., & Suttell, B. J. A study of genital symbols on the Rorschach test: Presentation of a method and results. *Journal of Abnormal and Social Psychology,* 1950, **45,** 286–295.

Pattie, F. A. The effect of hypnotically induced hostility on Rorschach responses.

Journal of Clinical Psychology, 1954, **10**, 161–164.

Paulsen, A. A. Personality development in the middle years of childhood. *American Journal of Orthopsychiatry,* 1954, **24**, 336–350.

Phillips, L., & Smith, J. G. *Rorschach interpretation: Advanced technique.* New York: Grune & Stratton, 1953.

Pine, F. Creativity and primary process: Sample variations. *Journal of Nervous and Mental Disease,* 1962, **134**, 506–511.

Pine, F., & Holt, R. R. Creativity and primary process: A study of adaptive regression. *Journal of Abnormal and Social Psychology,* 1960, **61**, 370–379.

Piotrowski, Z. A. A comparison of congenitally defective children with schizophrenic children in regard to personality structure and intelligence type. *Proceedings of the American Association on Mental Deficiency,* 1937, **42**, 78–90.

Piotrowski, Z. A. *Perceptanalysis.* New York: Macmillan, 1957.

Piotrowski, Z. A., & Bricklin, B. A long-term prognostic criterion for schizophrenics based on Rorschach data. *Psychiatric Quarterly Supplement,* 1958, **32**, 315–329.

Piotrowski, Z. A., & Bricklin, B. A second validation of a long-term Rorschach prognostic index for schizophrenic patients. *Journal of Consulting Psychology,* 1961, **25**, 123–128.

Pope, B., & Jensen, A. R. The Rorschach as an index of pathological thinking. *Journal of Projective Techniques,* 1957, **21**, 54–62.

Potkay, C. R. *The Rorschach clinician.* New York: Grune & Stratton, 1971.

Powers, W. T., & Hamlin, R. M. Relationship between diagnostic category and deviant verbalizations on the Rorschach. *Journal of Consulting Psychology,* 1955, **19**, 20–124.

Powers, W. T., & Hallin, R. M. The validity, bases, and process of clinical judgment, using a limited amount of projective test data. *Journal of Projective Techniques,* 1957, **21**, 286–293.

Powers, W. T., & Hamlin, R. M. A comparative analysis of deviant Rorschach response characteristics. *Journal of Consulting Psychology,* 1958, **22**, 123–128.

Pruitt, W. A., & Van de Castle, R. L. Dependency measures and welfare chronicity. *Journal of Consulting Psychology,* 1962, **26**, 559–560.

Pyle, W. H. *Examination of school children.* New York: Macmillan, 1913.

Pyle, W. H. A psychological study of bright and dull pupils. *Journal of Educational Psychology,* 1915, **6**, 151–156.

Quinlan, D. M., & Harrow, M. Boundary disturbances in schizophrenia. *Journal of Abnormal Psychology,* 1974, **83**, 533–541.

Quinlan, D. M., Harrow, M., Tucker, G., & Carlson, K. Varieties of "disordered" thinking on the Rorschach: Findings in schizophrenic and nonschizophrenic patients. *Journal of Abnormal Psychology,* 1972, **79**, 47–53.

Quirk, D. A., Quarrington, M., Neiger, S., & Slemon, A. G. The performance of acute psychotic patients on the index of pathological thinking and on selected signs of idiosyncrasy on the Rorschach. *Journal of Projective Techniques,* 1962, **26**, 431–441.

Rabin, A. I. A contribution to the "meaning" of Rorschach's inkblots via the semantic differential. *Journal of Consulting Psychology,* 1959, **23**, 368–372.

Rabkin, J. G. Psychoanalytic assessment of change in organization of thought after psychotherapy (Doctoral dissertation, New York University, 1967). *Dissertation Abstracts,* 1968, **28,** 4763-B. (University Microfilms No. 68-6098)

Rader, G. E. The prediction of overt aggressive verbal behavior from Rorschach content. *Journal of Projective Techniques,* 1957, **21,** 294-306.

Ramer, J. The Rorschach barrier score and social behavior. *Journal of Consulting Psychology,* 1963, **27,** 525-531.

Ramzy, I., & Pickard, P. M. A study in the reliability of scoring the Rorschach ink blot test. *Journal of General Psychology,* 1949, **40,** 3-10.

Rapaport, D., Gill, M., & Schafer, R. *Diagnostic psychological testing* (Vol. 2). Chicago: Year Book Publishers, 1946.

Rapaport, D., Gill, M., & Schafer, R. *Diagnostic psychological testing* (Rev. ed. by R. H. Holt). New York: International Universities Press, 1968.

Rav, J. Anatomy responses in the Rorschach test. *Journal of Projective Techniques.* 1951, **15,** 433-443.

Rawls, J. R., & Slack, G. K. Artists versus nonartists: Rorschach determinants and artistic creativity. *Journal of Projective Techniques and Personality Assessment,* 1968, **32,** 233-237.

Raychaudhuri, M., & Mukerji, K. Rorschach differentials of homosexuality in male convicts: An examination of Wheeler and Schafer signs. *Journal of Personality Assessment,* 1971, **35,** 22-26.

Reitman, E. E., & Cleveland, S. E. Changes in body image following sensory deprivation in schizophrenic and control groups. *Journal of Abnormal and Social Psychology,* 1964, **68,** 168-176.

Reitzell, J. M. A comparative study of hysterics, homosexuals, and alcoholics using content analysis of Rorschach responses. *Rorschach Research Exchange and Journal of Projective Techniques,* 1949, **13,** 127-141.

Renik, O. D., & Fisher, S. Induction of body image boundary changes in male subjects. *Journal of Projective Techniques and Personality Assessment,* 1968, **32,** 45-48.

Reznikoff, M. Review of the Rorschach. In O. K. Buros (Ed.), *The seventh mental measurements yearbook.* Highland Park, N. J.: Gryphon Press, 1972.

Richards, T. W. Personal significance of Rorschach figures. *Journal of Projective Techniques,* 1958, **22,** 97-101.

Richter, R. H., & Winter, W. D. Holtzman Inkblot correlates of creative potential. *Journal of Projective Techniques and Personality Assessment,* 1966, **30,** 62-67.

Rickers-Ovsiankina, M. The Rorschach test as applied to normal and schizophrenic subjects. *British Journal of Medical Psychology,* 1938, **17,** 227-257.

Rickers-Ovsiankina, M. Longitudinal approach to schizophrenia through the Rorschach method. *Journal of Clinical and Experimental Psychopathology,* 1954, **15,** 107-118.

Rieger, A. F. The Rorschach test and occupational personalities. *Journal of Applied Psychology,* 1949, **33,** 572-578.

Rieman, G. W. The effectiveness of Rorschach elements in the discrimination between neurotic and ambulatory schizophrenic subjects. *Journal of Consulting Psychology,* 1953, **17,** 25-31.

Roe, A. A psychological study of eminent biologists. *Psychological Monographs,*

1951, **65** (14, Whole No. 331).

Roe, A. Analysis of group Rorschachs of psychologists and anthropologists. *Journal of Projective Techniques,* 1952, **16,** 212–224.

Roe, A. Group Rorschachs of university faculties. *Journal of Consulting Psychology,* 1952, **16,** 18–22.

Rogers, L. S., Knauss, J., & Hammond, K. R. Predicting continuation in therapy by means of the Rorschach test. *Journal of Consulting Psychology,* 1951, **15,** 368–371.

Rogolsky, M. M. Artistic creativity and adaptive regression in third grade children. *Journal of Projective Techniques and Personality Assessment,* 1968, **32,** 53–62.

Rorschach, H. [*Psychodiagnostics*] (5th ed.). (P. Lemkau & B. Kronenberg, trans.). Berne, Switzerland: Verlag Hans Huber, 1942. (Originally published, 1921.)

Rosen, E. Symbolic meanings in the Rorschach cards: A statistical study. *Journal of Clinical Psychology,* 1951, **7,** 239–244.

Rosen, E. Connotative meanings of Rorschach inkblots, responses, and determinants. *Journal of Personality,* 1960, **28,** 413–426.

Rosenstiel, L. Capacity for empathy: A function of anxiety in the production of *H*-responses. *Journal of Projective Techniques and Personality Assessment,* 1969, **33,** 336–342.

Rosenstiel, L. Increase of hostility responses in the HIT after frustration. *Journal of Personality Assessment,* 1973, **37,** 22–24.

Rosenzwaig, S., Ludwig, D. J., & Adelman, S. Retest reliability of the Rosenzweig Picture-Frustration study and similar semiprojective techniques. *Journal of Personality Assessment,* 1975, **39,** 3–12.

Rosner, S. Inquiry: Partial or total. *Journal of Projective Techniques,* 1960, **24,** 49–51.

Rossi, A. M., & Neuman, G. G. A comparative study of Rorschach norms: Medical students. *Journal of Projective Techniques,* 1961, **25,** 334–338.

Rothstein, C., & Cohen, I. S. Hostility and dependency conflicts in peptic ulcer patients. *Psychological Reports,* 1958, **4,** 555–558.

Rust, R. M., & Ryan, F. J. The relationship of some Rorschach variables to academic behavior. *Journal of Personality,* 1953, **21,** 441–456.

Sanders, R., & Cleveland, S. E. The relationship between certain examiner personality variables and subjects' Rorschach scores. *Journal of Projective Techniques,* 1953, **17,** 34–50.

Sandler, J., & Ackner, B. Rorschach content analysis: An experimental investigation. *British Journal of Medical Psychology,* 1951, **24,** 180–201.

Sappenfield, B. R. Perception of masculinity-femininity in Rorschach blots and responses. *Journal of Clinical Psychology,* 1961, **17,** 373–376.

Sappenfield, B. R. Perception of attractive and repelling qualities in Rorschach blots and responses. *Journal of Clinical Psychology,* 1965, **21,** 308–311.

Schafer, R. *Psychoanalytic interpretation in Rorschach testing.* New York: Grune & Stratton, 1954.

Schwartz, S., & Giacoman, S. Convergent and discriminant validity of three measures of adjustment and three measures of social desirability. *Journal of Consulting and Clinical Psychology,* 1972, **39,** 239–242.

Sen, A. A statistical study of the Rorschach test. *British Journal of Psychology Stastist. Sect.,* 1950, **3,** 21–39.

Shaffer, L. F. Review of the Rorschach. In O. K. Buros (Ed.), *The fifth mental measurements yearbook.* Highland Park, N. J.: Gryphon Press, 1959.

Sharp, S. E. Individual psychology: A study in psychological method. *American Journal of Psychology,* 1899, **10,** 329–391.

Shatin, L. Psychoneurosis and psychosomatic reactions: A Rorschach contrast. *Journal of Consulting Psychology,* 1952, **16,** 220–225.

Shatin, L. Relationships between the Rorschach test and the Thematic Apperception Test. *Journal of Projective Techniques,* 1955, **19,** 317–331.

Shaw, B. Sex populars in the Rorschach test. *Journal of Abnormal and Social Psychology,* 1948, **43,** 466–470.

Shereshevski-Shere, E., Lasser, L. M., & Gottesfeld, B. H. An evaluation of anatomy content and *F+* percentage in the Rorschachs of alcoholics, schizophrenics, and normals. *Journal of Projective Techniques,* 1953, **17,** 229–233.

Shipman, W. G., Oken, D., Goldstein, I. B., Grinker, R. R., & Heath, H. A. Study in psychophysiology of muscle tension: II. Personality factors. *Archives of General Psychiatry,* 1964, **11,** 330–345.

Siegel, S. M. The relationship of hostility to authoritarianism. *Journal of Abnormal and Social Psychology,* 1956, **52,** 368–372.

Silverman, L. H. A study of the effects of subliminally presented aggressive stimuli on the production of pathologic thinking in a nonpsychiatric population. *Journal of Nervous and Mental Disease,* 1965, **141,** 443–455.

Silverman, L. H. A technique for the study of psychodynamic relationships: The effects of subliminally presented aggressive stimuli on the production of pathological thinking in a schizophrenic population. *Journal of Consulting Psychology,* 1966, **30,** 103–111.

Silverman, L. H., & Candell, P. On the relationship between aggressive activation, symbiotic merging, intactness of body boundaries, and manifest pathology in schizophrenics. *Journal of Nervous and Mental Disease,* 1970, **150,** 387–399.

Silverman, L. H., & Goldweber, A. M. A further study of the effects of subliminal aggressive stimulation on thinking. *Journal of Nervous and Mental Disease,* 1966, **143,** 463–472.

Silverman, L. H., Lapkin, B., & Rosenbaum, I. S. Manifestations of primary process thinking in schizophrenia. *Journal of Projective Techniques,* 1962, **26,** 117–127.

Sines, J. O. An approach to the study of the stimulus significance of the Rorschach inkblots. *Journal of Projective Techniques,* 1960, **24,** 64–66.

Singer, M. T., & Wynne, L. C. Differentiating characteristics of parents of childhood schizophrenics, childhood neurotics, and young adult schizophrenics. *American Journal of Psychiatry,* 1963, **120,** 234–243.

Singer, M. T., & Wynne, L. C. Thought disorder and family relations of schizophrenics: III. Methodology using projective techniques. *Archives of General Psychiatry,* 1965, **12,** 187–200. (a)

Singer, M. T., & Wynne, L. C. Thought disorder and family relations of schizophrenics: IV. Results and implications. *Archives of General Psychiatry,* 1965,

12, 201–212. (b)

Singer, M. T., & Wynne, L. C. Communication styles in parents of normals, neurotics and schizophrenics: Some findings using a new Rorschach scoring manual. In I. M. Cohen (Ed.), *Family structure, dynamics, and therapy* (Psychiatric Research Report No. 20). Washington, D.C.: American Psychiatric Association, 1966. (a)

Singer, M. T., & Wynne, L. C. Principles for scoring communication defects and deviances in parents of schizophrenics: Rorschach and TAT scoring manuals. *Psychiatry,* 1966, **29**, 260–288. (b)

Smith, J. R., & Coleman, J. C. The relationship between manifestations of hostility in projective tests and overt behavior. *Journal of Projective Techniques,* 1956, **20**, 326–334.

Sommer, R. Rorschach animal responses and intelligence. *Journal of Consulting Psychology,* 1957, **21**, 358.

Sommer, R., & Sommer, D. T. Assaultiveness and two types of Rorschach color responses. *Journal of Consulting Psychology,* 1958, **22**, 57–62.

Speisman, J. C., & Singer, M. T. Rorschach content correlates in five groups with organic pathology. *Journal of Projective Techniques,* 1961, **25**, 356–359.

Steffy, R. A., & Becker, W. C. Measurement of the severity of disorder in schizophrenia by means of the Holtzman Inkblot Test. *Journal of Consulting Psychology,* 1961, **25**, 555.

Steinzor, B. Rorschach responses of achieving and nonachieving college students of high ability. *American Journal of Orthopsychiatry,* 1944, **14**, 494–504.

Stephenson, W. *The study of behavior.* Chicago: University of Chicago Press, 1953.

Stone, N. M., & Schneider, R. E. Concurrent validity of the Wheeler signs of homosexuality in the Rorschach: (Ci/Rj). *Journal of Personality Assessment,* 1975, **39**, 573–579.

Storment, C. T., & Finney, B. C. Projection and behavior: A Rorschach study of assaultive mental hospital patients. *Journal of Projective Techniques,* 1953, **17**, 349–360.

Stotsky, B. A. A comparison of remitting and non-remitting schizophrenics on psychological tests. *Journal of Abnormal and Social Psychology,* 1952, **47**, 489–496.

Strauss, E. L. The Rorschach as an encounter. *Psychiatric Quarterly Supplement,* 1967, **41**, 255–261.

Sullivan, H. S. *Schizophrenia as a human process.* New York: Norton, 1962.

Sundberg, N. D. The practice of psychological testing in clinical services in the United States. *Ameriaan Psychologist,* 1961, **16**, 79–83.

Swartz, J. D. Pathognomic verbalizations in normals, psychotics, and mental retardates (Doctoral dissertation, University of Texas at Austin, 1969). *Dissertation Abstracts International,* 1970, **30**, 5703–5704B. (University Microfilms No. 70-10, 872)

Swartz, J. D., Cleland, C. C., Drew, C. J., & Witzke, D. B. The Holtzman Inkblot Technique as a measure of perceptual development in mental retardation. *Journal of Personality Assessment,* 1971, **35**, 320–325.

Swartz, J. D., Tapia, L. L., & Thorpe, J. S. Perceptual development of Mexican school children as measured by responses to the Holtzman Inkblot Technique. *Revista Interamericana de Psicologia,* 1967, **1,** 289–295.

Swift, J. W. Reliability of Rorschach scoring categories with preschool children. *Child Development,* 1944, **15,** 207–216.

Symonds, P. M. A contribution to our knowledge of the validity of the Rorschach. *Journal of Projective Techniques,* 1955, **19,** 152–162.

Taniguchi, M., De Vos, G., & Murakami, E. Identification of mother and father cards on the Rorschach by Japanese normal and delinquent adolescents. *Journal of Projective Techniques,* 1958, **22,** 453–460.

Thelen, M. H., & Ewing, D. R. Roles, functions, and training in clinical psychology: A survey of academic clinicians. *American Psychologist,* 1970, **25,** 550–554.

Thelen, M. H., Varble, D. L., & Johnson, J. Attitudes of academic clinical psychologists toward projective techniques. *American Psychologist,* 1968, **23,** 517–521.

Thorpe, J. S., & Swartz, J. D. Level of perceptual development as reflected in responses to the Holtzman Inkblot Technique. *Journal of Projective Techniques and Personality Assessment,* 1965, **29,** 380–386.

Thorpe, J. S., & Swartz, J. D. Perceptual organization: A developmental analysis by means of the·Holtzman Inkblot Technique. *Journal of Projective Techniques and Personality Assessment,* 1966, **30,** 447–451.

Towbin, A. P. Hostility in Rorschach content and overt aggressive behavior. *Journal of Abnormal and Social Psychology,* 1959, **58,** 312–316.

Tulchin, S. H. The pre-Rorschach use of inkblot tests. *Rorschach Research Exchange,* 1940, **4,** 1–7.

Tutko, T. A. Need for social approval and its effects on responses to projective tests (Doctoral dissertation, Northwestern University, 1963). *Dissertation Abstracts,* 1964, **24,** 3429. (University Microfilms No. 64-2535)

Ulett, G. A. *Rorschach introductory manual.* St. Louis, Mo.: Educational Publishers, 1950.

Ullmann, L. P., & Eck, R. A. Inkblot perception and the process-reactive distinction. *Journal of Clinical Psychology,* 1965, **21,** 311–313.

Ullmann, L. P., & Hunrichs, W. A. The role of anxiety in psychodiagnosis: Replication and extension. *Journal of Clinical Psychology,* 1958, **14,** 276–279.

Vernallis, F. F. Teeth-grinding: Some relationships to anxiety, hostility, and hyperactivity. *Journal of Clinical Psychology,* 1955, **11,** 389–391.

Vernon, P. E. The Rorschach ink-blot test. II. *British Journal of Medical Psychology,* 1933, **13,** 179–205.

Von Holt, H. W., Sengstake, C. B., Sonoda, B. C., & Draper, W. A. Orality, image fusions and concept-formation. *Journal of Projective Techniques,* 1960, **24,** 194–198.

Walker, R. G. A comparison of clinical manifestations of hostility with Rorschach and MAPS test performances. *Journal of Projective Techniques,* 1951, **15,** 444–460.

Wallace, J., & Sechrest, L. Frequency hypothesis and content analysis of projective techniques. *Journal of Consulting Psychology,* 1963, **27,** 387–393.

Wallen, R. The nature of color shock. *Journal of Abnormal and Social Psychology,* 1948, **43,** 346–356.

Walters, R. H. A preliminary analysis of the Rorschach records of fifty prison inmates. *Journal of Projective Techniques,* 1953, **17,** 437–446.

Ware, K., Fisher, S., & Cleveland, S. Body-image boundaries and adjustment to poliomyelitis. *Journal of Abnormal and Social Psychology,* 1957, **55,** 88–93.

Warner, S. J. An evaluation of the validity of Rorschach popular responses as differentiae of ambulatory schizophrenia. *Journal of Projective Techniques,* 1951, **15,** 268–275.

Watkins, J. G., & Stauffacher, J. C. An index of pathological thinking in the Rorschach. *Journal of Projective Techniques,* 1952, **16,** 276–286.

Weiner, I. B. *Psychodiagnosis in schizophrenia.* New York: John Wiley & Sons, 1966.

Weiss, A. A., & Winnik, H. A contribution to the meaning of anatomy responses on the Rorschach test. *Israel Annals of Psychiatry and Related Disciplines,* 1964, **1,** 265–276.

Weiss, L., & Masling, J. Further validation of a Rorschach measure of oral imagery: A study of six clinical groups. *Journal of Abnormal Psychology,* 1970, **76,** 83–87.

Werner, H. *Comparative psychology of mental development* (Rev. ed.). New York: Follett, 1948.

Westrope, M. R. Relations among Rorschach indices, manifest anxiety, and performance under stress. *Journal of Abnormal and Social Psychology,* 1953, **48,** 515–524.

Wheeler, W. M. An analysis of Rorschach indices of male homosexuality. *Rorschach Research Exchange and Journal of Projective Techniques,9,* **13,** 97–126.

Whipple, G. M. *Manual of mental and physical tests.* Baltimore, Md.: Warwick & York, 1910.

Whitaker, L. The Rorschach and Holtzman as measures of pathognomic verbalization. *Journal of Consulting Psychology,* 1965, **29,** 181–183.

Wiener, G. Neurotic depressives' and alcoholics' oral Rorschach percepts. *Journal of Projective Techniques,* 1956, **20,** 453–455.

Willi, J. Joint Rorschach testing of partner relationships. *Family Process,* 1969, **8,** 64–78.

Wirt, R. D. Ideational expression of hostile impulses. *Journal of Consulting Psychology,* 1956, **20,** 185–189.

Wishner, J. Rorschach intellectual indicators in neurotics. *American Journal of Orthopsychiatry,* 1948, **18,** 265–279.

Witkin, H. A., Lewis, H. B., Hertzman, M., Machover, K., Meissner, P. B., & Wapner, S. *Personality through perception.* New York: Harper & Row, 1954.

Wittenborn, J. R., & Holzberg, J. D. The Rorschach and descriptive diagnosis. *Journal of Consulting Psychology,* 1951, **15,** 460–463.

Wolf, I. Hostile acting out and Rorschach test content. *Journal of Projective Techniques,* 1957, **21,** 414–419.

Wright, N. A., & Zubek, J. P. Relationship between perceptual deprivation tolerance and adequacy of defenses as measured by the Rorschach. *Journal of*

Abnormal Psychology, 1969, **74,** 615–617.

Wynne, L. C. Consensus Rorschachs and related procedures for studying interpersonal patterns. *Journal of Projective Techniques and Personality Assessment,* 1968, **32,** 352–356.

Wynne, L.C., & Singer, M. T. Thought disorder and family relations of schizophrenics: I. A research strategy. *Archives of General Psychiatry,* 1963, **9,** 191–198. (a)

Wynne, L. C., & Singer, M. T. Thought disorder and family relations of schizophrenics: II. A classification of forms of thinking. *Archives of General Psychiatry,* 1963, **9,** 199–206. (b)

Wysocki, B. A. Assessment of intelligence level by the Rorschach test as compared with objective tests. *Journal of Educational Psychology,* 1957, **48,** 113–117.

Yamahiro, R. S., & Griffith, R. M. Validity of two indices of sexual deviancy. *Journal of Clinical Psychology,* 1960, **16,** 21–24.

Zax, M., & Benham, F. G. The stimulus value of the Rorschach inkblots as perceived by children. *Journal of Projective Techniques,* 1961, **25,** 233–237.

Zax, M., & Loiselle, R. H. Stimulus value of Rorschach inkblots as measured by the semantic differential. *Journal of Clinical Psychology,* 1960, **16,** 160–163. (a)

Zax, M., & Loiselle, R. H. The influence of card order on the stimulus value of the Rorschach inkblots. *Journal of Projective Techniques,* 1960, **24,** 218–221. (b)

Zax, M., Loiselle, R. H., & Karras, A. Stimulus characteristics of Rorschach inkblots as perceived by a schizophrenic sample. *Journal of Projective Techniques,* 1960, **24,** 439–443.

Zelin, M., & Sechrest, L. The validity of the "mother" and "father" cards of the Rorschach. *Journal of Projective Techniques,* 1963, **27,** 114–121.

Zimet, C. N., & Brackbill, G. A. The role of anxiety in psychodiagnosis. *Journal of Clinical Psychology,* 1956, **12,** 173–177.

Zimet, C. N., & Fine, H. J. Primary and secondary process thinking in two types of schizophrenia. *Journal of Projective Techniques and Personality Assessment,* 1965, **29,** 93–99.

Zimmerman, I. L., Lambert, N. M., & Class, L. A comparison of children's perceptions of Rorschach cards III, IV, and VII with independent ratings of parental adequacy, and effectiveness of school behavior. *Psychology in the Schools,* 1966, **3,** 258–263.

Zimny, G. H. Body image and physiological responses. *Journal of Psychosomatic Research,* 1965, **9,** 185–188.

Zubin, J. The non-projective aspects of the Rorschach experiment: I. Introduction. *Journal of Social Psychology,* 1956, **44,** 179–192.

Zubin, J., Eron, L. D., & Schumer, F. *An Experimental approach to projective techniques.* New York: John Wiley & Sons, 1965.

Zubin, J., Eron, L. D., & Sultan, F. A psychometric evaluation of the Rorschach experiment. *American Journal of Orthopsychiatry,* 1956, **26,** 773–782.

Zuckerman, M., Levitt, E. E., & Lubin, B. Concurrent and construct validity of direct and indirect measures of dependency. *Journal of Consulting Psychology*, 1961, **25**, 316–323.

Zuckerman, M., Persky, H., Eckman, K. M., & Hopkins, T. R. A multitrait multimethod measurement approach to the traits (or states) of anxiety, depression, and hostility. *Journal of Projective Techniques and Personality Assessment*, 1967, **31** (2), 39–48.

Zulliger, H. [*The Zulliger individual and group test*] (F. Salomon, Ed., & D. Dubrovsky, trans.). New York: International Universities Press, 1969. (Originally published, 1941.)

REFERENCE NOTES

1. Burt, C. *The Rorschach test*. Unpublished manuscript, University College, London, 1945.
2. Greenberg, E., & Aronow, E. Relationship between inkblot content and interpersonal distance. *New Jersey Psychologist*, 1975, **25** (4), 11.
3. De Vos, G. *Manual of criteria for scoring affective inferences*. Unpublished manuscript, 1955.
4. Holt, R. R. *Manual for the scoring of primary and secondary process manifestations in Rorschach responses*. New York: Research Center for Mental Health, New York University, 1968.
5. Mayman, M. *Form level scoring manual*. Unpublished manuscript, Menninger Foundation, 1960.

Author Index

Subject Index